MW00359053

American Taxation, American Slavery

AMERICAN TAXATION

AMERICAN SLAVERY

Robin L. Einhorn

The University of Chicago Press
Chicago & London

ROBIN L. EINHORN is professor of history at the University of California, Berkeley. She is author of *Property Rules: Political Economy in Chicago, 1833–1872* (1991, reissued with new preface, 2001), also published by the University of Chicago Press.

The University of Chicago Press, Chicago 60637
The University of Chicago Press, Ltd., London
© 2006 by The University of Chicago
All rights reserved. Published 2006
Printed in the United States of America

15 14 13 12 11 10 09 08 07 06   1 2 3 4 5
ISBN: 0-226-19487-6 (cloth)

Library of Congress CataloginginPublication Data

Einhorn, Robin L. (Robin Leigh), 1960–
   American taxation, American slavery / Robin Einhorn.
      p. cm.
   Includes bibliographical references and index.
   ISBN 0-226-19487-6 (cloth : alk. paper) 1. Slavery—Political aspects—United States—History. 2. Taxation—Political aspects—United States—History. 3. Slavery—Economic aspects—United States—History. 4. State rights. 5. United States—Politics and government—1775–1783. 6. United States—Politics and government—1783–1865.
I. Title.
   E441.E38 2006
   336.200973—dc22

                                                                2005030545

To jop3
inevitably

CONTENTS

TABLES, FIGURES, AND MAPS

ACKNOWLEDGMENTS

To Alice Yeomans, Ginny Irving, Patty Heard, and their colleagues at the Boalt Hall Law Library, University of California, Berkeley: thank you for turning a storage basement into an archive to make a wonderful collection of material accessible to me. Thanks also to the staffs of the National Archives at College Park, Baker Library at Harvard Business School, and Connecticut Historical Society. My work would have been much harder without the incredibly useful Library of Congress American Memory online collection, "A Century of Lawmaking for a New Nation: U.S. Congressional Documents and Debates, 1774–1875." For their first-rate research assistance, I am very grateful to Jason Scott Smith (yes, it's taken that long), Alejandra Dubcovsky, and Sparsh Khandeshi.

To the John Simon Guggenheim Memorial Foundation and Doreen N. Townsend Center for the Humanities at the University of California, Berkeley—and to the friends who helped persuade these institutions to support my research: a deep thank-you for the leaves from teaching and faith in this project, even when I had only a vague sense of what it was. Many thanks to Doug Mitchell, Tim McGovern, Maia Rigas, and the rest of the talented team at the University of Chicago Press. Thanks also to Christine Eduok of UC Berkeley, who made the maps, and to the Committee on Research, Institute of Governmental Studies, and Department of History, UC Berkeley, for additional financial assistance.

Early versions of this work were presented at the conferences of the Institute for Policy History. I thank Don Critchlow and Bill Glankler for building this critical venue for research in U.S. political history—and Joel Silbey, Bill Novak, Richard John, Margo Anderson, and Louis Gerteis for critical feedback there. Similarly, for helpful critiques at the Department of Political Science, UC San Diego; the Institute for Governmental Studies and Townsend Center, UC Berkeley; the Charles Warren Center, Harvard; and the German Historical Institute, I am grateful to Amy Bridges, Margaret Weir, Candace Slater, Tina Gillis, David Henkin, Sven Beckert, W. Elliot Brownlee, Christoph Strupp, and Alexander Neutzenadel. Still, I inflicted the real work-in-progress (the thinking out loud) on my students at Berkeley, and not least the alumni of 7A. Many thanks to you all.

Some of the arguments in this book (and a few paragraphs) first appeared in "Slavery and the Politics of Taxation in the Early United States," *Studies in American Political Development* 14 (2000): 156–83; "Species of Property: The American Property-Tax Uniformity Clauses Reconsidered," *Journal of Economic History* 61 (2001): 973–1007; and "Patrick Henry's Case against the Constitution: The Structural Problem with Slavery," *Journal of the Early Republic* 22 (2002): 549–73. For assistance and feedback with these, I thank Karen Orren, Jan deVries, Gavin Wright, John Lauritz Larson, John Wallis, Peter Wallenstein, and anonymous reviewers.

For generous readings and critiques of the manuscript, I am immensely grateful to Richard John, Jon Gjerde, Bob Middlekauff, Paddy Riley, John Peters, Richard Abrams, and anonymous reviewers. For similar generosity with parts of it, a hearty thanks to Charles Postel, David Hollinger, Tim Hampton, Leslie Kurke, Celeste Langan, Michael Lucey, Beth Berry, and Brad DeLong. I am wistfully grateful for what can only be called the mentoring of two late colleagues at Berkeley. It is still hard to grasp the loss of Jim Kettner and Mike Rogin.

This book is a history of American taxation in the two centuries before the Civil War. It is also an extended essay about democracy in America over this long period. Some readers may find the title misleading, but one of the main themes of this book is the source of the assumptions about American politics and American history that would encourage a reader to be misled in this way. This book is not about how taxation enslaved Americans. It is about how *slavery* enslaved Americans, including the white majorities who gained wealth and status from the enslavement of Africans and African Americans. This book is about how slavery undermined democracy in the long period when slaveholding "masters" ruled the United States.

We must stop beating around the bush on this issue. Slaveholding masters *did* rule much of the United States most of the time in this period. We can all agree that some of these masters had admirable qualities, that Thomas Jefferson was charming and eloquent, that James Madison was a talented political theorist, that George Washington was a brilliant general, and that Andrew Jackson fought for the interests of people who were not rich. Nevertheless, these men all owned human beings and, as politicians, defended the ownership of human beings—even when they believed that society would be better off if it acknowledged that "all men are created equal; that they are endowed by their Creator with certain unalienable rights," and so on. There was a Civil War for a reason, and this reason had very little to do with tariffs or railroads. The United States collapsed into one of the bloodiest wars of the nineteenth century (620,000 dead) because a series of political struggles in the 1850s demonstrated that it "cannot endure, permanently, half slave and half free." Americans were forced to decide, continuing in Abraham Lincoln's words, whether it would become "all one thing, or all the other." At Gettysburg,

1

Antietam, Vicksburg, Petersburg, and Atlanta, they decided that it would become all free. The masters finally lost control of American politics, though they certainly did not disappear altogether.[1]

This book operates on the assumption that we will gain much more than we can ever lose by taking these facts seriously. We do not celebrate our democratic traditions more faithfully by identifying them incorrectly. On the contrary, when we embrace slaveholders as the champions of liberty and democracy in our history, what we really promote is a cynical despair—not only about our political history but also about contemporary political life. There is a real tradition of liberty in the United States. There is also a real tradition of democracy, including a democracy practiced in formal political institutions. Rebels and outsiders are often fascinating people, and their stories produce great and inspiring histories. But it is hardly necessary to "give voice to the voiceless" to locate an American democratic tradition. It is only necessary to accept the reality that the stories the slaveholders liked to tell about themselves are misleading when they are not downright false. These stories are our most familiar historical set pieces, the ones in which the slaveholding champions of liberty and democracy defeat legions of monarchists and aristocrats (by which they usually meant northerners) on behalf of "the people."[2]

Writing about hobbits, J. R. R. Tolkien could have been describing our situation. Hobbits, it seems, were voracious consumers of their own history, though only when it was packaged in a familiar form. They were especially partial to genealogy. "Hobbits delighted in all such things, if they were accurate: they liked to have books filled with things that they already knew, set out fair and square with no contradictions."[3] Tolkien's joke here, of course, is that the "accuracy" of stories we already know depends on their familiarity rather than on a more meaningful measure of truth. For hobbits, the result of reading the same stories over and over again is that they know almost nothing about who they are or who they were in the past. They are profoundly surprised to learn that they actually have the capacity to be heroes. For Americans, whose familiar stories of slaveholding "founding fathers" are no longer quite as delightful as they used to be, the result is an unnecessary fatalism about our capacities to act on our ideals.

This book retells some of the most familiar set piece stories of American political history, such as the framing of the Constitution, as well as a number of other stories that are not nearly as well known. Yet even when the terrain seems most familiar, we actually will be proceeding on a relatively obscure path across it. The stories in this book will never be about the personalities of individual politicians, although certain politicians (especially James Madison) will play large roles in some of them. The stories in this book will always be about political institutions and struggles over how they should work. Specifically, they will always be about taxation, struggles over the power to tax, and struggles over the distribution of tax burdens.[4]

There is a story we already know about taxation in American history. In this story, the nation was born in a tax revolt. Impatient of government restraints on their liberty and resenting the costly pomp of parasitic kings and aristocrats, the colonists jettisoned this European baggage for a republican government that was small, weak, and frugal. The frugality was threatened in the nineteenth century, as "special interests" insisted on government subsidies (protective tariffs to help industry at the expense of the farmers), but agrarian "independence" held the field until after the Civil War, when the victorious North built a much stronger federal government. In the twentieth century, the floodgates opened. Liberals and socialists agitated for the programs that culminated in the welfare state and won the 1913 constitutional amendment that authorized the federal income tax. It has been a downhill slide ever since: government growing, tax burdens skyrocketing, and our liberty in more danger than George III ever posed.

The problem with this story is that it leaves out a lot. It leaves out the states, which did much of the taxing before the twentieth century; it leaves out the Revolution, which was not an inexpensive undertaking; and it leaves out slavery altogether. In this story, American liberty was most complete when millions of Americans were the chattel property of owners who could buy them, sell them, whip them, separate their families, and exert all manner of other arbitrary power over their lives. And if romanticizing the era of slavery (for its liberty!) is not a serious enough problem to damn this story, there is also the little matter of democracy. This story casts "the government" of the United States as an autonomous entity, whose relationship to the people is that it forces us to pay taxes to finance it and to do other intrusive paperwork in the guise of "regulation." Elections never enter into this story, as the significant decisions are made behind the scenes in conspiratorial (and undoubtedly smoke-filled) conclaves of insiders. In the radical libertarian world of this story, it is inconceivable that Americans might have wanted (and might still want) to use their (our) government to provide certain services, voting for candidates who promised to deliver them.

There is also another story we already know (or used to know) about American taxation, what we might call the old-fashioned "liberal" story of government growth. Here, government expanded in response to urban and industrial development, with taxes rising to pay for its new functions. This story agrees with the libertarian story on the early period, but it diverges in the industrial age. Small, weak, and frugal government was fine for an overwhelmingly agricultural society (this story also disapproves of the tariff), but the Industrial Revolution created entirely new bastions of private power and intolerable levels of inequality. Responding to urgent public demands, the government stepped in to protect ordinary people against exploitation: regulating the railroads, food and drug industries, building standards, wages, work hours, and working conditions, and then rescuing the elderly from squalid poverty. By the 1960s, the public had agreed (or been forced to agree) to use government power to promote racial justice: end segregation, enforce voting rights, combat discrimination in employment and housing. Meanwhile, the traditional government tasks of providing roads and schools came to include the interstate highways and great public universities. The traditional responsibilities for public lands came to include the national parks and vast irrigation projects. In the liberal world of this story, taxes rose because Americans wanted their governments to protect ordinary people against exploitation and to provide other services that "the market" could not or would not provide.[5]

This story also has problems. The idea that private bastions of power were new products of the industrial age erases slavery as completely as the libertarian story does, since slaveholders actually exerted far more power over slaves than industrial employers ever exerted over workers. It was a kind of power that nobody exerts over anybody else in the United States today—except, perhaps, within the gulag of our prison system. Still, the liberal story never featured an outright romance with slavery times. It treated the "agrarian" past mainly as the source of ideas about self-sufficiency and individualism that had to be overcome in the age of industry and big cities. Both the libertarian and liberal stories, moreover, neglect the importance of war, what Randolph Bourne (reacting to World War I) called "the health of the state." Governments have always grown fastest in wartime. Taxes have always risen more for war than welfare, regardless of whether we adopt the liberal view of the welfare state as a response to public demands or the libertarian view of it as an unjust imposition on hard-working taxpayers.

The crucial weakness of the liberal story, however, is that it is dated. Like old narratives of the Scopes "monkey trial" (1925)—which simply assumed that every reader obviously agreed that Darrow was right and Bryan was wrong, that John Scopes was right to teach evolution in his biology class— the liberal story of government growth as a "response to industrialism" was written before the conservative resurgence of the 1980s and 1990s. It simply assumed that its readers obviously agreed that the New Deal represented a progressive step toward a more democratic society, that Franklin Delano Roosevelt's four freedoms (of speech and religion, from want and fear) outlined a political program that everyone except a few crazy extremists supported. In our world, these assumptions are no longer warranted. Today, the former extremists run the country, championing "creationism," attacking regulation, and pledging to cut taxes no matter what the cuts do to the ability of our governments to provide the services people want, from law enforcement to social security and environmental protection (meanwhile running massive budget deficits). Today, the idea that democracy is desirable precisely because it allows the people to use their governments to distribute freedom and wealth more equally than they were distributed in the monarchies and aristocracies of the past actually prompts jeers from so-called "conservatives"—who dismiss it as the ancient heresy of a discredited "left."

But democracy is too important to be left solely to politicians and ideologues, regardless of whether they call themselves libertarians, liberals, or religious conservatives. And taxation is an especially useful vantage from which to renew a national conversation about democracy, both today and in our history. A brief theoretical excursion will illustrate why taxation provides such a useful vantage. All governments always tax. It is not necessary to accept the famous assertion of Oliver Wendell Holmes that taxes are "the price we pay for civilization" to acknowledge that taxation is a necessary aspect of government. Whether a government is a monarchy, aristocracy, democracy, or some more modern variation (say, a totalitarian regime), it will always tax. What makes the taxes of a democracy different from the taxes of the other forms of government is that in a democracy the people—personally or through the representatives they have chosen—decide why, how, and at what levels to tax themselves.

In a democracy, taxes are the way the people pool their resources to buy things that they cannot or prefer not to buy as individuals. These things might be armies, police, roads, schools, parks, or places with clean air and water. The people can decide to buy these things collectively; individuals can also decide to buy them individually. From the armies of Colombian drug lords to rent-a-cop security officers, for-profit toll roads, parochial or other private schools, theme parks, and certain Aegean islands, individuals can buy access to almost anything. By the same token, the people in a democracy *can* decide to restrict access to anything to the individuals who can afford to buy them individually. Thus, one of the perennial political decisions that the people make in a democracy is always which things *should* be purchased only by individuals and which should be purchased by the public for public use. Another perennial issue is how to finance the costs of the things the people decide to buy publicly, or, how to distribute the tax burden. The crucial point, however, is that in a democracy, both decisions—what to buy publicly and how to distribute the costs—are made by majority rule.

There are also other tax-related decisions that a democracy makes by majority rule. The people might decide to use taxation to promote or penalize certain behaviors. They might decide to make it easier to buy houses through income tax deductions for mortgage interest. They might decide to promote child-rearing by granting parents exemptions and credits. They might decide to persuade people to quit smoking or use public transportation through steep excises on tobacco and gasoline. They might decide to use tax incentives to persuade businesses to do any number of things: manufacture articles instead of importing them, offer health insurance to employees, hire veterans or welfare recipients. Many economists, at least since Adam Smith, have argued that taxes should not be used for nonrevenue purposes because these uses affect the distribution of tax burdens in complex ways and distort economic behavior in general. Nevertheless, most governments have always used taxes for nonrevenue purposes.[6] In a democracy, the power to decide whether and how to use taxes for these purposes belongs to the people.

When I began working on the history of American taxation and tax debates, I knew that I was going to end up writing a book about democracy, but I had no idea that this book was going to be about slavery. Having read many versions of the stories we already know, I thought about slavery the way it has usually been presented in American political history, as a "contradiction" or "unresolved problem" that sometimes intruded on the main story line. This is changing now. After some thirty years of magnificent research on the social, economic, and cultural history of slavery, political historians are finally starting to catch up, taking the "peculiar institution" more seriously than ever before.[7] It is not just that many of the "founding fathers" owned slaves. Nor is it that many of them felt guilty about owning slaves. It is that slavery was such a significant, even a foundational, institution in the early United States that it affected almost everything that happened in the political arena. It certainly affected taxation.

In hindsight, it is almost embarrassing to have "discovered" the significance of slavery. I knew that the history of taxation would contain untold stories—simply because very few historians had examined it—but I had no idea how significant these stories would turn out to be. I knew that the economist Joseph Schumpeter once quoted a lovely line about the importance of public finance from a colleague: "[T]he budget is the skeleton of the state, stripped of all misleading ideologies." Schumpeter added that taxation reveals "the thunder of world history" because taxes always have to be designed and redesigned to keep up with the changing structures of social, economic, and political life.[8] This rhetoric was inspiring, though not a guarantee that I would find thunder if I charted the history of American taxation in the dusty volumes of laws and debates that many other historians already had studied in search of other things.

But Schumpeter was right. There was thunder in the old books when I read them with an eye to taxation. The tax laws and debates told a story about American government I had never heard before. Early American governments were indeed small, weak, and frugal, while leading politicians did indeed celebrate the smallness, weakness, and frugality as signs of the "republican virtue" of a people who had thrown off parasitic kings and aristocrats. But the weak government and the celebration of "virtuous" weakness did not reflect the liberal story's "agrarian society." Agriculture was fully compatible with active governments that provided everything from roads and schools to the direct government support for religion that ended before the "industrial" age.[9] Nor did the weakness reflect the libertarian story's assumption that our "founding fathers" would have disapproved of the welfare state, which they obviously did not anticipate. Neither of these stories captured the meaning of the tax laws and debates of the long period before the Civil War, before the Industrial Revolution, and before the United States emerged as a world power.

Finally, I realized that the key to this meaning was slavery. The "states rights" arguments of proslavery politicians in the 1820s and 1830s are familiar. Nobody will be surprised to learn that they insisted that the federal government be kept weak in order to prevent it from interfering with southern slavery. But the history of taxation revealed a far more comprehensive impact of slavery on American politics—and much earlier than the 1820s. Here is the thunder. From the beginning of the colonial era, American governments were more democratic, stronger, and more competent where slavery was a marginal institution: in those colonies where most people were free and there were few slaves or slaveholders. American governments were more aristocratic, weaker, and less competent where slavery was a major institution in the economy and society: in those colonies where large fractions of the population were enslaved and there were many slaves and slaveholders. *Democracy and liberty produced stronger and more competent governments in early American history.* And, from the moment the colonies banded together to create the United States, slaveholders realized that strong, competent, and democratic governments were the only institutions in American life that posed credible threats to slavery.[10]

To put the main findings of this book in more general terms, the antigovernment rhetoric that continues to saturate our political life is rooted in slavery rather than liberty. The American mistrust of government is not part of our democratic heritage. It comes from slaveholding elites who had no experience with democratic governments where they lived and knew only one thing about democracy: that it threatened slavery. The idea that government is the primary danger to liberty has many sources, but one of its main sources in the United States involved the "liberty" of some people to hold others as chattel property. The allied idea that government is the primary danger to property rights also has many sources. In the early United States, however, it made the most sense where large amounts of the "property" consisted of human beings.

Readers will notice that these are not Jeffersonian arguments. But the Jeffersonian story is wrong. It was a political story framed for immediate needs, and it was a story that did more to frustrate liberty and democracy than to promote them, even though Jefferson was an intelligent man with a talent for inspirational political rhetoric. We must come to terms with the fact that one of the crucial achievements of our slaveholding "founding fathers"—especially Jefferson and Madison—was to work out a story about the origins of American politics, a story in which, not coincidentally, they were the heroes. This story was a brilliant accomplishment. It was so brilliant that it has remained the story that Americans have told and retold for two hundred years in the books filled with things that we already know. It is the story about the slaveholding champions of liberty and democracy in the United States.[11]

A few words are necessary about what this book is not. It does not try to catalog every colonial or state-level tax measure, trace the endless rounds of federal tariff revision, or explore the feelings of individual taxpayers struggling to pay their taxes. Nor does it present a statistical analysis of the size or economic impact of tax burdens.[12] These are important tasks that a history of taxation might undertake, but they are not the tasks that this book undertakes. All research strategies involve trade-offs. I have sacrificed the depth that can be achieved in a case study for the payoffs of comparative attention to a variety of government jurisdictions over a long swath of historical time. The purpose throughout is to use the history of tax policies and tax debates as a lens to focus in on when, where, and with what kinds of results democratic governments existed in the early United States. I know that some readers will be wary about delving into the arcane world of tax history. Since even the basic language for evaluating taxation is unfamiliar today, I have written a general guide to this language in the appendix. Still, one might well be justified in thinking that our current tax system is complicated enough without puzzling over taxes that no longer exist. All I can say is that I learned a lot about American history by studying the history of taxation. I can only hope you will agree, in the end, that it is worth the trip.

Here is the itinerary. The prologue begins in Europe to place colonial America into an international context and then crosses the Atlantic to sketch the struggles over "taxation without representation" that caused the American Revolution. The chapters in part 1 then move back to the beginning of English settlement in colonial North America. They offer a great deal of background about society and government in the colonies, but they focus on some of the most important colonial tax systems: describing their development, evaluating their main features, and showing how they fared when they had to cope with the cost of the Revolutionary War. Part 2 turns to the national level beginning in 1776. These chapters describe and analyze the series of decisions through which Congress came to rely on the tariff for revenue. While the significance of the tariff would lie in its industrial protectionism, these chapters show that its origin actually had little to do with industry and much more to do with the national politics of slavery during the Revolutionary War. This politics also shaped the U.S. Constitution, with its notorious "three-fifths" rule for representation and its more obscure apportionment rule for "direct taxes."

Finally, part 3 returns to the states, taking their stories to the eve of the Civil War. By some criteria, the northern and southern states seemed to converge on a series of common tax practices in the antebellum era. By others, they remained almost as distinct as they had always been. Freedom and slavery produced different societies, governments, and tax systems. They also produced different relationships to democracy. The irony is that, even as the nation veered toward its collapse, northerners who missed these realities helped to perpetuate the relationships associated with slavery—into the industrial era and beyond.

Taxation without Representation

On July 12, 1789, two days before the event we usually identify as the beginning of the French Revolution, a mob set out to demolish a wall that one of the most powerful corporations in France had been building around Paris for six years. The wall was being built by the Farmers General (*fermiers-généraux*), a corporation of tax farmers that had held the contract ("farm") to collect many of the monarchy's taxes since 1726. One of these taxes, the *entrées de Paris,* was a levy on goods brought into Paris, including food, beverages, and building materials. The *entrées* involved a bewildering array of rates on particular items and preferential rates on items intended for particular buyers. In 1774, the Farmers General stationed 453 collectors and guards at 29 toll gates across the roads into Paris, requiring that certain goods enter the city at certain gates. But because the gates had been erected fifty years earlier, decades of urban growth had made them easy to evade. A wall enclosing the whole city would solve the problem. It was a grand project. Designed by a leading architect, it featured richly ornamented customshouse pavilions at 66 toll gates plus broad inner and outer boulevards. By July 1789 it was almost finished, with 45 of the new customshouses in place. Almost everyone in France hated the tax farmers. Parisians especially hated the wall. If the Bastille prison, stormed on July 14, is the most famous symbol of the tyranny of the French Old Regime, the wall and its pavilions actually were the first targets of mob action in Paris. The tax farmers survived for five more years. The corporation stopped collecting taxes in 1790. Its last 28 partners were guillotined in 1794.[1]

There are several noteworthy aspects of the history of the Farmers General. Perhaps the most obvious is that it provides an object lesson about the perils of "privatizing" public services. Anyone who thinks that the U.S. Internal Revenue Service is an oppressive bureaucracy should consider the history of tax farming, the alternative that introduced the profit motive into the tax collection process. The Farmers General paid flat fees ("lease prices") to the crown and then collected as much as they could from the population. After they covered the lease prices and their operating costs, everything else they collected was profit. This incentive actually worked too well. The Farmers General was large, efficient, and ruthless. No government bureaucracy in France was nearly as well organized as this corporation. It featured regular advancement ladders and pay scales, its supervisors filed efficiency reports on their subordinates, and it deployed an army of uniformed guards (23,000 in 1784) to search for and seize contraband goods. For one of its more lucrative operations, the royal salt monopoly (*gabelles*), its guards made 4,000 seizures in homes and 10,500 arrests on the roads in one year. The Farmers General also had no trouble attracting executive talent; its partners received compensation packages equivalent to net annual incomes of between $2 million and $5 million today. The partner who came up with the idea of the Paris customs wall was an especially talented executive. We usually remember Antoine Lavoisier as the chemist who discovered the properties of oxygen rather than as the economist who applied modern research methods to the problem of tax evasion. He was a very capable tax farmer, and he was killed in 1794 for this reason.

Another obvious point is that there was no institution in colonial North America that was anything like the Farmers General. There was nothing as large, nothing as wealthy, nothing with the same administrative capacity, and nothing with comparable reach into the society (the ability to arrest 15,000 people). One might even say there was nothing as "modern." Nor were there any taxes that were nearly as regressive as the ones the Farmers General collected. Most of these taxes were "indirect" levies on consumption.[2] They fell into five main categories: customs taxes on imports and exports (*traits*), excise taxes on wine and other commodities (*aides*), salt taxes levied mainly through a royal monopoly on sales of salt (*gabelles*), tobacco taxes levied through a royal monopoly on the manufacture and sale of tobacco products (*tabac*), and registry taxes levied on legal instruments (*domaines*). The Farmers General also collected the internal customs at Paris (*entrées*) and similar entrance taxes at other cities (*octrois*). Most of these taxes raised the prices of goods that consumers would buy even at very high prices (goods with what economists call a "low elasticity of demand"). But if some of them could be justified with a claim that they taxed items that low-income consumers should have done without (liquor, tobacco), others were levied on absolute necessities: food and the salt that everyone needed before the advent of refrigeration. The efficiency and ruthlessness of the Farmers General only magnified the oppressiveness of a tax structure that depended on such regressive impositions.

France also levied "direct" taxes on wealth. The traditional direct tax, the *taille,* was a tax on the peasantry. It was apportioned to local communities and then distributed to individuals by rough estimates of their ability to pay. But the crucial feature of the *taille* was that it exempted a range of "privileged" groups. Clergy, nobles, courtiers, military officers, judges, administrators, professors, doctors, the residents of some provinces and certain cities (including Paris), and all 30,000 employees of the Farmers General enjoyed the "fiscal privilege" of *taille* exemption. The privilege, moreover, was tied to tracts of land as well as to people, which meant that it grew even more arbitrary as land changed hands over time. Even if the fiscal privileges of certain groups could be defended on theoretical grounds—by claiming, for example, that the nobility provided military service in lieu of taxes—there was no theoretical justification for exempting a wealthy commoner whose land was non-*taillable* because it once had belonged to a noble family. While the "indirect" taxes on consumption were highly regressive and imposed serious burdens on the poor, they at least had the advantage of universality compared to the *taille.* Even the privileged usually paid the consumption taxes when they bought taxed commodities.[3]

In the eighteenth century, as war costs created immense revenue demands, the monarchy instituted new direct taxes to draw revenue from the privileged. The first of the new "universal" taxes, the *capitation* (instituted in 1695), was more like an income tax than the poll tax its name suggests. It was levied at a scale of flat rates after an elaborate classification process sorted the taxpayers into brackets by various measures of wealth and social position. The other new direct taxes, the *dixièmes* (tenths) and *vingtièmes* (twentieths), were more precise. They taxed income from real estate, financial assets, business profits, professional earnings, officeholding, pensions, and other items. Taxpayers submitted returns of their income-producing assets, which officials verified in ever more comprehensive investigations. The new taxes did not relieve the *taillables,* who paid them as well as the *taille.* Nor did they blunt the regressive impact of the consumption taxes. But they did provoke the elites to condemn both the taxes and the increasingly competent administrators who levied them. A major reassessment effort after 1771 was especially galling ("the inquisition that is conducted in our houses and châteaux").[4] The grievances of the nobility against the "arbitrary" power of royal tax bureaucrats created a protest rhetoric that others would mobilize against the whole regime of regressive taxation and fiscal privilege. Needless to say, the outcome was not exactly what the "oppressed" nobles had in mind.

On the other side of the English Channel, meanwhile, taxation was also comprehensive and highly regressive. There were no tax farmers exploiting the population for profit in Britain after 1684, but there was a well-oiled bureaucracy collecting a very regressive consumption tax. Britain's leading revenue engine in the eighteenth century was the excise, which taxed alcoholic beverages, salt, leather, soap, candles, wire, paper, silk, starch, and other items. Collection was the responsibility of the Excise Office.[5] With 3,500 employees in 1730 and 4,800 in 1780, the Excise Office was no Farmers General, but it was the most elaborate *public* bureaucracy in Europe. Lines of authority were clear, from commissioners in London to collectors in the provinces, to "gaugers" who traversed local "rides" and "footwalks" measuring the quantities of taxed commodities at breweries, coffeehouses, pubs, grocers, chandlers, and so on. Training and supervision were thorough. Gaugers passed technical exams in mathematics, bookkeeping, accounting, penmanship, and the use of measuring devices. They were paid salaries rather than the kinds of fees that would tend to encourage overzealous collection, while underzealousness was curbed by regular rotations that prevented gaugers from establishing corrupt relationships with the tradesmen and merchants on particular rides and footwalks.

The most impressive aspect of the Excise Office was the way its employees internalized the norms of modern bureaucratic rationality. The commissioners ordered the use of thin paper to reduce postage costs, while gaugers wrote books to instruct others in their rarified skills ("the art of gauging"). The most famous exciseman, Thomas Paine, became an American patriot only after he lost his excise job. Paine petitioned Parliament to grant the excisemen pay raises on the grounds that only their poverty could undermine their commitment to honest and precise work.[6] His superiors were not amused. After they fired him, Paine sailed to Philadelphia to launch his new career as a revolutionary agitator and political theorist, first in America and later in France. The point, however, is that there was nothing else like the Excise Office in Britain or anywhere in Europe in the eighteenth century. There certainly was nothing like it in North America.

Customs duties on imports and exports were the second most lucrative revenue engines in Britain in peacetime (they fell dramatically when wars disrupted foreign trade). The Navigation System that encompassed these duties is probably most famous today as Adam Smith's target in *The Wealth of Nations* (1776). Smith attacked the duties because they favored what otherwise would be unprofitable economic activities and because they subsidized interest groups with good political connections at public expense ("employ taxation as an instrument, not of revenue, but of monopoly").[7] From an American perspective, the navigation duties are remembered as the only British taxes that the colonists paid. The customs duties were enormously complex. In addition to schedules of rates on particular items, hundreds of laws regulated the shipping and storage of goods. If merchants planned to reexport the goods they imported, they had to deposit the duties or give bonds to pay later, collecting drawbacks (refunds) when the exportation occurred. The system also included bounties for the exportation of some commodities.

Unlike the collection of the excise, customs collection was riddled with corruption. Not only did merchants scheme constantly to evade duties (for example, collecting drawbacks and then secretly relanding "exported" goods), but customs officials were also quite corrupt. They connived with merchants to lie about the weight and value of goods often enough to be caught in a series of well-publicized scandals. In the colonies, smuggling was known to be rampant, in no small part because many of the collectors stayed home in England, collecting their salaries and sending lower-paid subordinates to collect from the colonial merchants. The Customs Service compensated its employees with fees as well as salaries. The fees from duty payments were one thing. The fees that could be earned by seizing contraband goods and ships were quite another, sometimes producing violent clashes with smugglers and alleged smugglers (perhaps the targets of extortion) at ports in Britain and the colonies. In the colonies, many customs officials tried to use their remote postings to get as rich as possible as fast as possible, but the colonial merchants gave as good as they got. They harassed the customs men by such strategies as having a colonial assembly pass a law requiring officials to bring seizure cases before local juries, which could be counted on to side with the merchants. The authorities in London would veto ("disallow") a law like this, but the process of sending it across the ocean, reviewing it, and returning the veto took time. Struggles over the power to regulate customs enforcement generated much of the political wrangling that drew American attention to the limits of colonial political autonomy.[8]

The third major tax in the British revenue structure was a direct levy called the "land tax." From the Glorious Revolution (1688) to the end of Queen Anne's War (1714), it was the leading source of British tax revenue—but its contributions to the treasury then fell precipitously, just as the total tax burden skyrocketed to finance the wars of the eighteenth century.[9] While the French monarchy was alienating powerful elites with its *dixièmes* and *vingtièmes,* the British Parliament was protecting its constituents (the landowning gentry and aristocracy) by leaning more heavily on consumption taxes. It is not that the British necessarily paid higher consumption taxes than the French. Because the Farmers General collected the French consumption taxes, the levies on the population included the corporation's profits as well as the crown's revenue. Rather, it is that the British elites protected their interests more successfully.[10]

The amazing fact about the British land tax is that, throughout the entire eighteenth century, it continued to be levied according to an assessment completed in 1692. No serious property tax could rest on such a radically outdated valuation. The land tax was little more than a symbol that the landowning elites (or, really, their tenants) were paying their share. In 1799, to finance the Napoleonic wars, Parliament introduced the first British income tax to tap the proceeds of landed and commercial wealth.

Oddly, at the same time the landed elites were protecting their interests by ensuring that a rising excise displaced a falling land tax—piling the growing burden onto the disfranchised—spokesmen for these elites launched furious assaults on the excise. It was "a *whole System of Oppression,* and strike at the very Vitals of our *Constitution.*" It would reduce the British to the level of the enslaved French ("No Excise, No Wooden Shoes"). And, for anyone who was not worried yet, the inquisitorial gaugers were sexual predators:

No new EXCISE
With five hundred Eyes,
Shall henceforth your Wives or your Daughters surprize;
For it they had License to gage all your *Stocks,*
May also pretend to gage under their Smocks.

Some of the attacks on the excise emanated from rich merchants who resented having to answer to gaugers "who are not [their] *Equals,* or *Neighbours.*"[11] The gentry assault had less obvious sources, since the expanded excise was exactly what kept land taxes down. If French aristocrats had real, if overblown, grievances (assessors in their châteaux), British landed elites were simply biting the hand that fed them. They were doing this because of a larger political struggle in the 1720s and 1730s, which actually had little to do with taxation. One party to this struggle was the "court," centered in the ministry of Sir Robert Walpole and backed by commercial interests. The other party was the "country," led by a group of talented pamphleteers such as Viscount St. John Bolingbroke and the team of John Trenchard and Thomas Gordon, who wrote a series of tracts collected as *Cato's Letters.* The "country" base, backbench members of Parliament, represented an allegedly oppressed agricultural interest and, in the pamphleteers' view, were the only plausible defenders of an embattled "English liberty." Despite the huge impact that this rhetoric would have in America (where *Cato's Letters* was reprinted endlessly), the "oppression" of the excise actually lay in its regressivity. It helped the gentry and hurt the poor.[12]

Things were much better in the Netherlands and much worse in Spain.

In colonies where imperial rule did not include representative institutions (Mexico, India), they were even worse, as Spain and Britain used taxation for the straightforward purpose of moving wealth from colony to metropolis. King Charles III of Spain summarized his colonial project in succinct fiscal language: "To bring my royal revenues to their proper level."[13] But the point of this review should be clear without the detailed treatment of additional cases. As the American colonists famously phrased it, taxation without representation was tyranny.

Adam Smith ended *The Wealth of Nations* by urging Britain to abandon the American colonies. They were too expensive. They required peacetime subsidies and dragged Britain into costly wars. In the 1740s, King George's War (War of the Austrian Succession) "was principally undertaken on their account" and had cost over £40 million. In the 1750s and 1760s, the French and Indian War (Seven Years' War), "undertaken altogether on account of the colonies," had cost over £90 million. The national debt had doubled for a colonial project that was little more than a fantasy. "The rulers of Great Britain have, for more than a century, amused the people with the imagination that they possessed a great empire on the west side of the Atlantic," but this empire "has hitherto existed in imagination only." Colonies that "contribute neither revenue nor military force towards the support of the empire" were not really colonies. They were "a sort of splendid and showy equipage of the empire."

> If any of the provinces of the British empire cannot be made to contribute toward the support of the whole empire, it is surely time that Great Britain should free herself from the expence of defending those provinces in time of war, and of supporting any part of their civil or military establishments in time of peace, and endeavor to accommodate her future views and designs to the real mediocrity of her circumstances.[14]

Britain, of course, did not embrace its real mediocrity in 1776. Instead, it fought another war in America, this time against its rebellious colonists. Before this war broke out in Massachusetts in April 1775, most colonists would have resented Smith's charge that they had failed to support the empire with "revenue" and "military force." They thought they had contributed both, especially for the French and Indian War. By the time Smith's treatise appeared in March 1776, however, this argument was academic. Even if Smith was right (which he basically was), the colonists no longer cared.[15] As they informed a "candid world" on July 4, "these United Colonies are, and of right ought to be, FREE AND INDEPENDENT STATES."

One of the great ironies of the American Revolution is that the struggle over the power of the British Parliament to tax its colonies climaxed in an expensive war. Far from reducing taxes, the Revolutionary War raised them astronomically. To escape from the cost of Britain's national debt, Americans had to incur large debts of their own. If George III and Parliament had listened to Adam Smith, this outcome might have been different. But, since they did not listen to Adam Smith, the United States, Britain, and France (which entered the war on the American side in the last months of 1777) spent millions of dollars, pounds, and francs to decide whether the United States would secure its independence—and the power to shoulder its costs.

The general outline of the events that culminated in the Revolution is familiar. After the end of the French and Indian War in 1763, Parliament attempted to tax the colonies. During the war, it had directed the colonial assemblies to contribute men and money and backed its requests with promises of future reimbursements, which it paid. Now, however, with a crushing debt and a large army stationed in America to defend the colonists against Indians—who launched major attacks on the frontiers in 1764—the British authorities decided that the colonists should make more regular contributions. They unveiled this plan in the Revenue Act (1764), also known as the Sugar Act. Primarily a reform of the customs administration, this law actually reduced the duties on imported molasses, but it also announced Parliament's intention to levy a stamp tax in the colonies. Colonists complained, arguing that only their own assemblies could tax them for revenue (as opposed to taxes that were merely incidental to trade regulations), but these early protests paled next to the ones that erupted when Parliament passed the Stamp Act in 1765.[16]

The tax at issue in the Stamp Act was mild and relatively progressive. It was to be levied on a range of more and less official documents: court orders, ship clearances, deeds, mortgages, licenses, college diplomas, pamphlets, newspapers, and gambling paraphernalia. The tax was to be collected by requiring that the documents be printed or written on paper stamped with the treasury seal, which individuals would buy from stamp collectors. In the summer of 1765, the collectors sailed for the colonies with stacks of the paper, preparing to put the act into effect on November 1. Protests had already begun. The colonial assemblies passed resolves and the politicians wrote pamphlets, but the Stamp Act actually was nullified on the ground by well-organized mobs in the port towns that terrorized the collectors—sacking their houses, hanging and burning effigies of them, forcing them to resign before cheering and jeering crowds.

Americans argued that the Stamp Act was totally unreasonable. The power to lay taxes in the colonies, they contended, belonged solely to the assemblies of the individual colonies. As the North Carolina assembly put it, the Stamp Act violated "what we esteem our Inherent right, and Exclusive privilege of Imposing our own Taxes." The Boston town meeting proclaimed that it "annihilates our Charter Right to Govern and Tax ourselves." "If Taxes are laid upon us in any shape without ever having a Legal Representation where they are laid," Boston wondered, "are we not reduced from the Character of Free Subjects to the miserable state of Tributary Slaves?" The Stamp Act Congress, with delegates from nine of the colonies in attendance, made the same point: "That it is inseparably essential to the Freedom of a People, and the undoubted Right of Englishmen, that no Taxes be imposed on them, but with their Consent, given personally, or by their Representatives." John Adams put it succinctly: "A Parliament of Great Britain can have no more Right to tax the Colonies than a Parliament of Paris."[17]

With colonial merchants organizing boycotts of British goods ("nonimportation" pacts), the British merchants who stood to lose colonial business joined in the demand that Parliament repeal the Stamp Act, which Parliament did in March 1766. It accompanied the repeal with the face-saving Declaratory Act, which asserted that Parliament could legislate for the colonies "in all cases whatsoever." In hearings held before the repeal, Benjamin Franklin had explained to Parliament that the colonists, who revered the King and held Parliament in the highest esteem, objected only to British efforts to bypass their assemblies by levying "internal" taxes. "External" taxes on trade, he suggested (incorrectly), would be acceptable. The Townshend Plan (1767) was a package of "external" taxes. It levied duties on lead, glass, paper, paint, and tea imported into the colonies and added new reforms to the customs administration. The colonists reacted exactly as they had during the Stamp Act crisis, with everything from resolves and pamphlets to riots and boycotts that again brought the British merchants around. The British sent troops into the port towns. In Boston, daily clashes between soldiers and civilians climaxed in the Boston Massacre (1770) when panicked troops fired into a crowd. Parliament repealed the Townshend duties. As it had paired the Stamp Act repeal with the Declaratory Act, it tried to save face this time by leaving one of the duties in place. This, of course, was the duty on tea.

Yet this leftover tea duty was not what caused the Boston Tea Party in December 1773. Although colonists resented the duty, the resistance movement collapsed in a general relief at the repeal of the other Townshend duties. Colonists smuggled as much Dutch tea as they could, but they also bought plenty of taxed British tea. The problem was that they did not buy enough to save one of Britain's most important corporations. The East India Company had financed much of the British war effort in India during the Seven Years'

War. It also owed the government a lot of money. Rather than allow it to collapse, Parliament adopted a bailout scheme to save it in the colonies through
monopoly marketing. Under the Tea Act (1773), only a group of handpicked
merchants would sell the East India Company's tea. This plan would make
smuggled tea harder to sell, but it also would cut all but the handpicked merchants out of the tea market. Intimidation by groups with names like the "committee for tarring and feathering" persuaded most of the tea agents to resign
before the new shipments arrived. In Boston, however, the agent was Thomas
Hutchinson, the Massachusetts governor. Hutchinson was devoted to the
preservation of crown authority, angry that his house had been torn down in
the Stamp Act riots, and determined to sell the tea. Hence the Sons of Liberty
in "Mohawk" costumes making the harbor a "teapot."

Nobody was talking about taxes by this time. Parliament answered the Tea
Party with the Coercive Acts (1774). The main point was to punish Massachusetts: closing the port of Boston (a serious economic sanction) until the
colony reimbursed the East India Company for its tea and suspending all representative governments, from the assembly to town meetings. But if George
III and Parliament now intended to discipline the colonists, the colonists
now intended to resist. Massachusetts called a meeting to protest the Coercive
Acts. In September, twelve colonies sent delegates to Philadelphia for the First
Continental Congress (Georgia, hoping for British military assistance against
the Creeks, wanted to appear obedient at that moment). The Congress called
for a comprehensive trade boycott, this time of both British goods imported
into the colonies and colonial goods exported to Britain. Meanwhile, in Massachusetts, the conflict escalated quickly. In December 1774, Parliament sent
4,000 soldiers to occupy Boston (whose population was only 15,000). With
their regular governments suspended, the Massachusetts colonists set up in-
formal political institutions and commenced serious militia drills. Watching
British authority deteriorate from his headquarters on an island in Boston Harbor, General Thomas Gage sent a detachment of soldiers to secure weapons
the colonists were holding at Concord, Massachusetts. "Minutemen" engaged
these soldiers at Lexington, and the American Revolution began.

The Second Continental Congress turned itself into a national government. It urged the patriots in individual colonies to frame new constitutions,
drafted and issued the Declaration of Independence, and sent George Washington to Boston to assume command of the New England militias as the nucleus for a Continental Army. For tax revenue, Congress did what the British
had done during the French and Indian War. It made "requisitions" on the
states, asking them to lay taxes and apply the proceeds to the war effort. While
Congress was in no position to promise reimbursements, its requisitions pro-

vided that the states would settle up with each other after the war. Thus, the taxes that financed the Revolution were the taxes of the states.

Part 1 of this book will chart the development of the state tax systems in the colonial era and during the Revolutionary War. Part 2 will turn to national tax politics during and after the Revolution. Meanwhile, however, one point must be noticed now. The taxes that the colonies (and then states) levied looked very different from the taxes that European regimes levied in the eighteenth century. Some of the colonies (notably New York) leaned on consumption taxes, but most leaned on combinations of poll and property taxes, both at the colony level and at the local level. These tax systems were more progressive than the European systems, imposing relatively higher burdens on the rich and relatively lower burdens on the poor. The colony taxes were also levied at much lower rates, at least until the crisis of the Revolution. These tax systems did not involve anything resembling the oppressive taxation of Europe.

There were two main reasons for this difference. First, although the colonial tax systems had been utilized to meet war costs, they had not been the tax systems of sovereign governments with full responsibility for the costs of wars, war debts, and other spending. The colonies simply did not need to exploit their tax systems in the way that Britain, France, and the other sovereign regimes had to do to maintain their solvency. Second, the colonial taxes were levied by much more democratic governments. Historians have debated at length about how democratic these governments were. As we will see presently, some were far more democratic than others. But none involved kings and aristocrats—or at least not resident kings and aristocrats.[18] The right to vote, moreover, was distributed more broadly than in the only European regime where elections mattered. It is not clear what fraction of the male adults could vote for members of Parliament in the eighteenth century, but it is clear that larger fractions of the free male adults in the colonies could vote for members of the colonial assemblies. About three-fourths of them could vote in most of the colonies, though the word "free" makes a big difference. In colonies where 40 or 60 percent of the population was enslaved (the Virginia and South Carolina figures), the distribution of the right to vote among free male adults is not comparable to its distribution in colonies where only 2 percent of the population was enslaved (Massachusetts and Pennsylvania).[19] Still, from the standpoint of the taxpayers, the colonial governments were unusually democratic eighteenth-century governments. They levied unusually progressive eighteenth-century taxes as a result.

This history of American taxation is a history of taxation *with* representation. If it were to proceed along the comparative lines sketched in this prologue, it might tell a triumphalist story about American exceptionalism, about how the absence of monarchy and aristocracy in the United States created more democratic political institutions such as more progressive forms of taxation.[20] But we are proceeding in a different direction. Rather than trying to explain what did not happen in American history, we are looking at what actually did happen. The United States *does* have an exceptional history compared with European countries. The absence of monarchy and aristocracy is one obvious difference. Other differences include the fact that the Indians were weaker than the neighbors of most European regimes, that the population grew through mass immigration in addition to natural increase, and that the North American continent contained an abundant supply of natural resources, from the fertile land, timber, and fish that the colonists exploited to the gold, silver, and oil that became significant later. But there was another difference between the United States and European countries, one that should be obvious but that somehow always escapes the standard lists of the "exceptional" features of American history. This difference—that only the United States was half slave and half free in the eighteenth and nineteenth centuries— shaped what actually did happen in American politics in powerful ways.

PART I

Colonial Tax Systems

When the "embattled farmers" of Lexington and Concord started shooting at the British soldiers trying to confiscate their cache of weapons in 1775, nobody was planning for a long war between the American colonies and Great Britain. Had they considered the practical problems, such as how they would finance such a war, the Massachusetts militias might have held their fire and patriots in other colonies might have restrained their enthusiasm. Connecticut troops might not have seized Fort Ticonderoga, and the Continental Congress, which previously had organized nothing more complicated than a boycott, might not have sent George Washington to Boston to take charge of the New England militias. "The cause of Boston," Washington had declared in 1774, "now is and ever will be considered as the cause of America." This American cause turned out to require a long, bloody, and very expensive war. The payoff was the creation of the United States. But the cost was higher than most colonists might have wanted to pay if they had thought seriously about it at the outset.

Some of the colonies were in better shape to finance this war (and to fight it in general) than others. In particular, the New England colonies were in better shape than the rest. Their traditions of independent government and administrative sophistication served them well in the early years of the war. They had to "mobilize" their societies, but they did not have to create institutions from scratch. The southern colonies, meanwhile, experienced these years as a time of mass confusion. Living in terror of slave uprisings, which Africans and African Americans did their best to make real and British officials did their best to exploit, and losing their labor forces as the slaves took the opportunity of wartime chaos to decamp from the plantations, the gentry patriots of the South also had to create new government institutions without being sure they could count on the loyalty of their white social inferiors.[1] The middle states had their own problems. The British occupied New York City and Philadelphia for years at a time after evacuating Boston in 1776, and local populations divided over whether to repel the invaders or embrace the crown's law and order.

To the extent that the American Revolution was financed by taxation, it was financed by the states. The Continental Congress could not tax at all until the

1781 adoption of the Articles of Confederation, the tax power conferred by that document turned out to be totally unworkable, and Congress was never empowered to collect its own "impost" on imported goods. Congress could borrow money in various ways, but even borrowing required some tax revenue—to retire currency (pull it out of circulation) in order to support the value of the amount that continued to circulate, and to make the scheduled interest payments on loans. Congress levied these "taxes" by asking the states to tax. From 1775 to 1786, Congress sent the states a series of increasingly urgent requests known as "requisitions." From the perspective of the states, the requisitions compounded the burdens they already were shouldering to finance their own military operations. While Congress was trying to finance the Continental Army, the states were paying their own militias and the people who supplied them with food, clothing, and guns. When state legislatures had to decide how to allocate their limited resources, Congress did not always seem the most pressing creditor. By the end of the war, its requisitions were burdens the states could not bear even if they tried, although, by that point, most had wearied of trying.[2]

No state was very charitable about raising money for Congress. In his important study of the requisition system, Roger H. Brown reports that only three states raised more than half their quotas from 1781 through 1788 (New York, Pennsylvania, and South Carolina) and that the national average was 37 percent.[3] Brown makes two arguments about the meaning of these figures. His major argument is that the inability of the states to pay their requisitions caused the adoption of the U.S. Constitution. On this point, Brown is clearly right, and part 2 of this book will turn to the relationship between taxation and the Constitution directly. Second, however, Brown argues that the same dynamics operated in all of the states. Every state tried to pressure its citizens to pay, encountered mass resistance, and then retreated from the effort in a concession to majority sentiments. Brown notices that there were differences among the states—that some had stronger governments than others—but because he is explaining the origin of the Constitution, he stresses similarities. "The breakdown of taxation is the only phenomenon that occurred in all the states," he points out.[4]

But Brown's idea of a simultaneous "breakdown" in every state may conceal more than it illuminates, since it does not ask what broke in each state or how it broke. Brown does offer an explanation of who broke the state tax systems (or who applied the brakes to them), identifying "the popular classes," "the rural lower classes," or "impecunious farmers and rural artisans" as the obstacles to effective taxation. Unable to pay, they wielded their majority power to legislate tax relief.[5] Brown's story, therefore, is about how effective democratic politics at the state level bankrupted the national government—a problem that the Constitution finally solved.

The following chapters tell another story. Politics in Virginia was different from politics in Massachusetts, the governments of these states had little in common, and everything related to taxation worked very differently. Brown's story about effective democratic politics is the story of Massachusetts and other northern states, but it is not the story of Virginia and other southern states. These differences, moreover, were far older than the Revolution. They dated from the early years of colonial settlement and only increased with the development of colonial societies and elaboration of colonial governments over time. By the outbreak of the Revolution, northern colonies had sophisticated tax systems, competent and experienced (and annually elected) local officials, and long traditions of democratic political struggle between groups who had competing interests, including interests in who bore the tax burden. In the southern colonies, however, tax systems were primitive and local officials (elites who were appointed rather than elected) were far less capable of performing complex administrative tasks. In the North, the tax reforms of the revolutionary era extended what already were long traditions of incremental tax reforms. In the South, these reforms represented such ambitious breaks with the past that they could barely be implemented at all.[6]

The Jeffersonian story of the early United States describes New England as a bastion of elitism, ruled by merchants whose hegemony was reinforced by powerful ministers in a kind of commercial theocracy. This story portrays the South as a place where slavery elevated the status of poor white men, thereby creating a less hierarchical society (among whites) and a politics of "*herrenvolk* democracy."[7] The following survey of the societies, governments, and tax systems of several of the colonies and states, from their founding through the Revolution, illustrates the gulf between this Jeffersonian story and the truth.

1   Virginia

At the outbreak of the American Revolution, Virginia had an extraordinarily primitive tax system. It levied several different taxes, giving the system as a whole an air of complexity, but each tax in this system was primitive in design and simple to implement. Nothing in Virginia's tax system required local officials to perform complex administrative tasks and nothing imposed serious administrative burdens on taxpayers. Nothing in this system involved even a hint of the sacrifice of simplicity to equity that is the hallmark of modern taxation.

Virginia levied an annual poll tax on "tithables" (defined as free men plus enslaved men and women), which financed both the colony government and its local governments, and it taxed key exported and imported commodities at flat rates by volume (as in two shillings per hogshead of tobacco exported). It taxed carriages, levying one flat rate on four-wheel "chariots" and another on two-wheel "chairs," licensed taverns at flat annual rates, and charged fees for the use of its legal system. Landholders paid a small tax to the British crown or, in part of the colony, to a private proprietor. Known as the "quitrent," this tax levied a flat rate on each hundred-acre tract, regardless of its value, use, or location. Finally, Virginia taxed imported slaves at a percentage of the price paid by the purchaser. This was the only tax Virginia ever had levied on an ad valorem basis (at a percentage of the taxed item's value), and it was highly vulnerable to fraud, as the buyers and sellers of imported slaves colluded to report prices from transactions that nobody monitored. Yet the really striking fact about the history of taxation in colonial Virginia is that this oldest, largest, and richest of the thirteen colonies—whose ruling gentry were proud of their tradition of self-government—actually had never asked its tax officials to measure the value of anything.

The massive costs of the Revolutionary War forced Virginia's newly independent state government to modernize this tax system in a hurry. Virginians scrambled to implement drastic reforms that the northern colonies had learned to administer through more than a century of day-to-day practice. Suddenly, armed only with vague directions from the legislature, local officials were expected to determine the value of various forms of property held by individuals and then to use these valuations to assess and collect extremely high taxes. The officials were supposed to do all this while British warships blockaded the coast, marauding armies marched and pillaged around the countryside, African Americans abandoned the plantations in large numbers, and the inflation caused by huge emissions of depreciating paper money threw the financial system into disarray. Needless to say, the results were less than salutary.

Why did Virginia find itself in this mess? Why hadn't it developed a more sophisticated tax system earlier? The answers to these questions are complicated, but the crucial point is that Virginia *did* find itself in this mess during the Revolution because it *had not* developed a more sophisticated tax system earlier. In its one-hundred-fifty–year history as a colony, Virginia had developed only quite rudimentary public institutions. Its gentry gloried in the accomplishments of their House of Burgesses, which had asserted certain decision-making prerogatives against royal governors, but this gentry had acquired remarkably little experience in either framing or administering complex public policies of any kind. They simply were not equipped to defend their independence against a king who was determined to keep his empire. Looking back at the spectacle, we can applaud the quixotic faith of a confident gentry—it takes a special kind of person in an underdeveloped society to proclaim "Give me liberty or give me death" to a superpower—but we also must ask what was wrong with them. Where had the Virginians been all those years?

The short answer is they had been in two places. For much of the seventeenth century, Virginia was a charnel house. Dying almost as quickly as they arrived, from disease, warfare, and other violence, the survivors may have opted for simple institutions as the only ones they had any hope of being able to implement. By the eighteenth century, a more stable society with greater wealth had emerged, but the gentry class who emerged with it enjoyed the private worlds of their plantations, where they ruled as sovereigns over "families" of slaves, servants, and other dependents, far more than the public world of colonial government, whose political jockeying they loathed—though they did not loathe it enough to cede it to their social inferiors.[1] Virginia had little electoral politics. The assembly's lower house, the Burgesses, were the colony's only elected officials, its county governments consisting of gentry cliques who co-opted new members themselves. It also had little legislative politics in the modern sense of hammering out policies to arbitrate diverse and competing interests. Slavery, gentry rule, and the elite prerogatives that followed from sovereign mastership inhibited the development of Virginia's public institutions in the eighteenth century as effectively as social disorganization had done in the seventeenth.

The only policy system that Virginia elaborated with any vigor in the colonial period was tobacco inspection, an effort to protect the value of the colony's staple crop on the world market in the eighteenth century. Yet even the tobacco inspection system required its officials to make only yes-or-no decisions (to approve or reject proffered tobacco) rather than the more complex judgments that might have followed from a series of grades, like the ones Pennsylvania used for flour inspection.[2] Virginia's political elite, in short, embarked on the Revolutionary War with hardly any usable traditions of competent governance. Their primitive tax system exemplified a more general lack of sophistication in their public institutions. The war forced them to consider whether they wanted to solve these problems. It turned out that they didn't.

Society

Virginia was a terrible place in the seventeenth century. Epidemic diseases and rampant personal and organized violence yielded a life expectancy of about fifty for settlers who survived their first summer (the "seasoning" that killed half the people who arrived) and simply ravaged the Indian population of Britain's first mainland American settlement.[3] From 1622 to 1640, the English population of Virginia rose from about 2,000 to 8,000—but more than 15,000 settlers had arrived. As for the Indians, the Powhatan Confederacy was a well-organized network of 30 to 40 tribes when the English established Jamestown in 1607, but it had disintegrated by 1646. Of 28 tribes whose presence the English recorded in 1608, only 11 still existed in 1669. Over the same period, an Indian population of about 20,000 fell to about 2,000, with the survivors losing their independence, their land, most of their towns, and much else of what had comprised their way of life. They mounted two major attacks on the settlers, in 1622 and 1644. These efforts not only failed to dislodge the English but provoked massive reprisals and a long-term military response that can be described only as a policy of extermination.

Virginia's settlers did not treat one another all that much better than they treated Indians. Overwhelmingly male and with a variety of useless specialized occupations, the early groups of them would have starved if the energetic Captain John Smith had not established a dictatorship and forced them to grow food, and if Powhatan, the confederacy's leader, had not provided more food because he viewed them as pawns in his diplomatic relations with other Indian groups. The Virginia Company, which was chartered by James I in 1606, chose these settlers to pursue what turned out to be a series of hare-brained schemes to bring wealth back to England: goldsmiths and refiners to process gold that did not exist, glassmakers, silk dressers, perfumers, apothecaries, and a huge oversupply of "gentlemen," who paid their own way to Virginia but had no plans to engage in manual labor. Virginia actually fulfilled nobody's plans, and the settlers who survived were disappointed. They did not take their disappointment calmly. They reacted with extreme violence, toward each other and Indians, despite depending on the Indians for food. The ensuing disasters climaxed in the 1622 massacre of one-third of the settlers. The Virginia Company went bankrupt, and the crown took over the colony.

Meanwhile, the Virginia settlers had managed to find a crop they could grow profitably.[4] For all the criticism tobacco provoked, both in Europe and Virginia, it was what made the colony a viable venture. Tobacco was easy to grow, easy to ship, and easy to sell. A boom in the 1620s led to bust in the 1630s, when Virginia's tobacco production increased so dramatically that prices collapsed. By the 1650s, however, tobacco's still-falling prices were offset by lower production costs, and this staple crop was shaping a society that had begun to look permanent. The drastic death rates of the early years fell, the settlers supplemented their ubiquitous tobacco with corn, cattle, and hogs to feed themselves, and, after Powhatan's son Opechancanough failed to destroy the colony in a major 1644 attack, the region's Indians were defeated decisively.

Yet all was not well for the settlers. Most, and perhaps ninety percent of them, arrived as indentured servants, which meant that they sold the next four to seven years of their lives for the price of crossing the Atlantic.[5] They made these deals at English ports, turning themselves into commodities. They could be bought, sold, and even gambled away as the private property of the men who owned the remaining time of their contracts. Virginia landowners purchased servants in large numbers until about 1680, when a series of complex economic changes made them stop buying English servants and start buying African slaves. Most servants were male, especially in the early years, but increasing numbers of female servants and other migrants led to somewhat more balanced sex ratios by the 1690s, of about two women to every three men. Virginia's laws treated servants harshly. The courts punished servants who deprived their masters of labor (by running away, becoming pregnant, breaking other rules) by adding time to their terms. Masters used these and similar laws—which they made by controlling Virginia's assembly and enforced by controlling its courts—to squeeze additional time and labor out of their servants.

If male servants survived their terms, they had relatively good chances of acquiring land and perhaps even their own servants. But, as the likelihood that they would survive went up, the availability of land for them went down. The sharp decline in mortality that began in the 1650s was accompanied by an increased concentration of landownership in the hands of the small elite that began to be identifiable as Virginia's "gentry." The land most accessible to former servants, moreover, was located on the "frontier," in areas where Indians were still in a position to resist white encroachment. The fact that this land was located upriver from the landing places of the British tobacco fleets also forced small-scale farmers to depend on gentry planters in selling their tobacco and buying imported goods. Simmering conflicts between the gentry and poorer settlers exploded over specific issues. The major explosion, Bacon's Rebellion (1676), was sparked by the coastal gentry's rejection of an all-out war against all neighboring Indians, regardless of their diplomatic relations with the colony. Starting with genocidal raids against Indians, the rebellion expanded into a murderous civil war, with white yeomen, servants, and African slaves fighting together against the corrupt oligarchy centered on Governor William Berkeley. Bloodthirsty reprisals featuring extortion (sign over your property to us or we'll hang you) confirmed the rebels' view of their triumphant enemies. They also persuaded the royal commission that arrived with 1,000 soldiers to help Berkeley defeat the rebels to oust his regime as well. The Plant Cutters' Rebellion (1682) resulted from efforts to curtail tobacco production to raise prices. It was less serious than Bacon's Rebellion, though it too ended in a series of hangings.[6]

By 1700, Virginia had been transformed by the enslavement of Africans. Although some African slaves had toiled in Virginia since at least 1619, the large numbers arrived in the decades after 1680, and continued to arrive until the 1770s, when the Virginia planters decided they had as many slaves as they could use. In 1690, Africans and their African American children were seven percent of the population. From 1750 to 1780, they were *forty* percent of the population. The economic history of eighteenth-century Virginia is the history of slavery, and its social and cultural history reflected struggles by an increasingly American-born slave population to control their own community life and elaborate their own culture, with particular success in the quarters of the larger plantations.[7] In spite of (or really because of) its violence and exploitation, slavery turned Virginia into a more congenial place for whites, who generally treated one another with more respect than before. This is the era of the fabled Virginia gentry, the grand houses and families, and the men who led the American Revolution.

Virginia remained a terrible place for blacks and, as white settlement extended further westward, for ever more groups of Indians. For them, life in Virginia remained as violent as it ever had been for whites and a good deal more oppressive. As long as these very large facts are kept in mind, however, eighteenth-century Virginia looks like the society we normally think of as the world of George Washington and Thomas Jefferson. A majority of white families worked on land they owned, wealthy planters owned large labor forces of African and African American slaves, most white males could vote for representatives in the House of Burgesses, and while gentry slaveholders and yeoman farmers disagreed about a range of issues and developed increasingly divergent lifestyles, they made the Revolution together—as slaveholders and as farmers who hoped to be able to buy slaves in the future.

Government

The government of Virginia was hopelessly corrupt in the seventeenth century, and its institutions remained primitive in the eighteenth.[8] The Virginia Company allowed the settlers to establish rudimentary representative institutions that, under crown control, became the tripartite government of House of Burgesses, council, and governor by 1650. The burgesses were elected and the council was appointed by the governor, who in turn was appointed by the British crown. The governor also appointed Virginia's local officials, the county court commissioners who acted as judges, legislators, and executives in the counties. After 1654, the governor was required to appoint new county court commissioners from lists supplied by the incumbents. While this rule clearly represented a victory for local control, removing county jobs from the British patronage network, it was far from democratic. It created a system of self-perpetuating county oligarchies in which membership carried life tenure and essentially passed as a family heirloom. Virginia's voters did not win the right to elect their local government officials until 1851.[9]

Starting in 1662, meanwhile, the county court members, now known as justices of the peace, also served as county sheriffs, rotating the job among themselves to guarantee each a shot at the lucrative fees sheriffs received for their services. Rounding out the Virginia government system, vestries supervised religious affairs, levying taxes to pay ministers' salaries and build and maintain churches. Initially elected (when a new vestry was established), vestrymen served for decades at a time and chose new members themselves—in a self-perpetuation even more direct than the county court nomination lists.

Burgesses, county courts, and vestries usually were the same men, serving in all three posts simultaneously, although they stepped down from the county courts temporarily while serving as sheriffs. These men overwhelmingly were wealthy planters, the owners of large numbers of white servants in the seventeenth century and large numbers of enslaved Africans in the eighteenth. Members of the council tended to be even wealthier, while the governors were British aristocrats or near-aristocrats with connections to top crown officials in London.[10]

The crown also stationed other officials in Virginia, particularly to safeguard its customs revenue. Under the Navigation Acts, Virginia's tobacco was an "enumerated commodity," which meant it could be shipped only to British ports, where the customs were collected. Customs men in Virginia collected on imports and, for exports (tobacco), supervised the "bonds" that shippers posted to guarantee that they obeyed the navigation laws. When they disobeyed, the collectors tried to cash in the bonds, but Virginia's courts—like those of other colonies—often interfered to protect the shippers. To collect quitrents (the small flat-rate land taxes), the crown relied on the sheriffs, ensuring that minimal efforts to collect would be made. Virginia's receiver-general (the official in charge of all crown revenue) reported in 1762 that *none* of the sheriffs submitted their annual quitrent accounts. Still, Virginia was a lucrative possession for Britain. Its tobacco produced a great deal of customs revenue, and it even returned some money in quitrents.[11]

One of the most consistent themes in Virginia's tax laws, particularly in the seventeenth century, was the corruption of county officials, the sheriffs in particular. Sometimes they were charged with mere incompetence, but the frequency of complaints about their rapacity suggests that it was nearly boundless. Because sheriffs were responsible not only for tax collection but also for distraint (confiscation and sale of property for nonpayment of taxes), their opportunities for extortion and other forms of "oppression" were large. They pocketed revenue outright, sold tobacco (the unit of currency for tax payments) at unfairly high prices to people whose nonfarm occupations forced them to buy it at tax time, manipulated the conversion of tobacco into money to reap large profits on complex transactions, and treated some taxpayers quite arbitrarily in the distraint process, say, by confiscating livestock worth far more than the taxes they owed.[12] The taxpayers could seek redress from the county courts, but these courts consisted of the sheriffs' friends. We often think of political corruption as a phenomenon of the cities of later eras—the "machines" of Boss Tweed's New York or Richard J. Daley's Chicago—but no urban ward heeler ever could boast that he "seen my opportunities and I took 'em" with more alacrity than the gentry of colonial Virginia.[13]

Historians generally argue that corruption was rampant in the seventeenth century but not in the eighteenth. As Edmund Morgan phrases it, officeholding was "a principal way to wealth" only in the earlier period. By the 1730s, according to Morgan, Virginia's slave-based agricultural regime had become a more dependable mode of accumulation than outright theft from the public. Others credit the stability of gentry rule, the rise of "a conscientious, responsible ruling group" guided by norms of noblesse oblige and devotion to "the public interest."[14] Yet there are several reasons to be skeptical about this story. One is that its equation of oligarchic domination with responsible government serving "the public" is problematic from the start. Another is the "Robinson affair." When John Robinson died in 1766, it turned out that the man who had served as Virginia's treasurer since 1738—whom a governor had described as "the most popular man in the country"—had embezzled some £100,000, most of which was tied up in large illegal loans he had made to his friends over the years, including twenty Burgesses, half the council, and a host of other leading planters. This money was tax revenue, paid in paper currency that it had been Robinson's job to remove from circulation. Instead of burning it, he had "loaned" it out to the Virginia elite. The executor of Robinson's estate tried to shield his high-profile debtors from public scrutiny, but there was too much money involved. The scandal broke as Virginians were protesting Parliament's Stamp Act, claiming the colony should control its own public finances because "taxation without representation is tyranny."[15] Corruption was not the preserve of low-level political operatives in colonial Virginia. It lay at the heart of gentry rule.

Nevertheless, Virginia's tax legislation included vastly fewer references to "frauds" in the eighteenth century than in the seventeenth. But before concluding that all was well in Virginia's counties in the later period, we must notice the rhetoric that replaced the earlier complaints about theft. Year after year, the burgesses attacked their major tax instrument, the poll tax on tithables, as "grievous" and "burdensome." After reading the laws that repeat this theme so incessantly, it is tempting to conclude that the Virginia gentry longed to scrap the poll tax in favor of a more progressive alternative. But progressive taxation was not the issue. The burgesses attacked the poll tax in order to defend trade taxes they thought crown officials might disallow (since they could interfere with the trade that the crown taxed itself). Each one of these tax laws began with a "whereas" clause emphasizing that the trade taxes would permit Virginia to reduce its poll tax, which was "always grievous to the people of this colony."[16] The burgesses clearly disliked the poll tax, but they neglected to explain what made it "burdensome."

The Poll Tax

Virginia's annual "public levy," as well as its county and parish levies, were poll taxes on tithables, with the "tithables" defined to include free adult males, white male indentured servants, and adult slaves of both sexes (with "adult" defined as sixteen and up).[17] The House of Burgesses, county courts, and vestries set rates for these taxes as flat numbers of pounds of tobacco on each tithable in every taxpayer's household. To get a quick sense of how this tax worked, take as an example a public levy of 10 pounds of tobacco per tithable. If the taxpayer was a farmer who was a free adult male with one adult son living at home and no slaves or servants, his tax bill would be 20 pounds of tobacco: 10 for himself plus 10 for his son. If the taxpayer was a wealthy planter, a free adult male with two free adult sons at home, two white male servants, and fifteen enslaved Africans, his tax bill would be 200 pounds: 10 for himself, 20 for two sons, 20 for two servants, and 150 for 15 slaves. If the taxpayer was a free widow with two adult sons at home, two white female servants, and eight African slaves, finally, her tax bill would be 100 pounds: 20 for two sons plus 80 for eight slaves, with no charge for herself or the white female servants.

The poll tax initially was established in the first laws enacted by a Virginia assembly, in 1624, immediately after the crown took over from the Virginia Company. To send an agent to lobby in England and "for defraying such publique debts our troubles have brought upon us" (the reprisals against Powhatan for the 1622 massacre), this first assembly levied fourteen pounds of tobacco on "every male head above sixteen years of adge now living." Five years later, however, an attempt to clarify the law for paying the salaries of ministers offered a different criterion: "It is thought fitt that all those that worke in the ground of what qualitie or condition soever" pay tithes for the ministers. In the 1640s, the assembly added greater precision. It defined the taxpayers as the "masters" of families, making these masters "responsible for all the public duties, tithes and charges, due from all persons in their familys," and decided who the "tithable" members of these families were: "all negro men and women, and all other men from the age of 16 to 60."[18] There would be minor changes later, but the Virginia poll tax had assumed the form it would maintain until the Revolution.

Because the poll tax on tithables was radically different from the taxes we pay today, it is necessary to spell out some of its major implications. Conceptually, the poll tax was taxing the labor power at the disposal of taxpayers, casting this labor as a proxy for wealth, but also using race and gender categories as proxies for the kinds of labor it was associating with wealth. Kathleen M. Brown has explored the major assumptions that this conceptual operation entailed. First, the poll tax exempted labor that was assumed to be performed by white women, on the further assumption that this "women's work" (the production of households and reproduction of families) did not produce wealth. Second, it did tax the labor that was assumed to be performed by African and African American women, implying that they were not "women" in the same way that white women were, that they worked in fields instead of homes, producing tobacco instead of households and families. There is no need to enumerate the many ways in which these assumptions were false.

Brown argues that the sexist and racist assumptions built into Virginia's poll tax fostered harmful stereotypes about white women and black people, devaluing the very real labor of white women and reinforcing an assumption at the heart of the whole system of slavery: that Africans and African Americans were commodities rather than people, since only people have the gender identities that defined tax liability.[19] This analysis is surely correct, but it is important to be clear about exactly what is at stake in it. As a tax, the poll tax on tithables did not harm white women or black people. On the contrary, white women were exempted, while enslaved Africans had no reason to care about how white Virginians distributed their tax burdens. Rather, Brown's point is that Virginia's poll tax on tithables reflected and reinforced key cultural assumptions and that the regular deployment of these assumptions in daily life—in the ways in which individuals treated each other—undoubtedly did harm a large majority of the residents of Virginia.

Virginia's poll tax on tithables also had interesting and significant economic implications. Like all poll taxes, it was levied as a flat tax rate on every taxed person. Because flat tax rates do not vary with the wealth or income of the taxpayer, a poll tax generally is considered one of the most regressive forms of taxation. In a modern economy, a poll tax charging every adult $1,000 per year, for example, would burden the poor more heavily than the rich—because $1,000 is a larger proportion of a poor person's income. While the rich might be able to write their $1,000 checks without thinking twice, the poor would have to scrimp and save out of what they usually spent on food and clothing to put a $1,000 tax payment together. This outcome is the very definition of regressive taxation.

But colonial Virginia was not a modern economy, and its poll tax was not regressive in this sense. Because some tithables owned other tithables in colonial Virginia, the tax functioned both as a poll tax on free men *and* as a property tax on the owners of slaves and servants. For this reason, its economic incidence was more complex than the incidence of a modern poll tax would be. The Virginia poll tax was regressive at the low end of the wealth distribution, among men who were free but poor. These men owned no servants or slaves;

they paid for themselves and their adult sons, and they paid at flat rates that did not take their poverty into account, though the county courts could exempt men who were very poor (because they were "disabled to labor by reason of sicknes, lamenes or age").[20] Poor men paid a tax that functioned as a modern poll tax would function. But, through the rest of the wealth distribution, among what we might call the middle class and the rich, the incidence of the poll tax on tithables was roughly proportional, since the ownership of human beings was closely correlated with wealth: the wealthier a man (or woman) was, the more servants and slaves he (or she) tended to own. Thus, the middle class and the rich were paying something that resembled a property tax, with richer taxpayers who owned many tithables paying more than poorer taxpayers who owned few tithables.

The administrative implications of this tax were crucial. Virginia's poll tax on tithables was as simple as any tax can be. It was levied at only one rate rather than in a series of brackets. It also imposed no record-keeping burdens on taxpayers. Unlike a property tax, it did not require local officials to assess the value of property. Unlike an income tax, it did not require taxpayers to calculate and report the size of their incomes. Unlike an excise, it did not require producers of taxed commodities to keep production records or use uniform weights or containers to gauge tax liabilities. In fact, nothing was measured or reported except the number of "tithable" adults in a household at tax time. Nothing invited taxpayers to think they were being overcharged, and nothing invited debates about whether complicated rules were being applied fairly to individuals. Nor did anything tempt legislators to manipulate minute provisions to favor certain constituents. The poll tax had no complicated rules or minute provisions, though it did contain exemptions.[21] Because tax evasion could take only two forms—concealing tithables and falsifying the ages of young adults—enforcement could consist solely of inquiries into whether taxpayers were doing one or both of these things.

From an administrative perspective, the poll tax on tithables was an ideal tax for colonial Virginia. It required little administrative sophistication and no special skills beyond the ability to multiply tax rates by numbers of tithables. Taxpayers did not have to trust the discretion of their public officials, which was a good thing because Virginians did not trust their officials. The only real problem with the poll tax was its low-end regressivity. Everyone who was involved seems to have understood this problem, though rhetoric about it often cloaked other kinds of objections. The poll tax on tithables was "grievous" and "burdensome" to the poor because of its regressive economic incidence, but it posed an entirely different problem for the gentry. For the gentry, the problem with the poll tax was administrative.

Reform

Despite its simplicity, the poll tax did not work very well. Especially in the seventeenth century, the colony's laws chronicle a series of problems that focused on the county sheriffs, individually and in collusion with taxpayers. In 1644 the problem was sheriffs refusing to produce their accounts. In 1645 it was sheriffs who not only committed "extortion" but also "converted a great part" of the tax revenue "to their private benefit." In 1646 it was tithables missing from tax lists. In 1661 it was the "fraud of sheriffes in bringing in their lists" and, a year later, what should have been a predictable strategy for evasion: that "diverse persons purchase [white] women servants to work in the ground that thereby they may avoyd the payment of levies," to which the solution, briefly, was to order that white female agricultural laborers be "reputed tythable, and levies paid for them accordingly." In 1672, the problem was taxpayers lying about the ages of tithable teenagers, and in 1691 it was sheriffs exploiting taxpayers by picking "their own advantagious times" to demand payment.[22]

This series of complaints—which included only those serious enough to merit a formal notice in legislation—largely ended with the seventeenth century, primarily because Virginia restructured its tax system to reduce poll taxes sharply (when the rates rose again in the 1750s, the complaints reappeared).[23] Morgan reports that the "public levy" was only one-fourth as high, on average, from 1687 to 1700 as it had been from 1680 to 1686. From 1700 to 1750, the levy was below half its average rate from 1687 to 1700. Complete runs of county records survive from few counties, but Morgan found that the "county levies" in four counties were much lower in the 1740s and 1750s than in the 1690s: one-third of their former size in Norfolk, one-fourth in Northumberland, one-fifth in Lancaster, and one-seventh in Surry. The counties could slash their tax rates because the colony assumed one of their major expenses, the cost of being represented in the House of Burgesses (per diems and travel allowances for the members).[24] Poll taxes fell across the board, with lower rates reducing the stakes of enforcement.

It is not that Virginia had tackled the low-end regressivity problem. An early effort to do that failed completely. In 1645, to finance their reprisals for the 1644 Indian attack, Virginians attempted a radical reform: to supplement the poll tax with a property tax on land and livestock. "Whereas the anncient and vsual taxing of all people of this collony by the pole, equally, hath been found inconvenient and is become insupportable for the poorer sorte to beare," colony and county taxes henceforth would be "raised by equall proportions out of the visible estates in the colony."[25] The 1645 tax was very simple: twenty pounds of tobacco on each tithable person in addition to four pounds on each hundred acres of land, four on each cow, four on each sheep, two on each goat, and thirty-two on each horse. This tax also was uncollectable. In 1646, announcing that the property lists were defective, the assembly ordered that new lists be made and charged double rates to taxpayers who had concealed property in the first round. It then tried exhortation. The war against the Indians was expensive and the taxes "extraordinary and not in former times to be paraleld," but the assembly still "hoped that with more cheerfullness it will be entertained and discharged by the inhabitants." When exhortation did not work either, the assembly tried administrative reform, appointing collectors in 1647 to replace the sheriffs. In 1648, however, the assembly abandoned the property tax altogether. It was "repealed and made void," and the colony reverted to its "anncient and vsual" practice of taxing tithables "by the pole, equally."[26] Virginia's experiment with property taxation was a total failure.

The real innovation did not address the regressivity issue at all. The real innovation, a tax of two shillings per hogshead of tobacco exported, addressed what actually was Virginia's crucial tax problem: its lack of administrative capacity, or, the endemic political corruption of its county governments. By supplementing the poll tax with a trade tax rather than a property tax, the assembly reduced its reliance on the counties for revenue. The 1645 property tax had been an effort to address the regressivity problem (even if its livestock taxes probably seemed less than a boon for "the poorer sorte"), but the trade tax reform had nothing to do with tax equity, despite some of the rhetoric that accompanied it. The two-shilling tobacco tax bypassed the county sheriffs. This reform was about tax administration rather than tax incidence.

The assembly began this reform effort in 1658, contrasting "the burthensom and vnequall waie of layinge taxes by the pole" against "how just and proportionable it will be to impose the same on our commoditie made," meaning tobacco. Rather than taxing the labor that produced the tobacco, Virginia could tax the tobacco itself. This strategy not only would allow Virginia to escape its administrative burden, but also promised to solve two of its major economic problems. The assembly directed that the two-shilling tax be paid in money by the English merchants who came to buy Virginia's tobacco. This procedure would inject scarce currency into the economy and also encourage diversification, since Virginians might "produce other vsefull and beneficiall comodities" if their tobacco was taxed. Another law laid a ten-shilling tax on tobacco exported in non-English ships, which in practice were Dutch ships. When the English and Dutch shippers refused to post bonds to secure their payments, the assembly ordered them to appear to explain, which they apparently refused to do. The assembly backed down quickly. It repealed its first trade taxes because "certaine inconveniencies" made them impossible to collect. It reinstated the ten-shilling tax on the Dutch shippers, but the English shippers (who were most of the shippers) were able to reject the burden of Virginia's tax administration in the 1650s.[27]

Virginia seemed stuck with its "burthensom and vnequall" poll tax, but not for long. The colony's power in relation to the English tobacco merchants shifted in 1660, with the Restoration of the Stuarts after the English Civil War and interregnum of Oliver Cromwell (Virginia's leaders had taken the royalist side throughout England's political convulsions). Charles II now "graciously" approved the two-shilling tax on the English shippers and ten-shilling tax on the Dutch, although the latter became moot when Dutch ships were banished from Virginia waters by the Navigation Act, also in 1660. The point of this story, however, is the origin of the lucrative two-shilling tax on exported tobacco. Far from being forced on Virginia's planters by the royal bureaucracy, this tax originated as their own plan to solve their own tax problem by cutting the counties out of the process as much as possible. Royal customs officers collected the two shillings and remitted the tax to Virginia's government. Virginia had invited the king to take over part of its tax administration, and the king had accepted the invitation.[28]

Still, Virginia could not abandon its poll tax entirely. The burgesses continued to attack it on equity grounds ("Whereas through the great taxes, which of necessity must be layd upon the country poore men are most likely to suffer . . ."), but when the governor and the council offered a remedy, the burgesses would have none of it. In 1663, the governor and council "unanimously concluded . . . that the most equal way of paying taxes is by laying a levy upon land and not upon heads" and advised the burgesses to replace the poll tax with a land tax. The burgesses refused even to consider this suggestion.[29] To the burgesses, the poll tax was acceptable now that it was supplemented by a trade tax that royal officials collected on behalf of the colony.

Why didn't Virginia tax land in the seventeenth century? Why did it stick to the poll tax on tithables? Unfortunately, the record offers no definitive answer to these questions. If we take the rhetoric about the poll tax oppressing "poore men" seriously, the colony's failure to tax land looks like simple elitism, with the gentry rejecting a system that would have increased their own taxes. The deployment of the regressivity critique by the Bacon rebels of 1676 seems to bolster this interpretation. Giles Bland, who would be hanged for his participation in the rebellion (and who actually was a British customs inspector!), complained that men "who had nothing but their labors to maintain themselves, wives, and children, paid as deeply to the public as he that hath twenty thousand acres of land."[30] Yet the elitism interpretation is weakened by the fact that this assertion was false. The owners of thousands of acres were also the "masters" of "families" of tithables. It is far from clear that a land tax, much less a tax on land and livestock, would have been more progressive than the poll tax on tithables in seventeenth-century Virginia.

When the Bacon rebels complained about favoritism toward men with "twenty thousand acres," they probably were talking less about taxes than about a separate issue: the engrossment of huge tracts of unimproved land by the colony's gentry. Bacon's Rebellion was about access to land by poor men and the coastal gentry's unwillingness to fight the Indians aggressively enough to obtain increased supplies in the west.[31] As a tax on the agricultural labor force, Virginia's poll tax resembled a land tax that might have been levied on land that was cultivated—as opposed to a tax on the total holdings of individuals. The Bacon rebels wanted to tax all land and, especially, unimproved land. They may even have wanted to use the tax system to bring about a large-scale land re-form—by slapping heavy taxes on princely accumulations of unimproved land that could never be farmed in the foreseeable future. It is in this sense that the burgesses pursued an elitist policy by retaining the poll tax. Taxing labor rather than land favored the gentry by protecting large holdings of unimproved land.

It is also in this sense that the taxation of labor emerges as a principle rather than a mere expedient in the Virginia tax system. Whether it taxed laborers directly (the poll tax) or taxed the tobacco they produced (the two shillings per hogshead), Virginia was taxing the production of its staple crop rather than the wealth of its taxpayers. A land tax could have been framed to achieve the same result if it had been designed to tax cultivated land but exempt specula-tive and otherwise idle holdings. The poll tax was "burthensom and vnequall" for the same reason a land tax of this kind would have been, although even this land tax could have relieved poor men who were landless but "tithable." But the burgesses were not interested in the regressivity problem. Nor did anyone suggest that land be taxed ad valorem rather than at flat acreage rates. Valua-tion might have favored speculators (since unimproved land was worth less than cultivated land), but Virginia's political culture raised a larger obstacle: if its county officials could not even produce tolerably complete lists of the "tith-ables" (or collect flat per acre quitrents), they could hardly be entrusted with the immensely more complex task of assessing the value of property.

For almost a century after the 1660s, Virginia expanded its revenue base by expanding its trade taxes. The two-shilling tobacco tax was the first of a series in which Virginia enlisted royal customs officers as its tax collectors. It added a tax on imported servants in 1680, with different rules for "christian servants" and African slaves, and a tax on imported liquor in 1684. By 1701, the assembly was reenacting the liquor and slave duties at regular intervals. The renewal laws all touted the productivity of these taxes, explaining to crown officials (who had the power to veto them) that Virginia's taxpayers preferred them to the "griev-ous and burdensome" poll tax. This rhetoric endured. The liquor and slave taxes "have proved very usefull and advantageous, and that no better Expedient can be found to lessen the Levy by the Poll or defray the Charge of any Public Design" (1710). "[M]any years of Experience" proved them "the only Method easy to be born here in raising Funds," enabling Virginia to build public build-ings and pay defense costs "with Chearfulness" (1723). "[L]ong experience" proved the liquor tax "the most easy expedient for raising money," while the slave tax not only was "very easy to the subjects of this colony, and no ways bur-thensome to the traders in slaves," but also raised "a competent revenue" while "preventing or lessening a poll-tax" (1734). The slave tax "will be a great ease to the poorer sort of people, by lessening the levy by the poll" (1752). "[I]t hath been found by experience" that taxes on tobacco, slaves, and other items "are easy to the people, and not so burthensome as a poll tax" (1769).[32]

The 1723 renewal raised another issue. When the governor worried that the liquor and slave taxes violated his instructions, which barred him from approving laws that "may affect the Trade & Shipping of Great Brittain," the burgesses added a new argument. Before elaborating on what these taxes had enabled Virginia to accomplish (to build "a House of our Governor, A Noble Structure for the Supream Court of Justice, A Magazine for the Arms and Ammunition of our Country, And a public Goal [sic] for Debtors and Crimi-nals"), not to mention their military utility (since the Indians "may possible [sic] become our Enemies"), the burgesses explained that white Virginians were afraid of their enslaved labor force. Virginia needed the slave tax because of the "vast Numbers of Negro Slaves which are daily imported and increased among us" and "some late discovered Conspiracies among these Slaves wholly to destroy Your Majesties good Subjects Inhabiting here."[33] The crown ve-toed the liquor and slave tax in 1724, approving the liquor tax separately in 1727. Starting in 1732, it also approved the slave tax again, though only after redesigning it. The crown demanded that the tax be levied ad valorem and col-lected from slave buyers rather than levied at a flat rate per slave and collected from slave traders. Hence the relative sophistication of this tax in the Virginia system. The claim that it was intended to suppress the slave trade (as opposed to raising money from it) would not be revived until 1771, when the crown suddenly vetoed it again—and in the context of a much larger conflict.[34]

Revolution

This tax regime, based on the poll tax on tithables plus the trade taxes on to-bacco, liquor, and slaves, worked until the French and Indian War, and even survived that with minor changes. When Virginia's governor sent a young militia colonel (George Washington) to demand that the French evacuate Fort Duquesne (Pittsburgh) in 1754, they sparked a war that would engulf three separate continents. Britain and France fought the Seven Years' War in Europe, North America, and India, enlisting indigenous allies in the two latter locations, and at an enormous cost for all of the societies involved. The French monarchy never recovered, although it postponed its final crisis until 1789. Britain's heavy war spending provoked the well-known series of revenue measures that produced the American Revolution: the Sugar, Stamp, Townshend, Tea, and Coercive Acts. Virginia's war costs might have instructed the tobacco planters about what it took to finance a major military operation, but Parliament rescued them from having to try anything radical. It reimbursed the colonies for their war spending—before the new Grenville ministry made the fateful decision to insist on colonial contributions in 1764.[35]

To finance the French and Indian War, Virginia issued paper currency, providing for its redemption by hiking its traditional taxes. The premise of "currency finance" was that currency held its value if it was removed from circulation when taxpayers used it to pay their taxes.[36] The burgesses also directed the county sheriffs to pay their quitrent arrears ("Whereas many of the sheriffs of this colony have of late years to the great prejudice of his majesty, kept the money collected by them for his quit-rents . . . till judgment could be obtained against them at law . . ."), and added a land tax that piggybacked on the quitrent system: 1.25 shillings per 100 acres, to be collected "according to the rent rolls . . . for the collection of his majesty's quit-rents." Aside from the currency (the money that John Robinson failed to burn), Virginia made few innovations during the French and Indian War. It reassigned the collection of the tobacco tax from customs officers to its own tobacco inspectors (the inspection system was established in 1730) and added one new tax to its repertoire. The carriage tax instituted during the French and Indian War would remain a staple of Virginia's tax system through the 1840s.[37]

Nothing in this experience prepared Virginia for the staggering cost of the Revolutionary War. First of all, trade taxes were useless when trade stopped. Since nearly all Virginia's trade had been with Britain and the British West Indies in the late colonial era, the American protest strategies of "nonimportation" and "nonexportation" (designed to pressure the crown by hurting British merchants) had the same effect as the naval blockade that the British established once the shooting began.[38] Virginia had to tax its own citizens directly. It started off in 1775 and 1776 by issuing paper currency, planning to redeem it by hiking all of its internal taxes: the poll tax, per acre land tax, carriage tax, tavern license, and court fees (for writs). In a move that probably was more symbolic than lucrative, the state took over marriage licensing from the governor—Lord Dunmore, who, at that moment, was soliciting African American volunteer soldiers to help him suppress the rebellion in return for their freedom. The response was enthusiastic. As Virginia militias encountered these black troops, wearing sashes reading "Liberty to Negroes," the gentry started to understand that revolution was a game with high stakes.[39]

By 1777, the old fiscal expedients clearly were not working. With their paper money in a free fall of depreciation and the Continental Congress begging for money to sink its own rapidly depreciating currency, Virginians were ready to try a radical tax reform: ad valorem taxation of various forms of property, many of which Virginia had never taxed before: "That a tax or rate of ten shillings for every hundred pounds value . . . shall be paid for all manors, messuages [houses and house lots], lands, and tenements [rented real estate], slaves, mulatto servants to thirty one years of age, horses, mules, and plate [gold and silver]," and "the amount of all salaries, and of the neat income of all offices of profit" except those of military officers. If the valuation of land, slaves, buildings, animals, plate, and salaries was not revolutionary enough, the 1777 law added a tax on financial assets: two shillings per pound "for the amount of the annual interest received upon all debts bearing interest." There was a new flat tax on cattle (four pence per head), and increases to the old taxes: the tavern and marriage licenses, the carriage tax, and the tax on exported tobacco. Nor was the poll tax forgotten, though the new tax regime required modifications. This poll tax was levied on "tithables" over the age of twenty-one except soldiers and sailors and "except also slaves and mulatto servants to thirty one years of age, who, being property, are rated *ad valorem* as aforesaid." Any taxpayer who did not take an oath of allegiance to the Revolution would be charged double, all previous taxes scheduled to become due before 1784 were declared void, and—on top of all this—there was also a regular "public levy" based on the old definition of "tithables."[40]

The big question, of course, was how Virginia would manage the valuation of property. In what must be considered the most radical part of the whole plan, the commissioners in charge of the process were elected by "the freeholders and housekeepers of each county or corporation [city]." The three local commissioners had to be "able and discreet men" who lived in the county (or city), owned £800 of "visible property," and did not hold any of a large number of jobs that might create conflicts of interest. The commissioners divided their jurisdictions into districts and appointed two "assessors or appraisers" for each district, "discreet men" who owned land in the district. After taking oaths to act impartially, the assessors visited everyone in the district to take lists of taxable property, with the taxpayer swearing that "he or she hath not shifted or changed the possession of any of the said taxable articles, or used any fraud, covin, or device, in order to evade the assessment thereof." Then, the two assessors valued the property "as the same would in their judgment sell for in ready money," splitting the difference when they disagreed. They submitted their lists and assessments to the commissioners, who checked their results.[41]

So far, so good—except that it didn't work, in part because the rates were too low and in part because of the more basic problems that resulted from introducing such a radical reform. In 1778, the legislature tripled the property tax (to 1.5 percent), extended it to cash holdings ("all money exceeding five pounds which shall be in the possession of one person" on May 1), hiked the other taxes, added an excise on distilling and an impost on imported liquor, and increased the penalty for failing to take an oath to the revolutionary regime, from double to triple taxes. This 1778 law also addressed the inevitable result of trying to value all this property for the first time: "[W]hereas great inequality and injustice have arisen from the various opinions of assessors in the same county in the valuation of taxable property," the county commissioners and assessors were directed to hold meetings at the beginning of the process to "consult together and form some general mode which they shall pursue in rating the several articles of taxation."[42]

In 1779, with these consultations failing to produce consistent assessments of land and slaves, Virginia gave up on valuing its two main forms of wealth. For slaves, "it being supposed that the assessment on this kind of property may be rendered much more equal by way of poll-tax, so settled, as to bear the proportion of one and a half per cent. for their average value," the legislature levied £5 per poll "for all negro and mulatto servants and slaves," with discounts on slaves who "shall be incapable of labour, and become a charge to the owner." For land, the state instituted an incredible scheme—which abandoned valuation but pretended to continue to do it. Now, at the annual county meetings, the commissioners divided the county's land into as many as six categories and then polled the opinions of the assessors:

> The said commissioners . . . shall call on each assessor singly, to declare under the obligation of his oath or affirmation, what he thinks each several kind of the said land would sell for by the acre . . . which several opinions, together with their own, they shall state in writing for each kind of land separately, and shall add together the several sums at which the same kind of land is rated by the different commissioners and assessors, and then *divide the aggregate sum by the number of persons whose opinions were stated,* and shall take the quotient or result, or such sum near thereto, as to avoid the difficulty of fractions may be approved by a

majority of the said commissioners and assessors, as the average price of such kind of land.

The assessors used these "averages" to fix the taxes on individual landholders, which meant they decided only into which category particular tracts of land fell—although they still had to assess the value of town lots, ferry landings, mines, mills, "and other extraordinary buildings."[43]

In 1780, the opinion-poll assessment demonstrated its versatility. In response to the huge depreciation of Virginia's paper currency and the currency issued by the Continental Congress, the legislature directed the commissioners and assessors to offer their opinions of the prices that categories of land "would have sold for" in 1774—six years earlier, and before the many kinds of disruptions that the Revolutionary War had brought to Virginia! Of course, since these officials were only pretending to assess land values anyway, the precise methods by which they pretended to assess them made little difference. On the pretend-valuations, the legislature levied the 1.5 percent tax rate from 1778, required the tax to be paid in specie (which nobody had), and offered an option "in lieu" of that impossible rule. Any county that wanted to tax in "the money now in circulation" could levy £30 on each £100 of land value— as that value had been pretend-measured in specie at what it "would have sold for" in 1774. And, if these innovations failed to raise enough money, Virginia would try to sell the Williamsburg capitol and governor's palace (the government had just moved to Richmond) and land the state owned in Jamestown.[44]

The pretend-valuation scheme was Thomas Jefferson's idea. If it exemplified Jefferson's characteristically peculiar relationship to science and math, computing "quotients" from fantasy data, it also reflected a more general phenomenon: Virginians had never tried valuation before.[45] *Of course* they could not initiate a full-blown real estate assessment in 1777, much less assess the value of each enslaved person at what he or she would "sell for in ready money." With the value of the "money" depreciating as well, the 1777 tax plan simply was too ambitious for Virginia to implement during the Revolution. It was one thing for northern states to assess property during the Revolution. They also faced the currency depreciation problem, but some of them had been valuing various forms of property for more than a century. Local officials in Massachusetts had been doing it since the 1640s. Northern assessors did not have to be told—as Virginia's did in 1779—to value land at the price it would yield if sold "in moderate quantities as happens in the ordinary course of things" rather than at the price it would yield if all the land in a county were dumped on the market at once.[46]

Meanwhile, the legislature also had levied a separate tax in commodities (known as the "specific tax"), which followed the old poll tax on tithables: one bushel of wheat or two bushels of Indian corn, rye, or barley, or 10 pecks of oats, or 15 pounds of hemp ("all sound, clean, and merchantable"), or 28 pounds of inspected tobacco "for every man above sixteen years old, and every woman slave of like age." Needless to say, this tax caused massive problems. It required comprehensive commodity inspection, storage and transportation of perishable goods, and then either the sale of the commodities (to convert them into cash) or their delivery to moving armies with ever-changing needs. Once the armies were fighting in Virginia, moreover, farmers found their grain "impressed" into service. It must have been with relief that the legislature permitted payment in the certificates for impressed grain, though they also dropped the hemp and tobacco for a more useful but perishable commodity: two pounds of "good sound bacon" per poll.[47]

In 1781 and 1782, Virginia cleaned up its property tax, junking the pretend-valuations, elected tax commissioners, taxes on salaries and financial assets, and valuations of everything except land. Now, each county court appointed two "reputable freeholders." These county tax commissioners took sworn lists from taxpayers and levied a series of flat rates: 10 shillings on each free male over 21 and all slaves (except free men and slaves exempted by the county courts for old age or infirmity), 2 shillings per horse (except stud horses, taxed at "the sum which such horse covers one mare the season"), 3 pennies per cow, 6 shillings per wheel on carriages, £15 for a billiard table, and £5 for a tavern license. For land, the commissioners levied a 1.5 percent tax after assessing land values by determining an average value per acre for "each tract or parcel of land separately," handling town lots with regard to their "situation," and ignoring buildings altogether.[48]

The legislature also addressed the "equalization" problem, the inherent characteristic of property taxation that the assessments local officials produce are always incommensurate—and usually reflect competitive under-assessments, as local officials try to reduce local tax burdens.* The legislature

---

*Competitive underassessment works as follows. The assessors of some counties think: if we assess property at a lower proportion of its actual value than the assessors of other counties do, our taxes will be lower—since the state will levy the same tax rate on our low assessments and their high assessments. Then, assessors in the other counties, realizing that their taxpayers are being cheated, reduce their own assessments. Local assessments approach zero across the state, but they do so inconsistently, since the officials of each county are unsure about (1) exactly what the other counties are doing, and (2) exactly how low they can go without provoking disciplinary action by the state. The solution to this problem is to create a state-level board to "equalize" the local assessments.

assembled the counties into four districts (later, the Tidewater, Piedmont, Valley, and Trans-Allegheny "divisions" of Virginia), fixed an "average or standard" value of the land in each district, and appointed "John Pendleton, junior, and Samuel Jones, gentlemen" to go through the county tax books and adjust the assessments. For each of the four districts, Pendleton and Jones were to determine the average valuation per acre of the county assessments, compare the county averages to the legislated "average" for the district, and then "apply the difference to the account of every individual within the district, and add or deduct from the same accordingly."[49]

Virginia had created a workable land tax based on a decent approximation of relative land values. This was a huge accomplishment to emerge from wartime chaos in a state with no prior experience valuing property for taxation. Virginia's other big tax reform of the revolutionary era came in 1787, when the legislature abolished its poll tax on white men. The counties continued to levy the old poll tax on "tithables," but the legislature dispensed with the regressive part of this tax at the state level. From 1787 through the 1840s, the state only taxed slaves "by the poll." Its annual tax laws levied percentages on land valuation; flat rates on slaves, horses (except studs), and carriages; and license fees on taverns, some other businesses, and certain occupations. This tax system could be expanded to embrace other objects (as it was during the War of 1812), but it was levied in this primitive form, essentially unchanged, for the next sixty years.[50]

It is not that Virginia had neglected alternatives. In the 1780s, the legislature adopted a comprehensive program of trade taxes with its other reforms, but the U.S. Constitution took this revenue source away from the states in 1789. Under the Constitution, nobody could tax exports, and only the federal government could tax imports. The federal government probably gave more than it took, as the deals surrounding Alexander Hamilton's financial program offered Virginia a favorable accounting of its war spending—and a national capital on the Potomac, where slavery could be sanctioned and protected.[51] Virginians were notoriously unhappy about these deals, and particularly the federal assumption of state war debts, since they endorsed Hamilton's prediction (which turned out to be wrong) that the larger national debt it produced would create a powerful federal government. But these financial deals removed the cost of the Revolution from the state government's agenda, thereby allowing Virginia to retreat from the radical parts of its experience with taxation during the war.

Virginia simply could not send officials into the homes of individual taxpayers to value their possessions. It could not assess the value of slaves, and it could not tax houses or financial assets at all. It could require, as it did in 1782, that "every master or owner of a family" submit a list of taxable property on request, and it could use proxies for the value of taxable items (count the wheels of a carriage, establish the sex and race of a person).[52] But it could not undermine the authority of "masters" over their "families" by sending officials into their homes to inquire about silver plate and money in sums over £5, much less to haggle with them over the "value" of those family members "who, being property, are rated *ad valorem* as aforesaid." Jefferson's flat-rate slave tax and opinion-poll land valuation were realistic responses to this problem of mastership, though the opinion poll was not a realistic way to tax land.

At the outbreak of the Revolution, wealthy white men in Virginia were used to dealing with customs collectors on ships and in port. Many more white men (and women as well) were used to dealing with tobacco inspectors at public warehouses. But the "masters" were not used to having officials value their possessions, and the officials lacked experience with the technical and interpersonal skills the job required. Sovereign mastership circumscribed the options of the legislators who tried to make Virginia's tax system more productive, equitable, and sophisticated during the Revolution. They borrowed key features of the 1777 law from New England, where local officials had been valuing property since the seventeenth century, but they could not make it work. The New England story begins in the next chapter, though one observation can be made usefully here: comprehensive property taxes did not entail intolerable intrusions into the private affairs of the New England taxpayers. But, of course, these taxpayers also were not "masters" of "families" in quite the same way as Virginians.

By 1816, Jefferson had come to understand that there was another crucial difference. In New England, local officials were elected on an annual basis. John Adams famously noticed an oligarchic tendency in the New England towns (offices "which [have] ever depended only on the freest election of the people, have generally descended from generation to generation, in three or four families at most"), but Jefferson finally glimpsed the difference between this and the formal oligarchy of county court members appointed for life on the recommendations of the incumbents. New England's towns "are the vital principle of their governments," Jefferson wrote, "and have proved themselves the wisest invention ever devised by the wit of man for the perfect exercise of self-government and for its preservation." Virginia's counties were nothing of the kind. Virginia entered the Revolution with no comparable tradition of local "self-government." Some county courts started appointing tax commissioners even before the legislature abolished the elections "by the freeholders and housekeepers."[53] Slavery (mastership) was part of Virginia's tax problem during the Revolution. Another was the absence of a democratic tradition of citizen participation in local government.

Nor did Virginia launch such a tradition after the Revolution. The structure of Virginia's local governments changed in two ways. First, the disestablishment of religion abolished the old Anglican vestries, transferring their poor relief functions to "overseers of the poor," who levied the same poll tax on "tithables" that the self-perpetuating vestries had levied. Second, the county courts lost their judicial significance, as planters, merchants, and especially an articulate group of trained lawyers demanded a more professional approach to law (particularly debt litigation) than the "amateurs" of the county courts offered. Jefferson and James Madison led this movement to reform the old county courts—but only insofar as they functioned as courts. The reform did not touch them insofar as they functioned as the local governments of Virginia. As governments, the county courts emerged from the Revolution and persisted through the 1840s unchanged: as self-perpetuating oligarchies levying the old poll tax on "tithables."[54]

Many historians have pointed to the "conservatism" of the Revolution in Virginia. There was remarkably little change in the state's social structure and even less in its government. If the British crown no longer appointed the governor, the voters did not elect him either. Under both the 1776 and 1830 state constitutions, the legislature chose the governor of Virginia. The single most important change was the creation of a sizable free black community during and after the Revolution through escape, military service, self-purchase, and manumission. Almost 13,000 free people of color lived in Virginia in 1790, and more than 30,000 in 1810. Still, these figures comprised only 4 and 7 percent of the black population. Forty percent of Virginia's total population remained in bondage in the early republic, a figure that fell only when planters began to move and sell large numbers of slaves west and further south in the 1830s—and 31 percent of the Virginia population still was enslaved in 1860. This was not a democratic society, and it was not a society capable of sustaining sophisticated government institutions. It was an oligarchy of "masters." White yeomen and black slaves put serious pressure on it in the ensuing decades, but, in the end, it defended the prerogatives of its "masters" to the death.

Massachusetts

Most people know one thing about taxation in Massachusetts in the revolutionary era: the state's taxes grew so heavy and unfair that they sparked Shays's Rebellion in 1786. The farmers who shut down the courts in western Massachusetts to prevent prosecutions for unpaid taxes and private debts led Thomas Jefferson, writing from France, to pronounce "the blood of patriots & tyrants" to be the "natural manure" of the liberty tree. But those closer to home responded with less equanimity, especially by the early months of 1787, as armies rode around harassing people and four rebels died in a battle at the Springfield arsenal. The electorate responded in April and May. In a turnout triple that of the previous year, the voters ousted three-fifths of the house of representatives, half the senate, and the incumbent governor by a three-to-one margin. After the fighting stopped, the new state government pardoned the rebels, relieved the taxpayers, and suspended private debt lawsuits—the principal rebel demands all along. Nationally, the lesson seemed to be that not even Massachusetts could finance the Revolutionary War. No state could pay its soldiers, repay loans from its citizens at their par value, and meet the increasingly urgent pleas for money ("requisitions") of the Continental Congress.[1] Massachusetts tried and caused a rebellion. Most states did not try. The upshot was the U.S. Constitution.

The national consequences of Shays's Rebellion were extremely important, but the state-level crisis is even more illuminating. What made the Massachusetts government think it could finance the Revolution by imposing massive taxes on its citizens? How could an election permit politics as usual to resume after an armed rebellion? The answers to these questions point us to fundamental differences between Massachusetts and Virginia. First, Massachusetts *could* levy taxes that hurt. Its tax system broke down in 1786 when an intransigent legislature pushed it too hard in depression conditions (a currency shortage and a huge burden of unpaid private debts)—but there was a working tax system for it to push, one that triggered action by experienced local officials. Second, the electorate could make its preferences known quickly. Annual elections could arbitrate major conflicts of interest, such as the one between the eastern mercantile groups who wanted to pay the war debt and the western agrarian groups who could not bear the taxes to pay it. As a delegate to the Massachusetts ratification convention explained in 1788, criticizing the biennial elections of the U.S. Constitution, "had the last administration continued one year longer, our liberties would have been lost, and the country involved in blood; not so much, Sir, from their bad conduct, but from the suspicions of the people of them."[2] Elites exerted a great deal of power in Massachusetts. An aroused electorate, however, sent the elitist legislators who provoked Shays's Rebellion into a speedy retirement.

The Massachusetts polity looked very different from the Virginia polity in the 1770s and 1780s. Its government institutions were sophisticated, and its people knew how to use them. Its economy was complex, its politics messy, and its people articulate if not downright cheeky when dealing with authority figures. Massachusetts met the crisis of the Revolution with a productive tax system in place, one that built on an already well-developed seventeenth-century tax system. The first state constitution, adopted in 1780, acknowledged this colonial inheritance by tweaking the system with a minor reform. The constitution required the legislature (General Court) to use up-to-date information to apportion its taxes to the towns. As long as it continued to tax "polls and estates, in the manner that has hitherto been practised, in order that such assessments may be made with equality, there shall be a valuation of estates within the Commonwealth taken anew once in every ten years at least, and as much oftener as the General Court shall order."[3] It is hard to imagine a clearer illustration of the difference between Massachusetts and Virginia as polities. Nobody in Virginia could have made the assumption this clause contained: that the state would be capable of conducting a decennial (or "oftener") valuation of property.

By 1775, Massachusetts had been valuing various forms of property for taxation for 130 years and apportioning taxes to towns for 75 years. The General Court and the towns possessed the administrative capacity to make these procedures work. Officials and taxpayers knew how to negotiate their inherent political pitfalls, from individual appeals of local assessments to colony-wide adjustments for a changing economy. Massachusetts reformed its tax structure during the Revolution by adding the decennial valuation rule and modifying other details. But there was no reason—even after Shays's Rebellion—to abandon "the manner that has hitherto been practised" and start from scratch. In Massachusetts, tax reform was never the all-or-nothing proposition that it was in Virginia. It did not require the creation of an entirely new administrative apparatus. It was a matter of adjusting the system's details in response to political pressure. Massachusetts, in short, had a tax politics. As everyone familiar with the current U.S. tax system understands, the details are the game in any real tax politics—and, unlike Virginia, Massachusetts had a politics in which these details were the issues.

The primary engine of the Massachusetts tax system was the tax on "polls and estates." By the 1770s, this tax consisted of a poll tax on free male adults (sixteen and up) plus a property tax on "the incomes of all estates, both real and personal." The "estates" included land, houses, commercial and industrial buildings, wharves, ships, livestock, slaves, and "incomes or profits" from "any trade or faculty, business or employment" and "by money or commissions of profits." Town officials assessed the value of the estates, the General Court decided how to distribute the tax burden between polls and estates, and local governments added their own rates to the colony levies. This system required highly political decisions and competent administration at all levels of government. Massachusetts also taxed imported goods through an "impost," which levied flat rates by volume on wine, rum, and tobacco and an ad valorem rate on all other commodities. Its counties charged legal fees and licensed innkeepers, liquor retailers, and "victuallers." But the tax on "polls and estates"—so much more sophisticated than Virginia's poll tax on "tithables"—was the backbone of the Massachusetts tax system and persisted into the twentieth century.[4]

Massachusetts was a very different society from Virginia—before, during, and after the Revolution. If the most obvious difference was slavery (slaves were never more than 3 percent of the population, and the institution disintegrated during the Revolution), the nature of political life would have to run a close second. Massachusetts had a highly contentious and participatory politics, especially at the local level. It was not a society where clever members of a privileged gentry class periodically tried to junk one set of institutions for another. Its institutions evolved. By modern standards, colonial Massachusetts obviously was not a democratic society. Slavery was legal, even though it was rare. Women were disfranchised and, if married, prohibited from owning property. If we compare colonial Massachusetts with colonial Virginia, however, the New England colony looks rather better. History had been kinder to Massachusetts, from the 1630 arrival of the first Puritan ships to the moment when Paul Revere warned the minutemen that the British were moving by land. The political institutions Massachusetts developed over this period would almost be able to cope with the Revolution.

Society

The Puritans who settled the Massachusetts Bay colony had remarkably little in common with their counterparts in Virginia, even though both were English. Migrating in family groups rather than as young single men and aspiring to build a society rather than to seize a bonanza of gold and jewels, the Massachusetts settlers behaved more like enthusiastic townspeople who had found precious land than like disappointed conquistadors who had failed to find precious metals and stones. They treated each other with more respect and less violence than the Virginians and, for a forty-year period, even managed to live in peace with the local Indians. The Massachusetts settlers quarreled and sued each other regularly. They banished religious dissenters and, in four notorious instances, hanged them.[5] Still, theirs was a much less violent society than Virginia's, in no small part because it was a more equal society. Unlike the very poor and very rich single men who settled Virginia, the Massachusetts settlers were men *and* women, in an age range from infants to the elderly. Apart from religion, their main similarity to one another was a "middling" social status in England. These farmers and artisans, husbands and wives, parents, children, and short-term servants expected to work for a living in Massachusetts.

Massachusetts was also a much healthier place for the English than Virginia. Although winters were hard, there was no summer "seasoning" like that which ravaged the Virginia settler populations. In New England generally—Massachusetts, Connecticut, Rhode Island, Plymouth (folded into Massachusetts in 1691), and the towns that became New Hampshire in 1679—high life expectancies around seventy and the balanced sex ratios of a family-based migration yielded rapid growth. By 1700, 25,000 migrants had produced a population of 100,000. Disease, meanwhile, had catastrophic results for local Indians, especially along the Massachusetts coast. The coastal Indians (the Massachusetts) faced crushing epidemics of European diseases in the late-1610s, probably introduced by English fishermen, and then a disastrous outbreak of smallpox in 1633, soon after the Puritans arrived. Killing some nine-tenths of their population, the epidemics left the Massachusetts unable to resist the English as the Powhatan Confederacy had in Virginia.[6] They also left large tracts of land emptied of people, an outcome the Puritans regarded as a providential endorsement of their migration.

Away from the coast, Indians survived, despite the 1633 smallpox and subsequent outbreaks of disease. One result was a reordering of political and trade relations, both among Indian groups and between Indians and English settlers. Indians and Puritans established an interlocking polity on a landscape dotted with English and Indian villages. Alliances linked the fortunes of Indians and colonists: River Indians (in the Connecticut River Valley) with Massachusetts, Wampanoags with Plymouth, Mohegans and Pequots with Connecticut, and Narragansetts with Rhode Island. Indians acknowledged the jurisdictional claims of the colonies in return for protection, which the colonies delivered by building forts and sending militias. Indians defended land claims in colony courts, served in colony militias, collected wolf bounties from English towns, and worked for the English both as servants and wage laborers. They intermeshed their economic lives with those of the colonists to a surprising degree, though never on terms of equality.[7]

Two moments of unbridled violence punctuated this generally peaceful (if often strained) coexistence. The Pequot War (1637) threatened it. King Philip's War (1675–1676) destroyed it. Both wars had complex origins, in rivalries between English colonies, between Indian groups, and between colonists and Indians. Both enlisted Indians on both sides, with the Narragansetts joining the English against the Pequots and, in King Philip's War, various Indian groups fighting with and against the loose anti-English alliance that the Wampanoags established. Both involved murderous atrocities. The Pequot War climaxed when English and Narragansett fighters torched the Pequot town of Fort Mystic in May 1637, killing 600 to 700 men, women, and children. A similar massacre occurred during King Philip's War, when English, Mohegan, and Pequot troops killed anywhere from 400 to 1,100 Narragansett men, women, and children in the Great Swamp Fight of December 1675. The English also suffered civilian casualties—in King Philip's War, Indians attacked 52 of the 90 Puritan towns, destroying 12 of them—although these casualties were not on the scale of Fort Mystic or the Great Swamp Fight.[8]

Religion, of course, was an essential part of the Massachusetts experience. These settlers were Puritans on an "errand into the wilderness." They wanted to demonstrate to the world that church, state, and society could be remade according to God's intentions—and God apparently intended that political authority should be monopolized by "visible saints" who had experienced a conversion that suggested they were among his "elect." The demonstration part of the errand ended within a decade, as the English Civil War diverted the attention of English Puritans away from their movement's faraway colony. As the English Puritans won political power in a large and complex society, they opted for religious toleration. As the English Puritans lost power with the Restoration of the Stuarts in 1660, it was no longer up to them, and a leading outcome of the Glorious Revolution of 1688 (which overthrew the Stuarts again) was a settlement on toleration in England. Some Massachusetts Puritans suffered crises of confidence at these junctures, but most defended their godly polity until 1691, when the crown closed that option by rechartering Massachusetts as a royal colony.[9]

The Massachusetts Puritans built a more egalitarian society than that of England—and much less that of Virginia. The colony's government managed land distribution by granting land to towns, which then granted parcels to individuals on a freehold basis (without quitrents), in quantities that acknowledged social distinctions but provided farms to most families. The significance of this wide distribution of landownership cannot be overstated. Original town proprietors limited grants to newcomers, but later arrivals acquired grants for new towns, which proliferated across the landscape until King Philip's War temporarily reversed the expansion of English settlement. Family farmers in the towns produced grains, meat, and dairy products for local consumption, while a few large-scale commercial operations also flourished from the beginning: Boston and Salem merchants in the overseas shipping business, William Pynchon's fur trading and land development empire in the Connecticut Valley (employing unusually large numbers of tenant farmers and wage workers), and a group of wealthy town promoters who operated across the New England region, bearing the initial costs of town founding in return for land grants.[10]

By the 1650s, Massachusetts had established a diversified economy. Fishing, lumbering, and grazing produced goods for export to the sugar colonies of the West Indies, artisans milled grain and manufactured wood and leather products, merchants exploited international markets (soon to include the African slave trade), and a shipbuilding industry enabled the merchants to compete with English shippers. Some of the farmers, artisans, and merchants also employed nonfamily labor. In the Great Migration of the 1630s, almost one-fifth of the migrants were servants, with half of the migrating families including servants as members. These servants generally became free within two years of arriving, however, and they were not replaced by other bound laborers. Most residents who worked for nonfamily employers were young men and women who earned wages, though some Africans and Indians (chiefly war captives among the latter) were enslaved in Massachusetts throughout the colonial era. The existence of slavery had crucial moral implications and crucial implications for the lives of the enslaved Africans and Indians. It also had long-term implications for racist thinking and racial discrimination in Massachusetts. But the enormity of these facts must not distract us from others: that overwhelming majorities of the total population were free and that overwhelming majorities of the adult male population owned their own farms and tools. The Puritans did not build anything we would recognize as an equal society, but they built a remarkably equal seventeenth-century society. In some respects, it was a more equal society than our own.[11]

Massachusetts faced a series of crises in the late seventeenth century: King Philip's War (1675), the revocation of the colony's charter (1684), the imposition of an autocratic government called the Dominion of New England (established 1686, overthrown 1689), frontier wars against the Eastern Indians in Maine (1688, 1692) and a disastrous attempt to invade Canada (1690), the rechartering as a royal colony, which established an active crown presence in its political system (1691), and then the Salem witchcraft catastrophe (1692). The eighteenth-century society that emerged at the other end of this chaotic quarter century was a little more commercial, a little less self-righteous, and a lot more fully enmeshed in the British empire, which meant, among other things, participation in the empire's wars. Massachusetts made energetic and costly contributions to Britain's struggles against France in the eighteenth century, fighting against French Canadians and Indians in King William's War (1689–1697), Queen Anne's War (1702–1713), King George's War (1744–1748), and the French and Indian War (1754–1763). Combined with the relatively greater opportunities for agriculture and commerce in New York and Pennsylvania in the eighteenth century, the costs of these wars slowed the colony's growth and caused a currency inflation in which wages lagged behind a rising cost of living.[12]

Massachusetts became a less equal society in the eighteenth century. In the countryside, slavery and servitude remained rare and land remained widely distributed, but land itself became scarcer. One response was migration to the "frontier" lands of Maine, New Hampshire, and New York. Another was non-farm employment. In 1735, Boston was a bustling port town of 16,000. Its merchant elite built palatial houses and bought African slaves, who comprised 8.5 percent of the city's population in 1742—much more than anywhere else in the colony. But, as Gary Nash explains, Boston's prosperity did not last. The city was hit hard by the wars, the resulting taxes and inflation, a devastating smallpox epidemic in 1752, and a runaway fire in 1760. Its artisans, shopkeepers, and free working poor (especially sailors and laborers in construction and shipping) lost ground, owning less real estate and other property, and its public relief costs (especially for war widows) soared, from £500 per year in the 1730s to £1,900 in the 1760s—while it actually lost population, with key industries moving to neighboring towns.[13] Massachusetts became the society of the urban artisans, shopkeepers, and laborers whose 1765 Stamp Act riots provoked British repression; the professional politicians (Samuel Adams), aspiring lawyers (John Adams), and merchant princes (John Hancock) who organized the escalating protest movement; and the "embattled farmers" who engaged the redcoats at Lexington and Concord.

Government

The structure of the Massachusetts government was remarkably democratic throughout the colonial era. The tone of its politics changed as the seventeenth-century polity of the "visible saints" gave way to a vibrant and divisive eighteenth-century polity—with broad participation at all levels, bitter pamphlet wars, and periodic crowd actions (especially in Boston) in which the disfranchised and activists among the enfranchised called politicians to account for unpopular actions. Few members of this eighteenth-century polity seem to have enjoyed political conflict. They deplored it as their Puritan ancestors had, and as many Americans still do. They valued unity and consensus over division and partisan struggle, but, rather like us, they performed the latter with gusto.[14]

At no time was outright corruption a serious problem in colonial Massachusetts. Public officials sometimes made bad decisions, elitist decisions, and self-interested decisions (such as land grants to themselves), but, unlike their counterparts in Virginia, they did not steal from the public on a regular basis. While it is tempting to attribute their probity to Puritanism, its more likely origin lies in the colony's more democratic institutions and, especially, the annual elections that produced a public accountability unknown to Virginia. If we might trace these institutions to Puritanism in turn, they probably had more to do with the more egalitarian social structure of Massachusetts. Its government never faced the violent unrest of huge populations of mercilessly exploited servants and slaves. Nor was it the instrument for savage reprisals by masters. A more egalitarian society had the luxury of a more democratic political system, because the system did not exist for the very purpose of perpetuating drastically exploitative social relations. That was Virginia's problem, but it was not the problem of government in Massachusetts. Officeholding in Massachusetts never licensed elites to steal from their social inferiors.[15]

Under the first Massachusetts charter (1629–1684), the governor, deputy governor, and assembly all were elected annually, along with a range of town officials. The assembly (General Court) reorganized itself several times in the early years, but after 1644 it remained a bicameral representative assembly, consisting of a lower house of "deputies" elected by town meetings and an upper house of "assistants" (also known as "magistrates") elected at large. Under the second charter (1691–1774), the British crown appointed the governor, lieutenant governor, and several other top officials. Town meetings still elected the lower house (representatives), but the upper house (council) now was nominated jointly each year by the new representatives and incumbent council, subject to the governor's veto—which still was a more democratic process than in other royal colonies, where governors appointed the councils themselves.

Massachusetts also was divided into counties. Under the first charter, the county courts consisted of local magistrates plus "associates" nominated in town meetings and elected at large in the counties. Under the second, governors appointed justices of the peace (JPs). The county courts appointed sheriffs to enforce judgments and maintain jails. They also levied small county taxes, although county officials ordinarily were not responsible for collecting them. Judicial patronage turned the county seats into centers of gubernatorial ("court") influence in the eighteenth century, with JPs increasingly forming a progovernor bloc in the General Court. Nevertheless, annual elections (towns could and regularly did dump JP representatives) restrained the power of JPs, as did the limited role of county government. Where Virginia's counties were electoral districts and local governments in addition to judicial units, the counties of Massachusetts functioned almost solely as judicial units. In Massachusetts, towns were the primary units of local government, the ones that assessed and collected the taxes.[16]

The towns were complicated entities. They were governments, religious bodies, and land corporations in the seventeenth century. They were governments with certain responsibilities for religion and land in the eighteenth century. They were electoral districts for the General Court's lower house all along. Their crucial institutional expression was the "town meeting," although to say this is to say little. Town meetings always met annually to elect town officers. They almost always met again to elect General Court representatives, and they often met several more times to deliberate about town business ranging from hiring a minister or building a meetinghouse to dividing common lands or arbitrating various kinds of competing local interests. Some towns at some times observed the colony's suffrage laws, but other towns at other times ignored them, to permit either more or fewer men (but never women) to vote.[17] The most important events in the history of the towns changed their relationships to religion and land.

"In practice," as John Murrin has remarked for the seventeenth century, "town and church were scarcely distinguishable institutions." Generally, the first thing the founders of a new town did was make a religious covenant with one another. They then built a church ("meetinghouse") and hired a minister. The minister's salary was a leading cost of town government and subject to constant negotiation between ministers and town meetings. Ministers grumbled endlessly about low salaries and inadequate firewood. Towns responded by criticizing dull sermons, provoking theological disputes, and affirming that they, rather than the ministers, owned and controlled the churches. Another church-based conflict broke out as towns grew. As people settled on outlying lands, they demanded new meetinghouses closer to their homes. The financial implications of this demand caused immense political wrangling and, eventually, the creation of new towns out of the sprawling grants of the older ones. Religious disagreements increasingly inspired a third set of conflicts. Baptists, Quakers, and others demanded to be exempted from the taxes that paid the salaries of the Puritan ministers. The Great Awakening (1730s–1740s) intensified this kind of conflict as the Congregationalists (Puritans) themselves divided into New Light and Old Light factions. Now, many towns found it impossible to agree on a minister, and formal splits ensued. Once towns contained multiple churches, the churches became more independent of the towns—though the towns still taxed to support them, causing predictable struggles over the revenue.[18]

In the seventeenth century, the towns also played a role with no basis in English law: as land corporations owned by shareholding "proprietors." The General Court organized towns by making land grants to them, and the towns distributed the land by making grants to individuals. Rather like modern condo associations, the towns administered common property, assessed their members for its upkeep and improvement, approved sales to newcomers, and made regulations to enhance the value of the commons and the lands owned by individual members. Unlike condo associations, however, the towns distributed dividends to their shareholders in periodic divisions of existing common lands and other lands they acquired. The importance of these dividends led towns to maintain a distinction between the ownership of land and the ownership of shares in the corporation, which meant individuals could own house lots and farms in a town without gaining the right to profit from its divisions or to vote in its town meetings (which administered the land corporation's affairs). Although these arrangements clearly had major implications for political life in the towns, the precise implications they had are unclear. John Frederick Martin, who has made the closest study of them, calls the shareholding proprietors "an exclusive, privileged club" in each town but also shows that shareholding was dispersed among a majority of the taxpayers (household heads) in most towns, and sometimes among as many as four-fifths of them.[19]

Towns negotiated these complex roles with minimal interference from the county courts or the General Court. The losers in town-level conflicts sometimes appealed to these authorities, but the authorities allowed the towns a great deal of leeway in implementing the colony's laws—even about such things as the suffrage and tax structure. The major exception was the Dominion of New England in the 1680s. Among the provocative acts of Sir Edmund Andros, the autocratic governor of the dominion, was a direct assault on the towns (he also abolished the General Court and instituted Anglican worship in Puritan churches). Andros banned all town meetings except the annual ones to elect the town officers, who, he assumed (naively), would collect the taxes he ordered. Andros also declared town-based land titles to be illegal, an edict that affected most of the land titles in Massachusetts. Landowners were to apply to Andros for new titles, for which he would collect fees, and these new titles would require the payment of quitrents—a plan that went nowhere. Bostonians overthrew Andros in 1689, jailing him and other dominion officials. The colony reverted to a provisional version of its old government until the crown issued the new royal charter in 1691. Martin argues that this crisis democratized the towns even while it had the opposite effect at the colony level (inaugurating crown appointment of governors). To protect themselves against Andros, shareholding proprietors established separate land corporations that were independent of the town meetings. This move, according to Martin, "liberated" the towns from their proprietors, turning them into "fully public institutions" for the first time.[20]

There was another crucial feature of town government. One of the most striking aspects of Massachusetts politics (the one that Thomas Jefferson would applaud in 1816) was the broad participation in local officeholding. Town meeting moderators, selectmen (town councilmen), treasurers, and clerks usually were members of local elite families, but ordinary men in the towns rotated a series of other elected positions: constables, tax collectors, fence viewers, commodity and market inspectors, highway surveyors, tithingmen (to enforce liquor laws and the Sabbath), and hog reeves (for stray livestock). The minor offices did not confer high social status on their incumbents, but they did confer meaningful power over the regulation of daily life in the towns. Edward M. Cook, Jr., studying the eighteenth century, found that "virtually all adult males were officeholders over the long run" in agricultural towns and that half served as officeholders even in larger commercial towns.[21] Broad-based local officeholding diffused political responsibility and experience well beyond the elite who served in the General Court. With annual elections, it produced governments that belonged to "the people" more directly than anything that emerged from Virginia's elite patronage networks. In Virginia, the voters elected only the burgesses, and even that only at irregular intervals. In Massachusetts, ordinary free male adults actually ruled on a day-to-day basis. They did not fill the top slots of the local political hierarchies, but they voted for (and against) those who did every year.

The crown played a far smaller role in Massachusetts than in Virginia in the seventeenth century, mainly because Massachusetts produced no taxable staple like Virginia's tobacco. The settlers considered their 1629 charter a grant of complete political autonomy. Although nobody in London saw it that way, the English Civil War and then the London fire and plague (1660s) kept crown officials too busy to worry about this financially insignificant colony. The officials did little more than complain about Massachusetts, whose merchants flouted the customs laws with abandon (for example, by buying tobacco in Virginia and exporting it illegally to Europe). But in 1676, during the disastrous King Philip's War and amid a flurry of charges by non-Puritan elites, especially Anglican merchants and aristocratic land speculators, the crown sent a customs inspector to Boston. Edward Randolph, a true believer in crown prerogative and a cousin of the angriest speculator (John Mason, who thought he owned New Hampshire), set out on a mission to destroy the Puritan commonwealth. His reports to the crown denounced Massachusetts for all kinds of sins. It was too democratic (artisans in political offices). It was a dictatorship (wealthy non-Puritans excluded). It was an oligarchy (incumbents continually reelected). It was corrupt (the smuggling). When the crown revoked the 1629 charter and set up the dominion, Randolph was a top aide to Andros and then, in 1689, a fellow inmate in the Boston jail.[22]

The dominion and the 1691 charter introduced the crown into the Massachusetts polity, but two shifts in political power between the colony and the towns were also significant. In the initial years of settlement, the General Court was the locus of authority, directing every aspect of the settlement enterprise and issuing orders about very mundane local matters. Starting in the late-1630s, the towns were the locus of authority, operating with considerable autonomy from the General Court. Then, in the mid-1670s, the colony government reasserted itself, a shift that was enhanced by crown initiative after 1691. T. H. Breen explains these changes as functions of war and taxation. During the long peace that lasted from the late-1630s to the mid-1670s (from the Pequot War to King Philip's War), towns did most of the taxing, financing ministers' salaries, public buildings, and after 1642 the common schools that helped to produce a nearly universal literacy in Massachusetts. After the 1670s, however, the colony did most of the taxing, first for King Philip's War and then for the series of imperial wars. Breen argues that these high colony taxes tended to politicize (rather than alienate) the Massachusetts taxpayers. Especially because they exposed the regressivity of the colony's tax structure, they "opened a floodgate of political participation"—large town meetings devoted to fierce debates about financial issues.[23]

Nevertheless, the Massachusetts tax system inspired little generalized criticism. The tax laws contain nothing like the century of condemnations of the "grievous and burdensome" poll tax in Virginia. The reason is *not* that the Massachusetts tax structure was more progressive. A heavy reliance on poll taxes, plus property taxes on the land and livestock that even many of the poorest taxpayers owned, probably produced a tax incidence as regressive as Virginia's. Yet, as we have seen, the problems with the Virginia poll tax (at least from the perspective of the elites who wrote the laws) had little to do with its regressivity. They stemmed from its administration by sheriffs who stole the proceeds, winked at evasion by some taxpayers, and exploited others in various ways. Massachusetts did not have these problems. Taxpayers had trouble paying and collectors fell behind—most famously Samuel Adams in Boston, whose arrears reached £4,000 in 1767. But these were different problems from Virginia's. They are the routine problems of any tax administration rather than results of corruption. The General Court preferred low taxes to high taxes. Unlike the House of Burgesses, however, it was not afraid to tax. King Philip's War generated tax burdens twenty-six times higher than normal. Massachusetts raised this money, and more for the wars of the eighteenth century.[24]

Country Rates

Technically, Massachusetts had three separate tax systems over the course of the colonial era: apportioned property taxes from 1634 to 1645, unapportioned "country rates" on polls and property from 1646 to 1692, and apportioned taxes on "polls and estates" after 1692. The first shift, with its discontinuance of apportionment, probably reflected the political decentralization that occurred after the first settlement years, although this explanation cannot account for another major part of the change, the introduction of the poll tax—which did not reflect wartime revenue demands either. Massachusetts anticipated a war for a decade after 1643, when it interfered in a conflict between the Narragansetts and Mohegans (sponsoring the execution of the Narragansett leader Miantonomi by the Mohegan leader Uncas) and built a military alliance called the United Colonies of New England, but it actually enjoyed another thirty years of peace after these events.[25] The second shift, from "country rates" to the apportioned taxes on "polls and estates," is easier to explain. It clearly reflected the reemergence of the colony-level government, war spending, and the royal charter. Massachusetts also taxed imported goods for much of the colonial period, first liquor and then other commodities, although the trade taxes never displaced the direct taxes as its primary revenue engines.

Initially, the General Court simply apportioned total tax sums to towns. Its first tax, £50 to pay military salaries in September 1630 (the first ships arrived in June), apportioned this sum without offering any guidance on how the towns were to distribute their portions to individuals. The General Court levied £11 on Boston and Watertown, £7 on Charlestown and Dorchester, £5 on Roxbury, £3 on Medford and Salem, £2 on Wessaguscus (Weymouth), and

£1 on Nantasket. It apportioned several similar taxes for salaries and building projects until, in 1633, it adopted a more general language of taxation: "to defray publique charges."[26]

These early tax orders treated the towns as autonomous corporate entities, allowing them to decide for themselves how to raise their quotas. In 1634, however, the General Court directed the towns to distribute its taxes as well as their own (raised mainly to pay ministers) by levying property taxes rather than poll taxes. It rejected poll taxes explicitly: towns were to "levy every man according to his estate, & with consideration of all other his abilities, whatsoever, & not according to the number of his persons." In 1636, it expanded on the term "ability"—"hereafter, all men shalbe rated in all rates for their whole abilitie, wheresoever it lyes"—and also tried to tax nonresidents who owned property in the colony: "[T]hose that live out of this jurisdiction shall have their goods, stock, & land rated in the places where they are in being." This last part could never have worked; Massachusetts could hardly tax people it had banished to Rhode Island! In 1639, it even tried to tax the property Massachusetts residents owned in England, backing down from that implausible plan in 1641. Yet the striking part of these orders is the pure property tax regime they created. The General Court apportioned taxes to the towns and the towns distributed these sums and their own taxes according to holdings of "goods, stock, & land."[27] This regime did not last, but it offered a notably progressive starting point for taxation in Massachusetts.

The "country rate" system was inaugurated by a 1646 General Court order that added the poll tax, rules for valuing property, and the taxation of artisan incomes. This order tried to tax everything "proportionably" to everything else, though at the cost of an excessive complexity.[28] Most of its innovations survived, however, cleaned up and codified in the *Laws and Liberties of Massachusetts* (1648) as the system of country rates. A "rate" consisted of a 2.5 shilling poll tax and a penny per pound tax on the value of "all personall & real estates." Instead of apportioning sums to the towns, the General Court now simply levied a "rate" against the number of polls and the value of property. Each year, the colony treasurer sent warrants directing each town to hold a meeting to elect a commissioner. This commissioner and the town's selectmen then made a list of all males aged sixteen and older,

and a true estimation of all personall & real estates, being, or reputed to be the estate of all & everie the persons in the same town . . . according to just valuation . . . so neer as they can by all lawful wayes and means which they may use. *viz:* of houses, lands of all sorts as well unbroken up as other [except town common lands], mills, ships & all small vessells, merchantable goods, cranes, wharfes & all sorts of cattle [livestock] & all other known estate whatsoever; as also all visible estate either at sea or on shore.

The tax that resulted from this process was a combination poll tax and property tax: a 2.5 shilling tax on all adult males "except Magistrates and Elders of Churches" and men who were "disabled by sicknes, lamenes, or other infirmitie," plus a penny per pound tax on the property. The law also included an equalization process within counties, though not between them. After creating their lists of polls and estates, the town commissioners of each county met to "duly and carefully examin all the said lists and assessments" and to correct them "according to the true intent of this order, as they or the major part of them shall determi[ne]." The commissioners then sent the lists to the treasurer, who issued warrants to the town constables "to collect & levie the same."[29]

There were detailed provisions for handling specific types of property. For livestock, the system provided town officials with fixed valuations "for a more certein rule in rating of cattle." They were to exempt animals under a year old and then apply fixed valuations to others, such as £5 for a four-year-old cow, £3 for a horse two or three years of age, and 8 shillings for a goat, applying the penny per pound rate to the total. While the list of rateable property ("houses, lands of all sorts . . .") included most of the assets that farmers and merchants were likely to own, especially with its open-ended "other known estate whatsoever," the law handled artisans by directing town officials to estimate their incomes. "[A]ll such persons as by the advantage of their arts & trades are more enabled to help bear the publick charge than common laborours and workmen" were to be "rated for their returns & gains proportionable unto other men for the produce of their estates" and then charged the penny per pound tax on the result. The task of assessing these "returns & gains" would have been tricky; assessors could not estimate artisan incomes "proportionble unto other men" without a sense of the "produce" farmers gained from their taxed land and livestock and merchants gained from their taxed ships, wharfs, and goods. The more serious problem with the artisan income tax, however, was that towns rarely assessed it.[30]

The complexity of this 1648 law is unimpressive in comparison to today's federal income tax code, but it is stunning in the contemporary context of Virginia's poll tax on "tithables" or its abortive 1645 property tax, with the four pounds of tobacco per hundred acres of land. To imagine the country rates being implemented, we must imagine officials and taxpayers agreeing on (and haggling over) individual assessments of the value of various forms of property. The officials did not have to value every animal on every farm, but they had to decide how to value tracts of land, ships, stocks of mercantile goods, and, of course, "other known estate whatsoever"—and they must have done all this with the taxpayers watching closely. We then have to imagine the town commissioners at the county equalization meetings, developing adjustments and revising the town lists accordingly and then taking their revised lists home so the constables could collect from the taxpayers when the treasurer's warrants arrived. The fact that it actually is not all that hard to imagine the Massachusetts colonists doing these things illustrates a very important point. Looking back across three and a half centuries of history, Massachusetts simply looks less exotic than Virginia, despite all of the intellectual and cultural paraphernalia of Puritan religiosity. We can imagine the Massachusetts townspeople implementing this system because we can imagine ourselves doing it. But it is not possible to imagine the Virginia gentry executing a comparable administrative feat.

To say that the Massachusetts tax system looked recognizably modern in the seventeenth century is not to say that it was equitable—a claim few would make about today's U.S. tax system either. Yet the country rates established a tax equity standard, the one Adam Smith later called the "maxim" of tax equity: that each taxpayer should be charged "proportionately to his ability." The act of setting such a standard (which Virginia never did) invites us to evaluate how well this tax system lived up to its principles. Clearly, the poll tax poses a problem. Using the livestock valuations for comparison, the 2.5 shilling poll tax equaled the property tax on six four-year-old cows, twenty sheep, or thirty swine but was levied regardless of whether the taxpayers owned cows, sheep, or swine. Precisely because the country rate system established a tax equity standard, the poll tax could violate it conspicuously. In this sense, it resembles the regressive components of our own tax regime (such as sales taxes), which fit uneasily into a system that also, until very recently, allegedly rested on the principle of "ability to pay."[31]

Another aspect of the country rate system, however, reminds us that it was a seventeenth-century tax after all, rather than one for a modern society: "And for such servants and children as take not wages, their parents and masters shall pay for them, but such as take wages shall pay for themselves."[32] This complex little sentence governed the poll tax on unfree labor. Its conflation of "servants" with "children" (sons) suggests the marginality of unfree labor in Massachusetts, but it ratifies its existence at the same time that it suggests the greater significance of wage labor. In this poll tax, the labor of male adults was taxable to the people who controlled it rather than to the men who performed it. The men who performed the labor could be the taxpayers, their sons, apprentices, servants, slaves, or other dependent but able-bodied men in a household. Labor, in other words, was taxable property in Massachusetts, exactly as it was in Virginia, except that the country rates exempted all women's labor—again reflecting the marginal roles of servitude and slavery. This poll tax was framed on the premise that most taxpayers were men paying for their own labor and that of sons (with female taxpayers paying only for sons), but it covered the cases of servitude and slavery. Inasmuch as it was levied on male labor that people really did think of as property—and the tax treatment of artisans who profited from "the advantage of their arts & trades" plainly cast their skilled labor as an income-producing asset—the poll tax actually may not have seemed to violate the "ability to pay" standard in the seventeenth century.

Reforms in the 1650s attempted to shift more of the tax burden onto wealthier taxpayers. In 1651, the General Court addressed what would remain a huge problem in American property taxation into the twentieth century: the taxation of commercial wealth. The problem was that the property that merchants typically owned (especially their personal property) was less accessible to assessors than the property that farmers typically owned. Livestock was visible on a farm, but ships could be at sea or in foreign ports, goods could be held by agents, and paper assets could be anywhere. Thus, this law directed that the property of "marchants, shopkeepers and factors shall be assessed by the Rule of common estimation, according to the will and doom of the assessours, having regard to their stock & estate, be it presented to view or not, in whose hands soever it be." To protect the merchants against the discretionary "will and doom," meanwhile, the law added an appeals process: "[I]f any such merchants find themselves over valued, if they can make it appear to the Assessours, they are to be eased by them, if not by the next County Court." The General Court also shifted burdens more directly. In 1653, it cut the poll tax from 2.5 to 1.67 shillings, and in 1657 it slashed the cattle, oxen, and sheep valuations to offer a tax break to the farmers who were the vast majority of the taxpayers.[33]

Towns did not always implement the country rate system in the seventeenth century. As Martin phrases it, they "frequently ignored colony statutes." Yet Martin's chief example of such disobedience is instructive. Some towns, especially in their first years of settlement, taxed shares in their town land corporations instead of taxing the polls and property of their residents.[34] If this example clearly illustrates the town officials flouting the law, it does not illustrate a lack of local administrative capacity. A town policy of taxing proprietors would have created a tax exemption for nonshareholding settlers. It would have encouraged settlers to move to towns that offered the exemption, spurring their development without diluting the proprietors' shareholdings. Everyone gained: proprietors whose stakes grew more valuable as a result of town growth, nonproprietors who were exempted from taxes, and the colony that still got its tax revenue and, eventually, more revenue as a result of economic growth. What is most striking about this enforcement "failure," therefore, is that the towns crafted practical alternatives to the colony laws. Unlike Virginia's tax failures—sheriffs stealing the taxes, taxpayers concealing tithables, and an assembly that could solve its problems only by enlisting royal officials (in the tobacco export tax)—this tax "failure" illustrates the competence and sophistication of the local governments of Massachusetts.

Other failures were more serious. Not only did towns rarely assess artisan incomes, but the assessors in most agricultural towns ignored "merchantable goods," much less "other known estate whatsoever" and "all visible estate either at sea or on shore." Only the large seaport towns actually taxed the personal wealth of merchants and shopkeepers. Boston drew 46 percent of its property tax revenue from shipping and merchandise in 1688. This was unusual, although Boston also contained much more mercantile wealth than most other towns. "The poll tax generally was enforced to the letter of the law," according to a study of the town tax lists, but the property tax most often was "limited to real estate and livestock." Polls bore about 45 percent of the total tax burden until the 1653 poll tax cut, about one-third from then until the 1670s, and then about 45 percent again.[35] The "country rate" tax system was highly regressive.

It had another major drawback. The country rate system allowed towns to make various political adjustments, both within its parameters (when they assessed property) and outside them (when they taxed in different ways), but this system was inflexible at the colony level. After the General Court cut the livestock valuations in 1657, it made only minor changes—on the order of whether to exempt sheep—until the advent of royal government in 1691. From 1651 until then, the rates consisted of 1.67 shilling poll taxes and penny per pound levies on property. This was fine as long as the General Court levied only one rate each year and the towns levied most of the taxes for religion and education. It was *not* fine when the General Court levied twenty-six rates for King Philip's War and thirty-seven in 1689–1690 for the war against the French and the Eastern Indians.[36] Each rate doubled the poll tax, magnifying its regressive impact on poor taxpayers. Because there was no apportionment mechanism, moreover, high colony taxes invited equalization problems. Town officials could undervalue property and relieve polls with generous "sicknes, lamenes, or other infirmitie" exemptions, and the commissioners could vote to accept these results at their county meetings. The General Court could only pile on additional rates as the yield of each one fell and the geographical distribution of the tax burden grew ever less rational.

The system of country rates was designed for a decentralized government, and especially for one at peace with its neighbors. The General Court had apportioned taxes to the towns in the early settlement years, but the country rates reflected its waning authority for much of the rest of the seventeenth century.

Tax politics occurred within the towns rather than between them in this period. It occurred in town meetings rather than in the General Court. The General Court might have changed the system before the crown intervened, but the fact is that it did not—presumably because the towns liked local control over taxes and their General Court deputies defended their preferences. War, as Breen argues, changed the equation. But war alone did not change the tax system. Royal government brought apportionment back to Massachusetts.[37]

Polls and Estates

Massachusetts redesigned its tax system from 1692 to 1700, enacting eighteen different sets of rules until it settled on the details of its new tax on "polls and estates." This tax differed from the "country rates" in two crucial ways, both of which required highly politicized decision-making at the General Court level. The tax on polls and estates was apportioned to towns, and its valuation rules reflected more regular struggles between agricultural towns and commercial towns. Town officials still enjoyed leeway in its administration, but apportionment reduced the impact of their discretion. They could redistribute burdens within their towns, but not between their towns (or their county's towns) and others. To change their local quotas for colony taxes, towns now had to take their cases to the General Court as a whole: through their representatives, by petition, or both. The tax on polls and estates replaced the brittle country rate structure with a more flexible and politicized structure, designed by majority rule at the colony level.

It took a while for the General Court to work out the details of its new system—under the pressure of King William's War (1689-1697) and the close scrutiny of crown officials. Its first effort, in June 1692, levied a poll tax and ordered property valued by an entirely new rule: "[A]ll houses, lands, stock, goods and merchandizes and other estates whatsoever, real and personal, at a quarter part of one year's value or income thereof." Rather than assessing the property's value, as they had in the country rates, assessors now were to determine the annual income the property generated. By December 1692, it was clear the towns could not do this right away ("the rules therein given have not been fully understood, or at least not attended, which has occasioned an inequality, and the sum thereupon returned to fall greatly short of what was expected"), and the General Court tried again. For real estate, it listed its forms ("all houses, warehouses, tan-yards, orchards, pastures, meadows and lands, mills, cranes and wharffs") and directed that they "be estimated at seven years' income, as they are or may be let for in the respective places where they lye." For personal property, it fell back on the country rate rules. It fixed livestock valuations, treated "all shipping, goods, wares, merchandizes and trading stock and estate" by invoking "the rule of common estimation at the best discretion of the assessors," and revived the artisan income tax ("every handicraftsman, for his income, at discretion aforesaid"). This 1692 law also created the first explicit tax treatment of slaves in Massachusetts: "[E]very male slave of sixteen years old or upwards" was to be valued "at twenty pounds estate."[38]

The most interesting gyrations of the next several years involved the poll tax and the tax treatment of slaves. In June 1694, slaves were folded into the poll tax rather than handled (like livestock) as personal property with fixed valuations. This poll tax applied to free men eighteen and up (rather than sixteen) and, in an echo of Virginia's poll tax on "tithables," to slaves of both sexes ("all negro's, molatto's and Indian servants, as well male as female, of sixteen years old and upwards"). Free men became taxable at sixteen again in March 1695, and in June the General Court took the unprecedented (and unrepeated) step of charging independent women, declaring "all single women that live at their own hand" liable for poll taxes. This law shifted slaves back into the property tax as well. "All negro, molatto and Indian servants" were taxable at fourteen "unless disabled by infirmity," with men valued at £20 and women at £14. Massachusetts taxed slaves as personal property until 1777, using the rule it created in June 1696: "[A]ll Indian, melatto and negro servants to be estimated as other personal estate"—which meant the assessors valued each slave individually. The poll tax continued to apply to free men sixteen and up, exempting top officials, ministers, teachers, Harvard and all of its affiliates, and "such who through age, infirmity or extream poverty, in the discretion of the assessors, are rendered uncapable to contribute towards the public charge." The General Court had given serious thought to the tax treatment of age, sex, and race. It decided to lay the poll tax on free men, to exempt free women, and to tax slaves in the same way it taxed commercial property.[39]

For real estate valuation, the General Court retained the practice, introduced in 1692, of assessing by annual income rather than value. This was a general tax practice in England (in the local "rates" charged mainly to "occupiers" of real estate), but it made more sense in the English economy, where most of the occupiers were renters and the rents measured the "incomes" of the real estate. What this practice offered Massachusetts, where most occupiers were owners, was a way to favor farmers by facilitating underassessments of agricultural land. After experimenting with various multipliers, the General Court settled on six times the annual rental in 1700. Where there was no rent, the assessors were to "estimate" what land and houses "may reasonably be sett or lett for in the places where they lye" and multiply the result by six. This procedure had three consequences. First, six years of annual rent probably was less than half the full market value of real estate. Second, when annually elected local officials estimated the rent for owner-occupied land, we can assume they erred on the side of low valuations. Third, since urban real estate was rented more often, it would have been assessed at a higher fraction of its actual value.[40]

For personal property, meanwhile, farmers now enjoyed much lower livestock valuations than the ones in the country rates. Oxen and horses valued at £5 in 1688 were valued at only £2 in 1700, the cow valuation was halved, and the sheep and swine valuations fell 60 percent. The new figures were less than half of the actual value of the livestock. Commercial assets, however, were subject to "the rule of common estimation at the best discretion of the assessors," meaning that "shipping, goods, wares, merchandizes and trading stock and estate," artisan incomes, and slaves were supposed to be assessed at their full market value. We can assume they were not—it is an axiom of property taxation that no property is ever assessed at its full market value—but by 1700 the urban interests enjoyed no tax breaks like the legislated undervaluations of agricultural property. The urban groups fought back, winning reduced valuations for shipping, trading stock, and financial assets. Then, in a win for both farmers and artisans, the General Court expanded the artisan income tax in 1730 to embrace all "income by trade or faculty which any person or persons . . . do or shall exercise in gaining, by money or other estate not otherwise assessed, or commissions of profit in their improvement."[41] There were winners and losers in each of these decisions. But the crucial point is that they were all political decisions, made by an assembly whose town representatives defended the interests of their constituents.

This political process was even clearer when the General Court turned to apportionment. Nothing is more obvious in the Massachusetts statute books than the pages and pages, sometimes ten at a time, devoted to apportionments of the tax on polls and estates. These lists of towns with their tax quotas addressed the equalization problem of the country rates by instituting a process of colonywide negotiation. In its first incarnation, before the country rates, apportionment had involved few towns, 12 in 1634 and 23 in 1645, and even then it required the General Court to appoint special committees to work out quotas for "every towne proportionablely." But in 1694, the General Court assigned quotas to 83 towns. In 1772, it assigned them to 260. The council left this process to the lower house, which represented the towns; it tried to interfere to protect the "Maritime" towns in 1735, but backed off when the representatives called their participation a "very extraordinary" threat to the people's liberties. For several years, the lower house voted on each town quota individually, "the Respective Representatives having first had the Liberty to show the present circumstances of their town." Town selectmen also sometimes sent petitions claiming that local conditions—war, fire, disease, and even high winds that harmed beaches—warranted quota reductions. The apportionment negotiations rested on data compiled in periodic colonywide valuations; the town officials who compiled them presumably took care to protect local interests. Apportionment, in short, was a political process from start to finish.[42]

The design of the tax on polls and estates had complex effects on the poll tax. One of the main reasons this tax regime could be more productive than the country rates was that it allowed the General Court to manipulate the poll tax rate to prevent it from spiraling out of control when taxes were high, as they were in wartime. In the country rates, the poll tax doubled each time the General Court added a rate, reaching ridiculously high levels in King Philip's War and the early phases of King William's War. In the tax on polls and estates, however, the General Court fixed new poll tax rates in every tax levy. It also fixed them on the basis of data about the number of nonexempt male adults, which grew from about 16,000 in 1700 to about 60,000 in 1770. These rates still could get very high compared to their peacetime figures, reaching 10 shillings in 1710 (Queen Anne's War) and again in 1760 (French and Indian War) before falling back, with peace, to 2.5 shillings in 1720 and 3.33 shillings in 1770. The General Court tried to fix poll tax rates to ensure that the poll tax raised between 30 and 40 percent of the revenue, particularly in wartime. It raised more than half the total in the 1720s and 1730s, though the totals were relatively low in these peacetime decades.[43] Nevertheless, when a poll tax raises 40 percent of the revenue, a tax system is highly regressive. Like the country rates (and like Virginia's poll tax on tithables), the tax on polls and estates was very regressive at the low end of the wealth distribution.

But the tax on polls and estates was not equally regressive everywhere in Massachusetts. Its complex design, including the apportionment, made its impact more regressive in some towns than others. Each tax law levied a total sum and a specific poll tax. Town assessors first levied the poll tax on their nonexempt free adult males (delimiting the "nonexempt" category locally), then calculated and levied the property tax rate that would raise the rest of the town quota. This procedure had very different results in towns with different economic structures. Poor, recently settled, and frontier towns sometimes raised their entire quotas from poll tax—their quotas being so low that the poll tax met them. Richer, older, and especially seaport towns raised much more from property—their quotas being high primarily because of this property. The valuation of 1772 expressed its results as town quotas for each £1,000 of tax. Of 260 towns, Boston paid £92.3, Salem paid £26.6, and seven other towns paid more than £10, with the other 251 paying less than £10 apiece for each £1,000 of tax. Boston raised less of its quota from the poll tax than any other town, 16 percent compared to a colonywide average of almost 40 percent. The tax on polls and estates was not all that regressive in Boston, even though its poor men paid the poll tax (unless they persuaded the assessors to exempt them). It was extremely regressive in the western towns that, after the Revolution, erupted in Shays's Rebellion.[44]

The tax on polls and estates did not have to operate as regressively as it actually did in the eighteenth century. In the nineteenth century, Massachusetts modified it to cap poll taxes at low figures that included town, county, and other local tax levies that piggybacked on the state's tax structure. In the twentieth century, the poll tax was so low that the state did not bother to abolish it until 1963.[45] But in the eighteenth century, even if town assessors were generous in granting exemptions (as Boston's assessors were), the poll tax imposed serious burdens—especially when total tax levels ballooned to finance the Revolution.

Revolution

The high cost of the Revolutionary War inspired no root-and-branch tax reform effort in Massachusetts. Towns asked for and sometimes won abatements for war damages and economic hardships, such as the impact of British naval activity on fishing. Agricultural towns demanded relief from heavy taxes on polls and estates through a more vigorous taxation of imports, liquors, and other "luxury" goods presumed to be owned chiefly in port towns. This conflict had been broached during the French and Indian War and now assumed greater significance as the tax on polls and estates reached dizzying levels. Mainly, however, the tax politics that already was so well developed in Massachusetts continued through the Revolution. It acquired more intensity, but its issues and alignments were familiar.

Slavery was not part of this politics. The General Court made a conservative bow to the fact that slavery was disintegrating in Massachusetts in 1777. It dropped the valuation of slaves as property, reviving the seventeenth-century poll tax on unfree labor. In the new formulation, the poll tax applied to men sixteen and up "including negroes and molattoes (and such of these that are under the government of a master or mistress, to be taxed to the said master or mistress, respectively, in the same manner as minors and apprentices are taxed)." After a 1778 revision exempted female "negroes and molattoes" more explicitly, this language survived for another fifteen years. The General Court dropped the racial terminology in 1793 and the mistresses and apprentices in 1805. The poll tax still applied to men sixteen and up, with the tax on a "minor" charged to "his parent, master or guardian" if he resided under the "immediate government" of such a person. Otherwise, he paid his own poll tax. This formula still hinted at apprenticeship, but the Massachusetts tax code no longer recognized unfree labor by adults.[46]

The valuation rules and apportionments attracted more attention. In 1777, the General Court simplified the valuation of commercial and agricultural property. Now, all property (land, buildings, livestock, financial assets, merchandise, shipping, plate) was to be valued at its "price" on November 1. The same rule covered an expanded income and profits tax, on "income from any profession, faculty, handicraft, trade or employment; and also on the amount of all incomes and profits gained by trading by sea and on shore, and by means of advantages arising from the war, and the necessities of the community"—with the last phrase referring to price gouging. A 1779 amendment added a moral assessment of the price-gouging profits: assessors were "to have special regard to the way and manner in which the same have been made, as well as the *quantum* thereof, and to assess them at such rate, as they . . . shall judge to be just and reasonable," as long as it was not "more than five times the sum of the same amount in other kind of estate" (doubled to ten times five months later). The profits at issue involved farmers charging city dwellers high prices for food, and we can assume that the assessors in agricultural towns were not overzealous about them. The war profiteers and price gougers disappeared from the tax code in 1781, only to be replaced by a new political deal. All real and personal estate was assessed at 6 percent of its value, except unimproved land, which was assessed at only 2 percent of its value, while incomes and profits were assessed at their full value.[47] The losers here were artisans and professionals (lawyers and ministers), although some of the professionals benefited insofar as they owned the unimproved land that received the most favorable tax treatment—and both groups also undoubtedly persuaded local assessors to treat their incomes more gently in practice.

The politics of apportionment intensified as well. The 1780 constitution required that the process rest on valuations made decennially or "oftener." The General Court opted for "oftener," completing new valuations in 1779, 1781, and 1786. In a break with the practice of the colonial council, the state senate (now annually elected by the voters) demanded to participate in the 1781 negotiations. The representatives cited the clause of the 1780 constitution requiring money bills to originate in the lower house. The senate answered that this clause did not mention valuations. After the supreme court sided with the senate, the General Court resolved that five senators join a committee of as many representatives as the lower house chose to appoint. Town requests for abatements, meanwhile, raised issues ranging from large local army enlistments and the collapse of commerce and fishing to the complaint by Harpswell that forty-two rich men had left the town since the last valuation and the plea by the Gore section of Chesterfield that the General Court let them make their own assessments to "Remove oure Egyptian yoke" (assessment by Chesterfield).[48]

The most controversial issue, using imposts and excises to reduce tax burdens on polls and estates, aligned the ports against the agricultural towns. Massachusetts had taxed imported goods for much of the colonial era. After a ferocious political battle in 1754, it added an excise on liquor consumption, although this tax lapsed after the French and Indian War (and the receipt of a hefty reimbursement from London). During the Revolution, the General Court imposed an excise on distilling and retail liquor sales, which included a carriage tax aimed at urban elites: £5 on a coach or chariot, £3 on a phaeton or four-wheel chaise, 15 shillings on a fall-back chaise, 10 shillings on any other chaise, and 9 shillings on a sulkey or riding chair. The "whereas" clause for this tax cited the General Court's need for money and its intent to suppress immorality, luxury, and extravagance, by which the rural majority clearly meant the wealth of the port towns.[49]

The ensuing political struggle was entangled with another issue: how and with what level of energy Massachusetts would meet the requisitions of the Continental Congress. Commercial towns generally wanted to help Congress curb the currency depreciation (the runaway inflation) by leaning on the tax on polls and estates. Agricultural towns demanded relief. Scattered rioting escalated until the state had to send 1,200 militiamen to quell a 1782 outbreak. For the next two years, Massachusetts relied on imposts and excises for its own costs, sending Congress apologies rather than money. But in 1786, the General Court decided to pay Congress (and fund its state debt) through a huge levy on polls and estates, bolstered by strict rules designed to prevent local officials from granting tax relief through lenient or negligent collection. These actions precipitated Shays's Rebellion, and the electoral response to that caused the General Court to legislate tax relief in 1787, long before the U.S. Constitution and federal assumption of state debts solved the underlying problem—the cost of the Revolution—for good.[50]

Historians often remark on the "conservative" nature of the Revolution in Massachusetts, just as they do for Virginia. Despite the political and economic upheavals of the war years, there was little change in the state's social structure or in its government. Yet the things that survived the Revolution in Massachusetts were not quite the same as the things that survived in Virginia. A society in which 98 percent of the population was free became more egalitarian when African Americans ended slavery altogether, seizing their freedom during the Revolution by escape, self-purchase, manumission, and legal challenges based on the 1780 constitution's proclamation that "[a]ll men are born free and equal." Although the 1776 Virginia constitution similarly declared that "all men are by nature equally free and independent," that statement acquired no analogous legal force. Massachusetts was hardly a paradise for the 6,000 African Americans who lived in the state in 1790 or for the 10,000 who lived there in 1860. They suffered from and fought against the many expressions of American racism as 2 percent and then less than 1 percent of the state's population. Nevertheless, a colony in which slavery and servitude had always been rare turned into a full-fledged free state during the Revolution.[51]

Changes to the state government also enhanced the relatively democratic structure that already existed. Under the 1780 constitution, the Massachusetts voters elected their governor, senate, and house of representatives, directly and annually. The constitution required that both houses be apportioned according to the tax on polls and estates, with town representation in the lower house reflecting numbers of "rateable polls" and district seats in the senate reflecting "the proportion of the public taxes paid by the said districts"—a formula designed to reserve power for the port towns.[52] This system of legislative apportionment depended on the administrative capacity the constitution also recognized in its decennial (or "oftener") valuation rule. It relied on the ability of the citizens of Massachusetts, acting locally in the towns, to determine numbers of polls and values of estates. The tax on polls and estates remained the primary revenue engine of Massachusetts after the Revolution. As a system of regular data collection, it also formed the cornerstone of the state's system of representation.

The history of taxation in Massachusetts is a story about prosaic political struggles and incremental changes. It is a recognizably modern story in which various groups competed over the distribution of tax burdens. Farmers, artisans, merchants, and professionals sought favorable valuation rules. Town representatives contended over apportionments. Local assessors enjoyed a great deal of leeway in valuing property and granting poll tax exemptions. Massachusetts had a tax politics throughout its history, a politics that operated at all levels of government. Of all the groups involved, poor men who were taxed only (or mainly) for their "polls" defended their interests least effectively. No reform of this era addressed the system's basic regressivity. Thus, what is most striking about the Massachusetts tax system is not its equity, but its sophistication. Massachusetts could tax "all personall & real estates" starting in the 1640s because its annually elected local officials were capable of assessing the value of property. Taxpayers could trust in the competence and good faith of these officials—or at least trust them enough to allow such a sophisticated tax system to work.

3 Variations

In 1796, Secretary of the Treasury Oliver Wolcott, Jr., surveyed the state tax systems in search of patterns. Congress had asked him to design a national property tax. He had hoped the federal government could piggyback on the existing state tax systems, since "habit has rendered an acquiescence under the rules they impose, familiar." But once Wolcott looked at the state tax systems closely, he realized that this plan would never work. They were "utterly discordant and irreconcileable, in their original principles." The experience of the states offered no template for a national system. No two states taxed exactly the same things and, when they did tax the same things, they taxed them in different ways. The conclusion was clear: in 1796, there was no such thing as an "American" tax system.[1]

Nor had there ever been an "American" tax system in the colonial era. The differences between Virginia and Massachusetts were only the beginning. Several colonies borrowed their early tax laws from Virginia or Massachusetts (the oldest and largest colonies), but borrowing was never the whole story. Some borrowers exaggerated characteristics of the lenders. Next to the probity of Connecticut, Massachusetts was a cesspool of corruption. Next to the thievery of North Carolina, Virginia was a good–government paradise. Connecticut experienced something that looked like a scandal in 1663 when the General Court attacked the New London assessors "for theire corupt and deceatfull dealings" in assessing a "country rate," but the accusation really arose from a dispute between the town and colony over the value of local real estate. The town backed its assessors, and the General Court backed off. Rather than following the Massachusetts transition from "country rates" to "polls and estates," Connecticut devised an elaborate schedule of fixed land valuations that favored intensive uses on small holdings: tillage over pasture, short crop rotations over long ones, and, more generally, the society of small-scale family farmers that later would be identified as a Virginian ("Jeffersonian") ideal. North Carolina was another story. Unable to emulate Virginia's shift to the tax on exported tobacco, North Carolina remained at the mercy of the sheriffs who collected its poll tax on "tithables." In the 1750s and 1760s, they stole the proceeds with stunning regularity, particularly in the backcountry, meanwhile also holding property hostage to extortionate claims for official fees. When angry farmers calling themselves Regulators rebelled against the corruption of these county officials, elites who believed, as one actually said, that it was "Vain and a Crime for any Common Man to pretend to understand the Fee-Bill" crushed them with military force.[2]

Needless to say, Connecticut and North Carolina also approached the financial demands of the Revolution in different ways. Connecticut made incremental changes, all of them framed to increase the progressivity of its tax structure. It halved the poll tax on men of military age and supplemented taxes on carriages and large houses with taxes on other items owned primarily by the rich: clocks, watches, silver plate, cash and loans, and mercantile stock-in-trade. It extended its "faculty" tax from artisans, lawyers, and shopkeepers to include the "clear annual profits" of "physicians, surgeons, tavern-keepers, owners of mills, iron-works, ware-houses, work-houses, graziers, drovers, and others." Like Massachusetts, Connecticut also taxed price-gouging war profiteers ("persons who make a business of buying and selling the necessaries or conveniences of life and by engrossing the same or other artificial methods enhance the prices thereof and thereby make great gains to themselves"). And it justified all of these changes by reviving the seventeenth-century "ability to pay" rhetoric: "Whereas all persons by law rateable ought to be taxed for the support of government and the common defence in proportion to the value of their estates and annual incomes . . ." Connecticut did not change its treatment of agricultural land during the war, although it added unimproved land to the tax rolls—which could not have raised much money but fit with the general effort to increase progressivity. The state used the same system of land valuations in 1796 that the colony had framed in 1712, preserving its policy of favoring intensive land uses on small holdings.[3]

North Carolina attempted a root-and-branch reform—and failed completely. In 1777, a state whose officials had never levied anything but the poll tax on "tithables" suddenly instituted an ad valorem tax on "all the Lands, Lots, Houses, Slaves, Money, money-at-interest, Stock in trade, Horses and Cattle in this state." Every "Inhabitant" was to provide "a just and true amount [*sic*] of his or her Estate as aforesaid on oath" within a month, at which time "three honest and intelligent persons" would value it "as nearly as may be."

The legislature asserted that this tax "will tend to the ease of the inhabitants of this State and greatly relieve the poor people thereof," but the law actually handled the poor by charging every free man who owned less than £100 of property a 4-shilling poll tax, which equaled the tax on £100 of property. In 1778, the legislature abandoned the claim that this tax helped the poor. It also retreated from the assessment of slaves by fixing valuations: £700, £400, or £150 depending on age (£700 on ages 10 to 40), with exemptions for "slaves disabled by bodily infirmities or void of reason [!], such incapacity to be adjudged and certified by the County Court." A 1780 law directed assessors to value other kinds of property "in proportion to what the negroes were valued," a 1782 law gave up on taxing financial assets, and a 1784 law gave up altogether. North Carolina emerged from the Revolution with the most primitive (and idiosyncratic) tax structure in the nation: a flat per acre tax on all land, a poll tax equal to the tax on 300 acres and levied on free men and slaves of both sexes, and an ad valorem tax on urban real estate (of which there was little in North Carolina) that set the tax on each £100 of value equal to the tax on 300 acres or one poll.[4]

To the extent that there was any pattern from colony to colony or state to state, it was the only pattern that Oliver Wolcott was able to identify in 1796. It is the same pattern we have seen in Massachusetts and Virginia, further illustrated by this brief run through Connecticut and North Carolina. Northern taxes were more sophisticated than southern taxes. In particular, from early in their histories, northern colonies enjoyed sufficient levels of administrative capacity to assess the value of property. They did not always do so, but except for South Carolina (see below), no southern colony ever did. After the Revolution, many of the northern states continued to value property. Among the southern states, only Maryland attempted to implement a comprehensive valuation program. Virginia treated its 1782 land value equalization as a permanent assessment and levied flat-rate taxes on slaves, horses, and carriages. The other southern states dropped all but the pretense of assessing the value of property.

Wolcott explained this difference as a function of the different local government regimes of the northern and southern states. Local governments were more democratic in the North than the South. In the North, local communities elected their own local officials. In the South, state officials appointed local officials. Northern states could levy more sophisticated taxes, Wolcott thought, because they could rely on the competence and discretion of their elected local officials, delegating the responsibility to assess and collect state taxes to them. He located the boundary at Delaware. North of Delaware, the states assigned tax levies to "townships or counties, in which the assessing and collecting officers are chosen by the people, who are ultimately responsible for their conduct." South of Delaware, the states taxed individuals directly, and "the assessing and collecting officers are appointed by the Legislatures, State Executives, or by certain courts." The Delaware legislature apportioned its taxes to counties, "but, as the collectors are appointed by the [state] treasurer, the counties are not responsible." Wolcott's effort to be polite sacrificed clarity, but his point emerged nonetheless. In the southern states (the states "where the principle of local responsibility has not been adopted"), the tax structures were primitive ("the systems of taxation have been simplified, and more and more confined to visible and permanent objects").[5]

Wolcott was right about the roles of local officials in northern and southern communities. In the North, they answered to constituents who elected them locally and, in most states, annually. In the South, they did not answer to local communities unless dramatic misbehavior instigated popular protests. The elected local officials of the North were capable not only of performing complex administrative tasks but also of managing complex political tasks. They were capable of negotiating with their constituents about the messy details of property valuation, and they did so on a regular basis. Wolcott tried to be tactful. In the overheated partisan atmosphere of the 1790s (to which we will turn in chapter 5), Wolcott was a Federalist treasury secretary talking to congressional Republicans. He was also a New Englander talking to powerful southerners. But a historian with two hundred years of distance from the partisan struggles of the 1790s can dispense with Wolcott's roundabout language to make what really was a simple observation. In the early United States, the more democratic governments were the more competent governments—and these governments were located in the North.

There was also another big difference between the North and the South in the colonial and revolutionary eras, one that Wolcott could not gloss politely in the political context of the 1790s even if he understood its ramifications, which he probably did not. Wolcott said nothing about slavery except to notice how states taxed the owners of human "property." Yet, as he was fully aware, slavery was a crucial institution in the South but a marginal institution in the North, despite its prolonged death throes in some northern states.[6] As we have seen, Virginia's efforts to cope with the Revolution suggested a solution to the problem of how slavery influenced the difference between northern and southern taxation: that a culture of "sovereign mastership" made the assessment of property seem unduly intrusive to taxpayers who thought of themselves as the "masters" of "families." In Massachusetts, assessment was not and had never been considered unduly intrusive. It had been part of a larger town-based community life since the seventeenth century. Nor were the Massachusetts taxpayers "masters" of "families" in the same sense as their Virginia counterparts. Ultimately, it is impossible to disentangle the impact of slavery from the impact of local democracy. Tax structures were more sophisticated in the colonies (and states) where local governments were more democratic *and* where slavery was rare. Either way, they were more sophisticated in the North.

Rather than tracing the ins and outs of the history of taxation in every colony (and state), the rest of this chapter will focus on two additional variations. Pennsylvania and South Carolina are especially interesting because they did not borrow their institutions from any other colonies. Pennsylvania had democratic local government in its counties and townships and very little slavery. South Carolina had hardly any local government at all and exploited slavery on an extreme scale. Yet both enjoyed competent administration. During the Revolution, moreover, their representatives became major players in national tax debates. While the Pennsylvania story illustrates the role of local democracy without the fabled communalism of New England towns, the South Carolina story offers more evidence about how slavery influenced the development of taxation in the United States.

Pennsylvania

At first glance, the history of taxation in the Quaker colony seems paradoxical: low taxes but a comprehensive and sophisticated tax structure. The colony and its local governments taxed the value of "real and personal estates" as determined by elected local assessors and collected a limited poll tax from single men. In addition to this general tax system, the colony taxed certain imported goods and levied an excise on liquor retailers. Landowners paid quitrents (small flat-rate land taxes), and everyone paid fees when they used the legal system. The major elements of this tax structure were in place within fifteen years after the 1682 arrival of William Penn's first groups of settlers, and most of them persisted into the nineteenth century. Pennsylvania's taxes were less regressive than those of Massachusetts (or Virginia) because there were no across-the-board poll taxes, but Pennsylvania resembled Massachusetts in the ability of its local officials to assess the value of property. It also resembled Massachusetts in another way: Pennsylvania's tax system proved usable in the crisis of the Revolutionary War. The state made only minor changes to the tax system it inherited from the colony, even though heavy taxes caused serious collection problems, just as they did everywhere else. The structure of taxation in colonial Pennsylvania included several unique and interesting features, but the tax level is even more striking. Taxes were much lower in Pennsylvania than in either Virginia or Massachusetts.[7]

Two of Pennsylvania's most famous characteristics kept its taxes low, both of which reflected the influence of the Quakers who dominated the colony's politics from the 1680s through the 1760s. First, there was its pacifist tradition. Before he left England for Pennsylvania in 1682, William Penn sent an extraordinary letter to the Delaware Indians: "The king of the Countrey where I live [Charles II], hath given unto me a great Province therein," Penn explained, "but I desire to enjoy it with your Love and Consent, that we may always live together as Neighbours and friends." It never worked out quite that well, but Pennsylvania and the Delawares sustained a "Long Peace" for seventy years, until the French and Indian War—and the migration of masses of non-Quaker settlers who were not interested in either the "Love and Consent" of Indians or in buying (rather than seizing) Indian land—shattered the world in which peace had been possible. In addition to keeping peace with the Delawares, Pennsylvania limited its participation in Britain's imperial wars against France. Where Massachusetts responded energetically during King William's War (1690s), Queen Anne's War (1710s), and King George's War (1740s), Pennsylvania made only token contributions. Even so, the Quaker members of the assembly covered these violations of their pacifist principles with a legal fiction. They claimed to be raising taxes for the "King's [or Queen's] use," as though they had no idea how the crown would spend the proceeds. The point, however, is that until the French and Indian War (1754–1763), which involved major fighting in Pennsylvania, these contributions were small.[8]

The second characteristic was Pennsylvania's celebrated extension of religious liberty to a polyglot population of settlers. Quakers opposed the establishment of official religious creeds and never established a creed in the colony. They dominated politics because non-Quakers voted for them rather than because others could not hold the offices. But there was more to it than toleration for diverse beliefs. Pennsylvania did not tax for religion at all. There were no Anglican vestries like Virginia's. Nor did townships finance religion, as towns did in Massachusetts. In Pennsylvania, local governments financed poor relief, roads, bridges, courthouses, prisons, and other things, but they did not build churches or pay the salaries of ministers. The reason is clear. One of the core aspects of Quaker religious doctrine was a refusal to invest authority in a "hireling clergy." The Quakers recognized individuals (both men and women) as "ministers," but they did not pay them salaries. They also discouraged the expensive college educations that elevated clergy over laity in church-based denominations. Settlers who practiced church-based religions in Pennsylvania (Anglicans, Presbyterians, Lutherans, and others) paid their ministers voluntarily or by attracting subsidies from Europe rather than, like dissenters in other colonies, demanding shares of the tax proceeds.[9] Thus, in Pennsylvania, peace reduced taxes at the colony level and the absence of a religious establishment reduced taxes at the local level. By avoiding the costs of both war and religion, Pennsylvania maintained its sophisticated and competent governments cheaply.

There was a third way Pennsylvania kept its taxes down. In 1723, the colony established a public bank called the General Loan Office (GLO), which printed paper money and loaned it to Pennsylvania residents for long terms, in small amounts, and at low interest rates, with the loans secured by real estate holdings. The GLO was a great success. It supplemented scarce gold and silver with a stable currency (one that held its value without depreciating); provided investment capital to farmers, artisans, and merchants; and, through the interest that borrowers paid on their loans, yielded profits to the colony. These profits, in turn, allowed the colony to avoid general taxes or, more precisely, to permit its local governments to monopolize the general tax revenue. From 1718 to 1755, Pennsylvania relied solely on import taxes, the excise on retail liquor sales, and GLO profits to fund government at the colony level. This policy system depended on peace, and the French and Indian War destroyed every part of it. Once the GLO emitted large sums for war spending—using "currency finance" to borrow against future taxes—its currency became a fiat issue like any other. Despite onerous general taxes to retire it (collect and burn it as people paid their taxes in it), the paper now started to depreciate. Yet for thirty years, the Pennsylvania paper money operation had worked differently from those of most other colonies. They usually printed money to borrow. Pennsylvania printed money to lend.[10]

Quakers began to trickle into what became Pennsylvania, New Jersey, and Delaware in the 1670s, even before Charles II granted William Penn the charter to establish his Quaker "holy experiment." From 1682 to 1715, about 23,000 Quakers migrated into the area from England, Wales, and Ireland. Like the Puritans of Massachusetts, the Quakers of Pennsylvania migrated as families into a healthy environment, though where Puritans were the overwhelming majority in Massachusetts, Quakers were only about half the Pennsylvania settlers in the early decades. By the 1750s, after large-scale migrations from Britain and the German states, the Quakers had become a small minority in what they still considered "their" colony. Population estimates are rough, since Pennsylvania took no censuses—Quakers rejected the concept on principle, in the same way that they refused to take oaths (because oaths implied that people would lie without them) and addressed individuals as "thee" and "thou" (because "you" implied an undue respect for social hierarchy). Nevertheless, the colony's population seems to have grown quickly until 1700 (to 18,000), more slowly from 1700 to 1720 (to 31,000), and then very quickly again (to 120,000 in 1750 and 240,000 in 1770).[11]

Pennsylvania's staple crop was wheat, which millers turned into flour in the small towns that dotted the landscape and merchants shipped to the West Indies from Philadelphia. Calling only for seasonal labor, wheat allowed the settlers to combine their export crop with a diversified mix of other agricultural and industrial efforts, from livestock and dairying to wood fabrication, brewing, tanning, iron and other metal working, and shipbuilding. Throughout the colonial era, family members provided most of the farm labor even though many white immigrants arrived as bound servants from Britain, Ireland, and the German states, paying for their passage with about four years of labor. The wealthy also purchased African slaves, chiefly when wars disrupted the supply of white servants. There were more slaves in Pennsylvania than in Massachusetts, but not nearly as many as in southern colonies. Slaves were about 8 percent of the population in 1720 (2,000 slaves) and about 2 percent in 1750 (2,800 slaves) and 1770 (5,600 slaves). Pennsylvania generally deserved its reputation as "the best poor man's country in the world." Land got harder to buy as values rose, but favorable terms made tenancy a viable strategy for family farmers and probably an avenue of upward mobility. The city of Philadelphia grew slowly until about 1710 and then more steadily. Unlike Boston, it prospered during the eighteenth-century decades and actually boomed during the wars. Hard times struck in the 1720s and 1760s, but Philadelphia remained a magnet for ambitious natives and immigrants. Its population overtook Boston's at 15,000 in the 1750s. It remained the largest city on the continent until New York claimed that title in the 1770s.[12]

Electoral politics generally was a staid affair in colonial Pennsylvania, but it got raucous when the power of the Penns as the "proprietors" of the colony clashed with the Quaker settlers' legendary mistrust of authority. Charles II had granted the land and government to William Penn personally. Penn expected land sales and quitrents to produce income, and he also expected the settlers to tax themselves to reimburse his outlays on behalf of the colony. The settlers had other ideas. In the early decades, political parties connected to the proprietor and assembly leadership structured fierce partisan conflicts. Penn suffered a disabling stroke in 1712, and after his death in 1718 his heirs fought over his estate until 1732. With his daughter Hannah Penn exercising a loose supervision over the colony, conflict subsided in these years. In 1746, however, Penn's son Thomas became the chief proprietor and decided to assert his prerogatives aggressively. Thomas Penn exploited the crises of the French and Indian War and the ensuing Indian uprising known as Pontiac's Rebellion (1764). He urged crown officials to order a purge of Quakers from all public offices (he was an Anglican), and he courted frontier settlers who resented the Quaker policy of negotiating with Indians (as opposed to killing them). The assembly responded by asking crown officials to overthrow Penn and institute a royal government. As a way to secure their autonomy, this plan would have been questionable under any conditions. The fact that it reached London as Parliament was passing the Stamp Act rendered it ludicrous.[13]

Meanwhile, the first phase of this conflict, in the 1680s and 1690s, had democratized the government of Pennsylvania, as William Penn asked for money and the assembly granted it with strings attached. "For the love of God, me and the poor country," Penn begged the settlers, "be not so governmentish, so noisy and open in your dissatisfactions." But governmentish they were. A series of constitutional frames capped by the Charter of Privileges (1701) created an unusually powerful assembly. In Pennsylvania, the Penns appointed governors and councils, as the crown did in royal colonies, but the governors were weak and the councils had no legislative roles. The governors could veto bills; they could not dispense with elections for years at a time or prorogue recalcitrant assemblies. In Pennsylvania, the assembly was elected annually, met every year, and controlled all taxes except the proprietor's quitrents. It had one seriously undemocratic feature. Each county and the city of Philadelphia elected an at-large slate of a certain size. The assembly added new counties slowly and failed to adjust the sizes of the delegations. By the 1760s, it was badly malapportioned and dominated by the three oldest rural counties—the ones where Quakers still were the most influential.[14]

The local government structure was highly democratic. Initially, Penn appointed justices of the peace (JPs) to administer county courts like Virginia's. After 1701, however, the sheriffs faced the voters every three years (rather than being appointed by the JPs) and in 1711 the JPs yielded county governance to elected commissioners. County tax assessors were the first local officials to be chosen by popular election, starting in 1696, and the only county officials who were elected on an annual basis (the commissioners served staggered three-year terms). If the counties were the main local government units, Pennsylvania was also divided into townships. The townships never had the same responsibilities as New England towns—the proprietary distributed land, the counties elected the assembly, charitable organizations operated schools, and churches supported themselves—but township responsibilities grew over time. Township meetings elected local officials (constables, overseers of the poor, highway supervisors, and others), and the townships taxed to finance their activities. Philadelphia was different. It was a "closed corporation," which meant that it was governed by a council composed only of "freemen of the city." The council admitted individuals to "freeman" status, chose new council members, and rotated the mayoralty. While this arrangement resembled the self-perpetuating county courts of Virginia, the assembly never permitted the Philadelphia corporation to tax. Instead, the residents of the city (as opposed to its "freemen") elected assessors in the same way rural counties did, with the city's wards assuming the roles of the rural townships (electing constables and so on).[15]

The Pennsylvania assembly never legislated the details of its general tax, known as the "land tax," as comprehensively as the Massachusetts General Court laid out its "country rates" and tax on "polls and estates." After establishing the tax in the 1690s, the assembly made minor adjustments until 1717, in its last colony-level land tax until 1755. It then stripped much of the detail out of an important 1725 tax law for the counties, which later was extended to other local government units such as the townships. In effect, the vagueness of the 1725 law granted leeway to local communities to decide how to distribute their local burdens. When the assembly started to tax in earnest for the French and Indian War, another burst of legislation essentially created a dual structure: new and highly detailed colony-level provisions alongside the looser local regime. This dual structure lasted through the early years of the Revolutionary War, when the legislature adjusted the system again, including by repealing the 1725 law in 1780. Now, local taxes piggybacked on the revised state-level structure, and in 1787 the state was able to stop levying its land tax again. In a sense, Pennsylvania pioneered what became the United States tax policy under the Constitution: peacetime reliance on imposts, excises, and nontax revenues, with direct taxes held in reserve for emergencies and normally levied only by "local" governments.[16]

The Pennsylvania land tax had two unique features. One was the way it handled taxable property. The other was its limited poll tax. In both cases, the tax was framed to offer targeted tax breaks for certain behaviors. Massachusetts tried to tax "all" property and the labor of "all" men not disabled by "sickness, lameness, or other infirmity." Virginia taxed the "tithables," also with disability exemptions. Pennsylvania, however, extended tax breaks for debt, child rearing, and poor families, plus a tax penalty to promote marriage. Today, the federal income tax code favors similar circumstances (think of the mortgage interest deduction and child tax credit). Although the behaviors that the current income tax favors are not exactly the same as the ones the Pennsylvania land tax favored, they are similar enough to suggest that something "modern" was happening in Pennsylvania three hundred years ago.[17]

In his fascinating study of family strategies among the Quaker settlers, Barry Levy argues that this "modern" thing was a "family ideology." In the seventeenth century, according to Levy, Quakers developed the ideas many Americans still hold about what a family should be: a "child-centered" household formed by marriage and shielded by financial security. They developed this ideology to promote their religious imperatives. To keep their children in the sect, parents tried to shelter them from having to associate with "carnal talkers" (non-Quakers), which the children would have to do if their parents could not afford to support them at home or launch them into adulthood with property. In northwestern England and Wales, where many of the Pennsylvania Quakers came from, poverty frustrated this ambition. But in Pennsylvania, cheap and fertile land plus the reliable West Indies market for flour created a "child-rearing garden." In Pennsylvania, Quaker parents could afford to support daughters until they found Quaker husbands and amass large holdings of land to distribute to sons. The unique provisions of the Pennsylvania land tax clearly were framed to assist the settlers in pursuing this family strategy.[18]

What Pennsylvania called a "land tax" was a tax on land and livestock as well as holdings of unfree laborers (indentured servants and slaves). From the 1690s through the 1710s, the laws described it as a comprehensive tax on "all estates, real and personal." Yet this was not a tax on anything Massachusetts would have recognized as "all" property. In Pennsylvania, tax assessors were to determine the "clear value" of a taxpayer's estate, meaning its value after subtracting debts. They were also to exempt all household goods and tools ("implements used in trade and getting a livelihood") and to levy no taxes on anyone whose net ("clear") estate came in below a figure such as £30 or £50.[19] Massachusetts probably also exempted household goods and tools in practice; its long lists of taxable assets never mentioned them. But Massachusetts did not offer anything like Pennsylvania's exemption for the poor or its debt offset. It is not that Quakers favored the accumulation of debt; they actually were very wary about it. The difference probably stemmed from the Pennsylvania land system. In Massachusetts, the General Court granted land to towns that granted it to settlers in transactions that normally did not involve money. In Pennsylvania, however, the Penns *sold* land to settlers, in transactions that definitely involved money and may have involved credit. The Pennsylvania land tax favored the accumulation of debt to buy land—or to make other investments.

The exemption for the poor, meanwhile, was not a flat exemption floor. It was mainly a tax break for parents. The assembly first articulated this policy in 1693 in its first land tax. No taxes were to be levied on people "who have a great Charge of Children and become Indigent in the world & are Soe farr in Debt, that the Cleare vallue of their Reall and Personall Estate doth not amount to Thirty pounds." In 1696, the assembly loosened the rule so that assessors valued individual estates "having a due regard to such who have a great Charge of Children, whose clear value of both real & personal estate doth not amount to Thirty pounds." This formula permitted either a total tax exemption or a partial abatement. Really, it left the amount of "regard" that was "due" open to negotiation between assessors and taxpayers on a local basis. The 1725 county tax law made the rule looser still. Now, assessors were to "hav[e] due regard to such as are poor and have a charge of children" without any specified cutoff. Now, in other words, local communities determined what levels of poverty should trigger the tax break for parents. It is not clear exactly what decisions they made (without censuses, the tax-exempt simply disappear from the records), but it is likely that the answers varied from place to place and over time.[20]

The flip side of Pennsylvania's tax break for parents, and especially poor parents, was a punitive tax on poor "single freemen." Rather than a poll tax levied on all men (Massachusetts) or free men and slaves of both sexes (Virginia), this tax was levied only on unmarried men who had been out of servitude or apprenticeship for at least six months and who owned less than the amount of property that otherwise would trigger a property tax exemption. It was levied at a flat rate "per head," but it was not a poll tax. It was a minimum tax that penalized poor men who did not assume the "burden" of marriage. The six-month grace period after release from servitude or apprenticeship was a nice touch, but the burden this tax imposed in place of marriage was steep and regressive. In the 1725 version, single men over the age of twenty-one whose "clear" estate was worth less than £50 paid 3 shillings for each penny per pound tax that was levied on property, meaning that they paid a tax equal to the tax on £36 of property whether they owned £49 of property or none at all.[21] The "single freeman" tax was not nearly as regressive as the across-the-board poll taxes of other colonies. Nor did Pennsylvania place a value on the labor of men or enslaved women in relation to other kinds of property or the labor of other people (children and free women). The implications of this tax for ideas about gender were more direct. Pennsylvania placed a value on the "burden" of marriage for men—and refused to allow poor men to evade it.

There was one more significant tax break. Until 1755, Pennsylvania taxed only improved land rather than total landholdings. The 1693 law mandated "a due Regard" for "the many Tracts of Uncultivated and unprofitable Lands which produce rather a Charge than Profitt to the Owners thereof"—interestingly using the same language ("due regard") that later governed the tax break for parents. The next several tax laws did not mention unimproved land, although starting in 1717 taxpayers reported how much of their land was "sowed with corn [grain]," data that would have enabled assessors either to exempt other (unsowed) land or value it at lower rates. The 1725 law was more explicit. It exempted "all unsettled tracts or parcels of land" including tracts "formerly accustomed to be rated in assessments." This policy lasted through the thirty years when local taxes were the only land taxes. In 1755, however, the assembly explained that accumulations of unimproved land no longer reflected the Quaker family strategy of amassing land for sons. Now, speculators were holding "large tracts of valuable lands . . . without intention of improvement, but merely in expectation of receiving hereafter higher prices for private advantage." Instead of helping parents to launch their sons locally, these holdings were chasing the sons away, forcing "great numbers of people . . . to leave this province and settle in other colonies where lands are more easily purchased, to the manifest injury and charge of the public."[22]

The taxation of unimproved land was one of several major tax changes during the French and Indian War, and it was entangled in the lengthy struggle between the assembly and Thomas Penn. As the colony's most important land speculator but also as its proprietor, Penn demanded that his land be exempted from the assembly's war taxes. The assembly refused, and it was this conflict that, most directly, produced the tax on unimproved land. There were other changes. In 1758, Pennsylvania switched its assessment base from value to annual income ("the clear yearly value of the estates within this province"), with "yearly value" based on net rental income ("the clear value of the rents aris[ing] out of the premises") or, in the case of owner-occupied property, "estimated by the assessors according to their discretion and judgment." There was also a more detailed list of taxable assets. Taxpayers already had been reporting land (including the amounts "sowed with corn"), unfree people ("bound servants and negroes, with their ages"), and livestock ("cattle, horses, mares and sheep"). Now, they also reported other real estate ("grist-mills, saw-mills and all other mills, forges, furnaces, mines, house rents, ground rents") and, for a new tax, all "trades or occupations, and all offices and posts of profit." This tax on trades resembled the Massachusetts "faculty tax," apparently with a similarly spotty enforcement.[23]

The heavy taxes for the French and Indian War tested the limits of local responsibility for taxation in Pennsylvania. In 1764, the assembly narrowed the discretion of assessors by issuing more detailed assessment instructions. It framed valuation ranges for real estate (such as £30 to £60 per hundred acres for meadow in Bucks and Chester counties), fixed flat valuations for livestock (horses at two-thirds of a pound, cattle at one-third of a pound, sheep at a shilling) and for unfree people (white servants at £2.5, "negro or mulatto slaves" at £4), and explained how to impute the "yearly value" of owner-occupied real estate (compare it to rented real estate, with adjustments). These rules were to be applied using printed forms, but the assembly abandoned the forms two years later on the grounds that printing and distributing them was a waste of money. The fact is that Pennsylvania's local communities did not need printed forms. Taxpayers and their annually elected assessors were capable of working out acceptable distributions of their local tax burdens and had been doing that with only vague formal instructions since the 1690s. What they needed from the assembly was a response to the new problem that colonywide land taxes raised. They needed an equalization process to ensure that the various local assessments were comparable. In 1774, the assembly conceded that the 1764 rules were insufficient for this purpose; the taxes had been hard to collect because of "great inequality in rating and assessing [them,] either through a misconstruction of the law or for want of more clear and explicit directions." Finally, during the Revolutionary War, the state legislature addressed this problem in the same way Massachusetts had been addressing it for nearly a century. The legislature apportioned its taxes to the counties in flat sums, which local officials then distributed among local taxpayers.[24]

When Oliver Wolcott examined the Pennsylvania land tax in 1796, he found a structure that had changed very little in thirty years, despite the adoption of two entirely new constitutions (in 1776 and 1790), vast fiscal demands, and bitter political struggles during the Revolutionary War. Taxes levied on a monthly rather than an annual basis during the war reflected the depth of the emergency. So did a new military exemption from the single freeman tax. The Quakers had identified marriage as the duty poor men owed to society, but poor men now were exempted as either husbands or soldiers. The state returned to assessment by value (rather than "yearly value") and added new attention to personal property owned by the wealthy (gold and silver plate, pleasure carriages, commercial "wares and merchandise"). With apportionment solving the equalization problem, however, Pennsylvania no longer needed detailed valuation rules—even to raise huge sums to fund the Revolution. Now, assessors were instructed simply to value assets at what they "would sell for in ready money," or, "at and for so much as they would bona fide sell for, or are worth."[25] This local assessment process had been the heart of the Pennsylvania land tax since the 1690s. It was based on the assumption that taxpayers and annually elected assessors could work out the details through negotiations conducted on a local basis. More generally, it was based on the assumption that local democracy could produce the competent assessment of a sophisticated tax. The assumption appears to have been warranted. Pennsylvania had not taxed very much in the colonial era, but its local communities had learned how to tax effectively.[26]

South Carolina

Measured by its response to the requisitions of Congress during the Revolutionary War, South Carolina also had learned how to tax effectively. It sent

Congress 55 percent of its quotas from 1781 to 1788, essentially matching the 57 percent performance of Pennsylvania. No other southern state did as well—Virginia sent 44 percent, Maryland sent 29, North Carolina sent 3, Georgia sent zero—and South Carolina delivered all this money even though the war was more destructive there than in most other states.[27] If Pennsylvania exhibited the paradox of a low-tax polity establishing a sophisticated tax structure, South Carolina exhibited a different paradox: a polity of slaveholding "masters" doing the same thing. South Carolina was capable of assessing the value of property. It actually assessed commercial property throughout its history. It valued urban real estate (town lots, buildings, wharves) as well as the stock-in-trade and financial assets that usually challenge the administrators of ad valorem tax systems. But South Carolina did not value the wealth of its plantation economy. It levied flat taxes on each slave and each hundred acres of land and ignored improvements to plantation real estate (e.g., buildings, irrigation works). South Carolina's refusal to value this property was indeed a refusal, as opposed to a failure. It did not suffer from the administrative handicaps that, in Virginia, made anything more complex than a poll tax on "tithables" seem utopian. In South Carolina, the use of flat-rate taxation can only be attributed to the preferences of the "masters."

The South Carolina tax system included imposts, fees, and quitrents (paid to the crown), but its centerpiece was an annual law called the "Tax-Act." Sometimes published as a pamphlet, this law had two parts. One described the property tax, fixing the flat and ad valorem tax rates, naming "inquirers" and collectors for each parish, and laying out rules and deadlines. The other part, the "Schedule," was an appropriation law, a list of the people to be paid from the proceeds with the purposes and amounts of the payments. The assembly framed the Schedule by auditing claims for salaries and other payments, including slaveholders to be reimbursed because officials had executed their "criminal slaves"—an instance in which the colony was perfectly capable of valuing this "property." Once the assembly completed the Schedule, it subtracted revenue from its imposts and other funds and fixed property tax rates to raise the balance. Clearly, the most striking features of the Tax-Acts are their lists of reimbursable slaveholders. Their precision is also worth noting. Even levies over £100,000 were expressed to the farthing (fourth of a penny). Competent implementation followed, as crown officials acknowledged by using the colony's tax lists to maintain the quitrent rolls. South Carolina's administrative successes did not depend on anything like the democratic local governments of the North. The assembly *appointed* the parish inquirers. Yet unlike Virginia's sheriffs (who were members of self-perpetuating county courts), these men answered to the assembly—and probably were more competent as a result.[28]

Nor did South Carolina's successful taxation depend on regular political negotiations at the colony level. Its assembly performed nothing like the periodic reapportionments of the tax on "polls and estates" in Massachusetts. From 1719 to 1758, the Tax-Acts apportioned levies between Charleston and the rural parishes (taken together) but, over these forty years, the assembly modified the ratio only once: it charged Charleston one-sixth until the 1740s and one-fifth after that. The tax rates illustrated a similar rigidity. The flat rates on land and slaves rose and fell with the levies but were always equal to each other—as in 10 shillings on every hundred acres and on "all negroes and other slaves." After 1758, when the assembly levied its tax rates on a colonywide basis, it always pegged the ad valorem rates at half the flat rates—as in 10 shillings on land and slaves and 5 shillings on each £100 of urban real estate, money-at-interest, commercial stock-in-trade, and professional income. It is possible that the average hundred acres and average enslaved human being were both worth £50. If so, the assembly was levying a uniform tax on the value (really, the average value) of all forms of taxed property. Still, the rigidity of all this is peculiar. There was something very brittle about the South Carolina polity. It excelled at administration, but it could barely do politics at all.

Everyone who studies South Carolina in the colonial era—or, for that matter, during the Revolution or the nineteenth century—notices that it was an unusual place. It was cruel, it was deadly, and as a result of its vicious exploitation of slave labor, it boasted a seriously rich elite. South Carolina was the only one of the thirteen colonies in which enslaved Africans outnumbered free whites. As a white immigrant observed in 1737, it "looks more like a negro country than like a country settled by white people." From 1720 through the Revolution, slaves were over 60 percent of the population and even this figure is an understatement, since slavery was not distributed evenly across the colony. It was concentrated in the "lowcountry," a strip of compact parishes that extended sixty miles west from the coast. In 1760, slaves were over 90 percent of the population in three lowcountry parishes, over 80 percent in another eight, and over 70 percent in another two. In 1774, slaves were 78 percent of the lowcountry population overall. Charleston (spelled Charles Town or Charlestown until 1783) also had a black majority. Slaves performed all kinds of work in its urban economy, to the dismay of white artisans who resented the competition. The lowcountry actually looked rather like a West Indies sugar island; in 1760, blacks outnumbered whites by 5 to 1 in Barbados and 10 to 1 in Jamaica. But, on the continent, only the South Carolina population reflected the exploitation of slave labor on this scale.[29]

The white society of Charleston and the surrounding lowcountry parishes was small, rich, and as one historian summarizes it, "anxious." Another notes that "the prevailing atmosphere approached that of a beleaguered garrison." By 1760, there were still only 20,000 whites in the lowcountry, among 50,000 enslaved Africans. This total included only about 3,500 white male adults in the plantation areas and another 1,300 in the town (although many planters kept town houses in Charleston, living there for part of the year). The town population included artisans of modest means as well as wealthy merchants and wealthier merchant-planters, but most whites in the plantation areas were rich and, by the end of the colonial era, spectacularly rich. The leading study of the colonial wealth structure reports that the average free person in the South Carolina lowcountry owned 4.5 times as much wealth as the average free person in the South as a whole and 10 times as much wealth as the average free person in the North. This opulence came at a staggering price, even for the rich whites themselves. Whites in the South Carolina lowcountry lived in constant fear of two things: stunning mortality from a disease environment that did not abate over time (as Virginia's did) and the threat of slave rebellions and other violent resistance. They coped with the diseases by chewing quinine bark, fleeing for the summer, arranging for the care of their ubiquitous orphans, and wearing their ability to survive as a badge of local identity. They coped with the threat of slave revolts by deploying patrols and striving for political unity against their "Domestic Enemy."[30]

South Carolina was established by land grants that Charles II made in 1663 and 1665 to a group of aristocrats called the True and Absolute Lords Proprietors of Carolina. Many of these men had participated in colonial projects in Barbados and Virginia, and some were prominent in English politics. Today, their main claim to fame is that they employed John Locke to help draft the Fundamental Constitutions (1669), a bizarre document that mixed forward-looking Lockean institutions (representative government, religious toleration) with a quasi-feudal pipe dream: vast land grants to a hereditary aristocracy of landgraves, caciques, and manor lords, plus a hereditary caste of leetmen and leetwomen bound to the land (liable to be bought and sold with the land). It also proclaimed another aspiration. "Every freeman," it declared, "shall have absolute power and authority over his negro slaves." As an expression of the influence of the Barbados experience—most of the earliest settlers, free whites and enslaved blacks, actually came from Barbados—this clause sketched different intentions from the ones that had animated the Virginia enterprise sixty years earlier. Slavery came late to Virginia, to an agricultural regime forged around the labor of white servants entitled to eventual freedom. South Carolina never attracted many white servants, even when it offered bounties to shippers for "any white male servants, Irish only excepted" and required slaveholders to buy one for every six slaves they owned.[31]

In fact, the colony attracted few people at all. Before the "rice revolution" of the 1710s, it was little more than a commercial outpost, with a population of 2,400 whites and 1,500 blacks in 1690 and 7,000 whites and 4,000 blacks in 1710. While the proprietors dreamed of leetmen and landgraves, the men on the scene extracted South Carolina's resources and shipped them out. They sent deerskins and naval stores (tar, pitch, turpentine) to England and lumber and slaves to the West Indies. Indians played several roles in this commerce. As hunters and trading partners, they supplied the deerskins in return for guns, ammunition, iron utensils, cloth, and rum. In the slave trade, meanwhile, they acted as military allies—until they became the export commodities. Other colonists sometimes sold Indian slaves to the West Indies (New Englanders did it after the Pequot War and King Philip's War), but only South Carolina fomented wars for the purpose of supplying a commercial slave trade in Indian captives. The colony's militias played small roles in this fighting, which depended on old hatreds and rivalries among native peoples. Savannahs fought to enslave Westos and then Catawbas fought to enslave Savannahs. Yamasees fought to enslave Tuscaroras and then Cherokees fought to enslave Yamasees. The Yamasees attempted to break the cycle. In the Yamasee War (1715–16), a pan-Indian coalition of coastal groups and stronger Creeks and Choctaws from the interior almost destroyed the colony. Only the decision of the Cherokees to reject the Yamasee overtures and side with South Carolina (against their old enemies, the Creeks) saved it at its most vulnerable juncture.[32]

Despite the provision in the Fundamental Constitutions for "absolute power" over "negro slaves," slavery was a relatively loose institution in these years. As Peter Wood has explained, black and white "pioneers" worked together to acquire food, build homes, and wage the colony's many wars, against the Spanish and French as well as Indians. Slaves hunted, fished, worked the Charleston docks, transported goods by river and land, and powered the forest industries: felling trees, sawing lumber, fabricating staves, assembling barrels, and producing the naval stores. The Yamasee War disrupted the forest industries. In 1725, Britain revoked the bounty it had paid on naval stores for twenty years, but South Carolina never looked back. Its elites had found a more profitable way to employ their slave labor force. By 1720, the colony was no longer an exporter of slaves, but a voracious importer.[33]

The rapid adoption of rice as an export staple (later supplemented by indigo) created the lowcountry society of wealthy white planters and enslaved black majorities. The population now grew, to 30,000 blacks and 15,000 whites in 1740, despite shocking mortality among both. Rice was even more labor-intensive than Virginia's tobacco, requiring construction and maintenance of irrigation works, months of weeding in flooded fields, and laborious postharvest processing. "[F]or a large portion of the year," in Ira Berlin's words, "slaves labored knee-deep in stagnant muck, surrounded by buzzing insects, under the scorching sun." Africans did somewhat better than Europeans in the lowcountry disease environment, but this work regimen, poor diets, and squalid living conditions proved murderous anyway. Planters responded by importing Africans in huge numbers. The term "importing" masks the horrors of the Atlantic slave trade, not least the notorious "middle passage," but South Carolina's heavy importations also meant something else. Because two-thirds of the imported Africans were men, the large importations skewed sex ratios and made it difficult for the men to form families. Where the Virginia slave population, with more balanced sex ratios, reproduced itself by natural increase, deaths outnumbered births in South Carolina. Planters increased importations accordingly, skewing the sex ratios further and magnifying the misery of the men they enslaved.[34]

Few things are as dangerous as a population of angry and lonely young men subjected to extreme exploitation. The single most violent upshot was the Stono Rebellion (1739). A group of about sixty blacks killed twenty whites, skirmished with militias, and marched toward the Florida border until the militias caught up and killed most of them, some with theatrical brutality. To the South Carolina elites, the lesson seemed obvious. They had to import fewer blacks and attract more whites. After Stono, the assembly slapped a prohibitive duty on slave importations, which reduced them by 90 percent in the 1740s, although they returned to the earlier levels in the 1750s. It also promoted a plan to get white settlers into the colony. The "township scheme" originated before Stono as a way to protect the lowcountry against Indians rather than Africans. Fortified settlements of "poor Protestants" from Europe would provide a buffer between the lowcountry and the Catawbas and Cherokees. After Stono, the plan also promised to attract white men who would defend the lowcountry against slave revolts. The colony furnished tools, food for a year, and transportation from Charleston, plus a ten-year tax exemption. The crown, which recently had bought out the proprietors, granted land in small parcels (much smaller than holdings in the lowcountry) and a ten-year exemption from quitrents. The townships did not turn out exactly as planned, but the incentives eventually attracted white migrants, especially after the British defeat of the Cherokees in the French and Indian War ended effective Indian resistance to settlement. By 1768, more than 75,000 free whites and 6,500 enslaved blacks lived in the backcountry.[35]

Politics was chaotic in the early years, chiefly as a result of religious struggles between Anglicans and dissenters (until the Anglican Church was established in 1704), monopoly claims to the Indian trade in deerskins and slaves

(governors took Indian "presents" instead of salaries until 1707), and two implications of the fact that the colony was a war zone: botched military expedi-
tions sparked recriminations, while colonists and proprietors fought over costs
(especially unstable paper money). Political disputes tended to climax in the
assembly jailing its opponents until they apologized for various affronts, and
outright revolts overthrew the proprietors in 1719 (after the Yamasee War) and
in 1728 (during a sharp economic downturn and another Yamasee attack). The
crown bought out the True and Absolute Lords in 1729 and dispatched a competent governor. Because this move came at the height of the rice boom, it is not
clear whether politics quieted because of the advent of crown sovereignty, the
influx of wealth (despite the downturn), or the dangers posed by slavery on
the larger scale. By the time of Stono, however, the colony's elites were cultivating the unity they later celebrated as "the harmony we were famous for."[36]

The government of South Carolina was highly centralized. Despite the
creation of some local institutions, power was concentrated in the assembly.
Elected parish vestries handled poor relief, but the assembly funded the Anglican establishment. Self-perpetuating road commissions handled public works,
but the assembly appointed commissioners for many projects. Charleston residents elected local officials starting in the 1740s, but the assembly decided
matters as local as where to build certain sewers. Justices of the peace tried and
sentenced slaves for capital crimes, but whites had to travel to Charleston for
civil and criminal cases. The appointment of inquirers and collectors in each
Tax-Act reflected the same pattern. As for the assembly, representation based
on the parishes produced reasonable apportionments in the lowcountry.
When the backcountry settlers arrived, however, the assembly added new
parishes very slowly. By the late 1760s, the backcountry held two out of forty-
seven seats to represent three-fourths of the white population. The failure to
create local governments also caused other problems. Too far from Charleston
to use the courts effectively, the backcountry settlers suffered from murderous
banditry and then a reign of terror by vigilantes ("Regulators"), whose targets
quickly expanded from criminal gangs to anyone who seemed insufficiently
awed by the local elite.[37]

Because it included no poll taxes on white men, the South Carolina tax
structure was the most progressive on the continent. The colony experi-
mented with poll taxes once, in the 1730s, but otherwise avoided them. An
"anxious" elite who staked their safety on their ability to attract "poor Protestants" probably rejected poll taxes as disincentives to immigration (the poll
taxes of the 1730s reiterated the exemption for "township" settlers). Yet small
white populations would have undermined the productivity of poll taxes anyway. In 1756, South Carolina inaugurated a punitive poll tax that resembled

Pennsylvania's tax on "single freemen"—but aimed at a different group. Pennsylvania targeted poor men who did not marry. South Carolina targeted poor men and women who were not white: "all free negroes, mulattoes and mustees, from ten to sixty years of age, who pay no other part of the taxes imposed by this Act." Levied at the same rates as the colony's slave taxes, this tax imposed steep burdens on people too poor to own property (unlike the slaveholders who paid the slave taxes). Nevertheless, since there were probably fewer than 1,000 free people of color, this tax was not really a revenue device. It was a way to harass free blacks by charging them their taxable "value" as slaves. It may also have been a way to enslave them: their freedom was a valuable asset to seize and sell for nonpayment.[38]

The property tax was the heart of the South Carolina tax system. It was sophisticated and comprehensive even in the chaotic seventeenth-century decades. It changed over time, but it did not "evolve." It was reshaped in response to changes in the colony's wealth structure. Thus, in the seventeenth century, when the colony was a commercial outpost, the tax was an ad valorem levy on all property and income, emphasizing commercial wealth and the salaries of proprietary officials. In the 1710s, with the advent of the "rice revolution," a major reform created separate rural and urban taxes, with flat rates on land and slaves in the country and ad valorem taxation in Charleston. As the mercantile and plantation elites merged into the super-rich merchant-planters of the late colonial era, the colony extended ad valorem taxation to financial assets in rural areas and, in 1759, all but abolished the rural-urban split. The surge of smallholding farmers into the backcountry was the only major economic change that inspired no tax reform, clearly because it was also the only major change that did not reshape the wealth structure of the lowcountry elite. The history of taxation in South Carolina is not a story about how ordinary settlers pooled their resources to buy roads, schools, and courthouses. But, as the absence of poll taxes suggests, it is not a story about how elites imposed burdens on their (white) social inferiors either. It is a story about how elites distributed burdens among themselves. "Ordinary" white settlers were basically irrelevant to this story until the backcountry tax exemptions ran out. The backcountry residents then began to complain about a serious inequity in the tax structure, though they could not win the attention of the lowcountry elites until after the Revolution.

The seventeenth-century tax rivaled the Massachusetts "country rates" in its sensitivity to the ways in which wealth was held. The oldest surviving tax law, from 1686, levied £500 for defense against a Spanish attack. This sum was to be "equally assessed, imposed and leavyed upon the severall inhabitants, merchants and others . . . according to their several estates, stores and abilities, and according to the profits indifferently computed of every pub-licque officer . . . by his respective office or any other imployment whatsoever." The colony levied this property tax, along with taxes on imports, exports, and tavern licenses until the Yamasee War, adapting its language as significant ag-ricultural operations developed. In 1703, for a £4,000 tax, commissioners listed not only "the estates, goods, merchandizes, stockes, abilities, offices and places of profitts, of what kind and nature soever," but agricultural assets as well: "the number of neat cattle, horses, sheeps, swine; white servants with their trades and time they have to serve; slaves, their sexes, ages, trades and capacities; the quantity of lands, the place the same lyes in, and the buildinges and improvements thereon." A board of assessors then used this information, including the characteristics of the human "property," to make the assessment and distribute the tax burden "indifferently, equally, and impartially."[39]

This tax did not work very well. The assembly levied another £4,000 in 1704 but then avoided property taxation until the Yamasee War, surviving on paper money emissions, imposts, and plunder—literally instructing its sol-diers to sell as many Indian slaves as they could capture. The text of a 1713 property tax law has been lost, but in 1715, with the Yamasee War underway, the assembly tried to raise £60,000, a much larger tax than it had levied before. It made two changes. The 1715 law directed assessors to go easy on financial assets ("money at interest") by valuing them "with due regard to the hazard and uncertainty of such money at interest, by reason of the present war." It also added an exemption for anyone whose tax would come in under 2.5 shillings. But the assembly realized that it could not fund the Yamasee War with its seventeenth-century tax system. It could not value the plantation assets that the "rice revolution" was turning into the core of the wealth structure. In 1716, the assembly repealed the 1715 tax ("all and every matter and thing that hath hith-erto been done or transacted . . . is hereby declared null and void") and cre-ated a tax structure designed to tap the plantation wealth without valuing it.[40]

The 1716 Tax-Act levied flat taxes on rural land and slaves and an ad val-orem tax on a much broader range of property in Charleston. As the assembly described it, this tax was to be "equally and indifferently raised, imposed and levied upon the lands and negroes of the several inhabitants, planters and others residing, living or otherwise interested" in South Carolina, and on "the several estates, real and personal, stocks and abilities of the several merchants and other inhabitants, living or residing within the limits of the town plot of Charlestown." The town paid one-sixth of the total and the rural parishes paid the rest. For the rural tax, parish inquirers took sworn statements from tax-payers to their holdings of land and "negroes or Indian slaves, men, women or children." A board of assessors then levied 5 shillings on each hundred acres, calculated how much that raised, and levied the rest "by way of poll, or so much per head, on all the negroe and Indian slaves, mustees and mulattoes . . . without any manner of difference or distinction of age or sex, save that any Indian slave being reputed of much less value than a negroe" warranted a 50 percent tax break. Nor did the assembly neglect the resulting racial classification loophole. To "prevent all doubts and scruples that may arise what ought to be rated on mustees, mulattoes, &c. all such slaves as are not entirely Indian shall be accounted as negroe."[41]

The assembly presented the town tax apologetically. Charleston required different rules because the wealth there "consist[s] mostly in town lots and the . . . buildings and improvements thereon, and also in goods, wares and merchandizes, ready money, &c. whereby according to the aforegoing method for the raising the tax on lands and negroes only, the said merchants and other inhabitants . . . would be in great measure exempted from paying their proportionable part of the said tax." So, the Charleston tax was levied ad valorem "on the real and personal estates, stocks and abilities," including slaves who worked mainly in town. The town assessors enjoyed considerable leeway on the details, though "for their better direction" they were instructed to take written accounts "of all such real and personal estates, negroes, stocks and abilities." Charleston officials handled the town lots and houses owned by taxpayers who usually lived in the country, and the rural officials handled the rural land and slaves owned by Charleston residents.[42]

South Carolina levied a version of this property tax almost every year from 1716 to 1758, charging Charleston one-sixth and later one-fifth of the total. The assembly dispensed with the rural assessors in 1723, now setting rates on slaves equal to the rates on land, but most changes tended to assimilate the tax treatment of town and country. This process started early. In 1719, rural officials started to levy an ad valorem tax on the stock-in-trade of storekeepers (the "divers persons" who "keep publick storehouses, and in the same do vend great quantities of goods and merchandizes"). In the 1740s, they also started to tax financial holdings: money at interest and, later, income from annuities. In 1736, the Charleston assessors lost the power to value slaves in the town (they were to use the colonywide rates) and, when the financial taxes were introduced, their rates also applied within Charleston. Yet the key urban-rural distinction survived. A 1731 effort to value rural land (but not improvements) failed completely. The assembly gave up after extending the assessment deadline three times and scolding officials who "valued all the lands in their respective parishes at one price." In the town, South Carolina could value real estate ("lots of land, buildings and wharves"), merchandise, negotiable paper, "Book-Debts," and the "Profits of Trades, Factorage, Faculties and

Professions (the Clergy excepted)." But while it could value some of the *intangible* wealth of the lowcountry planters, it could not value the *tangible* property of anyone except storekeepers outside of Charleston.[43]

As the Yamasee War had prompted the colony to create this tax structure, the French and Indian War prompted the next major reorganization. Again, the assembly tried to use its existing tax system to raise much larger sums than before. It hiked the land and slave rates from 16 to 36 shillings as the levies jumped from £62,000 (1755) to £166,000 (1758). But if the punitive poll tax on "free negroes, mulattoes, and mestizoes," inaugurated in 1756, offered little help, a 1758 attempt to tax cattle raised in large-scale ranch operations was the end of the line. The assembly decided to solve its tax problem in Charleston. It removed the cap on the town's contribution and levied a series of rates that ostensibly applied everywhere in the colony: flat rates on land, slaves, and "free negroes," all equal to each other, and ad valorem rates on urban real estate, commercial stock-in-trade, financial assets (money at interest), and occupations—all pegged at half the flat rates except annuity income, which was taxed slightly more heavily. In case anyone doubted the assembly's intentions for Charleston, the occupation tax now extended to the town's artisans by naming "handicraft Trades" along with the factorage, faculties, and professions.[44]

This tax structure was controversial from the start. Charleston taxpayers complained that they paid the overwhelming bulk of the ad valorem taxes. Having lost their 20 percent cap, they paid 26 percent of the total tax in 1759 and 28 percent in 1765. Without knowing what share of the colony's wealth they owned, it is not clear whether we ought to sympathize, although one fact was clear to them: their taxes had risen. The backcountry settlers also resented this tax (as "very unequal and grievous"), and on much firmer grounds. With the "township" exemptions expiring and other settlers arriving without exemptions, the use of one flat rate to tax the land of frontier farmers and lowcountry rice planters was patently outrageous. A hundred-acre backcountry tract was worth vastly less than a hundred-acre lowcountry tract. Both sets of critics thought across-the-board ad valorem taxes would yield more equitable results. The lowcountry planters who dominated the assembly refused to oblige (together, Charleston and the backcountry held only one-sixth of the seats), but they did take an action that mollified their critics. They stopped passing Tax-Acts. From 1770 to 1777, South Carolina relied solely on its imposts and paper money emissions. As a way to depoliticize the colony's own taxation—while rallying resistance to British taxation in the escalating imperial conflict—an extended property-tax holiday was hard to beat.[45]

But this would not do once there was a Revolutionary War to finance. In

1777, the state legislature passed a Tax-Act exactly like the last colonial Tax-Acts. The old opposition renewed, but only Charleston won timely relief. In 1778, the legislature accompanied a tenfold hike of the flat rates (on land, slaves, and free blacks) with only a fourfold hike of the ad valorem rates (on urban real estate, money at interest, stock-in-trade, and faculties), recouping some of the loss by adding a new flat tax on carriages and double taxes on the property of "absentees" (Tories). The war was disastrous in South Carolina. The British took Charleston in May 1780 and held it until January 1783, ransacking the lowcountry plantations periodically. In the backcountry, enmities dating from the Regulator era produced partisan warfare so nasty that the officers of both regular armies recoiled at the carnage they helped to stoke. Slaveholders lost one-fourth of their human "property" as 25,000 African Americans escaped from their masters, were confiscated by British masters, or died in the fighting. Meanwhile, new constitutions in 1776 and 1778 reapportioned the legislature, increasing the representation of Charleston and especially the backcountry. The state's most radical politicians championed serious tax reforms: exempt artisans from the faculty tax, double the taxes on slaves and large landholdings (over 20,000 acres), and levy special taxes on people who held more than £10,000 in cash. These proposals all failed. The legislature passed no Tax-Acts from 1780 until 1783—and then actually exempted financial assets altogether.[46]

The backcountry came into its own after the end of the war. The assembly set up county courts in 1785 and, after seven years of debate, moved the capital from Charleston to Columbia in 1790. But the land tax came first. In 1784, the backcountry won something that resembled an ad valorem land tax. Land allegedly was now taxed at the same percentage rate as stock-in-trade and faculties, but tracts of land actually were categorized rather than assessed. A schedule of 22 categories fixed per acre valuations ranging from a high of £6 ($26) for the best lowcountry land ("tide swamp, not generally affected by the salts or freshes, of the first quality") down to a low of one shilling (20 cents) for the worst backcountry land ("oak and hickory high lands above the old Indian boundary" of the "third quality"). Analyzing the tax returns, Jerome Nadelhaft has shown that this reform produced a substantial redistribution of burdens. Land taxes in two lowcountry parishes more than doubled, while those in backcountry areas fell by almost half in one case and by almost three-fourths in another. As Nadelhaft explains, this redistribution was part of a larger political deal. The backcountry had gained more representation, but the lowcountry still held the majority. The planters accepted these tax hikes because the state constitution required that future reapportionments, including one scheduled for the next year, reflect the distribution of the state's white population *and* its taxable property. "Increased taxation," in Nadelhaft's words, "was the price planters agreed to pay to justify their political dominance."[47]

South Carolina did not start sending its inquirers onto the plantations to value the wealth of the "masters." The state now levied categorical taxes on agricultural land; flat taxes on slaves and carriages; ad valorem taxes on urban real estate, stock-in-trade, and "faculties"; poll taxes on free blacks; and no taxes on financial assets. Because it taxed some commercial wealth, this tax structure remained more sophisticated than its Virginia counterpart. But because it taxed the two leading forms of wealth (land and slaves) without valuing particular tracts or particular people, it did not compare with the tax structures of Pennsylvania or Massachusetts. Oliver Wolcott was undoubtedly right about the significance of annually elected local assessors. Democratic local governments legitimized valuations of property in northern states by ensuring that "the people" controlled them on the ground. Yet the South Carolina experience shows that local government was not the whole story. South Carolina once valued all assets. Even after the "rice revolution," it valued urban wealth and the financial assets of planters. But it did not send assessors onto the plantations to value tangible wealth: land, buildings, irrigation works, livestock, plate, carriages, or enslaved people. Charleston and the backcountry championed ad valorem to shift more of the burden onto the lowcountry planters. Ultimately, the planters agreed to pay—but not to tolerate assessments of their wealth.

Looking Forward

In a sense, every one of the thirteen colonies had a "unique" tax system. Some colonies had borrowed the poll tax on "tithables" or the "country rates," but each made its own history of taxation. Nor did any two states respond in exactly the same way to the financial demands of the Revolution, even though they all faced the same pressures. As Wolcott found in 1796, the state tax systems were still "utterly discordant and irreconcilable, in their original principles." The big differences between these systems were not simply matters of carriages, plate, financial assets, or "faculties." Nor were they matters of progressivity or regressivity, such as whether certain states levied poll taxes. They were differences in basic structure. They reflected different assumptions about what local governments could do, and especially about who could negotiate about what at the local level. Every state taxed land, but variation also trumped similarity there. Some states valued land, some levied flat per acre rates, and others fixed arbitrary valuations. Some of the arbitrary valuations approximated relative land values, some (like Connecticut's) aimed at larger social policy objectives, and others were just plain arbitrary. Some states taxed only land, while others taxed a "real estate" that included buildings and improvements.

Today, there is an American system of state and local taxation. The states rely on income taxes that generally piggyback on the federal income tax; retail sales taxes that vary only in their rates and exemptions (e.g., food and clothing); excises on gasoline, liquor, and tobacco that vary only in their rates; and fees (automobile registration) and gambling operations (lotteries) that also use similar structures. There is more variation at the local government level, especially as a result of the "tax revolts" of the 1970s, when measures like California's Proposition 13 (1978) decoupled real estate valuations from market values in complex ways. These "reforms" forced local governments to rely more heavily on their own retail sales taxes, business taxes, fees, fines (hence the importance of parking tickets), and taxes on the hospitality industries that try to shift burdens onto nonresidents. Some of the largest cities (such as New York) also levy their own income taxes. Some of the smallest states avoid income taxes by drawing revenue from major industries such as gambling in Nevada or oil in Alaska or, like New Hampshire, by bucking the national trend with defiance ("Live Free or Die"). Nevertheless, there is a recognizable *system* of state and local taxation in the United States today.

This system came into being in the nineteenth century. Starting in the 1830s, the state tax systems grew more similar. State legislatures and the conventions that wrote and revised state constitutions copied from each other more systematically than before. This development is the subject of part 3 of this book. Meanwhile, at the close of the revolutionary era, the state tax systems differed fundamentally. Wolcott, writing for a hostile Congress in 1796, emphasized the absence of patterns even while he noticed one particular pattern. Northern states generally taxed larger ranges of objects in more sophisticated ways. Wolcott attributed the difference to the local government regimes of the North and South. Today, our local governments echo this difference. Towns and townships are the main units in the North. Counties are the main units in the South. The county officials now are elected rather than appointed, but the sectional distinction endures despite an incredible proliferation of local government forms: cities with various regimes (strong mayor, city manager, and so on) and thousands of special-purpose districts that borrow and tax (for schools, water, transportation, parks, and, in some states, even mosquito abatement). There were 87,525 local governments in the United States in 2002.[48] The eighteenth-century scene was simpler, but the difference between North and South was starker. Local officials were elected in the North and appointed in the South. Wolcott thought the more democratic governments were the more competent governments, that democracy itself allowed states to levy more sophisticated taxes. The histories of Virginia, Massachusetts, and Pennsylvania bear him out. South Carolina, however, suggests another dynamic.

The "masters" who bought and sold enslaved Africans in South Carolina knew the value of their human property. They also knew the value of their land. The planters of Virginia may have been confused, though their affectations of commercial naiveté should be approached with suspicion. Yet when the crown demanded that duties on imported slaves be levied ad valorem on buyers rather than at flat rates on sellers, Virginia complied while South Carolina refined its previous practice: flat rates that distinguished children from adults. In 1721, it had levied £10 on imported slaves aged ten and older and £5 on slaves under the age of ten ("sucking children excepted"), plus a punitive £50 on the sellers of slaves who had been exported from other colonies "for their ill behaviour or misdemeanors." In 1740, in the nearly prohibitive duty that followed the Stono Rebellion, South Carolina started to charge buyers rather than sellers. It also shifted the basis of the rates from age to height: £100 on slaves 4'2" or taller, £50 on slaves from 3'2" to 4'2", and £25 on slaves shorter than 3'2" (except the "sucking children"). A provision referring disputes about heights to two JPs, whose decisions were final, points to an explanation for these bizarre rules. Height silenced the Africans. This tax could be levied without asking them about their ages or any of the other characteristics that determined their "value." Since the Africans were imported for sale, these questions were both asked and answered. But they were neither asked nor answered for tax purposes.[49]

South Carolina's combination of flat-rate taxes on plantations with ad valorem taxes on commercial property (in Charleston and elsewhere) only makes sense in this context. In South Carolina, flat-rate taxation was never an accommodation to administrative incompetence, as the persistence of the poll tax on "tithables" in Virginia may well have been. In South Carolina, the refusal to value tangible rural property can only have reflected a refusal to invite assessors onto the plantations to ask the slaves about the composition and value of their masters' property—or to ask the masters in the presence of the slaves. Slaves might not know much about holdings of money at interest or annuities, but who else would the diligent assessor ask about the real estate, livestock, luxury furnishings (such as silver plate), or taxable (enslaved) human beings? The fact that many of the South Carolina planters were absentees, who delegated day-to-day decisions to black "drivers" as well as white overseers, only increases the likelihood that in South Carolina the diligent assessor would ask slaves.

Every colony (and then state) where slavery was a significant institution taxed the owners of slaves for their human property. These taxes often fixed age ranges to exempt "unproductive" children and elderly slaves, but in the colonial era they all levied a single flat rate, or, taxed the slaves "by the poll." Before the Revolution, no southern colony except South Carolina levied an ad valorem property tax of any kind. While South Carolina maintained its colonial tax structure until after the end of the Revolutionary War, other southern states attempted ambitious reforms. Virginia, North Carolina, and Maryland all replaced the poll tax on "tithables" with across-the-board ad valorem property taxes in 1777. They tried to assess the value of enslaved people along with other kinds of property. Virginia and North Carolina quickly gave up, reviving slave taxation "by the poll," but Maryland remained committed to ad valorem.

Maryland is especially interesting because the innovation it made during the Revolution later influenced other states. Maryland was the first state to write a clause into its constitution to limit the power of its legislature to design taxes. By 1860, twenty constitutions contained such clauses; only thirteen permitted legislatures to design taxes at will. The first state constitution of Massachusetts (1780), as we have seen, required that taxes be "proportional and reasonable" and that property be reassessed every ten years as long as the state continued to levy the tax on "polls and estates." Less specifically, the first Pennsylvania constitution (1776) urged the legislature to determine that the purposes of its taxes were "of more service to the community than the money would be, if not collected, which being well observed, taxes can never be burthens." Maryland's first constitution (1776) went much further:

> That the levying taxes by the poll is grievous and oppressive, and ought to be abolished; that paupers ought not to be assessed for the support of government; but every other person in the State ought to contribute his proportion of public taxes for the support of government, according to his actual worth, in real or personal property, within the State; yet fines, duties, or taxes, may properly and justly be imposed or laid, with a political view, for the good government and benefit of the community.[50]

By later standards, "with a political view" sounds highly permissive. As other states adapted the Maryland constitutional innovation in the nineteenth century, they tightened its language. Yet by the standard of the revolutionary era, this clause imposed a serious limit on legislative discretion. It prescribed what taxes the legislature could and could not levy in unique detail.

Maryland would be the future. A detailed analysis must await our return to the history of state and local taxation in part 3 below. For now, however, the important thing to notice is what the Maryland constitution banned. It banned all poll taxes and, in particular, the poll tax on "tithables" that had been Maryland's principal tax in the colonial era. Maryland now had to levy property taxes. The property taxes had to be levied ad valorem rather than at flat rates and levied on all property rather than only on certain items. In nineteenth-century language, they had to be "uniform" and "universal"—"uniform" in levying the same tax rates on different kinds of property ("real or personal") and "universal" in taxing all kinds of property (the "actual worth" of the tax-payers). As we will see, the crux of all this was that Maryland could not decide to do what Connecticut did: use its tax rates to promote social policies. In Connecticut, the policies at issue involved agricultural land use. In Maryland, they could have involved slavery and, especially, attempts to limit or abolish it through heavy taxation. Maryland had abandoned the core fiction of the poll tax on "tithables," that free men and slaves were taxed in the same way as "persons." Maryland no longer taxed "persons." In the new fiction, Maryland taxed slaves as "property" in the same way as other property.

Like Virginia and North Carolina, Maryland actually retreated from assessing the value of most slaves. In 1781, the legislature directed that enslaved children under 8 be valued at £10, children 8 to 14 at £25, men 14 to 45 at £70, women 14 to 36 at £60, and older men and women at "a true proportioned value" to these figures. Assessors were to raise the valuations of skilled male slaves according to "their respective trades and their proficiency therein" and to reduce the valuations of slaves who "shall not be perfect in [their] limbs or sight, or from the want of health or any visible infirmity [are] rendered incapable to perform [their] usual and proper labour." But Maryland retreated no further than this. It used versions of these categories all the way down to the Civil War. In fact, Maryland taxed slaves the way South Carolina taxed land: it levied what it called an ad valorem tax but avoided the actual assessment of value.[51]

Historians have tended to emphasize similarities among the governments of the thirteen colonies. This strategy makes sense of the Revolution as a movement that involved all of them. It also rests on important facts about the structures of the colonial governments and the dynamics of colonial politics. Every colony had a governor and an assembly. Voters elected the members of at least one of two houses everywhere. In most colonies, struggles between the governors and assemblies structured a great deal of political life. Governors were caught between instructions from London and resistance from assemblies, but most governors were the crown's men. Over time, the assemblies wrested the power of the purse from governors and appointed upper houses, which meant that they wrested it from the crown. This development played a significant role in causing the American Revolution. It created deep suspicions between assemblies and governors and informed the colonial argument that taxes such as the Stamp Act and Townshend duties were tyrannical abuses of power.[52]

Historians have paid less attention to local governments or to the public policies (such as tax policies) of the colonial assemblies.[53] Although the crown demanded *that* the colonies raise taxes, especially to pay salaries to governors and fund wars, the crown rarely prescribed *how* the colonies should raise taxes. The assemblies made those decisions from the beginning. Different assemblies made different decisions. Northern assemblies generally made decisions predicated on the ability of annually elected local officials to negotiate the valuation of property. Southern assemblies generally kept things simpler. When the shooting started at Lexington and Concord, the northern colonies were in better shape than the southern colonies to raise men and money for the struggle. Their more democratic governments enjoyed greater authority on the ground. Nor did they have to worry about how huge numbers of enslaved African Americans would respond to wartime chaos or British offers of liberty. The Revolution changed many aspects of American politics, but the most dramatic break with the past did not happen within the colonies that turned themselves into states. It was the creation of the United States. The representatives of colonies that had worked out entirely different policy traditions over more than a century of history now had to figure out how to fight a war together. For our purposes, they had to figure out how to finance a war together. They had to create an American tax policy.

PART II

National Tax Politics

During the Revolutionary War, the United States developed a tax structure that endured until the twentieth century. The heart of this tax structure was an intergovernmental division of labor in which the federal government relied on the tariff while the state and local governments relied on property taxes. There were extraordinary moments when this arrangement broke down; during the Civil War, it broke down completely. There were also always other taxes. Starting in 1791, Congress levied the whiskey excise, which is most famous for provoking the Whiskey Rebellion in western Pennsylvania in 1794. Congress also levied "direct taxes" on land, houses, and slaves in 1798 and during the War of 1812. Meanwhile, many states continued to levy poll taxes, some taxed the income from certain occupations, and several raised substantial revenues from taxes on banks—which a few found so lucrative that they were able to confine property taxation to local government financing for decades at a time.[1] Nevertheless, until the advent of income taxation (first in the states and then at the federal level), the principal taxes in the American system were the federal tariff and the state and local property taxes.

Figure 1 illustrates the outcome of this policy at the national level. Taxes other than the tariff—direct taxes and the levies known collectively as the "internal revenue" (the category that included the whiskey excise)—imposed small slices of the federal tax burden in the early republic. Congress abolished its entire nontariff revenue structure in 1801, revived it in 1813 to finance the War of 1812, and then abolished it again in 1817. From 1817 until the Civil War, the tariff was the only federal tax. The state and local governments continued to impose a variety of levies, of which their property taxes were the most important.[2] This was the intergovernmental tax arrangement that emerged from the Revolution.

Nobody planned to create this arrangement. Nobody wrote a political economy treatise showing that it was the best way to finance American governments. The decisions that created this tax system were decisions about other things. In particular, they were decisions about how to avoid talking about slavery. From the moment the Second Continental Congress turned itself into a national government in 1776, its members realized that national tax decisions

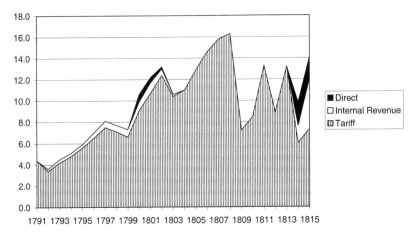

Figure 1. Federal Tax Revenue, 1791–1815 (millions of dollars). SOURCE: Davis Dewey, *Financial History of the United States* (1939), pp. 112, 126, 142.

raised different political problems from state tax decisions. In northern states, tax decisions hinged on routine political struggles over the distribution of tax burdens. In southern states, they hinged on the distribution of burdens in the context of oligarchic local governments with limited capacities. But, except in Maryland, state-level tax debates did not reflect the idea that slavery raised especially difficult problems. Northern states began to abolish slavery in the revolutionary era, using constitutional mandates, judicial decisions, and "gradual emancipation" laws (promises that slaves born after certain dates would be freed when they reached certain ages). Southern states made antislavery gestures as well, prohibiting the importation of slaves and permitting slaveholders to free slaves if they chose to do so.[3] But these developments did not involve taxation. At the state level, tax decisions were about the distribution of tax burdens.

National tax decisions were different. While they too involved the distribution of tax burdens and the problem of limited administrative capacity, they hinged on fears that the "property" of southern slaveholders would be vulnerable in national decisions made by majority rule—even when the majorities at issue consisted only of white men. The problem was not that northerners intended to abolish southern slavery. Rather, it was that any decision about taxes had to include an accommodation to the sectional geography of slavery. The fact that there were few slaves in the North and many slaves in the South had huge implications for the distribution of burdens to the white taxpayers of northern and southern states. When northerners tried to use this fact to favor their constituents by imposing higher burdens on the South, southerners accused them of threatening the institution of slavery. When southerners tried to use it to favor their constituents by imposing higher burdens on the North, northerners were forced into the position of actually threatening the institution of slavery. This game had very little to do with the emancipation of African Americans. It had a lot to do with the ostensible dedication of its white participants to the self-evident truth that "all men are created equal."

The "founding fathers" told a different story about national struggles over taxation and other policies in the early republic. They located the essence of these struggles in conflicts over class interests: rich versus poor, creditors versus debtors, merchants versus farmers and artisans. Strikingly, the elite side of the opposition was usually figured as the same people: commercial elites in the urban North. This story erased the characteristic class conflict of southern politics, slaveholding planters versus yeoman farmers, almost as effectively as it erased slavery itself. Class conflict was extremely important in the early republic. It structured much of political life at the state level in every state. The magic of this story of national politics was that it construed the national elite as a small group of northerners and counted southerners who owned dozens (if not hundreds) of human beings among the downtrodden "people." Many Americans contributed dialogue for this story. If it is possible to award an authorial credit, however, that credit must be shared by two slaveholding Virginians. Thomas Jefferson and James Madison took the lead in fashioning this story of American politics and in backing the story with political power.

Jefferson and Madison usually told the story in the romantic idiom that historians have called "republican ideology." A direct descendant of the British "country" opposition to Robert Walpole in the 1720s and 1730s, republican ideology spread in the colonial era through the circulation of *Cato's Letters* and allied tracts, and grew far more influential as colonists mobilized it in the struggle against Britain in the 1760s and 1770s. In its British form, republican ideology emphasized an idealization of country life, a mistrust of commerce and cities, and an anxiety that cabals of political insiders were constantly scheming to subvert liberty. It portrayed the country as a place where benevolent gentlemen, jealous only of their own "independence," protected their grateful social inferiors against threats from the city (London), which it condemned as a morass of greed, poverty, conspiracy, and corruption. In its American form, the ideology broadened the population who counted among the "independent" and dropped the part about the grateful social inferiors—only to revive it later with reference to enslaved African Americans. In a somewhat schizophrenic turn, it also celebrated urban artisans despite its bias toward rural life.[4]

At its core, republican ideology was a theory about the preservation of liberty. Its central idea was that the "independent" part of the community had to remain on guard for the signs that a tyrant was deploying his lackeys in a con-spiratorial plot to corrupt the government and "enslave" the people.[5] There were four specific signs: high taxes, large public debts, standing armies, and "swarms" of government officials. The beauty of republican ideology in the 1760s and 1770s was that it seemed to predict the whole series of British mea-sures from the Stamp Act through the Coercive Acts and the outbreak of the war. George III obviously was a tyrant: he tried to tax the colonies to fund his huge debt, stationed a standing army in the colonies, and commissioned swarms of officials (stamp collectors, tea agents) to prey on the people and cor-rupt their political institutions. Yet the most striking feature of the ideology in that context was its use of the term "slavery" as a metaphor for political defeat. Here lay the answer to Samuel Johnson's notorious question: "How is it that we hear the loudest yelps for liberty from the drivers of negroes?"[6]

Jefferson's paean to country life in *Notes on the State of Virginia* (1785) was a classic of "republican" thinking. "Those who labour in the earth are the chosen people of God . . . whose breasts he has made his peculiar deposit for substantial and genuine virtue." Americans should concentrate on agriculture rather than industry ("let our workshops remain in Europe") because urban-ization would destroy liberty: "The mobs of great cities add just so much to the support of pure government, as sores do to the strength of the human body."[7] In the 1790s, the Jeffersonian crusade against Alexander Hamilton retailed the ideology with all the trappings. Hamilton was the American Wal-pole. His Federalist party consisted of monarchists, urban commercial elites, and the corrupt lackeys of both. In language that annihilated the distance of sixty years and an ocean (not to mention a revolution), one Jeffersonian politi-cian claimed that the whiskey excise would "let loose a swarm of harpies, who, under the denomination of revenue officers, will range through the country, prying into every man's house and affairs." But there was a solution. Under the leadership of Jefferson and Madison, "the people" could defeat the American tyrants as they had defeated the British tyrants. The Jeffersonian "Revolution of 1800" had nothing to do with slaveholders taking over the federal govern-ment. It brought "the people" to power.[8]

One reason this story has persuaded so many historians is that some of the people who told it in the North actually were poor farmers and artisans. In the more democratic societies of northern states, widespread literacy enabled "plebeian" writers to articulate their political views more effectively than their southern counterparts ever could. In the more democratic polities of northern states, concrete political experience taught the plebeian groups how to organize against commercial elites in ways that poor southern yeomen rarely could or-ganize against their local elites. In the South, meanwhile, wealthy slaveholders who were confident about their power at home did not articulate their own class interests as explicitly as their northern counterparts did. As a result, they left behind fewer elitist statements for us to use against them. But democracy is not about consensus, much less about confident oligarchy. Democracy is about political struggle between groups with incompatible interests. Democratic political struggles are real struggles—and they sound like real struggles. Ironically, therefore, we have taken what actually is evidence of the existence of a vibrant democratic politics in the North and used it as evidence that slaveholding oligarchs were the champions of the American "common man."[9]

National tax debates during the Revolutionary War rarely invoked this "republican" story, which was not elaborated as a full-fledged case against American tyrants (as opposed to British tyrants) until the 1790s. Meanwhile, the debates that produced the first American tax structure—the tariff for the national government and property taxes for the states—hinged explicitly on the implications of the sectional geography of American slavery.

Before the Civil War, federal taxation was almost completely synonymous with the tariff. Except for three years during and immediately after the War of 1812, this tax on goods imported into the United States always raised more than 90 percent of the total federal tax revenue—and usually more than 99 percent of it. The tariff also played a huge role in antebellum politics. It was the focus of the Nullification Crisis, when South Carolina responded to the 1828 "tariff of abominations" by making it a crime for U.S. officials to collect it and then asserting the state's right to secede from the Union if Congress did not reduce it (which Congress did). The federal government relied on the tariff for two main reasons: it was easier to collect than other taxes and it subsidized the domestic producers of the goods that it taxed.[1] Yet the historical origin of the tariff lay in a separate issue. In addition to its administrative and economic characteristics, a tax on imports offered a political advantage over other forms of taxation. Congress could design a tax on imports without talking about slavery. The irony here is extraordinary. The tax that southerners would resent and resist so famously—because it forced them to subsidize northern industry—originated in a political accommodation to slavery during the Revolution.

The story of the tariff's origin is complex. Spanning the entire period from 1776 to 1789, it involved the efforts of three distinct national governments to finance the American Revolution: the quasi-legal Second Continental Congress (1776–1781), the Confederation Congress under the Articles of Confederation (1781–1788), and the federal government under the U.S. Constitution. It involved issues ranging from currency inflation and debt settlement to the framing of the three governments themselves. It also involved a structural issue that linked taxation to representation. Both taxation and representation required decisions about apportionments, about how to allocate tax burdens in one case and how to allocate voting power in the other. Apportionment decisions, however, created huge political difficulties. Regardless of whether the apportionments rested on population or wealth, they had to include decisions about how to treat slaves: how to count them as persons or how to count them as property.

These decisions were inherently controversial, pitting the interests of northern states with few slaves against the interests of southern states with many slaves. On top of these conflicts of interest, decisions about how to count slaves also opened discussions of slavery itself, in which northerners tended to make unflattering observations. The "founding fathers" hated discussions about slavery. Southerners hated them because, in the revolutionary era, even many slaveholders considered slavery an immoral institution, a violation of the egalitarian ideals of the Revolution, and a threat to their personal safety. They had no intention of taking any steps toward abolishing it, but they could not allow northerners to play on their guilt and fear in negotiations about other matters. Northerners hated these discussions because they threatened to destroy the new nation. Hardly any of them were abolitionists. Most did not care at all about African American freedom. But in negotiations about issues affecting their (white) constituents, northerners found it hard to remain silent about what everyone understood to be a crime against humanity—and northerners knew that southerners tended to react badly when this silence was broken.[2]

For representation, the apportionment problem had to be solved in some way. After some debate, the Continental Congress decided to apportion representation by granting each state one vote, a plan that endured under the Articles of Confederation ("In determining questions in the united states, in Congress assembled, each state shall have one vote"). The Constitution solved the problem by creating the complicated but familiar plan of a bicameral congress plus an electoral college: the Senate with two votes per state, the House of Representatives based on a population count that included three-fifths of the slaves, and the electoral college summing these figures to set each state's vote for president equal to the size of its congressional delegation (to "the whole Number of Senators and Representatives to which the State may be entitled in the Congress").[3]

For taxation, however, the Continental Congress discovered a way to evade the problem of apportionment. Their evasive strategy was the "impost," designed in 1781 as a flat 5 percent ad valorem duty on all imported goods and modified in 1783 to add higher duties on imported drinks and spices. The impost had several virtues as a form of taxation, but one of its major ones was its automatic character. Merchants would pay the tax when they imported goods, recouping their payments from consumers by charging higher retail prices.

Thus, the economic incidence of the impost (its distribution to groups of tax-payers) depended on the consumption of imported goods rather than on formal decisions by Congress. The impost required no apportionments, no decisions that would force Congress to talk about slavery—and almost everyone who served in Congress liked it for this reason. Yet the Articles of Confederation made the impost impossible to enact. Congress approved it unanimously in 1781 and by a large majority in 1783, but every state legislature also had to approve for it to go into effect. Rhode Island refused to approve the 1781 impost. New York held out against the 1783 impost. When the champions of the Constitution attacked the "imbecility" of the Articles of Confederation, they were talking about these rounds of state legislative action and the power of a single state to frustrate the rest. Mostly, they were talking about the defeat of the impost.[4]

We are used to thinking about the impost debates as battles over "centralization," with the defenders of state sovereignty opposing the defenders of centralized power in a long struggle that climaxed with the adoption of the Constitution. This was the story several participants told at the time, and nobody told it as consistently as the Rhode Island congressional delegates. The Rhode Islanders rarely mentioned their state's direct economic interest in defeating the national impost: Rhode Island had its own lucrative state impost. Merchants who imported goods through Rhode Island ports often sold them—at prices hiked to recoup the tax—in neighboring states such as Connecticut. The consumers of Connecticut, therefore, were paying Rhode Island taxes. Not surprisingly, Connecticut supported the national impost, preferring to fund the nation instead of the state of Rhode Island. Yet the Rhode Islanders ignored this issue to paint their opposition to the national impost as a principled stand against centralization. David Howell demanded that the states retain "the absolute controul over their own purse strings." His colleague Jonathan Arnold traced pro-impost pamphlets to "the United Efforts of a Junto" and dismissed speeches favoring the impost in Congress as utter hypocrisy. The impost, Arnold sneered after one session, "was extolled as the infallible, grand Political Catholicon, by which every evil was to be avoided, and every advantage derived." A surprising number of historians have endorsed Arnold's analysis over the years, agreeing with him that support for the impost was merely a "violent & stubborn" smokescreen for another objective: "to engross more Powers to Congress."[5]

The Rhode Island delegates infuriated their colleagues from other states. If some, such as Alexander Hamilton, later championed the creation of a strong national government, at this point most simply wanted the impost. Lengthy debates in 1783 about how to make other taxes work impressed a generation of American politicians with the imperative of relying on import taxes at the national level. Apportionment was only part of the problem. Slavery was a huge institution in the American political economy. It was impossible to discuss the economy seriously without talking about slavery—and it was impossible to design any tax but the impost without discussing the economy seriously. In a sense, Jonathan Arnold was right. His fellow delegates did indeed treat the impost as a panacea (though they might have objected to "Catholicon"). But the crucial issue is what problem they treated the impost as a panacea *for*. It would have given Congress a tax base that was independent of the state legislatures, as the Rhode Islanders complained, but it also solved a very different problem. The impost was the only tax Congress could adopt without talking about slavery. One delegate who learned this lesson from the 1783 debate was the young James Madison of Virginia. But there was a related lesson that Madison did not learn (could not have learned) from his experience in Congress under the Articles of Confederation. In Congress under the Constitution, the impost inevitably would turn into the protective tariff.

The Problem

On July 30, 1776, less than a month after adopting the Declaration of Independence, the Continental Congress received an ultimatum from one of its members. "If it is debated, whether their Slaves are their Property," Thomas Lynch of South Carolina warned, "there is an End of the Confederation." The general context for this first of the long series of threats to emerge from the planters of South Carolina (until they made good on them in December 1860) was the effort of the Second Continental Congress to adopt what eventually became the Articles of Confederation. The specific context was the debate about a tax clause for the Articles and a draft proposing that Congress apportion national tax burdens to the states according "to the Number of Inhabitants of every Age, Sex and Quality, except Indians not paying Taxes."[6]

The first voice to be raised was that of Samuel Chase (Maryland), who moved to insert the word "white" before "Inhabitants." The southern states obviously would pay much less if the word "white" were inserted. Congress had no data on the precise distribution of either the total population or the black population. Even today, we have good estimates of the total and slave populations, but not of the black population including free people of color. Nevertheless, with slaves comprising 4 percent of the northern population (New Hampshire to Pennsylvania) and 37 percent of the southern population (Delaware to Georgia), Congress did not need precise figures to agree that inserting the word "white" would make a huge difference in the distribution of tax burdens. After two days of debate, Congress defeated Chase's amendment seven to five. Every state from New Hampshire to Pennsylvania voted no, every state from Delaware to South Carolina voted yes, and the Georgia delegates divided for some reason (so that their vote did not count). Meanwhile, Chase's proposal to exclude slaves from the tax apportionment had initiated a dangerous debate, with stakes rather higher than Chase seems to have intended.[7]

Chase began with a theoretical analysis. Taxes should be fixed in proportion to wealth, he explained ("this was in theory the true rule"), but Congress would be incapable of measuring wealth. "[F]rom a variety of difficulties," the wealth rule "could never be adopted in practice," since the "value of the property in every state could never be estimated justly & equally." Chase was willing to accept population as a "tolerably good" proxy for wealth, conceding that it was "the best Rule We can lay down," but he was not willing to accept a population rule that counted southern wealth when it did not also count northern wealth. "The Negroes are wealth," as Chase put it, "and as such cannot be distinguished from the lands or personalities held in those states where there are few slaves." Using total population would "tax the Southern states according to their numbers & their wealth conjunctly, while the Northern [states] would be taxed on numbers only." Anticipating what would emerge as the "great compromise" of the 1787 Constitutional Convention, Chase linked taxation to representation. "If Negroes are taken into the Computation of Numbers, to ascertain Wealth, they ought to be in settling the Representation." Yet Chase did not want to count African Americans for representation either, on the grounds "that Negroes in fact should not be considered as members of the state more than cattle & that they have no more interest in it." Besides, he added, many slaves actually were not valuable: "The young and old Negroes are a Burthen to their owners."

John Adams tried to answer Chase by arguing that slavery was irrelevant, that "it was of no consequence by what name you called your people, whether by that of freemen or of slaves." "Certainly 500 freemen produce no more profits, no greater surplus for the paiment of taxes than 500 slaves." The "fallacy" in Chase's argument, according to Adams, stemmed from "the use of the word 'property' here, & it's application to some of the people of the state." But James Wilson (Pennsylvania) would have none of this. The problem was not merely verbal. Slavery obviously was relevant—and not only for tax incidence. Excluding slaves from the tax apportionment base created an incentive to expand slavery. "It will be the greatest Encouragement to continue Slave keeping, and to increase them." Slavery "is attended with many Inconveniences," Wilson noted with considerable understatement, although the inconvenience he cited affected nonslaveholding whites rather than either slaves or their owners. Slavery crowded out free labor, as slaveholding planters monopolized the land to "prevent freemen cultivating a Country."

On the issue of wealth and taxes, Wilson thought Adams had conceded too much. Slaves *did* produce "a greater surplus for taxation." Free men might work harder, "but they consume the most also." Slaveholders imposed low levels of consumption on slaves to extract greater profits: "The slave is neither fed nor clothed so expensively as a freeman." Slaveholders also deployed enslaved women as agricultural field laborers. Wilson exaggerated when he claimed that "white women are exempted from labour generally," but he was right about "negro women" performing agricultural field labor in much larger numbers. Because of the agricultural labor of enslaved women, "the Southern states have an advantage as the article now stands." The total population formula actually favored the South because the labor force (population that produced "profits") was a larger fraction of the South's total population than of the North's total population. Finally, Wilson lit into the hypocrisy of Chase's position. He knew how southern tax systems worked. He knew they charged poll taxes on all "labourers whether they be black or white." Nor would he accept the bit about how children and the elderly made slavery a "burthen" to slaveholders. Southerners could not have it both ways on the profitability of slave labor. "It has sometimes been said that slavery is necessary because the commodities [the slaves] raise would be too dear for market if cultivated by freemen; but now it is said that the labor of the slave is the dearest." Southerners who answered abolitionists by claiming that they depended on slave labor because it was cheaper than free labor could not now try to evade their share of the tax burden by claiming that slave labor was more expensive.[8]

This speech was too much for Thomas Lynch. Wilson had committed the unpardonable sin of suggesting that there might be something objectionable about slavery. After delivering his ultimatum ("there is an End of the Confederation"), Lynch endorsed Chase's economic analysis. The total population rule would apportion taxes on southern property but not northern property. "Our Slaves being our Property," Lynch asked, "why should they be taxed more than the Land, Sheep, Cattle, Horses, &c." He then defended the institution of slavery itself. The economy of South Carolina depended on slavery. "It is not in the Ability, or Inclination of freemen to do the Work that the Negroes do," Lynch argued—although nobody really thought it was "inclination" that put enslaved Africans to work in the deadly rice fields of South Carolina.

Yet if Lynch had found James Wilson's speech offensive, he was about to suffer worse treatment at the hands of a much more famous and much more widely respected delegate from Pennsylvania. Benjamin Franklin was the only real celebrity member of Congress. When Lynch threatened to destroy the new nation, Franklin lost patience. Moving beyond Wilson's economic argument, Franklin alluded to the long history of African resistance and revolt, not least in South Carolina itself: "Slaves rather weaken than strengthen the State," Franklin observed. As to slaves being property just like "Sheep, Cattle, Horses, &c.," Franklin refused to mince words. Sheep were totally different from slaves: "Sheep will never make any Insurrections."

Franklin, of course, was no longer talking about taxes at all. Franklin was talking about slavery. He was threatening Lynch and other southern planters with their greatest fear, that the men and women they exploited so mercilessly would take the opportunity of the revolutionary upheaval to kill them. The planters could negotiate about taxes, but if they insisted that the vast populations they held in bondage entitled them to favorable tax treatment, they could not expect northerners to remain silent about what the institution of slavery really was—and about what it meant to be a planter perched atop the southern volcano. Franklin reminded them that they were vulnerable in a way northern whites simply were not, even though slavery existed to some degree in every state. Lynch's threats might scare a John Adams, whose state had been a battlefield for more than a year. It might also scare a James Wilson, who had been wary about independence all along. But it could not scare an old hand at high-stakes politics at the colonial and imperial levels. Thomas Lynch did not scare Benjamin Franklin.

But the debate was not over. Edward Rutledge (South Carolina), William Hooper (North Carolina), and Benjamin Harrison (Virginia) all rehearsed the point Chase and Lynch had made about the low productivity of slave labor. Rutledge repeated the idea that old and young slaves "cannot work," Hooper added that "[a] Negro works under the Impulse of fear—has no Care of his Masters Interest," and Harrison proposed that each slave be counted as half a person for tax purposes because "slaves did not do so much work as freemen." Perhaps chastened by Franklin, Rutledge and Hooper also expressed pious antislavery sentiments, with Rutledge claiming that he "shall be happy to get rid of the idea of Slavery" and Hooper "wish[ing] to see the day that Slaves are not necessary." The main point they made, however, was that southern slaveholders were victims of slavery—and therefore should gain a tax break at the expense of northerners who did not suffer from owning unproductive workers. This was an outrageous argument, and the southern delegates made it one after another.

A different voice turned out to be decisive, though not right away. John Witherspoon of New Jersey was no Franklin, but the words of the president and professor of theology, history, and French at the College of New Jersey (now Princeton University) carried weight. Unlike the other speakers, Witherspoon believed that a property-based (rather than population-based) apportionment could actually work. He suggested a new theoretical basis, arguing that "the value of lands & houses was the best estimate of the wealth of a nation" and adding "that it was practicable to obtain such a valuation." Witherspoon then turned to Wilson's observation that southern poll taxes had been levied on both free men and slaves throughout the colonial era. Taxation at the national level, the professor explained, was a different political problem from taxation at the colony level: "[T]he cases are not parallel. In the Southern colonies slaves pervade the whole colony; but they do not pervade the whole continent." Like many academic analyses, this last point really just restated the problem. Slavery was crucial in the South and marginal in the North, but a national decision about taxes required a national decision about slavery. The problem was that the United States was already almost what Abraham Lincoln would call it in his "House Divided" speech in 1857. In July 1776, at the very moment of its birth, the United States was already almost "half slave and half free."

The Absurdity of Article 8

Witherspoon was totally wrong in claiming that an apportionment based on "the value of lands & houses" was "practicable." We know he was wrong because his formula was adopted in Article 8 of the Articles of Confederation:

> All charges of war, and all other expences . . . for the common defence or general welfare . . . shall be defrayed out of a common treasury, which shall be supplied by the several states, in proportion to the value of all land within each state . . . as such land and the buildings and improvements thereon shall be estimated according to such a mode as the united states in congress assembled, shall from time to time direct and appoint.

In retrospect, it is difficult to believe that Congress adopted—or that the states ratified—such a wildly unworkable scheme. To imagine an apportionment based on the total value of real estate (land, buildings, and other improvements), we must imagine Congress designing and supervising an assessment of this property. We must imagine them doing one of the following: (1) sending a corps of trained assessors into the states, (2) relying on state officials to observe uniform rules, or (3) letting state officials proceed and then agreeing on how to equalize incommensurate results. Not only must we imagine one of these scenarios unfolding, but, if we are to take the text of the article seriously (as a plan for financing "charges of war"), we must imagine it unfolding during the

Revolutionary War. From the vantage of Valley Forge, where the Continental Army shivered and starved because Congress could not manage to deliver its most vital supplies, the prospects for a national real estate assessment were dim.

A great deal of ink has been spilled over the question of why the army suffered at Valley Forge in the winter of 1777–78. The answer is not the Articles of Confederation; they were not even adopted by Congress until November 1777 and not ratified by all the state legislatures until February 1781. Nevertheless, historians generally trace both the weaknesses of the Articles and the larger series of administrative catastrophes exemplified by Valley Forge to the same sources: a localized jealousy of central authority, an unwillingness to entrust Congress with power, and a defense of the independent sovereignty of the state legislatures. Some historians have applauded the states for resisting a centralized tyranny, some have attacked the states for starving the army, and some have pointed to a larger ideological framework. In this "ideological" view, members of the revolutionary generation interpreted all political action as part of a titanic struggle between "power" and "liberty," with the conflict between these abstractions making it difficult for anyone to imagine a more workable system—even if state-based politicians had been willing to give up concrete power to politicians operating at the national level.[9]

The Articles of Confederation did create an intentionally weak national structure. "Each state," article 2 declared, "retains its sovereignty, freedom and independence, and every Power, Jurisdiction and right, which is not by this confederation expressly delegated to the United States in Congress assembled." Article 3 described the confederation as the diplomatic assembly of a military alliance, as something more like NATO than like the federal government under the U.S. Constitution: "The said states hereby severally enter into a firm league of friendship with each other, for their common defence, the security of their Liberties, and their mutual general welfare, binding themselves to assist each other, against all force offered to, or attacks made upon them, or any of them. . . ." In article 4, the vision was of something more like the modern European Union, with free migration and trade between states, extradition of fugitives ("any Person guilty of, or charged with treason, felony, or other high misdemeanor in any state"), mutual recognition of judicial proceedings ("full faith and credit"), and mutual recognition of the individual rights ("privileges and immunities") of the "free inhabitants" of each state.[10]

The tax system the Articles created, moreover, depended directly on the state legislatures. After it laid out the real estate apportionment, article 8 delegated decisions about how the states raised their apportioned quotas to them. "The taxes for paying" the quotas, the article concluded, "shall be laid and levied by the authority and direction of the legislatures of the several states."

Congress was empowered only to set deadlines; the states were to pay "within the time agreed upon by the united states in congress assembled." This final sentence of article 8 authorized the "requisition system" of national taxation, in which Congress literally "requested" the states to lay taxes and deliver the proceeds. As Roger H. Brown has shown in detail, this state-based system had a serious problem: the states could not pay their requisitions. Relying on the states to fund the Revolutionary War might be considered to be visionary at best and foolhardy at worst, but it actually was not how Congress funded the war. Congress funded the Revolution in exactly the same way every government always funds wars: by borrowing money and struggling to tax just enough to persuade lenders that they could hope to be repaid in the end (assuming the United States won).[11]

The absurdity of article 8 did not lie in the requisition system itself. Although the states could not raise the money Congress kept pleading with them to send, the idea of relying on the states to assess and collect taxes was perfectly reasonable in 1776 and 1777. Every state already had a tax system. Some of these systems were more sophisticated than others, but, for Congress to tax, it would have had to create a system to manage assessment and collection from scratch. Should this national system rely on officials who were elected by town meetings in some states and appointed by governors in other states? Should Congress create its own tax bureaucracy? What kinds of taxes should Congress levy? Should it tax only real estate or should it also tax slaves, ships, and financial assets? What should the states continue to tax? Enforcement raised additional problems. What sanctions would Congress impose on individuals who failed to pay, and how would it impose sanctions on individuals? Before the United States had come close to winning the war—and when Britain was blockading American ports, ruling out trade taxes as realistic sources of revenue—relying on the existing state tax systems was the only practical option. Accordingly, it was the only option Congress considered in framing the Articles.[12]

Congress actually had been apportioning things that resembled tax quotas since the start of the war. It had been borrowing money by issuing paper currency, hoping that the states could pull enough of it out of circulation to prevent it from depreciating. The plan was for Congress to print money ("bills of credit") and to spend it to pay soldiers and buy supplies, while the states protected its value by removing quotas of it from circulation. The states would collect the bills as people used them to pay their taxes, punch them with round one-inch holes "to render them unpassable," and then send them to Philadelphia to be burned. In July 1775, Congress resolved to fix the currency quotas using the total population of each state: "the number of Inhabitants, of all ages, including negroes and mulattoes." Yet because these numbers "cannot, at present, be ascertained," the delegates negotiated a guess at the population to fix an apportionment in flat dollar figures. Six months later, Congress asked the states to take censuses ("to ascertain, by the most impartial and effectual means in their power, the number of inhabitants in each respective [state]"), a request with which only four states complied by 1783. In any case, Congress turned the currency quotas into taxes in November 1777 in what technically was its first "requisition." The delegates negotiated a similar apportionment in flat dollar figures, adding a proviso they also inserted into subsequent requisitions: that the figures were provisional, that each state would be credited for its payments, that the state accounts eventually would be settled using the formula in the Articles of Confederation (in November 1777, "the confederation hereafter to be adopted and ratified by the several states"), and that all over- and underpayments by individual states would bear 6 percent interest.[13]

Requisitions never stopped the currency from depreciating. The states could not redeem enough continental currency, and they also issued currencies of their own to fund the recruitment of continental troops and their own militias, fortifications, and other costs. Depreciation reached crisis proportions. The states tried price fixing and legal tender laws, which made it a crime to discount the currency in transactions. Predictably, these strategies did not work either. Congress stopped issuing paper money in late 1779 and made an official devaluation (40 to 1) in March 1780. Meanwhile, they tried to end-run the currency problem by requisitioning specific supplies. Instead of asking the states to support the currency so the commissary department could spend it to buy what the army needed, Congress apportioned quotas of commodities (flour, corn, beef, rum, hay, and so on) to the states, setting a price scale at which each state would be credited for its contributions in the final settlement of accounts. As E. James Ferguson points out, the state governments had an option Congress's commissary agents did not have—they could "bypass the market entirely" by levying taxes payable in the commodities—but this plan also added another layer of political decision making (the state legislatures) to the procurement process. After 1779, the army mostly supplied itself by impressment. In what amounted to a system of forced loans, officers simply took what they needed, sometimes by force, from people living near the scene of their operations and issued "certificates" promising eventual payment.[14] Nevertheless, despite all the weaknesses of the requisition system, Congress simply had to incorporate it into the Articles of Confederation. There was no alternative to relying on the existing state tax systems.

The absurdity of article 8 lay elsewhere. The real estate apportionment reintroduced the very administrative dilemma that the requisition system successfully dodged: there could be no real estate apportionment without serious administrative capacity at the national level. The states could not step into this breach. When the real estate apportionment was inserted into the Articles in October 1777, no southern state had ever assessed the value of real estate before. Some of the northern states also had not done it recently; Connecticut had not valued real estate for sixty-five years. Virginia, Maryland, and North Carolina were embarking on ambitious plans in 1777 to introduce property valuation into their tax systems for the first time, but all three quickly adopted shortcuts for determining land values, and Virginia and North Carolina both gave up on valuing buildings altogether—much less the other "improvements" mentioned in article 8. Nor was this all. Even if there had been rooms filled with tidy assessment books in every state capital, the idea that they would have contained comparable valuation data is ludicrous on its face. If taxes were going to be apportioned to the states by the value of "land and the buildings and improvements thereon," Congress would have to figure out how to assess real estate on a national basis. The real estate apportionment, in short, required a strong national government. It could work only if the states obeyed highly detailed directives from Congress or if Congress bypassed the states to build its own assessment bureaucracy.[15]

The incorporation of the real estate apportionment into the Articles of Confederation had nothing to do with state sovereignty or fears of central authority. Nor did it reflect an ideological framework that defined politics as a perpetual struggle between "power" and "liberty." The real estate apportionment solved only one problem: the fact that apportionments by population forced northerners and southerners to talk about slavery. If Congress decided not to count heads, then they would not have to decide whose heads to count. The real estate apportionment actually was not a plan for apportioning taxes at all. It was a way to get the Articles framed without talking about slavery. John Witherspoon may have suggested it in 1776 because he thought real estate "was the best estimate of the wealth of a nation," but Congress ignored him that summer. They shelved the Articles for over a year, in part because they could not agree on a tax article, though also because they could not agree on two other issues: a representation plan and a way to handle the extensive western land claims of certain states.[16]

When Congress returned to the Articles in the fall of 1777, the delegates were determined to hammer them out. They wanted to persuade the French that the United States was a credible ally (France entered the war after the American victory at Saratoga in October), and they wanted to persuade Americans that they could deal with the currency. Congress spent five days debating the tax article. They rejected apportionments by total population and total property ("the value of all property except household goods and wearing apparel"), with the latter an incredibly impractical suggestion. Not only would Congress have to figure out how to treat shipping and financial assets, which were far more difficult to assess than real estate, but they also would have to figure out how to treat slaves. Were delegates really envisioning a national assessment of the "value" of every slave in the United States? Because nobody took notes on the 1777 debate, it is impossible to know exactly who favored this plan. The only delegate who wrote about favoring it, however, was a southerner. Cornelius Harnett (North Carolina) thought "property in general" was the "most equitable" basis for the apportionment, though he was willing to accept real estate. Everyone who described the debate agreed that New Englanders united on population, but that, as William Williams (Connecticut) put it, they were "very strongly & forceably opposed." On the debate as a whole, Henry Laurens (South Carolina) reported that "some sensible things have been said, & as much nonsense as ever I heard in so short a space."[17]

Congress finally adopted the real estate plan by a close and starkly sectional vote. Four New England states (New Hampshire, Massachusetts, Connecticut, Rhode Island) voted no, four southern states (Maryland, Virginia, North Carolina, South Carolina) voted yes, and two middle-state delegations (New York and Pennsylvania) divided. In the end, the decision rested with the two delegates from New Jersey, including John Witherspoon, and they voted for the real estate apportionment. Delegates who wrote home about what Congress had done attributed the result to concrete calculations about how a real estate apportionment would affect various states. New Englanders opposed real estate because land in New England was more valuable than land in the other states, mainly because it was settled and farmed more intensively. Southerners supported real estate because their apportionments would reflect the lower value of southern land and omit slaves entirely. "The Eastern people [New Englanders] were very much against" the real estate plan, Harnett of North Carolina explained: "[K]nowing their Lands to be very Valuable, they were for settling the Quota by the Number of Inhabitants including Slaves, [which] would have ruined Poor No. Carolina." Nathaniel Folsom (New Hampshire), conversely, attacked the real estate plan for favoring the South: "[I]t appears to me that one third part of the we[a]lth of the Southern States which consists in negroes is left out and no Notice taken of them, in determining their ability to pay taxes, notwithstanding that it is by them that they procure their wealth."[18]

Folsom hoped to reopen the question once the state legislatures had seen the Articles, but his colleagues dashed that hope in June 1778 by rejecting every single one of the thirty-six amendments the states proposed. Seven states had offered amendments, with five of them addressing article 8. Connecticut wanted to replace real estate with total population. Massachusetts proposed that the decision be left up to Congress "so that the rule of apportionment may be varied, from time to time, by Congress, until experience shall have shewed what rule of apportionment will be most equal and consequently most just." South Carolina wanted two changes. First, in an amendment that made sense (if a real estate apportionment made sense at all), South Carolina asked that the quotas be reapportioned on the basis of new valuations every ten years. Rhode Island and New Jersey also asked for reapportionments and new valuations, using five-year intervals. But South Carolina proposed another amendment that could only have made matters worse. Instead of the valuations of real estate being made, as article 8 directed, "according to such a mode as the united states in congress assembled, shall from time to time direct and appoint," South Carolina asked that the Articles stipulate that the valuations be made "by persons to be appointed by the legislatures of the respective states."[19] Presumably, South Carolina envisioned a political process in which each state turned in whatever figures it decided to send—and Congress based the apportionments on these figures. When, after seeing the incommensurate data, some delegates suggested (as they inevitably would) that the figures had to be equalized, others would answer that each state was the best judge of the value of its own land and buildings, and that the Articles barred Congress from tampering with the numbers the "sovereign" legislatures had approved.

It is worth emphasizing that the real estate apportionment was not a national real estate tax. It was an apportionment formula for distributing tax quotas to the states, in the expectation that the states would meet their quotas in various ways and by levying various taxes. The real estate apportionment was a way to distribute the quotas for the requisition system. The principal reason the issue of western land claims was so controversial was that states without claims faced the prospect of levying onerous taxes to meet their requisitions while other states met theirs from land sales. Maryland, the most insistent of the "landless" states, refused to ratify the Articles of Confederation until February 1781 because it took neighboring Virginia until then to accept the idea of ceding its western claims to the United States. Maryland would not agree to a plan that forced it to tax for its quotas while permitting Virginia (which allegedly extended to the South Seas) to meet its obligations by selling land.

It is also worth repeating that the requisition system was a reasonable accommodation to the reality that Congress could not tax on its own during the war. Congress had to rely on the states to design and collect taxes. But the use of real estate value to apportion the requisitions was not reasonable. It was not reasonable when John Witherspoon proposed it in 1776, when southerners endorsed it unanimously in 1777, or when Congress rejected the state amendments in 1778. Five years later, when Congress was embroiled in an impossible effort to make the real estate apportionment work, two veterans of the original 1776 debate claimed that nobody ever had wanted to insert such an unworkable scheme into the Articles. Everyone had realized that population was more practical from an administrative standpoint (easier to count), but everyone also had realized that population had an insurmountable political drawback. A population rule required a decision about how to count slaves. The real estate apportionment, as James Wilson (Pennsylvania) recalled, was "the effect of the impossibility of compromising the different ideas of the Eastern and Southern states as to the value of Slaves compared with the Whites." More specifically, Abraham Clark (New Jersey) remembered "that the Southern States [would] have agreed to numbers, in preference to the value of land if ½ their slaves only [should] be included; but that the Eastern States would not concur in that proportion."[20]

As Jack Rakove has shown, the delegates shared one objective in designing the Articles, an objective that overrode every disagreement on specifics. Congress wanted to frame and adopt Articles of Confederation. Almost any Articles seemed better than no Articles in 1777 and 1778, even though, thanks to Maryland, there actually was no ratified document until 1781. The imperatives of the French alliance and currency depreciation (which Congress addressed through the November 1777 requisition, with its provisional quotas, state accounts, and future settlement) trumped even the obvious and fundamental absurdity of the real estate apportionment. If this was what it took to get the Articles framed, then this would be part of the Articles. Richard Henry Lee (Virginia), one of few delegates whose correspondence crossed the sectional divide, struck a philosophical pose in writing to Roger Sherman (Connecticut). Compromise was essential. Nobody could "rigidly insist on having everything correspondent to the partial views of every State. On such terms we can never confederate." Lee tried to persuade the New Englander that Virginia would have done better with population than real estate, since Virginia could only expect to get richer and real estate values rose "in proportion to the influx of wealth." Virginia actually was making a sacrifice by accepting real estate. "I doubt extremely whether Virginia will not pay more by the pres[e]nt mode than if it had been determined by numbers."[21]

Lee was responding to a letter in which Sherman had informed him that the real estate scheme was "impracticable." In the same terms Samuel Chase had used in his initial speech on the subject, Sherman praised a population rule as "the best that can be devised." He then offered a compromise on how to count slaves. Congress could exempt "all under ten years old or any other age that may be agreed on." Sherman was willing to bargain about slavery. He told Lee that population was a better basis for the tax apportionment in theory and practice. It was better in theory because "Wealth principally arises from the labour of Men." It was better in practice because "the States can neither agree to nor practise the mode voted by Congress."[22] Sherman may have been wrong in his labor theory of value, but he was right about what would happen, in 1783, when Congress tried to implement the real estate apportionment. By then, it turned out, other members of Congress also were ready to consider a bargain about slavery.

The Impost

Before any such bargaining could begin, however, Congress had to try and fail with a different strategy. Three weeks before Maryland ratified the Articles of Confederation, in February 1781, Congress asked the states to amend article 8 by granting the national government an alternative source of revenue, the 5 percent impost on imported goods and "prizes" (enemy ships and goods captured by privateers). The impost became a practical alternative in 1781 because, after France entered the war on the American side in the last months of 1777, its navy started to weaken the British blockade of American ports, enabling several to reopen for business. The impost became an attractive alternative in 1781 because the requisition system was clearly failing—so clearly that members of Congress worried that the United States could not attract additional European loans without offering better security to the lenders. The impost was intended, as an early draft put it, to enable Congress to budget "certain stated funds" to the foreign debt in order "to provide for the discharge of such foreign debts as the United States have already contracted and to enable them to procure such farther credit as the public exigencies may require."[23]

The impost was not a new idea. Gouverneur Morris (New York) had proposed it as part of a larger tax package in 1778 and Thomas Burke (North Carolina) had suggested it to substitute for other taxes in March 1780 (in the debate about the 40-to-1 currency devaluation). In August 1780, Congress also considered a 2.5 percent tax on exports (which would have meant southern tobacco in particular) and prizes. In February 1781, however, Congress decided to tax imports rather than exports and then considered a detailed schedule of enumerated duties for particular goods. This effort must have involved delicate negotiations, though their precise content is not clear because the journals in 1781 did not record debates in "committee of the whole" (this was one reason to use the parliamentary device of a committee of the whole). But, after nine sessions in committee, Congress dropped the enumerated rates for the flat 5 percent ad valorem duty on all imported goods except war materiel ("arms, ammunition, cloathing . . ."), along with the duty on prizes. In addition to the enumerated rate schedule, which may have been designed to charge higher rates on luxury goods, Congress also rejected the idea of letting individual states use the money raised at their own ports to meet their own requisitions—a plan whose patent unfairness never stopped the states with open ports from claiming that it was reasonable.[24]

The impost had several advantages over other kinds of taxes. First, it could be levied and collected with a minimum of administrative capacity. Rather than resting on population censuses or wealth assessments, the impost required only small customs establishments in the ports and a few revenue cutters to prevent flagrant smuggling.[25] Second, the impost avoided the problem of the depreciating currency. Merchants who had access to acceptable forms of money "advanced" the tax to the government, shifting it to consumers through whatever cash or credit arrangements happened to prevail in their ordinary retail transactions. Third, nobody knew who finally would pay the tax. Merchants complained about the cost of "advancing" it, but everyone else assumed they would raise retail prices enough to recover profits when they shifted it to consumers. "In this view," as Congress informed Massachusetts in April 1781, "no tax could have been devised, under our present circumstances, which afforded a prospect of more equality and impartiality, or of less objection, or discontent." Congress also explained to Massachusetts why states could not be permitted to apply the proceeds to their own quotas:

> The states, whose commerce is the most flourishing, will appear in the first instance to contribute largely to the common treasury. But remotely the consumer, wherever he resides, must bear the burthen. And the merchant who advances [the tax], will take care to receive full interest. Even if it should be admitted, that states which enjoy the greatest commercial advantages [that is, states whose ports were not occupied or blockaded by the British] may be exposed to a share of the duty beyond their strict proportion, might it not be considered as a just tribute for peculiar blessings denied by the fortune of a common war to their less happy sister states? Blessings purchased perhaps by their sufferings and secured by their resistance against invaders, who might otherwise have had leisure to close all the avenues to commerce[?][26]

The uncertain ultimate incidence of the impost became "equality and impartiality" more through wish than analysis, but, as long as it was kept low (5 percent) and simple (no enumerated rates), nobody had much incentive to investigate its economic details. In any case, the impost's crucial advantage was political rather than economic. Congress did not have to decide what any state's "strict proportion" of the impost might be. Since it would not be apportioned, Congress could levy the impost without exploring either the structure of the economy or the distribution of the population. Congress, in short, could levy the impost without talking about slavery.

But there was a problem. The Articles of Confederation *required* Congress to apportion its taxes to the states, and the document was very hard to amend. The absurdity of the real estate apportionment in article 8 was compounded by the amendment rule in article 13. To change the Articles, "any alteration" had to be adopted by Congress and "afterwards confirmed by the legislatures of every state." No matter what advantages the impost offered, unanimous approval by every state legislature was too much to ask. It had taken four years to coax every legislature to ratify the Articles in the first place. Eight states had approved the impost by the fall of 1781, Congress had decided that two (South Carolina and Georgia) initially were not necessary since they were under British occupation, and two more approved in the summer of 1782. That made twelve states. As Maryland had frustrated the other twelve states on the Articles, Rhode Island now frustrated them on the impost, first by delay and then, when Congress called on the Rhode Island legislature for "an immediate definitive answer," by what James Madison described as a "unanimous & final veto" by "this perverse sister" in November 1782.[27]

Meanwhile, Congress struggled to make requisitions now that article 8 ostensibly was a binding constitutional rule. Rather than trying to assess real estate, however, Congress based the state quotas on the seat-of-the-pants estimate of total population from 1775 (they also still had no population data, "as no actual numeration of the inhabitants of each State hath yet been obtained by Congress"). Congress continued to promise that each state would be credited for its payments plus interest until the settlement of state accounts ("until the quotas shall be finally ascertained, agreeably to the Articles of Confederation"), but delegates dismissed the idea of a wartime real estate valuation. In April 1781, adopting the report of a committee chaired by Samuel Adams, Congress explained that "the attainment of such an estimate, *flagrante bello,* is difficult; perhaps in some states, which are the seat of war, impracticable; in every view it must be remote." In April 1782, in a letter drafted by a committee chaired by James Madison, Congress again stated the obvious: that "a valuation of land throughout the United States," although it was prescribed by article 8, "was under present circumstances manifestly unattainable." There would be a real estate apportionment eventually, Congress insisted, but not *flagrante bello.*[28]

Yet the politics of allocating the requisitions intensified once even the requisition system violated article 8. It had always been hard to fix the state quotas. "[U]pon my representing the Circumstances of our State," a Rhode Island delegate had gloated to his state's governor in 1777, "Twenty thousand were taken off and put upon Massachusetts." But it was one thing to use the 1775 guess at the state populations before the Articles had been ratified, and quite another to use it when the "constitution" of the United States mandated another rule. In framing its November 1781 requisition, Congress rejected a motion by the Maryland delegates to increase Connecticut's quota. New Hampshire then complained that it had been "overrated," and demanded a reduced quota for the September 1782 requisition. Congress refused New Hampshire's request—at which point the debate degenerated into a free-for-all. In the course of trying to adopt an apportionment of $1.2 million worked out by a "grand committee" (a committee with a member from every state), the delegates voted down motions to shift $9,000 from Massachusetts to Virginia, to shift $2,800 from Rhode Island to New Jersey, to reduce the Connecticut quota by $33,200, to shift $13,750 from Maryland to Connecticut, to reduce the New York quota by $9,600, to shift $3,000 from Pennsylvania to Virginia, and to cut the Georgia quota in half "in consideration of the ravages of the war." Congress finally adopted the grand committee report unchanged.[29] Clearly, however, quotas framed on a basis other than the one mandated in article 8— quotas framed on the basis of a 1775 guess at the population—faced legitimacy problems by 1782. Even if the states could not have met their quotas anyway, the article 8 mandate to apportion by real estate invited them to decide that their quotas not only were too high but had been set in an unconstitutional way—and to use this fact to justify their failures to pay them.

In addition to the impost, Congress also took another step to sort out its finances in 1781. As the capstone of a larger administrative reorganization, they appointed Robert Morris to the new office of "superintendent of finance." Morris, a Philadelphia merchant with an extensive network of commercial correspondents, used his network and personal credit to buy supplies and deliver them to the army, more effectively than anyone had done before. Morris quickly became a lightening rod for criticism, in part because of his role in an ugly 1779 dispute sparked by the American envoys in Europe, and in part because his financial and procurement operations, which mingled the nation's finances with his own, inevitably raised suspicions that he was exploiting the war effort for private gain. These suspicions were heightened when Morris addressed the currency mess by establishing a central bank backed by his personal credit, issuing a new paper currency that everyone called the "Morris notes." Morris suggested that Congress ask the states to authorize other national taxes to supplement the impost, specifically a land tax, poll tax, and liquor excise. Congress ignored these proposals. The delegates appreciated Morris's financial and logistical accomplishments, but, when it came to the politics of taxation, they trusted their own judgments more than they trusted the political acumen of their financier.[30]

Morris became the lobbyist-in-chief for the impost. He organized the "public creditors" (Americans who had loaned money to the United States by buying instruments known as "loan office certificates") to pressure the state legislatures to ratify the impost and, after that failed, to demand that Congress take other steps to resume interest payments that had been suspended in 1780. In the early months of 1783, Morris also may have played a role in a shadowy effort to organize the continental army officers, who threatened (or almost threatened) to stage a military coup unless Congress redressed their very real grievances: months of back wages and efforts to rescind the pensions they had been promised. The so-called Newburgh Conspiracy, in which Alexander Hamilton also was implicated, dissolved when George Washington made a dramatic speech to the erstwhile mutineers, informing them that he disapproved of any move against the civilian government, no matter how ineffectual that government was. Regardless of what the officers thought of Congress, their loyalty to Washington was beyond question, and the coup ended before it began (if anyone actually had been planning a coup).[31]

The most significant development of 1782 was the end of the war. Charles Cornwallis surrendered to Washington at Yorktown in October 1781, the British House of Commons voted to end offensive operations in America in March 1782, and the United States and Britain signed a treaty in which Britain acknowledged American independence in October. Americans learned in December that the British envoy had been instructed to sign such a treaty at the negotiations in Paris, though the treaty itself did not cross the Atlantic until March 1783. Americans, including the army encamped at Newburgh, waited anxiously through these months. Several members of Congress worried that Rhode Island's rejection of the impost (November 1782) would encourage Britain to prolong the war—although it is hard to imagine that either George III or Parliament cared about the impost one way or the other. The people who cared were Americans: the public creditors, the army, the state legislatures, Robert Morris, Congress, and others who considered the financial crisis a test of the viability of the United States as a nation.

The impost was a plan to address the absurdity of the tax program written into the Articles of Confederation by enabling Congress to supplement the requisitions with another tax. Opponents such as the indefatigable David Howell of Rhode Island assailed it as the "ent[e]ring wedge" for the establishment of a Leviathan state, or at least for the land tax, poll tax, and liquor excise that Morris had proposed. As Morris and Congress pressured the Rhode Island legislature, Howell's rhetoric grew more inflammatory. By urging his state to hold firm, he was defending "the Rights of the poor, the Weak and the Ignorant against the Rapacity, the Violence and the Intrigue of the Rich, the powerful and the Subtle." This was nonsense, but Howell's colleague Jonathan Arnold identified the alternative to the impost correctly. "The Eighth Article points out the method of Ascertaining the Quotas of the States in all pecuniary requisitions, [and] the *Equity & Justice of the mode is not contested.*" Yet the Rhode Islanders were rewriting history when they called the Articles of Confederation "a work of time & great Wisdom."[32] Having joined Congress in 1782 (Howell in August, Arnold in October), they may not have understood how the Articles had been framed—much less how the Articles had come to include the real estate apportionment. There was a reason the Rhode Islanders heard nobody questioning the "equity and justice" of article 8. Equity and justice were irrelevant if a real estate valuation was "manifestly unattainable."

Actually, Congress *had* "contested" the justice of the real estate rule. In February 1782 (before Howell arrived), they had decided to abandon it. On Morris's recommendation, Congress announced that they intended to settle the state accounts right away—that it was "indispensably necessary to settle and adjust, and finally to determine the proportions to be borne by the several states of the cost of the war" up to January 1, 1782. Real estate would not work for two reasons. First, "from the present situation of some of the states," it "cannot, with any degree of certainty, be proceeded on." Second, however, because the war itself had affected the value of real estate in various places at various times, using a valuation from any one point in time would produce "manifest injustice." Since the real estate rule was both impractical *and* unjust, Congress asked the states for two things: (1) to amend the Articles by permitting Congress "to assume and adopt such principles as, from the particular circumstances of the several states, at different periods, may appear just and equitable, without being wholly confined by the rule laid down in the eighth Article," and (2) to send "all such documents and information as they may judge most proper to assist the judgment of Congress in forming just estimates of the value and abilities of each state." Nothing came of these resolutions. As Ferguson explains, no settlement between the states could proceed until there was a total of what Congress and the states had spent on the war, and this part of the accounting took much longer than anyone had realized it would. Nor did the states act on Congress's 1782 plan for making the settlement.[33]

With the war ending, the *flagrante bello* argument against attempting to assess the value of real estate seemed to diminish in force. Now, delegates including Howell and John Rutledge (South Carolina) urged their colleagues to give it a try. Real estate, after all, was the rule that the Articles specified. By the beginning of 1783, a confluence of circumstances—the war's end, the impost's defeat, the public creditors' pressure, the army's unrest, and, in addition, Robert Morris's threat to resign if Congress did not secure a revenue source more adequate than the trickle from requisitions—persuaded Congress to initiate a wide-ranging debate about the nation's financial alternatives. Congress had adopted the real estate apportionment in 1777 to avoid debates about how to count slaves in an apportionment that used population. Congress had adopted the impost in 1781 to avoid the impractical real estate apportionment. In 1783, Congress ran out of evasive options. If the delegates were going to talk seriously about taxation, they were going to have to talk about slavery.

Three-Fifths

From the perspective of U.S. history generally, the significance of the 1783 tax debate is that it produced the infamous "three-fifths ratio" for counting the population of enslaved African Americans. From the perspective of the history of U.S. taxation, the significance of this debate is that it left its participants with a deeper appreciation for the political advantages of the impost. Although these two outcomes obviously exist on different moral planes, the three-fifths ratio and the impost actually were closely related. Both emerged from the 1783 tax debate as alternatives to the real estate apportionment, as two sides of one effort to amend the unworkable article 8 in order to save the Articles of Confederation. Both of these strategies failed. The Articles could not be saved—because they were too hard to amend. The Articles would be replaced altogether by the U.S. Constitution. The three-fifths ratio and the impost survived this transition, though in altered forms. The Constitution turned the three-fifths ratio into a representation plan. In 1789, the first Congress under the Constitution turned the impost into the tariff.

Over the first four months of 1783, Congress discussed the various aspects of its financial crisis nearly every day until, on April 18, they sent the states a package of proposals to address it. The United States owed over $42 million to foreign lenders and, among Americans, to the army, the public creditors, and people who had "become creditors in the first instance involuntarily"— holders of the "certificates" issued by army officers who had "impressed" supplies. The annual interest on this debt amounted to $2.4 million. Congress asked the states to fund the interest by (1) approving an impost projected to raise almost $1 million per year; (2) agreeing to meet the quotas of a long-term requisition of $1.5 million per year; and (3) completing their compliance with the western land cession deal that had persuaded Maryland to ratify the Articles (Virginia in particular was still dragging its feet) so that the nation could raise money by selling land. There was also a fourth proposal. Congress asked the states to amend article 8 to replace real estate with a version of population: "the whole number of white and other free citizens and inhabitants, of every age, sex and condition . . . and three-fifths of all other persons not comprehended in the foregoing description, except Indians, not paying taxes, in each State." This, of course, was the formula that would become the "three-fifths clause" of the U.S. Constitution.[34]

The impost that Congress proposed in 1783 was somewhat different from the one it had proposed two years earlier. First, with the advent of peace, there would be no more privateers capturing prizes, so the 1783 impost dropped the prize duty of the earlier tax. Second, Congress added enumerated duties (fixed rates per gallon or pound) on the classic objects of consumption taxation: hard liquor and "luxury" goods that did not compete with domestic products (wine, tea, pepper, sugar, molasses, cocoa, and coffee). The 1783 impost consisted of these duties plus the 5 percent ad valorem on other imported commodities. Third, Congress addressed one of Rhode Island's key objections to the 1781 impost. The Rhode Island legislature had said that allowing "Officers unknown and unaccountable to them" to collect taxes at the Rhode Island ports would violate the state's constitution. Congress therefore provided "that the collectors of the said duties shall be appointed by the states, within which their offices are to be respectively exercised," with the proviso that these officers still would be accountable to and removable by Congress. Finally, in a concession to Rhode Island and Virginia, Congress added a more explicit sunset provision. As in 1781, impost revenue could be spent only to service the war debt, but the 1783 tax would expire in twenty-five years regardless of whether the debt had been extinguished.[35]

The long-term requisition also would last for twenty-five years, with its proceeds dedicated to the war debt. Far less radically than Robert Morris's proposals for a national land tax, poll tax, and liquor excise—which Congress never took seriously—this plan relied on the states to levy taxes "of such nature as they may judge most convenient" as long as these taxes were "substantial and effectual" and guaranteed to last for twenty-five years. This requisition, in other words, would not depend on the vagaries of annual state compliance (the "delays and uncertainties incident to a revenue to be established and collected, from time to time, by thirteen independent authorities"). Congress set "temporary" state quotas resembling those of all the previous requisitions (based on the 1775 guess at the total population), proposing that these quotas remain in effect "until the rule of the Confederation can be carried into practice" (i.e., until Congress figured out how to make a national real estate valuation). Finally, Congress promised to adjust the quotas in the future, a prospect that would become more realistic if the states endorsed the three-fifths population amendment. The quotas would be "fixed and equalized, from time to time, according to the rule which is or may be prescribed by the Articles of Confederation."[36]

Before Congress could agree to any of this, however, they had to dispense with the real estate apportionment. The Rhode Island delegates favored the effort to make real estate work as the only way to stave off the impost. Many of the southerners, meanwhile, thought their states would gain if the real estate was assessed at its value in 1783, since most of the recent fighting had taken place in the South. The North Carolina delegates championed real estate consistently, less because of war damage than because the relative economic backwardness of North Carolina made the real estate rule "more favorable for us than for most other states in the Union. Other states must pay for their large Towns & lands highly cultivated, while we have few towns and much wood land." Samuel Osgood (Massachusetts) thought his state might benefit, "provided we can obtain a Valuation as nearly Right as we have Reason to expect," though he worried as he heard his colleagues talking about how a valuation might work and wrote home for copies of the Massachusetts valuation laws ("They know so very little about such Acts this Way"). Still, most delegates continued to cling to the hope that Rhode Island would ratify the 1781 impost—until December 1782, when a committee that had set off to cajole them turned back on the news that Virginia suddenly had revoked its approval.[37] With the 1781 impost now unquestionably dead, Congress turned in earnest to real estate.

They began with a draft that bore obvious marks of its southern origin. Written by John Rutledge (South Carolina), this draft required the state legislatures to create districts and appoint commissioners who were "principal freeholders, resident in the district[s]." The commissioners would value the real estate and the governors would send Congress the results.[38] The fact that tax assessors in northern states were popularly elected at the local level—that northern legislatures could not just appoint "principal freeholders" to value property—might have posed an obstacle to this plan if other, more fundamental obstacles had not taken precedence.

According to James Madison, whose notes provide the best record of these debates, the Connecticut delegates initially tried to postpone the real estate valuation by "alledging" that the *flagrante bello* argument still applied, that a valuation would be impractical until the British had evacuated New York City. Madison and his colleagues were skeptical, "apprehending" that they really wanted to shield "the flourishing state of Connecticut," whose prosperity "compared with the Southern States, would render a valuation at this crisis unfavorable to [Connecticut]." Then, Madison and Alexander Hamilton, inaugurating the partnership that lasted through their work on the *Federalist* essays in 1788, assaulted the real estate apportionment head on. The war was not the problem. Real estate was "chimerical" under any conditions. Rutledge's plan to get the states to do the valuation could never work, since "their interests would give a biass to the judgments or . . . at least suspicions of such biass [would] prevail." Nor could Congress correct or equalize the state results "without giving extreme offence to the suspected party." But if Congress did not rely on the states, the valuation "could not be executed but at an expence, delay & uncertainty which were inadmissable." Thus, Madison and Hamilton argued, the states could not trust each other to do the valuation, but Congress also could not act on its own—lacking the administrative capacity, the political authority, or both. Instead of attempting to implement article 8, Congress should ask the states to amend it, to "exchange" real estate for a rule that was "more simple, easy, & equal"—which, of course, could only mean population.[39]

Other delegates, however, insisted on trying to make Rutledge's plan work. Madison and Hamilton agreed to indulge them, Hamilton with open contempt: he was ready to talk about the real estate plan "in order that its impracticabil[it]y & futility might become manifest." Nor was he alone. Eliphalet Dyer (Connecticut) proposed, as a joke, to let the states do the valuation with the proviso "that each of the States should cheat equally." But talk of outright cheating missed the real point, which was that the state tax systems had never been designed to be comparable. Madison finally killed Rutledge's plan by comparing the operation of state-level property taxes in Virginia and Pennsylvania. Apparently, the "average valuation" of land was 50 percent higher in Virginia than Pennsylvania, although "the real value" of land in Pennsylvania "was confessedly" three times as high. It is not clear where Madison got these figures—or whether they rested on actual assessment data—but they did the job. Madison had raised "apprehensions" about asking the states for anything more complicated than "a report of simple facts."[40]

Congress then adopted a plan even less practical than state valuations. The states would return the simple facts: numbers of acres of land, numbers of buildings "distinguishing dwelling houses from other buildings," and population figures "distinguishing white from black." Using this data, the delegates would "make a just and true estimate of the value of all lands . . . and of the buildings and improvements thereon" (the article 8 formula) and then use this "estimate" to settle the state accounts and make further requisitions. And the states somehow would endorse this procedure and immediately start sending money! "The whole report," according to Madison, "was agreed to with great reluctance by almost all." Hamilton found it preposterous. Article 8 clearly "intended an *actual* and *specific* valuation . . . not a mere general estimate" hammered out in Philadelphia, much less an estimate that actually would rest on population figures, which were "totally foreign to the confederation." Madison also noted the irony. "Who could have supposed that such a measure could ever have been the offspring of a zealous & scrupulous respect for the Confederation?" Hugh Williamson (North Carolina) was happier. He praised the resolution to do something that looked vaguely like a valuation as one "which the Southern States have carried with great difficulty." Yet even Williamson admitted that this plan had defects ("it is not so good as we wished, but the best we could get"). Congress sent it to the states, which ignored it.[41]

From the beginning, Hamilton was "most strenuous" about the need to amend article 8 to replace real estate with population. Madison also favored a population amendment, though only if it included "certain qualifications as to Slaves." In a private memorandum, Madison defined these "qualifications" as "reckoning two slaves as equal to one free man," the very position that his predecessor, Benjamin Harrison, had advocated in the 1776 debate. James Wilson, the man who had provoked Thomas Lynch's ultimatum in that debate, also was ready to reopen the issue. Others were less sure that this was a good idea. Once the North Carolina delegates finally were ready to abandon real estate ("it would be an even chance which would come first[:] The fixing the quotas or the day of Judgment"), they warmed to the unofficial offers of New Englanders to make a "considerable allowance for slaves" by excluding those younger than sixteen. The North Carolinians thought "the Southern States" might be able to extract an even better deal from their colleagues "for the sake of preventing Jealousies, a Contention and delay," but they also worried about what the New Englanders might say if Congress launched a formal debate: "[W]e fear that if an attempt should be made to alter or amend the mode of fixing the quota, those very men would again talk of a Slave being equal to a white man."[42]

Congress finally bit the bullet at the end of March. Unfortunately, it is not clear what, if anything, the New England delegates said about slavery. We can be sure that they did not make stirring speeches about human equality, but the delegates guaranteed that nobody else would ever know exactly what they said by voting to hold the entire finance debate in secret—so that they did not write letters describing it. Madison took notes, but while his notes resemble transcripts for other phases of the debate, they shift into a summary mode for March 28, the day Congress produced the three-fifths ratio. These notes record that the New Englanders favored a ratio of 3 slaves to 4 free people, that southerners countered with 2-to-1, 3-to-1, and 4-to-1, that Madison himself proposed 3-to-5 "to give a proof of the sincerity of his professions of liberality," and that James Wilson agreed to "sacrifice his opinion to this compromise." Madison also quoted Hugh Williamson (North Carolina) criticizing slavery in the same breath in which he demanded a tax break for slave states, saying that "he was principled agst. slavery; but that he thought slaves an incumbrance to Society instead of increasing its ability to pay taxes." But Madison declined to identify other arguments with individual speakers. Alexander Hamilton, whose letters analyzed other aspects of the tax problem in detail, was absent from Congress on March 28.[43]

Madison's summary suggests that southerners avoided the forthright definition of slavery that had grounded the southern position in 1776 ("The Negroes are wealth") and that, perhaps as a result, nobody repeated John Adams's answer: the "fallacy" of using "the word 'property' here" to identify "some of the people" of the southern states. Four delegates who had been present for the 1776 debate were there in 1783, but only one speaker from the earlier round (James Wilson) was present for the reprise. Samuel Chase was back in Maryland. Thomas Lynch had died in a shipwreck. John Adams and Benjamin Franklin were in Europe, negotiating the peace treaty and securing foreign loans. This time, when southerners demanded favorable tax treatment to offset the losses they sustained as a result of owning human beings—and accompanied these demands with pious antislavery rhetoric—nobody was prepared to call them to account as Franklin had done in 1776. This time, there is no evidence that anyone pointed to the long history of African American resistance and revolt or to its recent expressions during the Revolutionary War. This time, at least according to Madison's record, the delegates treated slavery as though it was just another economic institution. This time, Madison's three-fifths solution could be presented as a slaveholder's show of "liberality."

These terms favored the southerners. They rang the changes on the low productivity of slave labor. Since slaves had "no interest in their labor," they "did as little as possible" and also refused to think about their work (they "omitted every exertion of thought requisite to facilitate & expedite it"). Adding to the 1776 argument, southerners now also asserted that slaveholders did not exploit child labor as fully as free parents did ("Slaves were not put to labour as young as the children of laboring families"). Because slaves were poor workers and slaveholders treated children well, the South should pay less than the North in taxes that otherwise were apportioned by population. Madison handled the northern response gingerly. "The arguments used by those who were for rating slaves high" emphasized the underconsumption analysis that James Wilson had offered in 1776, though without his earlier glosses on the labor of enslaved women or what it meant to insist that slave labor was unprofitable (that slavery should be abolished). According to Madison, the northerners stuck to simple economics: whatever slaveholders lost from poor work habits they more than made back by imposing low standards of living ("the expence of feeding & cloathing [slaves] was as far below that incident to freemen, as their industry & ingenuity were below those of freemen"). New Englanders also argued that the South benefited from its warm weather and rich soil, as opposed to "the rigorous climate & inferior fertility" of their states, and there was some debate about how import and export figures might be relevant for evaluating the ability of the northern and southern economies to bear tax burdens.[44]

Even if this debate went every bit as smoothly as Madison's account suggests, Congress rejected the population amendment on March 28, in part because Hamilton's absence left New York represented by only a single delegate (so that its vote, in favor, did not count). On April 1, however, with Hamilton back to fill out the New York delegation and perhaps to persuade others (from Connecticut, Massachusetts, and South Carolina) to change their minds, Congress agreed to add the three-fifths ratio to the repertoire of American politics. "Those who voted differently from their former votes," Madison reported, "were influenced by the conviction of the necessity of the change [replacing real estate with population] & despair on both sides of a more favorable rate of the Slaves." The state legislatures were less willing to agree. By March 1786, nine had ratified the amendment, but South Carolina, Georgia, and two of the New England states (New Hampshire and Rhode Island) had not. As Congress continued to make requisitions, real estate remained the ostensible apportionment rule and the 1775 guess at the total population remained the actual apportionment rule.[45]

The real estate apportionment, in fairness, solved the problem it was intended to solve. It enabled Congress to frame the Articles of Confederation in 1777. As a plan to allocate "charges of war" to the states, however, it was wildly unrealistic. Once Congress was ready to admit that no serious tax plan could rest on the real estate apportionment, they confronted the issue they had avoided since Thomas Lynch threatened to destroy the new nation in 1776. Southerners did not win everything they demanded in 1783, but they won quite a lot. Northerners had swallowed an unspeakably twisted argument: the evil of slavery justified tax breaks for slaveholding states! In order to buy peace with the South (or, as the North Carolinians had put it, to avoid "Jealousies, a Contention and delay"), northerners had agreed to levy higher taxes on their own constituents to compensate southerners—who had the audacity to claim to be "principled agst. slavery"—for the "incumbrance" of owning large numbers of human beings. Madison's personal preference for a 2-to-1 ratio is highly significant in this context. The northern concession was not made merely to South Carolina, a small state whose economy had been undermined seriously by the war (not least by the "loss" of 25,000 slaves, one-fourth of the prewar slave population). It was made to the South generally and, most of all, to Virginia—the largest state, the one with the largest slave population (of about 236,000 in 1783), and the one whose interests were championed by a leader as savvy and articulate as James Madison.[46]

The three-fifths population amendment was an attempt to save the requisition system. It was predicated on the idea that the states were not paying their requisitions because their quotas had never been apportioned in accordance with article 8 and because everyone recognized that the state accounts could never be settled if the settlement had to depend on a national real estate valuation. Money that a state sent to Congress under these conditions was little more than a gift to the other states, and no state was eager to lay heavy taxes on its citizens in order to subsidize the laggards in others. The absurdity of article 8 had produced a race to the bottom. But, as the delegates also understood, it was far from clear that this analysis of the states' failure to pay was correct. It was far from clear that they would be capable of paying their requisitions even if they agreed that their quotas had been fixed in a legitimate way.[47] The three-fifths amendment did not address this problem. The impost amendment did.

From Impost to Tariff

The main difference between the impost debates of 1781 and 1783 is that the impost was the only national tax Congress considered in 1781. In 1783, however, Congress also considered Robert Morris's taxes: the land tax, poll tax, and liquor excise. In Morris's plan, Congress would ask the states to authorize these taxes as well as the impost. Congress actually disposed of them quickly. Even a cursory look at their economic implications persuaded the delegates to stick to the impost, with its uncertain shifting and opaque ultimate incidence. When Morris persisted, Congress rejected his whole program, with the "impropriety" of part of it (according to Madison) "being generally proclaimed."[48] Because the 1783 impost debate also involved these other taxes, Madison and his colleagues learned exactly why the impost was desirable. The other taxes could have solved the problem of relying on the states to meet requisitions, but the impost had a unique advantage. As the only tax Congress could enact without serious economic inquiry, it was also the only tax they could enact without considering the economic implications of slavery.

Morris had made this point clearly, so clearly that his report on these taxes may actually have been intended to persuade Congress that it could *not* adopt them. First, Morris proposed to tax land at flat rates per acre rather than ad valorem. This would solve the problem of a national valuation, but Morris also argued that a flat-rate land tax would deter land speculation by taxing large uncultivated tracts at heavy rates in proportion to their value. It might even break up large landholdings to create a more egalitarian distribution of land. Since Morris was deeply involved in land speculation, along with many members of Congress, it is not clear how this argument was supposed to make the land tax appealing. Could Morris have been joking when he praised it as "an Agrarian Law without the Iniquity"? Morris also managed to present unattractive arguments for the liquor excise. Its most persuasive defense, the invisibility of consumption taxes, was already a part of the case for the impost ("Of all Taxes, those on the Consumption of Articles are most agreable; because, being mingled with the price, they are less sensible to the People"), but it went downhill from there. The liquor excise would be an effective sumptuary regulation, "a Means of compelling Vice to support the Cause of Virtue," and its regressivity was a good thing: it would "draw from the Idle and Dissolute that Contribution to the public Service, which they will not otherwise make." Morris may actually have wanted to impose a regressive tax and a sumptuary law, hoping to improve the morals of the poor and force them to work harder. Some historians have portrayed him as exactly this kind of an elitist. Still, this project did not exist in the same political universe with support for an "Agrarian Law."[49]

The best part of the report was its argument for the poll tax. First, its regressivity was not really a problem because American wages were high; poll taxes were "extremely oppressive" in Europe, but "where three Days of labor produce Sustenance for a week, it is not unreasonable to ask two Days out of a year." Second, Congress could use the poll tax receipts to keep tabs on the population, requiring men to pay new poll taxes when they moved from one state to another as a "useful Regulation of Police." And if the idea of national identity cards seemed a stretch, Morris also had a way to deal with the problem of slavery. The poll tax he proposed was different from that of any state. Northern poll taxes were levied on male adults or "single freemen." Southern poll taxes were levied on free male adults and slaves of both sexes, usually between certain ages. Morris proposed to tax free male adults and male slaves aged 16 to 60. The first thing everyone would notice about this proposal was its exemption of female slaves. Morris may have intended it to balance the northern and southern tax burdens (he did not explain), but any attempt to levy a poll tax that exempted enslaved women obviously would have provoked a debate about the value of their labor. Nobody in Congress would have wanted to initiate such a debate in 1783. Morris, in short, could not have crafted a better explanation of the political virtues of the impost.[50]

Madison, meanwhile, acknowledged the problems that other taxes would create when he proposed poll taxes and land taxes "under certain qualifications." He may not have explained the qualifications to his colleagues (he recorded them in a footnote to his account of the debate), but they involved "rating blacks some what lower than whites" in the poll tax and "considering the value of land in each State to be in an inverse proportion" to its population density. The idea here was that densely populated states (particularly in New England) would pay higher poll taxes for their large populations, while sparsely populated states (particularly in the South) would pay higher land taxes for their huge tracts of unimproved acreage. And, of course, the South would benefit from the slave discount. Congress would apportion aggregate poll-and-land tax quotas to the states, and each state would apportion its quota to districts "on a like or any other equalizing principle."[51] Madison probably knew that this plan made no sense, that it conflated the problem of apportioning quotas with the problem of designing actual taxes, and that it solved neither one. Congress would not be able to frame these quotas, and the states would not be able to levy these taxes. Yet by thinking through the economic logic of this and other tax schemes, Madison came to appreciate exactly what made the impost the indispensable national tax.

Other delegates came to the same realization. "After opening and discussing a variety of questions," Joseph Jones (Virginia) reported, "no object has been yet discovered, to which so few objections lie, as the impost duty formerly recommended to the States." When Congress tried to frame other taxes, "difficulties apparently insurmountable presented themselves in almost every stage of the business, owing to the different circumstances of the several States." John Taylor Gilman (New Hampshire) tried to explain the problem by comparing it to state-level tax politics: "[I]f we find so great difficulty in Ascertaining the proportion of Each Town & Parish, what may we Expect between State & State?" John Francis Mercer (Virginia), who opposed the 1781 impost as a member of the Virginia legislature, changed his mind after experiencing the 1783 debate for himself. Requisitions could not be made to work ("the thing is impossible"), and when Congress considered taxes other than the impost, they were "hemmed in on all sides with difficulties that appear insurmountable." Hence his conversion: the impost "in every light will be found the best calculated of any that can be devised to produce large sums in the correct mode." As Eliphalet Dyer (Connecticut) summarized the conversations around him, the impost "is said in general to be the only plan which appears feasable."[52]

The central fact was that nobody could predict the ultimate economic incidence of the impost—that nobody knew exactly how its burden would be shifted through the economy after merchants "advanced" it at the ports. Put another way, the central fact was that Congress would not have to decide how to distribute the impost burden, either to groups of taxpayers or to individual states. No compilations of data about land, buildings, or population "distinguishing white from black" could be relevant. There was no reason to collect such data or to argue about its implications. If nobody knew who bore the burden, then nobody could claim that his state was "overrated," the perennial problem of the requisition quotas. Some of the impost's proponents, such as Dyer of Connecticut, stressed the idea that individuals could choose to avoid the tax burden by choosing not to buy imported goods, and especially the hard liquor and other drinks and spices on which the 1783 impost levied the enumerated rates. "The People have been so harassed with taxes & Collectors," he explained in reference to state taxes, "that they feel galled, fretted, Impatient, & many really unable to pay." Shouldn't Congress try something that "will leave every one pretty much at his Choice whether to pay or not? & when he does pay, not to know or feel it?"[53]

As Dyer no doubt understood (but failed to say), there was another side to this argument. Connecticut's merchants could not compete with their counterparts in Boston, Providence, or New York City. The very features that Dyer praised in the national impost made state imposts extremely attractive to other states—and had been staples of tax politics in Massachusetts since the French and Indian War. Massachusetts, not to mention Rhode Island, could employ import taxes as substitutes for heavy tax burdens on polls and property. Their legislatures could enjoy the same uncertainty, invisibility, and "voluntary" payment that Congress would enjoy from the national impost. Once the British had evacuated New York City, New York State could do the same. Connecticut could not. Nor could New Jersey, since imported goods entered its markets through New York and Pennsylvania. Nor could North Carolina, whose imported goods entered through Virginia and South Carolina. The fact that the "importing" states could shift part of their state taxes onto their neighbors, and apply the proceeds to their own requisitions, only enhanced the preference of these states for state imposts over the national impost and for requisitions over the only tax Congress could levy itself. For the states to grant the national impost unanimously, every importing state had to cede these advantages to the nation—which was still too much to ask. Rhode Island ratified the 1783 impost, but this time New York held out alone.[54]

The U.S. Constitution was many things, but one of them was a device to ensure that the national government could levy the impost. The Constitution and its tax provisions will be the subjects of the next chapter. Here, it is sufficient to note the first clause of article 1, section 8 (the powers of Congress): "To lay and collect Taxes, Duties, Imposts and Excises," as long as the "Duties, Imposts and Excises" are "uniform throughout the United States." Many aspects of the Constitution proved controversial in Philadelphia and again in the state ratification process. But the impost was not controversial. As a tax, it had never been controversial. Congress and twelve state legislatures had endorsed it twice. Most of the Constitution's opponents ("Antifederalists") continued to endorse the impost as a solution short of junking the Articles altogether. The defeat of the national impost, in both rounds, by a state defending its own tax base illustrates the reality that the problem was never an objection to the impost as a tax. The problem was that the states had incurred large debts during the war, including the backlog of requisitions, and some hoped to meet these obligations with state imposts rather than heavy taxes on polls and property (like the one that provoked Shays's Rebellion in Massachusetts). Alexander Hamilton's finance program, including the federal assumption of state debts, would address the only powerful objection to the national impost: Congress rescued the states from their war debts and funded the enlarged national debt by taxing imported goods.[55]

But the federal government under the Constitution did not levy the impost. It levied the tariff. Rather than the flat ad valorem tax on all imported goods plus "revenue duties" on liquor and tropical produce, the first session of the first Congress adopted the protective tariff—a tax that subsidized ("protected") domestic manufacturers by hiking the prices of competing imported products. In his 1791 "Report on Manufactures," Hamilton would make the theoretical case for protectionism as an industrial policy, urging Congress to use the tariff (as well as bounties and other measures) to promote the development of American manufacturing. Yet Congress enacted the first protective tariff in 1789, two years before Hamilton submitted his treatise. As Hamilton noted in his report, the tariff was already "sanctioned by the laws of the United States."[56] It was already sanctioned because Madison, no fan of protectionism, tried to make the impost the first accomplishment of the first Congress under the Constitution.

In theory, the impost could have become law far more easily under the Constitution. It had to pass both houses of Congress and win the president's approval, but the whole point of the Constitution as a way to "energize" the national government was to dispense with the rounds of state legislative action that had thwarted the impost under the Articles. In practice, however, the new regime generated new obstacles, which Madison seems not to have anticipated, despite his celebrated mastery of the Constitution (on display in the Philadelphia convention, his *Federalist* essays, and the Virginia ratification convention). The Constitution transformed the legislative process *within* Congress. Under the Articles, the members of Congress had no reason to suppose that the states would endorse deals that the members made with each other. They not only cited the threat of state resistance in debate, but they actively stoked it—as David Howell did by urging the Rhode Island legislature to resist the 1781 impost. But, under the Constitution, the deals congressmen made with each other (and the president) were the law.[57] The Articles had placed a premium on simplicity in tax measures that thirteen legislatures had to endorse. The Constitution offered no such premium. Now, Congress *was* a legislature. Now, congressmen were free to strike deals. When the commitment to import taxation met the deal making authorized by these new legislative conditions, some degree of protectionism was inevitable. The Constitution turned the impost into the tariff.

As the floor manager of the first session of the first House of Representatives, Madison introduced the impost with a speech about how the United States, "having recovered from the state of imbecility that heretofore prevented a performance of its duty, ought, in its first act, to revive those principles of honor and honesty that have too long lain dormant." Citing a lack of detailed commercial data and the need to act quickly, he proposed that Congress adopt only those rates "as are likely to occasion the least difficulty," the 1783 rates that had "received, generally, the approbation of the several States of the Union." As soon as he did this, however, Thomas Fitzsimons (Pennsylvania) proposed to add a long list of rates on manufactured goods "calculated to encourage the productions of our country, and protect our infant manufacturers." Madison responded by stressing the urgency of passing a law in time to capture revenue from the spring import season (it was already April) and by arguing that revenue and protectionism were separate issues that should not be "confusedly blended." But when Elias Boudinot (New Jersey), the next speaker, asked why Fitzsimons had left glass off his list, it was all over. The politics of the impost had succumbed to the politics of the tariff.[58]

The impost's principal political advantage diminished in that moment. Congressmen had decided to think about the economy rather than only the revenue, initiating the tariff politics that later generations knew only too well: Pennsylvanians leading the charge for protective duties, southerners objecting to taxes that would force their constituents to subsidize the development of northern industry, New Englanders balancing the competing claims of import merchants (who preferred low tariffs) and manufacturers (who preferred high tariffs), and everyone engaging in the log-rolling and other strategic behaviors that would make tariff politics a paradigmatic case for twentieth-century political scientists investigating the legislative process.[59] Meanwhile, in 1789, the debate about particular rates for particular commodities dragged on day after day, from April 8 to May 15 in the House, with the Senate reviving it in mid-June by adding a few items of its own. Sooner or later, as congressmen argued about the economic impact of the provisions of their evolving bill, someone was bound to point to the role of slavery in any realistic analysis of the American economy.

That someone was Fitzsimons. Tiring of southern attacks on his protectionist program, he opened the dangerous question of the identity of the "consumers" who bore the tax burdens on imported goods. Tariffs on such items as beer, candles, cheese, soap, and boots did not burden the South disproportionately—because slaveholders did not permit slaves to consume them at anything like the rates at which northern free people did. In an echo of James Wilson's earlier argument that slaveholders profited by enforcing low standards of living on slaves, Fitzsimons said he "never could conceive that the consumption of those articles by the negroes of South Carolina could contribute to the revenue as much as that of the white inhabitants of the Eastern States." Fisher Ames (Massachusetts) also dismissed the claim that southerners suffered from a uniquely heavy dependence on imports, adding a dig at the South's aristocratic plantation society. New England's greater social equality offset the lavish consumption of imports by rich southern planters. "Admitting the people of New England to live more moderate than the opulent citizens of Virginia and Carolina, yet they have not such a number of blacks among them, whose living is wretched, consequently the average consumption per head will be nearly the same."[60]

Salt and molasses also caused flare-ups. After Thomas Tudor Tucker (South Carolina) attacked the regressivity of a duty on salt, calling it worse than a poll tax ("the most odious of all taxes") because the poor consumed more salt than the rich ("the poor consume greater quantities of salted provision than the rich"), John Laurance (New York) refused to let this South Carolina planter pose as the poor man's friend by ignoring slavery. In fact, Laurance argued, "the rich are generally more profuse in their [salt] consumption than the poor; they have more servants and dependents also to consume it." Madison then jumped in to concede the point. A salt tax would not be regressive in the South because slavery caused the wealthy to buy more salt than the poor (in Madison's incredible language, "because the species of property there consists of mouths that consume salt in the same proportion as the whites"). On molasses, the imported raw material for the New England rum industry, southern demands for high rates—buttressed by moralistic appeals to the virtues of temperance—pushed George Thatcher (Massachusetts) beyond consumption or economics: "If the pernicious effects of New England rum have been justly lamented, what can be urged for negro slavery?" Madison rushed to soften this blow, certain that Thatcher had not expressed "either the deliberate temper of his own mind or the good sense of his constituents," but the damage was done. James Jackson (Georgia) felt compelled "to observe, that however slavery may be condemned in the Eastern States, it is impossible to cultivate the Southern country without their assistance."[61]

Thatcher actually had done more than insult southern slaveholders. He had created a new problem by alluding to imported slaves. "Suppose a member from Massachusetts was to propose an impost on negroes" as high as southerners were proposing for molasses? "[W]hat would you hear from the Southern gentlemen, if fifty dollars was the sum to be laid?" Congress, of course, could not levy a $50 slave duty. The slave-trade clause of the Constitution capped any such tax at $10. In addition to barring Congress from prohibiting slave imports before 1808, it permitted a tax of up to $10 per imported slave. Now, Josiah Parker (Virginia), calling himself a reluctant slaveholder and attacking the "inhuman" slave trade as "contrary to the Revolution principles," introduced the $10 tax. South Carolina and Georgia representatives responded with predictable outrage. Jackson (Georgia) "knew this business was viewed in an odious light to the eastward, because the people were capable of doing their own work, and had no occasion for slaves," but this was not Georgia's situation (its "people" could not do their own work). Yet Jackson reserved his anger for Virginians. They already "had [their] complement of slaves" and "ought to let their neighbors get supplied, before they imposed such a burthen upon importation." Northerners, for their part, urged that this "subject of some delicacy" not be permitted to derail the revenue bill, with Roger Sherman (Connecticut) declaring that he "could not reconcile himself to the insertion of human beings as an article of duty, among goods, wares, and merchandise."[62]

Congress seemed to have come full circle. After all the efforts to avoid repeating the 1776 debate about whether to consider enslaved African Americans as persons or property for tax purposes—and whether to consider what slavery itself really was—the logic of tax politics had brought these issues back. Still, even if "it was the fashion of the day to favor the liberty of slaves," as Jackson scoffed, it was no longer 1776. Madison may have been blindsided by the political logic that turned the impost into the tariff, but he was ready for the inevitable discussion of slavery that ensued. In 1776, Chase, Lynch, Hooper, Harrison, and Rutledge were not ready for the northern hostility to slavery. Nor was Thomas Jefferson, who took notes on the 1776 debate but apparently did not say a word. In 1789, James Madison was ready. He had honed his skills in the Confederation Congress and the Philadelphia convention. He knew how to talk to northerners about slavery and how to shape debates so that they ended up strengthening rather than weakening the institution. A crude ultimatum ("there is an end of the Confederation") or a defense of slavery itself (Jackson: the slaves "were better off in their present situation than they would be if they were manumitted") only invited northerners to affirm the basic immorality of slavery—to proclaim, as Fisher Ames did, that "he detested it from his soul." Madison realized that there was a better way.[63]

Madison wrung a significant proslavery victory from this debate: duty-free slave imports. His strategy was complex. It is not clear if Parker was in on it, but Madison showed the northern and Deep South members what a little rhetorical and parliamentary sophistication could achieve. He endorsed Parker's motion to adopt the $10 slave duty by attacking slavery in general and the slave trade in particular. His point, however, was that the question at issue was narrow. Because the tariff was framed to levy a 5 percent ad valorem duty on all goods without enumerated rates, and because, on average, $10 was 5 percent of the value of an imported slave, the only question Parker had raised was whether to enumerate slaves explicitly or to leave them in the 5 percent category with other commodities. Congress, Madison claimed (outrageously), had been working on the assumption that the 5 percent category included slaves. But if they did not make the slave duty explicit, it would not be collected. "The collector may mistake; for he would not presume to apply the term goods, wares, and merchandise to any person whatsoever." Sherman, who had been very concerned about the Constitution's rhetorical approach to slavery at Philadelphia, now dismissed this possibility. It would be unconstitutional to interpret the language "goods, wares, and merchandise" as applying to slaves. The Constitution "does not consider these persons as species of property; it speaks of them as persons." Once Sherman offered this clear statement of the "original intent" of Congress to exempt slaves from the 5 percent duty, Madison announced his realization that the slave tax required a separate bill and asked Parker to withdraw his motion, which Parker immediately did. Congress referred the $10 slave tax to a committee chaired by Parker, whose report was postponed to the next session. It was never revived.[64]

The second session of the first Congress waged a more famous battle over the slave trade, initiated by petitions from Quakers and the Pennsylvania Abolition Society (Benjamin Franklin was prominent among the latter). This battle ended by killing the $10 slave tax. Congress *never* levied it. They banned the slave trade in 1808, the first opportunity under the slave-trade clause, but slaves entered the United States duty-free until then. Historians have made much of the anti-slave-trade rhetoric of Virginians in the early republic, but these debates suggest that they never had any intention of acting against the slave trade. Joseph J. Ellis, summarizing their behavior in the famous debate, notes that the Virginians "talked northern but thought southern." Ellis wisely avoids the question of "[w]hether they were living a paradox or a lie," a psychological issue that cannot be resolved definitively.[65] The political upshot is clearer. Madison attacked slavery and the slave trade as directly as any northerner. He thereby silenced the northerners while alerting the Deep South members to pay attention. Jackson got nowhere by defending slavery. Madison won duty-free slave imports for Jackson's constituents through the strategy southerners had been developing since 1776: condemn slavery while demanding that the institution be favored.

In the end, the 1789 tariff was moderately protectionist. Fitzsimons won protection for most of the items he introduced, from cheese, candles, and soap to cordage, shoes, coal, clothing, and carriages. In the typical fashion of tariff politics, New England was paid off with duties on imported fish and preferences for American shipping, and the South was paid off with generally lower "revenue" duties on liquor, sugar, and the like. If a fifty cent tax on imported boots may have been prohibitive, most protected goods were rated at 7.5 and 10 percent ad valorem.[66] The Philadelphia artisans were winners in the details of this tax and the creditors of the United States were winners in that there now finally was a tax to fund interest on the U.S. debt. Consumers in Connecticut, Delaware, New Jersey, and the still unrepresented North Carolina (which would not ratify the Constitution until November) were winners in that they no longer had to pay the state-level taxes of their neighbors. Yet this policy victory had a price. A detailed tax bill inevitably provoked debate about the economic impact of its provisions. Once congressmen decided to talk about the economy, they could not avoid talking about slavery.

Tariff politics never again resembled the unanimous adoption of an unanalyzed impost by a Congress that considered it a panacea, as had been the case under the Articles of Confederation. Protectionism politicized import taxation, generating the articulation of competing economic analyses in which slavery necessarily became one of the relevant variables. Nevertheless, import taxes retained an advantage over other taxes in this regard. Nobody ever knew exactly who paid the tariff. The question of what assumptions to use in estimating its final incidence (particularly what kinds of market conditions favored or thwarted shifting by importers and price hikes by manufacturers) kept economists busy into the twentieth century. This uncertainty favored the tariff. Although the tariff never reaped the full political advantages of the impost, congressmen knew they would face more divisive debates if they considered a tax with a more transparent incidence. Advocates of the 1789 tariff constantly raised the specter of debates about a "direct tax." If this bill failed, they warned, Congress would have to discuss the "direct" alternatives that everyone understood to be dynamite (and that are the subject of the next chapter).

The long-term dominance of the tariff in the federal revenue system can be explained by stressing the advantages that made the impost attractive to the Continental Congress in the first place. The tariff required less administrative capacity than other taxes to collect. Its payment in the first instance by merchants avoided currency problems, insulated most people from contact with federal collectors, and made the tax "invisible" (if not quite "voluntary") to the consumers who ultimately paid it. The politics of the tariff's protectionism would cut both ways. It would create strong and enduring pro-tariff constituencies, but it also would create strong and enduring opposition. The crucial difference between the impost and tariff, however, was that the simplicity of the impost discouraged examinations of its economic incidence. From its introduction in 1781 to its demise in 1786, the impost provoked remarkably little economic analysis of any kind. In the impost, the Continental Congress found a tax it could adopt without exploring the structure of the economy and, therefore, without talking about slavery. The Articles of Confederation made this tax impossible to enact and the Constitution turned it into something else. Yet the impost, which was never levied, is one of the most influential tax policies in American history.

Historians generally have considered the impost a strategy to "centralize" the American government. Taking their cues from its opponents, they have missed the problem that the impost was intended to solve. The impost could be levied without apportionments. It could be levied without considering slavery. The impost was aimed at precisely the problem that the real estate apportionment might have solved if it had been at all practical. But the United States could not perform a national real estate valuation in the revolutionary era. Hardly anyone thought it could, though the truly remarkable thing is how few of the "founding fathers" bothered to think about the real estate scheme until 1783, when they had to junk it. John Witherspoon had offered a plan to get the Articles through a Congress unable to compromise about slavery in 1776, even if that plan only pretended to be a way to allocate "charges of war." A Congress that could compromise about slavery in 1783 added the three-fifths ratio to the repertoire of American politics, although the states rejected that effort to apportion by population. The impost solved the problem of how to tax without any apportionments. It solved the problem of how to allocate national tax burdens without talking about slavery. Its legacy was the tariff.

5   Direct Taxes

The adoption of the Constitution solved the core tax problem of the national government under the Articles of Confederation. Where the Congress under the Articles could not tax at all except through requisitions—asking the state legislatures to tax and deliver the proceeds—the Congress under the Constitution could rely on the impost (tariff). There were fiscal crises under the Constitution, particularly before 1815 when wars disrupted foreign trade seriously enough to undermine tariff receipts, but the new government never suffered from the abject dependence ("imbecility") of its predecessor. The tariff was usually a reliable revenue engine. Its proceeds cut the national debt from $83 million in 1801 to $45 million in 1812. The costs of the War of 1812 increased the debt to $127 million in 1816, but lucrative tariffs on a thriving international commerce enabled the United States to pay it off altogether in 1835. From 1817 to 1861, the tariff was the *only* federal tax.[1]

This fiscal triumph fulfilled the intentions of the framers of the Constitution. Although the men who wrote the Constitution in the summer of 1787 did not expect the impost to turn into a protective tariff, they did intend to use taxes on imported goods to finance the new government. After the six-year struggle to amend article 8 to grant Congress the impost, the framers thought they knew the solution to the problem of public finance in the United States. They placed their trust in the impost not only because they thought it would be lucrative and easy to collect (from a few merchants at the ports rather than individual taxpayers scattered across the country), but also because they thought they had learned a political lesson in earlier tax debates: that imposts, with their uncertain ultimate incidence, could minimize the dangers of distributing tax burdens across a nation that was half slave and half free.

Yet the Constitution also introduced a new apportionment problem, which is still part of the document. In two clauses, the three-fifths clause and the direct tax clause, the Constitution requires that "direct taxes" be apportioned to the states by population.[2] Today, these taxes must be apportioned to the states by total population. Originally, however, they had to be apportioned by "population" as that term was defined in the three-fifths clause: "adding to the whole number of free persons, including those bound to service for a term of years, and excluding Indians not taxed, three-fifths of all other persons." Unlike the real estate apportionment of the Articles of Confederation, which could never be implemented at all, the direct tax provision of the Constitution proved usable in emergency situations. It actually was implemented four times: once in 1798, twice during the War of 1812, and once during the Civil War. This reservation of "direct taxes" for emergencies also fulfilled the framers' intentions. It was the flip side of their plan to rely on the impost in normal conditions. The apportionment rule was intended to preempt future debates about how to apportion these taxes. Like the real estate apportionment of the Articles—and like the impost itself—it was intended to prevent the tax debates that would politicize slavery.

The framers gave little thought to how apportioned "direct taxes" would work in practice. Some imagined that these levies would be requisitions, with each state framing its own taxes and collecting them independently, presumably using its existing state tax system. Others imagined that they would be national taxes on land, slaves, or property generally, which Congress would design and the federal government would collect. Congress ultimately managed to compromise these visions. The direct taxes of 1798, 1813, and 1815 were national taxes on land, houses, and slaves; the 1861 tax was a national tax on real estate. The 1798 tax invited no state participation, but the other three offered states 15 percent discounts if they treated the taxes as requisitions by "assuming" their quotas. Seven states (of eighteen) assumed the 1813 tax and four assumed the 1815 tax. The policy worked better during the Civil War. Every jurisdiction except the state of Delaware, the territory of Colorado, and the states that identified themselves as the Confederate States of America assumed their quotas of the 1861 direct tax.[3]

The real problems with the apportionment of direct taxes lay elsewhere. First, it was and remains an almost laughably unfair way to distribute the tax burden. To levy an apportioned tax, Congress must fix a population-based quota for every state and then levy the separate tax rates in each state that will raise these quotaed sums (or allow the states to "assume" the quotas). Table 1 illustrates the results of this procedure by imagining that Congress levied the federal income tax as an apportioned direct tax today. The table shows the

Table 1: The Federal Income Tax as an Apportioned Direct Tax Today

	Personal Income per Capita 2001	Resident Population April 1, 2000	State Quotas of $1 Trillion Tax	Average Tax Rate (percent)
TEN RICHEST STATES				
Connecticut	38,732	3,405,565	12,101,278,996	9.2
Massachusetts	35,512	6,349,097	22,560,777,483	10.0
New Jersey	35,149	8,414,350	29,899,413,729	10.1
New York	32,876	18,976,457	67,430,632,070	10.8
Maryland	32,118	5,296,486	18,820,446,764	11.1
New Hampshire	31,159	1,235,786	4,391,221,769	11.4
Colorado	30,549	4,301,261	15,284,030,519	11.6
Minnesota	30,213	4,919,479	17,480,796,253	11.8
Illinois	30,141	12,419,293	44,130,512,711	11.8
California	29,848	33,871,648	120,358,960,258	11.9
TEN POOREST STATES				
South Carolina	22,714	4,012,012	14,256,217,851	15.6
Idaho	22,473	1,293,953	4,597,911,436	15.8
Alabama	22,443	4,447,100	15,802,252,437	15.8
Louisiana	22,394	4,468,976	15,879,986,258	15.9
Utah	22,070	2,233,169	7,935,306,216	16.1
Montana	21,872	902,195	3,205,844,964	16.2
New Mexico	21,135	1,819,046	6,463,768,318	16.8
Arkansas	20,890	2,673,400	9,499,615,854	17.0
West Virginia	20,884	1,808,344	6,425,740,006	17.0
Mississippi	19,852	2,844,658	10,108,161,232	17.9
UNITED STATES	27,813	281,421,906	1,000,000,000,000	12.8

NOTE: The tax rates in the last column are the average for every person in a state, including people who earn income and pay income tax, but also including people (such as children) who do not.

SOURCE: U.S. Census Bureau, "Uncle Sam's Reference Shelf: State Rankings from the Statistical Abstract of the United States," http://www.census.gov/statab/www/ranks.html.

effects on twenty states, the ten richest and ten poorest, with "rich" and "poor" measured by per capita income. In 2002, the income tax on individuals raised slightly more than $1 trillion. The third column of the table fixes the state quotas for this $1 trillion and the fourth column sets the average tax rates to raise these quotaed sums. The result is ludicrous. If Congress levied the income tax as an apportioned direct tax, the rates would be lower in rich states and higher in poor states. Residents of Connecticut, with the highest incomes in the nation, would pay an average of 9.2 percent of their incomes; residents of Mississippi, with the lowest incomes in the nation, would pay 17.9 percent. Nobody (except perhaps the residents of Connecticut) would want the federal government to tax in this way—which is the principal reason it has not taxed in this way since 1861.[4]

Another problem is that the Constitution does not define the term "direct tax." Although several of the framers and a handful of the nation's early legislators proposed definitions—and many lawyers, judges, and legal scholars have weighed in over the two centuries since then—the question of whether any particular tax should be defined as a direct tax appears to remain open even today.[5] The Supreme Court has spoken to the issue twice. The first case was bizarre. In *Hylton v. U.S.* (1796), the parties stipulated to fictitious "facts" and the U.S. government paid both legal teams. The case was concocted to test the claim that a tax on pleasure carriages was a "direct tax." The Court ruled that the carriage tax was not a direct tax because an apportionment would produce absurd results—even more absurd than the income tax example of table 1. If Congress fixed state quotas by population and then taxed the carriages, the tax on the carriages in any particular state would depend on the number of carriages in that state. Table 2 illustrates this outcome by imagining that the carriage tax had been levied as an apportioned direct tax. In Delaware, with the most carriages per person, carriage owners would have paid 73 cents per carriage, while in Georgia, with the fewest carriages per person, they would have paid $5.69 per carriage. Thus, the Court ruled that the carriage tax could not possibly be a "direct tax" under the Constitution: "As all direct taxes must be *apportioned,* it is evident that the Constitution contemplated none as direct but such *as could be apportioned.*" The justices added that only a land tax or a poll tax definitely would count as a direct tax under the Constitution.[6]

The Supreme Court spoke a second time in *Pollock v. Farmers' Loan and Trust Company* (1895), which declared a federal income tax to be unconstitutional because it was a "direct tax" and therefore subject to the apportionment rule. For a century, the *Hylton* ruling had been the authoritative word on the term "direct tax." In a series of cases upholding the constitutionality of the taxes levied to finance the Civil War, the Supreme Court had invoked *Hylton* to quash claims that various levies were direct taxes. In one case, *Springer v. U.S.* (1880), the Court had ruled on an income tax explicitly, citing *Hylton* to affirm that it was not a direct tax. *Pollock,* which was about an income tax that Congress enacted in 1894, overturned the *Springer* decision.[7] Income taxes were "direct taxes" and therefore had to be apportioned by population. The Court was not proposing that income taxes be levied in accordance with table 1. It was saying that because the income tax was a direct tax that could

Table 2: The 1794 Carriage Tax as an Apportioned Direct Tax, 1796

	Population (three-fifths) 1790	Tax Quota (dollars)	Number of Carriages	Carriages per 1,000 (three-fifths)	Tax per Carriage (dollars)
Delaware	55,541	621	847	15.2	0.73
New Jersey	179,570	2,006	2,195	12.2	0.91
Maryland	278,514	3,112	1,942	7.0	1.60
South Carolina	206,235	2,304	1,385	6.7	1.66
Rhode Island	68,729	768	446	6.5	1.72
Massachusetts	475,257	5,310	2,972	6.3	1.79
New York	331,590	3,705	1,811	5.5	2.05
Connecticut	237,037	2,648	1,288	5.4	2.06
Virginia	699,282	7,813	2,663	3.8	2.93
New Hampshire	141,836	1,585	418	2.9	3.79
North Carolina	387,946	4,335	1,100	2.8	3.94
Pennsylvania	432,878	4,837	1,178	2.7	4.11
Georgia	70,842	792	139	2.0	5.69
TOTAL	3,650,668	40,790	18,384	5.0	2.22

NOTE: The Virginia figures include Kentucky, the North Carolina figures include Tennessee, the Massachusetts figures include Maine, and Vermont is excluded entirely. The quotas are computed from the actual yield of the carriage tax in fiscal year 1795–96 ($40,790).

SOURCE: Tench Coxe, "Internal Revenues," February 21, 1798, ASP-F, 1: 565; Seventh Census, 1850, ix.

not be apportioned, the Constitution prohibited Congress from levying it. *Pollock* galvanized the supporters of income taxation, especially westerners and southerners who wanted to reduce their tariff burdens by using the income tax to tap the greater wealth of the Northeast (which also enjoyed most of the subsidies from tariff protection). They finally won the adoption of the Sixteenth Amendment in 1913. Because the amendment exempts income taxes from the apportionment rule without removing the rule from the Constitution, other taxes can still run afoul of it if the Supreme Court decides to construe them as "direct taxes."[8]

Slavery and the three-fifths rule were significant historical footnotes in the debates about *Pollock* and the Sixteenth Amendment. In the early republic, however, they lay at the heart of all discussions about apportioned direct taxes. From the 1787 Philadelphia convention through the ratification debates, the *Hylton* case, and the congressional maneuvering that produced the direct taxes of 1798 and 1813, efforts to define and levy apportioned direct taxes were always about the tax implications of slavery. It could not have been otherwise. The apportionment rule *was* a rule about slavery ("the whole number of free persons" plus "three-fifths of all other persons"), and most glosses on the term "direct taxes" assumed that it applied to slave taxes. Laws that imposed direct taxes also required a third accommodation to slavery. The apportionment rule addressed the distribution of burdens between states, but direct taxes also distributed burdens *within* states, including between slaveholders and nonslaveholders in the southern states. The politics of direct taxation under the apportionment rule turned out to be much more complicated than anyone had realized when the Philadelphia convention placed the rule into the Constitution in 1787. Nobody grasped its full implications until Congress framed an actual direct tax in the late 1790s.

Philadelphia

The story of how the Philadelphia convention came to insert the apportionment rule into the Constitution has been told many times. It is the story of the origin of the three-fifths clause.[9] In February 1787, Congress authorized a convention to gather in Philadelphia "for the sole and express purpose of revising the Articles of Confederation." Delegates from every state except a suspicious Rhode Island met in late May and, within a week, decided to replace the Articles with an entirely new frame of government. The stumbling block was representation. Delegates from large states (Virginia, Massachusetts, Pennsylvania) wanted to apportion the new Congress by population, delegates from small states (New Jersey, Delaware, Connecticut) wanted to keep the one-state-one-vote system of the Articles, and everyone understood that a population rule would require a decision about whether and how to count slaves. On June 30, James Madison, who was promoting Virginia's large-state interest in an apportioned Congress, insisted that the convention should not even be talking about whether to apportion. The small-state argument depended on a false premise about American politics. "[T]he States were divided into different interests not by their difference of size, but of other circumstances; the most material of which resulted partly from climate, but principally from the effects of their having or not having slaves." In fact, "the great division of interests in the U. States . . . did not lie between the large & small States: it lay between the Northern and Southern."[10]

The idea that taxation might be relevant for apportioning Congress was part of this debate from the beginning. The Virginia Plan, which was introduced at the start of the convention and which framed much of the ensuing debate, said nothing about how the new government should tax. Its representation clause, however, assumed that the requisition system of the Articles would persist into the new regime. "[T]he rights of suffrage in the National Legislature," it suggested, "ought to be proportioned to the Quotas of contribution, or to the number of free inhabitants, as the one or the other rule may seem best in different cases [in the two branches of Congress that the plan also proposed]."[11] Presumably, these "Quotas of contribution" would rest on population, which could be counted using the 1775 rule ("the number of Inhabitants, of all ages, including negroes and mulattoes") but was more likely to be counted using the 1783 rule ("the whole number of white and other free citizens and inhabitants, of every age, sex and condition . . . and three-fifths of all other persons"). Only one thing was certain. These tax quotas would not depend on a national valuation of real estate.

The idea of using tax quotas to apportion representation conflicted with another important idea—that the new government would rely on the impost. The political advantage of the impost had always been that it could not be apportioned at all. Nobody could know how much revenue the ports of each state would raise, much less how the tax would be shifted through the economy as merchants sold the taxed goods to consumers. Rufus King (Massachusetts) made this point as soon as the Virginia Plan was presented. Representation could not be apportioned by tax quotas, since "the revenue might hereafter be so collected by the general Govt. that the sums respectively drawn from the States would not appear; and would besides be continually varying." If Congress relied on the impost, there would be no tax quotas to use for representation. Madison, who had just tried to remove "free inhabitants" on the grounds that a discussion of slavery would "divert" the convention "from the general question" of whether to apportion the new Congress at all, now endorsed King's critique of the tax quota alternative.[12]

Over the course of the convention, some delegates connected taxation and representation on a theoretical basis. Since "money was power," Pierce Butler (South Carolina) argued, "the States ought to have weight in the Govt.—in proportion to their wealth." Gouverneur Morris (Pennsylvania) agreed. "Life and liberty were generally said to be of more value, than property," but "property was the main object of Society." Wealth therefore "ought to be one measure of the influence due to those who were to be affected by the Governmt." Taxation offered an obvious way to measure wealth. Several of the state constitutions "represented" wealth by using tax data in legislative apportionments, favoring richer districts such as Boston in Massachusetts and the lowcountry parishes in South Carolina (whose wealth included their massive slave populations). Butler clearly hoped that a representation-by-wealth model would benefit his rich little state. Morris's intentions are less apparent. But other delegates rejected the whole idea of the representation of wealth. James Wilson

(Pennsylvania) "could not agree that property was the sole or the primary object of Governt. & Society. The cultivation & improvement of the human mind was the most noble object." Since governments were supposed to protect "*personal* rights" as well as property rights, population was "surely the natural & precise measure of Representation."[13]

The elitist claims of Butler and Morris aside, the issue was not whether the Constitution should "represent" property. It was how to count slaves when the population was counted, given that the institution of slavery treated enslaved people as property. Once the delegates agreed to the compromise that settled the fight between the large and small states—one house apportioned by population, one giving every state the same vote—they turned to the problem of how to count the population to apportion what would become the House of Representatives. The compromise measure had proposed the three-fifths ratio from the 1783 tax debate. The predictable argument about slavery ensued. In 1776 and 1783, when the subject was taxes, northerners had wanted to count all of the slaves, while southerners had wanted to count none of the slaves. Changing the subject to representation reversed these positions, especially obviously to veterans of the earlier rounds. Ten of the delegates had participated in the 1783 debate, including Madison, Hamilton, Wilson, Rutledge (South Carolina), and Williamson (North Carolina). A few others, including Wilson, Benjamin Franklin, Elbridge Gerry (Massachusetts), and Roger Sherman (Connecticut), had participated in the 1776 debate over the Articles.[14]

The result was a deadlock. Southerners demanded the "security" they would gain from additional seats in Congress. Charles Pinckney (South Carolina) merged the defense of slavery with the defense of property generally: the South should be granted extra representation so "that property in slaves should not be exposed to danger under a Govt. instituted for the protection of property." Using a southern rhetorical strategy dating from 1776, Edmund Randolph (Virginia) conceded the moral point to insist on this political point. "He lamented that such a species of property existed. But as it did exist the holders of it would require this security." Northerners, meanwhile, emphasized the logical anomaly of three-fifths representation. Wilson made this point the same way others did. "Are they [slaves] admitted as Citizens? Then why are they not admitted on an equality with White Citizens? Are they admitted as property? then why is not other property admitted into the computation?" But Wilson also spoke as a veteran of 1776 and 1783. "These were difficulties however which he thought must be overruled by the necessity of compromise."[15]

So far, nobody had mentioned "direct taxes." Nobody had said much about taxes at all. According to Madison, "it seemed to be understood on all hands [that taxes] would be principally levied on imports and exports," that the new government would rely on the impost. Gouverneur Morris made the critical move the next day. To break the deadlock over how to count slaves in apportioning the House of Representatives, Morris proposed "that taxation shall be in proportion to Representation." When George Mason (Virginia) pointed out that this language could render the impost unconstitutional ("It might drive the Legislature to the plan of Requisitions"), Morris modified his motion "by restraining the rule to *direct* taxation." Now, it would not affect the impost. "With regard to indirect taxes on *exports* & imports & on consumption, the rule would be inapplicable." Wilson located the virtue of Morris's formula in a hope that it could obscure the meaning of three-fifths representation. By adopting it, the delegates could pretend that they were not doing what they actually were doing: "representing" slaves in order to ensure that *their* interests (in the abolition of slavery) would never prevail. He "observed that less umbrage would perhaps be taken agst. an admission of the slaves into the Rule of representation, if it should be so expressed as to make them indirectly only an ingredient in the rule, by saying that they should enter into the rule of taxation: and as representation was to be according to taxation, the end would be equally attained."[16]

Pinckney issued another demand to count all of the slaves ("The blacks are the labourers, the peasants of the Southern States: they are as productive of pecuniary resources as those of the Northern States"), and Butler defended the southerners' position by charging that northerners were abolitionists ("The security the Southn. States want is that their negroes may not be taken from them which some gentlemen within or without doors, have a very good mind to do"). But Morris had broken the deadlock. By inserting the reference to taxation into the apportionment rule, he had enabled the convention to reach an agreement. Madison savored the new political logic of the fraction he had devised in 1783. "He liked the present motion, because it tended to moderate the views both of the opponents & advocates for rating very high, the negroes." Four days later, the convention adopted the three-fifths rule to apportion both representation and "direct Taxation." The crucial bargains on representation had been struck. Congress would consist of two houses, the Senate granting each state the same vote and the House apportioned by the three-fifths rule.[17]

But what kind of bargain was the insertion of "direct taxes" into the three-fifths clause? Among its perplexing characteristics was the fact that it did *not* make the apportionment of the House of Representatives depend on taxation. It made the apportionment of certain ("direct") taxes depend on the composition of the House of Representatives. Even though nobody knew exactly which taxes would count as "direct," nobody expected Congress to levy these taxes on a regular basis. Everyone expected Congress to depend on the impost most of the time. The link between taxation and representation in the three-fifths clause reversed the logic of the Virginia Plan, with its "Quotas of contribution," as well as the claims for the representation of "property." Rather than using taxes to determine representation, the three-fifths clause used representation to determine taxation—but only when Congress levied "direct taxes." As some delegates started to notice the difference, they began to doubt that the apportionment of direct taxes was a good idea. Morris seemed to think he could just edit it out once it had helped the convention to agree on the representation issue: "He had only meant it as a bridge to assist us over a certain gulph; having passed the gulph the bridge may be removed."[18]

Introducing the term "direct taxes" into the three-fifths clause also had another impact on the debates. It raised the prospect of the new Congress taxing property. Some delegates already had considered the idea that the impost might not always raise enough money. The New Jersey Plan, whose main feature was one-state-one-vote representation, proposed what Congress had proposed to the states in 1783: the impost supplemented by requisitions, with the requisitions apportioned to the states by the three-fifths rule. But the three-fifths clause suggested something else: that *Congress* might levy these supplementary taxes. Delegates began to think about what this could mean when they turned to the powers of Congress. When Roger Sherman proposed a description of these powers that did not mention "direct taxation," Morris criticized the omission for implying that "for the deficiencies of taxes on consumption . . . the Genl. Govt. should recur on quotas & requisitions, which are subversive of the idea of Govt." Morris, who had worked for Robert Morris (no relation) during the war, had written at least one of the reports that urged Congress to levy land taxes, poll taxes, and liquor excises—the taxes Congress rejected in 1783. Now, Morris was trying to grant the new Congress a tax power that would make it stronger than many other delegates were ready to make it. He was using taxation to test their commitment to a powerful national government. Sherman rejected the bait. "Some provision he supposed must be made for supplying the deficiency of other taxation, but he had not formed any."[19]

On July 26, the convention adjourned for ten days while its "committee of detail" wrote a full draft of the Constitution. As Jack Rakove notes, the committee's primary innovation was to enumerate—rather than describe—the things Congress could and could not do.[20] The tax power headed the first list: Congress "shall have the power to lay and collect taxes, duties, imposts, and excises." The second list concentrated on limiting the tax power, though it also banned titles of nobility. It applied the three-fifths rule to "proportions of direct taxation," barred Congress from taxing exports, barred Congress from either taxing or banning the slave trade ("the migration or importation of such persons as the several States shall think proper to admit"), and required that supermajorities ("two thirds of the members present in each House") consent to any regulation of foreign trade ("navigation act"). It also placed a new restraint on the tax power, one that clearly followed from southern fears about what could happen if Congress (rather than the states) levied the taxes that met impost deficiencies: "No capitation tax shall be laid, unless in proportion to the Census hereinbefore directed to be taken." This clause reinforced the use of the three-fifths rule for "direct taxation." Congress could not levy any tax "by the poll" unless it reduced the burden in the South by the three-fifths rule. For unknown reasons, the committee missed the core of the three-fifths compromise, its apportionment of the House of Representatives. When the delegates reconvened, they fixed that problem immediately. But three-fifths representation *plus* the new limits on congressional power yielded a draft that was extremely pro-South and proslavery.[21]

The first problem was the combination of three-fifths representation with unlimited slave importations. Rufus King "never could agree to let them be imported without limitation & then be represented in the Natl. Legislature." Gouverneur Morris went further:

> The admission of slaves into the Representation when fairly explained comes to this: that the inhabitant of Georgia and S. C. who goes to the Coast of Africa, and in defiance of the most sacred laws of humanity tears away his fellow creatures from their dearest connections & damns them to the most cruel bondages, shall have more votes in a Govt. instituted for protection of the rights of mankind [a shift from Morris's earlier claim that governments exist to protect "property"], than the Citizen of Pa or N. Jersey who views with a laudable horror, so nefarious a practice.[22]

Morris then turned to the tax provisions. Banning export taxes to restrict the impost to imported goods not only would deprive Congress of revenue, but would force northerners to pay most of the taxes. Morris explained this point with the old underconsumption analysis of how slaveholders profited from slavery. Consumption taxes "will fall heavier" on the North because slaveholders denied slaves most of the goods on which Congress would levy its "taxes, duties, imposts, and excises." In an import tax, "the bohea tea used by a Northern freeman, will pay more tax than the whole consumption of the miserable slave, which consists of nothing more than his physical subsistence and the rag that covers his nakedness." Congress could even the score only by taxing the South's staple crops, by levying something like Virginia's traditional tax on exported tobacco. Morris, for his part, "would sooner submit himself to a tax for paying for all the Negroes in the U. States. [in order to abolish slavery] than saddle posterity with such a Constitution."[23]

But what about the power to levy "direct taxes"? Morris, who had baited Sherman on the need for this power, now predicted that Congress would not use it, dismissing the significance of the compromise he had brokered. "Let it not be said that direct taxation is to be proportioned to representation. It is idle to suppose that the Genl Govt. can stretch its hand directly into the pockets of the people scattered over so vast a Country." In reality, Congress would be able to tax only "through the medium of exports imports & excises." The convention did not return to this issue for two more weeks. Even by then, few delegates had thought it through. Some expected "direct taxes" to be requisitions. Luther Martin (Maryland) expressed this idea: "Direct taxation should not be used but in cases of absolute necessity; and then the States will be best Judges of the mode." It actually was not clear either what "direct taxes" were or who would levy them. Among tax scholars, the most famous passage in the records of the convention is the one where Rufus King "asked what was the precise meaning of *direct* taxation? No one answd."[24]

Despite his generally erratic behavior at the convention, Gouverneur Morris offered fairly consistent answers to King's question. Direct taxes were not taxes "on *exports* & imports & on consumption." Like the poll and property taxes of the states, they stretched a government's hand "directly into the pockets of the people." Direct taxes were hard to levy and harder to pay, which was exactly why Congress would avoid them. The states had never been able to collect them in sufficient amounts to meet their requisitions; Shays's Rebellion (1786) only dramatized what was already an old problem. Whether Congress or the states levied these taxes was immaterial to the reason why imposts were better. Direct taxes required lump-sum payments and universal access to currency. Imposts were fronted by merchants who had access to currency and shifted through the economy in all kinds of cash and credit transactions. "For a long time," as Morris explained, "the people of America will not have money to pay direct taxes. Seize and sell their effects and you push them into Revolts."[25]

In mid-September, as the convention ran through its final draft, delegates made two more attempts to change the "direct tax" provisions. One failed, the other succeeded. The failure was an effort by John Dickinson (Delaware) and James Wilson to remove the apportionment of direct taxes from the three-fifths clause. The words "and direct taxes," they argued, were "improperly placed in a clause relating merely to the Constitution of the House of Representatives." Morris, who had suggested this change earlier ("having passed the gulph the bridge may be removed"), now defended the inclusion of direct taxes with the same argument Wilson made initially. The point was to divert attention. Direct taxes should remain in the clause "in order to exclude the appearance of counting the Negroes in *the Representation*—The including of them may now be referred to the object of direct taxes, and incidentally only to that of Representation."[26]

The success, the next day, turned the capitation clause framed by the committee of detail into the direct tax clause of the Constitution. The draft clause read "No capitation tax shall be laid . . ." George Read (Delaware) now moved to insert the words "or other direct tax" after the word "capitation." Read was thinking about the final settlement of state accounts for the cost of the Revolutionary War. The requisitions of Congress all included a proviso that these accounts would be settled by the rule specified in the Articles of Confederation, whatever that rule turned out to be. Now that there would be no Articles of Confederation, Read worried that the accounts might be settled using the rule Congress had used to make the requisitions, the 1775 guess at the total population. Read "was afraid that some liberty might . . . be taken to saddle the States with a readjustment by this rule, of past Requisitions of Congs—and that his amendment by giving another cast to the meaning would take away the pretext."[27] Now, the slaves who comprised 15 percent of the population of Delaware (in 1790) would be counted by the three-fifths rule in the settlement. Read's concern about the settlement was trivial (the Constitution already gave the slave states enough power to defend their interests in that), but his objective was significant: to grant the South yet another form of constitutional "protection."

Ultimately, the apportionment of direct taxes appeared in the Constitution twice, in the three-fifths clause ("Representatives and direct taxes shall be apportioned . . .") and the direct tax clause ("No capitation, or other direct, tax shall be laid, unless in proportion to the census or enumeration herein before directed to be taken"). The amendment clause made a third reference to it. Like the slave trade clause, the direct tax clause could not be amended until 1808. The tax power, meanwhile, was hedged slightly from its original draft. Congress can "lay and collect taxes, duties, imposts, and excises" as long as they are "uniform throughout the United States" (the same everywhere in the country). The impost was restricted to imports by the prohibition of export taxes and protected against state encroachments in a clause barring the states from taxing foreign trade "except what may be absolutely necessary" to administer their "inspection laws." Finally, in the slave trade clause, the Constitution allowed Congress to levy the tax of up to $10 on imported slaves.[28] Anyone who thinks of governments as profit-maximizing entities, bound to exploit every form of taxation that is not expressly forbidden in a constitution, would do well to remember that Congress never levied this tax.

The export tax ban turned out to be a reasonable trade-off for dropping the supermajority rule for a "navigation act." Madison, who came from a state that had relied on its tobacco export tax for most of its colonial history, endorsed export taxation as "proper in itself" and as a task of the national government. The states could not be allowed to raise their own revenue in this way because the ports of some states exported the crops of other states. Morris's argument that export taxes were necessary to balance the sectional impact of consumption taxes ("the bohea tea used by a Northern freeman" versus "the whole consumption of the miserable slave") was on target as well. What Madison and Morris did not foresee (what nobody seems to have foreseen) was that the impost would become a protective tariff.[29] If the Constitution had required supermajorities to regulate foreign trade, this outcome might have been different. The impost might have remained the tax that Congress had designed in 1783: one ad valorem rate on most goods plus higher rates on drinks and spices. It might have remained a consumption tax rather than both a consumption tax and a subsidy for manufacturing. The industrial Northeast would enjoy the last laugh on the constrained federal tax power in the late nineteenth century. If the Constitution had required the supermajorities, however, the North probably would have borne most of the tax burden.

But, more generally, southerners had won most of what they demanded again. When the committee of detail was appointed, General Charles Pinckney insisted that it incorporate explicit protections for slavery into its draft. (In an aristocratic version of family values, South Carolina had sent two Charles Pinckneys to Philadelphia.) The general "reminded the Convention that if the Committee should fail to insert some security to the Southern States agst. an emancipation of slaves, and taxes on exports, he shd. be bound by duty to his State to vote agst. their Report."[30] The committee returned with unlimited slave importations, the export tax ban, the "navigation act" supermajorities, and the three-fifths rule for a "capitation tax." Although nobody explained the reasoning behind the capitation clause at the convention, its intention was clear enough. If Congress levied a national poll tax (like Virginia's colonial poll tax on "tithables"), the tax would have to be reduced in the South by an apportionment using the three-fifths rule. More important, Congress could not levy a flat-rate ("by the poll") national slave tax that would fall mainly on the South. More important still, Congress could not levy this tax at a very high rate. The purpose of a tax of $1 per slave would be to draw revenue from southern slaveholders. The purpose of a tax of $100 per slave would be to abolish slavery in the United States.

During the 1783 tax debate, the northern members of Congress had kept their cool. They had preserved amicable relations with their southern colleagues by avoiding the direct criticism of slavery that had been explosive in 1776. They had not even attacked the idea that somebody could be "principled agst. slavery" while he demanded a proslavery tax break (since slaves were "an incumbrance to Society instead of increasing its ability to pay taxes"). The 1787 convention went less smoothly. The text from the committee of detail was too pro-South and proslavery to be swallowed in silence. Morris took the lead, contrasting the "prosperity & happiness" of the middle states against "the misery & poverty which overspread the barren wastes of Va. Maryd. & the other States having slaves." Yet even the normally cautious Oliver Ellsworth (Connecticut) lost his temper when a Virginian blamed slavery on New Englanders. During the debate about banning the slave trade, which Virginians favored, George Mason elaborated Thomas Jefferson's complaint in *Notes on the State of Virginia* (1785) that slavery victimized slaveholders through its "pernicious effects on manners" ("Every master of slaves is born a petty tyrant"). In Mason's version, however, the Virginia tyrants were victimized by New England merchants, whose "lust of gain" sustained the slave trade. Ellsworth did not bother with the economic fallacy of Mason's charge—that somebody had to be buying the slaves. He went right for the Virginia pretension to moral superiority. Where Morris struck a glancing blow with his economic argument, Ellsworth hit the real mark precisely. "As he had never owned a slave [he] could not judge of the effects of slavery on character," but "if it was to be considered in a moral light we ought to go farther and free those already in the Country."[31]

There it was, and from an unlikely source. Like Roger Sherman, also from Connecticut, Ellsworth was a compromiser par excellence, willing to trade the freedom of African Americans in a heartbeat to win an advantage for his constituents.[32] The South Carolina delegates jumped to the defense of slavery. Charles Pinckney "cited the case of Greece Rome & other antient States" and "the sanction" of the European "modern States." General Charles Pinckney added that "S. Carolina & Georgia cannot do without slaves," that slave importations also would benefit New England ("The more slaves, the more produce to employ the carrying trade"), and that the Virginia opposition was hypocrisy. "As to Virginia she will gain by stopping the importations. Her slaves will rise in value, & she has more than she wants." But Ellsworth was not talking to the South Carolinians. Nor was Morris, whose "barren wastes" featured Virginia and Maryland. Ellsworth and Morris were talking to the Virginians. They were talking to the delegates of the largest state and the one with the most slaves and slaveholders. They were talking to Edmund Randolph, who "lamented that such a species of property existed" but believed that, "as it did exist," slave states should gain extra representation. They were talking to George Mason, who attacked the "evil of having slaves" but opposed anything that might threaten slavery. And, of course, they were talking to James Madison, who knew perfectly well that "the great division of interests in the U. States" did not arise from how anyone talked about slavery, but "principally from the effects of their having or not having slaves."[33]

Today, the most famous quotations from the Philadelphia debates come from the northern attacks on three-fifths representation. They sound like defenses of slavery and clearly are hurtful descriptions of African Americans. William Paterson (New Jersey): "He could regard negroes [*sic*] slaves in no light but as property. They are no[t] free agents, have no personal liberty, no faculty of acquiring property, but on the contrary are themselves property, & like other property entirely at the will of the Master." Elbridge Gerry (Massachusetts): "Why then shd. the blacks, who were property in the South, be in the rule of representation more than the cattle & horses of the North."[34] But we must remember that this debate referred back to older ones. Gerry was there in 1776, when Samuel Chase (Maryland) asserted "that Negroes in fact should not be considered as members of the state more than cattle & that they have no more interest in it." He had listened to Thomas Lynch (South Carolina): "Our Slaves being our Property, why should they be taxed more than the Land, Sheep, Cattle, Horses, &c." The comparison of slaves to livestock did not originate in 1787, in a representation debate, or in northern voices. It was the southern case for low tax quotas in 1776. We might wish that Paterson and Gerry had avoided this language, but they were not saying that African Americans should be property or resembled livestock. They were pointing to the hypocrisy of the slaveholders.

The apportionment of direct taxes entered the Constitution as a byproduct of the debate about how to count slaves in the apportionment of representation. As "a bridge to assist us over a certain gulph," it served its purpose. Now, however, the significant question shifted from how it would affect the debates of the Philadelphia convention to how it would affect the government under the Constitution. Now, somebody had to figure out what it meant. Gouverneur Morris's remarks in the debates fell far short of a legally adequate definition of the term "direct tax." Nor would anyone have access to them until the publication of Madison's notes of the debates in the 1830s. The term "direct tax" was only part of the problem. The meaning of "apportionment" in this context was not obvious either. The apportionment of direct taxes clearly imposed a limit on the federal tax power. It clearly placed an obstacle in the path of a national direct tax. The open questions were how powerful a limit, what kind of an obstacle, and who would benefit from the fact that the Constitution contained such a rule.

Ratification

The struggle over the ratification of the Constitution made the first interpretive pass at the apportionment of direct taxes. Federalists (pro-ratification) and Antifederalists (anti-ratification) clashed in pamphlets, essays, street demonstrations, and several riots, but especially in the series of state conventions that actually decided whether to ratify the Constitution. Except in Virginia, Federalists and Antifederalists devoted little attention to the apportionment of direct taxes. Even in Virginia, they missed its principal implications. The delegates at Philadelphia may have had a reasonable excuse for failing to think through the apportionment of direct taxes. They assumed that the new government would rely on the impost. But the ratification struggle proceeded from a different assumption: that Congress would exercise every power the Constitution conferred *and* every power it did not withhold explicitly. Everyone seemed to agree that Congress would enjoy an "unlimited" tax power. Federalists thought this was good, since it rescued the United States from the "imbecility" of the Articles of Confederation. Antifederalists thought it was bad, since it granted financial autonomy to the Leviathan that would swallow the states, destroy individual liberty, and institute monarchy and/or aristocracy in the United States. Southern Antifederalists also worried that this unlimited tax power posed a threat to slavery. Nobody seemed to realize that apportioned direct taxes would be very difficult for Congress to levy.[35]

The ratification struggle followed from one of the major innovations of the Philadelphia convention—one of its major usurpations of power in the Antifederalist view, comparable to its initial decision to disregard its instructions (to revise the Articles) by framing a completely new government. In one terse sentence, the Constitution established a procedure to launch the new government that dispensed with the existing Congress, the state legislatures, and the unanimity rule that had frustrated earlier efforts to amend the Articles: "The ratification of the conventions of nine States shall be sufficient for the establishment of this Constitution between the States so ratifying the same."[36] The battle to shape public opinion, elect delegates to the state conventions, and then persuade them to endorse or reject the Constitution began the moment the Philadelphia convention released its text to the public. The Philadelphia debates had been kept secret, which itself had aroused widespread suspicion. Several of the Philadelphia delegates, meanwhile, had abandoned the convention in disgust (John Lansing and Robert Yates of New York) or stayed on but refused to sign the Constitution in the end (Elbridge Gerry of Massachusetts, Luther Martin of Maryland, George Mason and Edmund Randolph of Virginia). Randolph ultimately decided to support ratification; the others became leading Antifederalists.

Because they agreed that the tax provisions of the Constitution made the new Congress much more powerful than the Congress under the Articles, Federalists and Antifederalists were all far more impressed by the breadth of the new tax power than by its limits. No aspect of this power was remotely as significant as the fact that it made the new Congress financially independent of the state legislatures. Congress still could decide to ask the states to tax and deliver the proceeds, but it would never be forced to rely on requisitions again. Almost every tax-related argument in the entire ratification struggle focused on this transformation of the American political system. Essayists and debaters might be talking about duties, imposts, and excises or about capitations and other direct taxes, but they usually were talking about this redistribution of power between the states and the national government.[37]

For this reason, everyone drew the same conclusion from the Constitution's references to "direct taxes": that Congress would be able to levy them. A second conclusion followed in turn: that Congress might encroach on the tax bases of the states. As Alexander Hamilton explained in the *Federalist,* the Constitution established a "concurrent jurisdiction" over internal taxes (all taxes except those on foreign trade). Congress and the states could levy similar taxes, much as Congress and the states both levy income taxes today. The outcome for the states, according to Hamilton, would depend on "the prudence and firmness of the people; who, as they will hold the scales in their own hands, it is to be hoped, will always take care to preserve the constitutional equilibrium between the General and the State Governments." To Antifederalists, however, the integrity of the states was much too important to entrust to a hope of "prudence and firmness." They thought Congress was highly likely to preempt the state tax bases and thereby destroy the state governments. "After satisfying their uncontrouled demands," as Patrick Henry phrased this point in Virginia, "what can be left for the States? Not a sufficiency even to defray the expence of their internal administration. They must therefore glide imperceptibly and gradually out of existence." Henry, orator that he was, also said it more dramatically. He would never permit Congress to encroach on the tax base of his state: "I tell you, they shall not have the soul of Virginia."[38]

When Federalists and Antifederalists noticed the apportionment rule, their concern was usually the impact of the three-fifths ratio on their own states. Would an apportionment of direct taxes in this manner favor the northern states because some slaves were counted, or the southern states because some slaves were not counted? Tables 3 and 4 illustrate what was at stake in this argument. Both tables apportion a tax to the states by the three-fifths rule, reporting the average burden *per free person* on the assumption that only free people counted as taxpayers. We might prefer a more sophisticated calculation. We might want to see the average burden per household head, which would be a closer approximation to the average burden per taxpayer and control for variations in family size in the states. The Antifederalist who called himself Cato (and may have been New York Governor George Clinton) hinted at this idea by predicting that the population-based apportionment would encourage Congress to levy a national poll tax, which would oppress poor men because they had many children ("more prolific wives than the rich").[39] But, since we are talking about a hypothetical tax anyway, the simpler calculation will suffice. The point is the difference between the sets of figures. In table 3, the average tax is higher in southern states. In table 4, the average tax is higher in northern states.

The two tables reflect two equally plausible interpretations of the politics of a direct tax apportionment, both of which can be backed with evidence from the Philadelphia debates. The first interpretation (table 3) reflects a "compromise" gloss on the three-fifths clause. Here, the insertion of "direct taxes" into the three-fifths clause was a compromise in which southerners accepted higher taxes in return for extra representation. Madison described the deal in this way when he said he "liked the present motion, because it tended to moderate the views both of the opponents & advocates for rating very high, the negroes." The second interpretation (table 4) reflects a "southern victory" gloss on the direct tax clause. Here, southerners won lower taxes *and* extra representation. This view draws support from the fact that the committee of detail wrote the "capitation tax" clause after General Charles Pinckney insisted that they insert "some security to the Southern States agst. an emancipation of slaves" into their draft.

Unsurprisingly, the positions of Federalists and Antifederalists on which was the correct interpretation of the apportionment rule—whether it is represented more accurately in table 3 or table 4—depended on where they lived. In the North, Federalists who were defending the Constitution presented the "compromise" gloss (lower taxes in the North), while Antifederalists who were attacking the Constitution presented the "southern victory" gloss (lower taxes in the South). A bizarre colloquy in Massachusetts framed the problem as a matter of the productivity of different kinds of people. Speaking for the Federalists, Rufus King asserted that "five Negro children of South-Carolina, are to pay as much tax as the three governours of New-Hampshire, Massachusetts, and Connecticut." Samuel Nasson offered the Antifederalist response.

Table 3: Apportioning a $1 Tax per Capita ("Federal"): "Compromise" Gloss

	1790	1800	1810	1820	1830	1840	1850	1860
NORTHEAST	1.01	1.01	1.00	1.00	1.00	1.00	1.00	1.00
ME	1.00	1.00	1.00	1.00	1.00	1.00	1.00	1.00
NH	1.00	1.00	1.00	1.00	1.00	1.00	1.00	1.00
MA	1.00	1.00	1.00	1.00	1.00	1.00	1.00	1.00
RI	1.01	1.00	1.00	1.00	1.00	1.00	1.00	1.00
CT	1.01	1.00	1.00	1.00	1.00	1.00	1.00	1.00
VT	1.00	1.00	1.00	1.00	1.00	1.00	1.00	1.00
NY	1.04	1.02	1.01	1.00	1.00	1.00	1.00	1.00
NJ	1.04	1.04	1.03	1.02	1.00	1.00	1.00	1.00
PA	1.01	1.00	1.00	1.00	1.00	1.00	1.00	1.00
NORTHWEST		1.01	1.00	1.00	1.00	1.00	1.00	1.00
OH		1.00	1.00	1.00	1.00	1.00	1.00	1.00
IN		1.02	1.01	1.00	1.00	1.00	1.00	1.00
IL			1.01	1.01	1.00	1.00	1.00	1.00
MI			1.00	1.00	1.00	1.00	1.00	1.00
WI						1.00	1.00	1.00
IA						1.00	1.00	1.00
CA							1.00	1.00
KS								1.00
MN								1.00
OR								1.00
UPPER SOUTH	1.19	1.20	1.20	1.18	1.18	1.18	1.17	1.16
DE	1.11	1.06	1.04	1.04	1.03	1.02	1.02	1.01
MD	1.29	1.27	1.25	1.21	1.18	1.14	1.11	1.09
VA	1.39	1.39	1.40	1.40	1.38	1.34	1.30	1.27
NC	1.21	1.23	1.26	1.28	1.30	1.29	1.30	1.30
KY	1.12	1.13	1.15	1.17	1.19	1.18	1.16	1.15
TN	1.06	1.09	1.12	1.14	1.16	1.17	1.19	1.20
MO				1.11	1.13	1.11	1.09	1.06
ARK				1.08	1.11	1.15	1.17	1.21
LOWER SOUTH	1.39	1.39	1.48	1.47	1.53	1.56	1.52	1.54
SC	1.45	1.44	1.54	1.63	1.71	1.73	1.81	1.80
GA	1.33	1.35	1.43	1.47	1.44	1.41	1.44	1.47
MS		1.39	1.44	1.46	1.56	1.65	1.63	1.74
LA			1.50	1.49	1.62	1.55	1.54	1.53
AL				1.29	1.37	1.45	1.48	1.49
FL					1.48	1.54	1.49	1.47
TX							1.23	1.26
TOTAL	1.13	1.12	1.12	1.11	1.11	1.10	1.10	1.09

SOURCE: Calculated from Seventh Census, 1850, ix; Eighth Census, 1860, 598–99.

Table 4: Apportioning a $1 Tax per Capita ("Federal"): "Southern Victory" Gloss

	1790	1800	1810	1820	1830	1840	1850	1860
NORTHEAST	.99	1.00	1.00	1.00	1.00	1.00	1.00	1.00
ME	1.00	1.00	1.00	1.00	1.00	1.00	1.00	1.00
NH	1.00	1.00	1.00	1.00	1.00	1.00	1.00	1.00
MA	1.00	1.00	1.00	1.00	1.00	1.00	1.00	1.00
RI	.99	1.00	1.00	1.00	1.00	1.00	1.00	1.00
CT	1.00	1.00	1.00	1.00	1.00	1.00	1.00	1.00
VT	1.00	1.00	1.00	1.00	1.00	1.00	1.00	1.00
NY	.97	.99	.99	1.00	1.00	1.00	1.00	1.00
NJ	.98	.98	.98	.99	1.00	1.00	1.00	1.00
PA	1.00	1.00	1.00	1.00	1.00	1.00	1.00	1.00
NORTHWEST		.99	1.00	1.00	1.00	1.00	1.00	1.00
OH		1.00	1.00	1.00	1.00	1.00	1.00	1.00
IN		.99	1.00	1.00	1.00	1.00	1.00	1.00
IL			.99	.99	1.00	1.00	1.00	1.00
MI			1.00	1.00	1.00	1.00	1.00	1.00
WI						1.00	1.00	1.00
IA						1.00	1.00	1.00
CA							1.00	1.00
KS								1.00
MN								1.00
OR								1.00
UPPER SOUTH	.91	.91	.90	.91	.91	.91	.92	.92
DE	.94	.96	.98	.98	.98	.99	.99	.99
MD	.87	.88	.88	.89	.91	.92	.94	.95
VA	.84	.84	.84	.84	.84	.86	.87	.88
NC	.90	.89	.88	.87	.87	.87	.87	.87
KY	.94	.93	.92	.91	.90	.91	.91	.92
TN	.96	.95	.93	.92	.92	.91	.90	.90
MO			.94	.94	.93	.94	.95	.96
ARK				.95	.94	.92	.91	.90
LOWER SOUTH	.84	.84	.82	.83	.81	.81	.82	.82
SC	.83	.83	.81	.79	.78	.78	.77	.77
GA	.86	.85	.83	.82	.83	.84	.83	.83
MS		.84	.83	.83	.81	.79	.80	.78
LA			.82	.82	.80	.81	.81	.81
AL				.87	.85	.83	.82	.82
FL					.82	.81	.82	.82
TX							.89	.88
TOTAL	.93	.93	.93	.94	.94	.94	.94	.95

SOURCE: See table 3.

King had neglected "the other side of the question," that "three of our infants in the cradle, are to be rated as high as five of the working negroes of Virginia." In the South, these positions were reversed. Federalists defended the Constitution with the "southern victory" gloss (lower taxes in the South); Antifederalists attacked the Constitution with the "compromise" gloss (lower taxes in the North). Edward Rutledge offered the Federalist version in South Carolina: "All the free people (and there are few others) in the Northern States are to be taxed . . . whereas only the free people, and two fifths [actually, three-fifths] of the slaves, in the Southern States, are to be rated, in the apportioning of taxes." William Goudy responded for the Antifederalists in North Carolina: "I wish not to be represented with negroes, especially if it increases my burdens."[40]

The fact that the "compromise" view of table 3 has a more familiar ring today than the "southern victory" view of table 4 must not be taken as evidence that it was more persuasive in 1788. The notion that every imperfect aspect of the Constitution stems from a "compromise" has been more than two hundred years in the making. In any case, both tables illustrate what actually was a more significant point: that apportioned direct taxes would be very difficult for Congress to levy. Using the 1790 figures in table 3, if a tax that imposed $1.00 per free person in Massachusetts and $1.04 in New York (over 21,000 African Americans were enslaved in New York in 1790) imposed $1.39 in Virginia and $1.45 in South Carolina, how was Congress supposed to assemble majorities in both houses to enact it? If the Constitution's recent adoption lent legitimacy to this distribution in 1790, no such help would be forthcoming in 1850, when the tax imposed $1.00 in northern states but $1.30 in Virginia, $1.48 in Alabama, and $1.81 in South Carolina. Nor do the table 4 figures change this outcome. Even if the 1850 tax imposed $1.00 in northern states but only 87 cents in Virginia, 82 cents in Alabama, and 77 cents in South Carolina, Congress would be able to enact it only in a very grave national emergency.

The problem with tables 3 and 4 as representations of the distribution of an apportioned direct tax is that they assume that the tax at issue is levied on something distributed fairly evenly across the country. King, Nasson, Rutledge, and Goudy were talking about a poll tax, a land tax, or a general tax on "property." But, as several Virginians realized, there actually was no reason to assume that the tax would take one of these forms. The Constitution required that direct taxes be apportioned, but it did not define "direct taxes." The reason Virginians paid unusual attention to the apportionment rule is that Virginia's leading Antifederalist, Patrick Henry, was especially concerned about the Constitution's grant of the tax power. Virginia's tax base may have been its "soul," but Henry was also worried about a prohibitive slave tax that could "compel the Southern States to liberate their negroes." It was "a picture so horrid, so wretched, so dreadful, that I need no longer dwell upon it," but dwell on it he did. At one point, Henry apparently summarized the threat with an appalling clarity. He roared at the convention: "*They'll free your niggers!*"[41]

Every southern convention debated about whether the Constitution would tend to protect or threaten the institution of slavery, with Federalists citing protections and Antifederalists citing threats. Virginia was no different from South Carolina in this sense. But Virginia was different from South Carolina in the sense that Virginia politicians habitually "lamented" the fact that they owned human beings. George Mason presented the full treatment in an Antifederalist argument. Slaves were "far from being a desirable property. But it will involve us in great difficulties and infelicity to be now deprived of them." The Constitution should contain an ironclad protection for slavery, a clause to "prevent the Northern and Eastern [New England] States from meddling with our whole property of that kind . . . which we have acquired under our former laws, and the loss of which would bring ruin on a great many people." Federalists answered that Virginians had nothing to fear. They pointed to three-fifths representation, the slave trade clause, and the fugitive slave clause (slaves who escaped across state lines had to be "delivered up on Claim by the Party" who owned them). Madison insisted that northerners could not touch slavery, since abolition would be a "usurpation of power" under the Constitution. Nor would they even want to touch slavery: "I believe such an idea never entered into any American breast, nor do I believe it ever will." The only people who would *ever* think about abolishing slavery, Madison argued, were hysterical slaveholders "who substitute unsupported suspicions to reasons."[42]

But Patrick Henry was not interested in a clause to prevent the abolition of slavery. Like other Virginians, he acknowledged the immorality of slavery ("we ought to lament and deplore the necessity of holding our fellow-men in bondage") while rejecting abolition ("We ought to possess them in the manner we have inherited them from our ancestors, as their manumission is incompatible with the felicity of the country").[43] Yet Henry was more concerned about taxation than about other threats to slavery. He was concerned about taxation because he understood that Virginians had been playing a dangerous game at the national level. Conceding the moral point to win the political point was a high-risk maneuver. It was one thing to play this game under the Articles of Confederation, when important decisions could be blocked by the veto of a single state legislature. But it would be quite another thing to play it under the Constitution. Even if the Constitution did not really institute majority rule (the Senate, three-fifths representation, state control of the suffrage, the electoral college), it did permit its version of a national majority to make everyday political decisions autonomously. Now, there would be a national tax politics involving much more than the old dickering over state quotas. Now, Congress would actually decide how to distribute the tax burden among particular categories of taxpayers.

The problem, as Henry saw it, was that northerners could not be expected to shrug off the Virginia line on slavery indefinitely. If Madison was right that abolition had "never entered into any American breast" (which he was not), it was only because northerners had not yet been forced to think about slavery very much. Virginians already grasped the full moral implications of slavery. One might even say they wallowed in them, casting themselves as the tragic heroes of a classical drama. Henry thought it was unrealistic to expect northerners to share this vision. They would "have no feeling for your interests" when they thought about slavery and they would use the powers of Congress under the Constitution to abolish it. "Among ten thousand implied powers which they may assume," Henry threatened,

> they may, if we be engaged in war, liberate every one of your slaves if they please. And this must and will be done by men, a majority of whom have not a common interest with you. . . . slavery is detested—we feel its fatal effects—we deplore it with all the pity of humanity. Let all these considerations, at some future period, press with full force on the minds of Congress. Let that urbanity, which I trust will distinguish America, and the necessity of national defence:—Let all these things operate on their minds. They will search that paper [the Constitution], and see if they have power of manumission.

The Constitution would create perennial tax debates in which the evil of slavery would "press" on the minds of northerners. Unlike Virginians, however, northerners would fail to appreciate how "dreadful and ruinous" abolition would be ("I see a great deal of the property of the people of Virginia in jeopardy, and their peace and tranquility gone away") because northerners would lack "ties of sympathy and fellow-feeling for those whose interest would be affected by their [slaves'] emancipation."[44] Never mind that the population with an "interest" in emancipation included people other than slaveholders— that African Americans had a pressing stake in the abolition of slavery. Henry's point was that northerners would not understand. As Virginians kept demanding tax breaks on the grounds that slavery was a lamentable evil that impoverished them, northerners eventually would seize on the truth in this rhetoric. Instead of compensating the Virginia slaveholders for their victimization by slavery, northerners would search for a way to abolish the institution.

Henry also went further. Not only would everyday tax debates impress northerners with the need to abolish slavery, but the tax power would provide them a way to do it. Henry thought northerners searching for a constitutional warrant for abolition would look at the preamble, the statement that the Constitution was intended to "provide for the common defense, promote the general welfare," and so on. He thought they would look at the elastic clause, which authorizes Congress to do anything "necessary and proper for carrying into execution the foregoing powers, and all other powers" of the federal government. Above all, however, Henry thought they would look at the tax power—because nothing in it would "prevent Congress from interfering with that property by laying a grievous and enormous tax on it, so as to compel owners to emancipate their slaves rather than pay the tax."[45]

But was this true? Did the Constitution prevent Congress from levying prohibitive slave taxes or not? Everyone involved in the Virginia debate assumed that the answer to this question hinged on an interpretation of the apportionment rule—that the slave tax in question would be a "direct tax." Federalists tried to evade the problem by predicting that Congress would levy direct taxes only in emergencies such as wars, but Henry was saying that wars were precisely when the "full force" would press. George Nicholas tried a version of the table 4 argument, the "southern victory" gloss on the apportionment rule. Since the requisition system mobilized Virginia's own slave taxes, which are "laid on all our negroes," the Constitution actually would reduce taxes on slaveholders: "two-fifths are exempted." Finally, Federalists argued that the apportionment rule made a prohibitive slave tax impossible to levy. Madison concentrated on this point: "From the mode of representation and taxation, Congress cannot lay such a tax on slaves as will amount to manumission. . . . The taxation of this State being equal only to its representation, such a tax cannot be laid . . ."[46] Yet this argument begged the central question, which was how the link between representation and taxation would work in practice.

Edmund Randolph had suggested the missing piece early in the convention, after George Mason attacked direct taxation by men with "neither knowledge of our situation, nor a common interest with us, nor a fellow-feeling for us." There was no need to worry. "It is a matter of very little consequence, how it [a direct tax] will be imposed, since it must be clearly laid on the most productive article in each particular State." Perhaps, but this observation did not strengthen the Federalist case. If the *design* of a direct tax was a separate problem from its *apportionment,* the apportionment rule might not protect slavery—since it said nothing about tax design. Henry elaborated: "The oppression arising from taxation, is not from the amount but, from the mode." Virginia's total liability would be regulated by the apportionment rule, "yet the proportion of Virginia being once fixed, might be laid on blacks and blacks only. For the mode of raising the proportion of each State being to be directed by Congress, they might make slaves the sole object to raise it of." Mason agreed. "For instance, if 500,000 dollars were to be raised, they might lay the whole of the proportion of the Southern States on the blacks, or any one species of property: So that by laying taxes too heavily on slaves, they might totally annihilate that kind of property." Attention to tax design represented a breakthrough in the interpretation of the apportionment rule. At the same time, however, it raised the stakes of Henry's rhetorical question: what in the Constitution would "prevent the adoption of the most oppressive mode of taxation in the Southern States, as there is a majority in favor of the Northern States?"[47]

Mason's estimate of the tax that would threaten to abolish slavery in the South was much too low. The tax would have to be 20 or 50 times higher *and* be levied solely on slaves before it would pose a significant threat. Yet his example of a slave tax as an apportioned direct tax also suggests another important point. Consider table 5, which apportions Mason's $500,000 with one difference. Where Mason's tax laid "the whole of the proportion of the Southern States on the blacks," table 5 lays the whole tax on the slaveholders of every state. In the South, where this tax is identical to Mason's example, the burdens on slaveholders are quite light: 26 cents per slave in South Carolina, 31 cents in Virginia, 37 cents in Maryland, 51 cents in North Carolina. In the North, however, the burdens are much higher: over $2 per slave in New York and New Jersey, almost $10 in Rhode Island, $12 in Connecticut, $16 in Pennsylvania, and an obviously prohibitive $123 per slave in New Hampshire. The Virginians had realized that the "mode" of taxation under the apportionment rule made a difference. They had not realized what kind of a difference it made. They had missed the real joker in the apportionment rule: higher rates where there were fewer of the taxed things (or people). This would be the issue in *Hylton* in regard to the distribution of carriages. Except in an income tax covered by the Sixteenth Amendment, it is still the issue in regard to the distribution of income or wealth. In the table 1 example, the rates are low in Connecticut and high in Mississippi because of this perverse effect of the apportionment rule.

Meanwhile, John Marshall (the future Chief Justice) addressed the threat of a prohibitive slave tax in a different way, evading the complexities of the apportionment rule. When Congress levied a direct tax, Marshall suggested, it actually could levy thirteen separate taxes, each framed by a state delegation in the House of Representatives. "Where is the absurdity of having thirteen revenues?" Who could think that Virginia's congressmen, "selected from all parts of the State, chosen because they know the situation of the people, will be unable to determine so as to make the tax equal on, and convenient for, the people at large?" Surely, they would work out the best mix of the "well understood" objects of direct taxation: land, slaves, "stock of all kinds, and a few other articles of domestic property." Would Virginia's own congressmen de-

Table 5: Apportioning George Mason's $500,000 Tax as a National Slave Tax, 1790

	Free Population	Slave Population	Tax Quota	Tax per Slave
New Hampshire	141,741	158	19,426	122.95
Massachusetts	475,257	0	65,092	***
Rhode Island	68,158	952	9,413	9.89
Connecticut	235,382	2,759	32,465	11.77
New York	318,796	21,324	45,415	2.13
New Jersey	172,716	11,423	24,594	2.15
Pennsylvania	430,636	3,737	59,288	15.87
Delaware	50,209	8,887	7,607	0.86
Maryland	216,692	103,036	38,146	0.37
Virginia	516,128	305,257	95,775	0.31
North Carolina	325,553	103,989	53,134	0.51
South Carolina	141,979	107,094	28,246	0.26
Georgia	53,284	29,264	9,703	0.33

NOTE: The Virginia figures include Kentucky, the North Carolina figures include Tennessee, the Massachusetts figures include Maine, and Vermont is excluded entirely.

SOURCE: Calculated from Seventh Census, 1850, ix.

sign a tax "so as to oppress us? What benefit will they have by it? Will it be promotive of their re-election?" Madison recognized a great idea when he heard one. He added another step. When the Virginia congressmen designed the Virginia tax, "they may even refer to the State systems of taxation."[48] Direct taxes could look a lot like requisitions after all.

Congress might decide to frame direct taxes in this way, but it might also decide to frame them in some other way. The Constitution required that direct taxes be apportioned to the states by the three-fifths rule, leaving everything else to the imagination. The Antifederalist who called himself Cato imagined a poll tax that would oppress poor men with "prolific wives." Rufus King and Samuel Nasson imagined the tax treatment of black children, white children, Virginia slaves, and New England governors. Patrick Henry and George Mason imagined a prohibitive slave tax. John Marshall imagined "thirteen revenues." The questions the Philadelphia convention had left open remained open as the states ratified the Constitution and established the new government. Everyone knew that the new Congress was stronger than the old Congress. Everyone knew that the states had been cut out of the national legislative process. Nobody knew what "direct taxes" were, how Congress would levy them, or who would benefit from the apportionment rule.

Congress

The emergency that forced Congress to answer these questions arrived in the late 1790s. For all the advantages of a tax structure that relied on the tariff, this reliance also left the United States vulnerable to a disruption of international trade. The European war sparked by the French Revolution, and especially the naval war between Britain and France, produced that disruption.[49] The United States declared its neutrality and attempted to secure it through diplomatic efforts in London and Paris. American shippers profited from the disruption of European shipping at first, sailing into belligerent ports under a neutral flag. Since the United States had no navy to protect its own commerce, however, diplomacy could not persuade the powerful belligerents to respect its neutrality forever. French and British attacks on American shipping not only drove Congress to invest in the establishment of the U.S. Navy and in a buildup of land forces (preparing for an invasion), but also threatened the delicate financial arrangements through which Congress and the Treasury had funded the Revolutionary War debt.[50]

By the time Congress considered direct taxation in a serious way, the advent of national political parties also had created a new context for tax debates. The Republicans (Jeffersonians) and the Federalists fought famously about taxation in general, with the Republicans demanding frugal government and the Federalists demanding responsible government, but they also clashed over issues of tax design—such as whether an apportioned direct tax should include a slave tax. These disputes did not resemble any of the disputes of the 1780s. They were not about whether to leave tax design to the states (requisitions), whether the three-fifths rule favored the North or the South, or whether Congress could abolish slavery by levying a prohibitive slave tax. Instead, they were about a specifically partisan concern: how apportioned direct taxes would affect party constituencies within particular states. In 1797, this partisan consideration provoked a debate that surprised even the congressmen who participated in it. New England Federalists opposed a slave tax and Virginia Republicans demanded a slave tax! "[I]t was a very extraordinary thing," as Richard Brent (R-VA) observed, "that gentlemen who represented States where there were no slaves, should oppose a tax on that species of property, and that the Southern States where slavery existed, should be advocating that tax."[51]

Extraordinary indeed. By the late 1790s, American politicians finally understood the full implications of the apportionment rule. The truth that eluded them as "founding fathers" struck them forcibly once they were partisans battling for control of the government. Decisions about the design of apportioned direct taxes did not affect the distribution of burdens *between* states, since that was fixed in the Constitution. They determined the distribution of burdens *within* states. In the North, they distributed burdens to farmers, merchants, and artisans. In the South, they distributed burdens to yeoman farmers and slaveholding planters. The stakes in decisions about what to tax and how to tax it involved class interests rather than sectional interests. But, because of the sectional geography of American slavery, they involved two separate arrays of class interests. To Republican and Federalist politicians, these sectional arrays of class interests were the crucial political facts. In a way that the "founding fathers" had not begun to anticipate, the politics of an apportioned direct tax turned out to hinge on slavery indirectly—as partisans appealed to class interests in a nation that was half slave and half free.

The "founding fathers" actually had not anticipated the emergence of political parties at all. Even though some states (such as Pennsylvania) had long histories of party politics by the 1780s, many politicians feared that the mobilization of "factions" would undermine the stability of the republic. Many more dismissed partisan organizing as evidence of disreputable personal ambition or as a sign of dependence that was unbecoming in a statesman or an intelligent citizen. Jefferson captured this attitude in 1789, boasting that he had "never submitted the whole system of my opinions to the creed of any party of men whatever."[52] In less than five years, however, a national two-party system had come to structure most American political debate, with Jefferson as the nation's leading partisan organizer. The Republicans (Jeffersonians) and the Federalists contested elections at both the national and state levels. They also struggled endlessly with each other in Congress. The apportionment of direct taxes acquired its true meaning in the context of this partisan struggle because every aspect of national policy making did.

The origin of the two parties is hard to summarize because it involved battles among the leading "founding fathers"—Washington, Hamilton, and John Adams on one side, Jefferson and Madison on the other. They all wrote eloquent accounts of their goals and what they took to be those of their opponents, which partisan newspapers amplified by hurling accusations of outright treason routinely. Historians have sorted and resorted this mountain of evidence to identify the policy disputes, ideological commitments, and electoral coalitions that distinguished Republicans from Federalists. Despite disagreements and conflicting sympathies among historians, however, several key characteristics of these parties by the mid-1790s are clear: (1) most Federalists were northerners and most Republicans were southerners, with the partisan centers of gravity located in New England and Virginia (see table 6 for an illustration with reference to the House of Representatives); (2) this sectional divide made the Republicans into the more proslavery party, regardless

Table 6: Party Representation in Congress, 1795–1799

	4th Congress 1795–1797		5th Congress 1797–1799	
	Fed	Rep	Fed	Rep
NEW ENGLAND	**24**	**5**	**25**	**4**
Connecticut	7	0	7	0
Massachusetts	11	3	11	3
New Hampshire	3	1	4	0
Rhode Island	2	0	2	0
Vermont	1	1	1	1
MIDDLE	**14**	**15**	**18**	**12**
Delaware	0	1	1	0
New Jersey	5	0	5	0
New York	5	5	6	4
Pennsylvania	4	9	6	8
UPPER SOUTH	**7**	**33**	**11**	**29**
Kentucky	0	2	0	2
Maryland	4	4	6	2
North Carolina	1	9	1	9
Tennessee	0	1	0	1
Virginia	2	17	4	15
LOWER SOUTH	**2**	**6**	**3**	**5**
Georgia	0	2	0	2
South Carolina	2	4	3	3
TOTAL	**47**	**59**	**57**	**50**

SOURCE: Kenneth C. Martis, *The Historical Atlas of Political Parties in the United States Congress, 1789–1989* (New York, 1989), 73–76. By-elections shifted three seats in the 4th Congress and two in the 5th.

of how individual Republicans and Federalists talked about slavery; (3) this sectional divide also shaped partisan attitudes toward competent administration, with Federalists devoted to it and Republicans suspicious of it; and (4) the Federalists never recovered from the Republican victory in the middle states (New York, Pennsylvania) that is usually called the "Revolution of 1800."[53]

An early sign of the impact of partisan politics on the meaning of apportioned direct taxes was the appearance of arguments in favor of their imposition. In the 1780s, everyone had agreed that the taxes most likely to count as "direct" (on land, polls, slaves, or property generally) were undesirable levies to be reserved for emergencies. Now, however, Republicans endorsed these taxes because they could embody republican virtue and promote active citizenship. Unlike taxes that shifted into consumer prices, direct taxes were honest levies that could mobilize citizens into the political process. In fact, Congress should levy them *because* they would hurt the taxpayers. All tax systems, Madison argued in 1792, should "include a proportion of such as by their direct operation keep the people awake, along with those, which being wrapped up in other payments, may leave them asleep, to misapplications of their money." John Smilie (R-PA) insisted in 1794 that "taxes ought to be raised in such a way, that the public might not only pay them, but at the same time, *feel* them. This would teach them to think a little better in what way their money goes," causing "an abridgement of the expenses of the Federal Government." In 1797, Jefferson endorsed a direct tax to "awaken our constituents, and call for inspection into past proceedings" that had increased the national debt.[54]

These were partisan arguments. As Uriah Tracy (F-CT) sputtered in response to Smilie in 1794, they were assertions "that, when taxes are to be raised, Government is in duty bound to give the people who pay these taxes, *as much trouble as possible!*" The spectacle of prominent national leaders promoting tax plans intended to discredit the federal government was peculiar, even if it is perfectly recognizable today. The spectacle of these politicians clothing a strategic maneuver in the garb of transparency and simplicity enraged their opponents, though it also is less jarring to our more jaded ear for political rhetoric. The temptation to dismiss this rhetoric as utterly hypocritical is weakened by the fact that it fit into a larger system of ideas. Jefferson, Madison, and Smilie really did value transparency and simplicity as republican (or Republican) virtues—Jefferson also thought "[t]he accounts of the US. ought to be, and may be, made, as simple as those of a common farmer."[55] Still, strategic demands for odious taxes were hardly expressions of the virtuous innocence of the common farmer. The Jeffersonians wanted to take over the government from the Federalists in the 1790s—and they wanted Congress to levy the worst possible taxes to help them do it.

Federalists wanted to avoid direct taxes for the same reasons that everyone had wanted to avoid them before. They were the taxes that the Congress under the Articles could not design in 1783 ("hemmed in on all sides by difficulties that appear insurmountable") and the taxes that the states could not collect at rates high enough to meet requisitions and state-level war costs ("The people have been so harassed with taxes & Collectors that they feel galled, fretted, Impatient, & many really unable to pay"). Federalists did *not* want to stretch the government's hand "directly into the pockets of the people" and could not believe that the Republicans really wanted to do that either. When the adoption of the controversial plan to fund the Revolutionary War debt required Congress to supplement the 1789 tariff with another tax in 1791, Congress followed Alexander Hamilton's recommendation to levy the ill-fated whiskey excise. When Congress needed more money in 1794, it added a package of other small taxes, again on Hamilton's advice. The 1794 package consisted of a sales tax on auctions, excises on snuff and sugar, a license fee on retailers of imported liquor, and the carriage tax that provoked the *Hylton* litigation.[56]

Collectively, the whiskey excise and the 1794 taxes were known as the "internal revenue" or "internal duties." This classification distinguished them from the tariff (an external duty) and from the direct taxes that the Constitution subjected to the apportionment rule. The category also had an administrative meaning: customs officers collected the tariff and internal revenue officers collected these taxes. Most were also "indirect" in an economic sense. Except the carriage tax, which was a property tax on carriage owners (hence *Hylton*), the internal duties were supposed to work in the same way as the tariff. The distillers, auctioneers, snuff millers, sugar refiners, and liquor retailers were supposed to pay them and then shift them to consumers. Although the Republicans complained that the excises unleashed "a swarm of harpies" to "range through the country, prying into every man's house and affairs," the Federalists liked these taxes precisely because they did *not* require collectors to fan out across rural America. What Samuel Smith (R-MD) said of the tariff was true of most of the internal duties. "We ought to keep friends with the merchants," Smith explained, "for they are the collectors of duties for the United States."[57]

The whiskey excise was more complicated. While much of its revenue came from large-scale distillers such as the New England rum producers, the situation was different in rural areas and especially in "frontier" areas. In these places, small-scale and part-time distillers consumed much of their own output. What really made the whiskey tax different from the other "indirect" taxes, however, was the fact that the government tried to collect it from some of the small-scale operators. In his fine recent study of tariff collection in the 1790s, Frederick Dalzell has shown that "a smoothly running system hummed steadily" in the major ports, where merchants paid the taxes on large ships and cargoes to raise most of the revenue. Customs officers had less success with small-fry shippers (coasting vessels) and in commercial "backwaters" (the coast of Maine), but they usually winked at such violations anyway. In most frontier areas, officials also winked at the small-fry distillers; in Kentucky, the whiskey excise was essentially a dead letter. But, for reasons that are not altogether clear, President Washington and Treasury Secretary Hamilton refused to wink at the small-fry distillers of western Pennsylvania. When their determination to collect became obvious, it was the Stamp Act riots all over again:

violent intimidation of collectors, local militia drilling, and a draconian federal response. In October 1794, Washington and Hamilton rode out to Pittsburgh with an army of 13,000 militiamen to suppress the Whiskey Rebellion.[58]

The most important way in which the Whiskey Rebellion affected American tax politics was by jump-starting the political career of one of its leaders. Albert Gallatin had arrived in the United States during the Revolutionary War as a well-educated young aristocrat from Geneva. He taught French at Harvard and dabbled in land speculation in Virginia until his inheritance came through in 1786, at which point he bought a farm near Pittsburgh and immersed himself in the local political scene—where anger at Philadelphia elites created Antifederalists in the 1780s and Jeffersonians in the 1790s. The Whiskey Rebellion was Gallatin's opportunity. Elected to Congress in 1794 from the district at its center and as a result of his active participation (which he later called his "only political sin"), Gallatin emerged immediately as the Republican point man on finance. He could do something that no other Republican could: challenge Alexander Hamilton's authority as the American expert on public finance and political economy.[59]

Gallatin's main project in the late 1790s was a tireless demand that Congress levy a direct tax. He was not interested in provoking another tax rebellion. Nor was he attracted by romantic appeals to "country" simplicity and honest taxation. Gallatin wanted Congress to levy a national land tax in order to convert northern Federalists into northern Republicans. His strategy was not simple, but it was clear. The Republicans could win in the North only by alienating the mass of ordinary farmers from their Federalist loyalties. The best way to do this, in turn, was to exploit divisions between farmers and merchants in the northern states. Gallatin thought an apportioned national land tax could do the trick. He outlined this strategy in *A Sketch of the Finances of the United States* (1796). Most of the book was an attack on Hamilton's handling of the debt, which made the point that Congress needed a large source of new tax revenue. But Gallatin could not resist flaunting his real discovery—about the within-state effects of the apportionment rule. An apportioned land tax would burden northern farmers more heavily than anyone else because the northern populations included large numbers of artisans. The presence of these artisans would raise the quotas apportioned to the northern states, while a land tax would impose the burdens on farmers. "If a land tax presses harder upon the landholders of the North," as Gallatin phrased it, "it is because the proportion of cultivators is less and that of manufacturers is greater than to the South."[60]

Gallatin omitted the punch line, but other congressmen supplied it as soon as his land tax reached the floor of the House of Representatives in 1797. The Ways and Means Committee had amended Gallatin's plan in order to levy the direct tax on slaves as well as on land, setting off the "extraordinary" debate in which the northern Federalists opposed the slave tax and the southern Republicans demanded it. The point of levying the tax on both land and slaves was to reduce the burdens on yeoman farmers in southern states. Wealthy planters would bear larger shares of the southern state quotas if they paid slave taxes in addition to land taxes. But, in the North, where there were few slaves or slaveholders, the tax would still be Gallatin's original land tax. Despite Gallatin's talk about artisans, everyone knew that the key was the tax treatment of *merchants*. A tax on land and slaves would show ordinary farmers in southern states that the slaveholding elite (Republican) was paying its share, while a tax that exempted commercial assets showed ordinary farmers in northern states that the merchant elite (Federalist) was *not* paying its share. This tax was designed to mute class conflict in the South and exacerbate class conflict in the North—in order to help the Republicans and hurt the Federalists.

New Englanders knew what was at stake. Jeremiah Smith (F-NH) "was aware that a tax on slaves would lighten the tax on land in the Southern States, and therefore he did not wonder at the Representatives from those States wishing it to take place; but, by so apportioning the tax, would not the land-holders in the Southern States pay less than the land-holders in parts of the Union where no slaves were kept?" A slave tax would make the burden fall "more equally" in the South, but it would do nothing of the kind in the North. Elisha Potter (F-RI) added the details. While both elites and nonelites owned land, elites also owned substantial amounts of "personal property." Southern planters owned slaves; northern merchants owned commercial and financial assets. The tax on land and slaves would fall "on the personal property of the Southern States, which, no doubt, they would be glad of," but exempt the personal property of the northern states. Potter "saw no reason why the personal property of those [southern] States should be made to bear a part of the proposed burden, whilst personal property in other States was suffered to go free. It was a hard case . . . that a man who possessed three or four hundred dollars in land, should be made to pay a portion of the direct tax, whilst men of affluence, who possessed many thousands in public securities, or loaned on interest, should pay nothing."[61]

While Gallatin pretended that the New Englanders were talking about live-stock instead of commercial assets ("it might seem somewhat wrong to introduce negroes in the one case and not cattle in the other"), Virginians trotted out the claim that they were victimized by the lamentable institution of slavery. "As he lived in a country which was unfortunately *cursed* with negroes," Thomas Claiborne (R-VA) supported the slave tax "for the sake of making the tax bear, in some degree, equally in the Southern States." John Page (R-VA) blandly asserted that freedom made tax equity less important in the North. "If a person living in a State where slavery did not exist, paid something more for his land, the difference was certainly not equal to the satisfaction he must enjoy in reflecting, that his State was free from that evil." Tax equity followed naturally from slavery, Page argued, since it was easier to count slaves than to value commercial assets. Northerners who "complain that the Southern States would pay the tax with greater facility than them . . . might . . . as well complain against the richness of their soil, or the warmness of their climate." Nobody had criticized slavery in this debate, but Page accused the New Englanders of hypocrisy anyway. It was "extraordinary that, whilst they [southerners] were upbraided with holding a species of property peculiar to their country, they should also be upbraided with wishing to pay a duty upon that property." Richard Brent (R-VA) was also suspicious. "He could not help believing that the real object of gentlemen had not been avowed. It was something hidden and unseen."[62]

The New England Federalists *had* avowed their objective: to avoid the trap that Gallatin and the Virginians had set for them. If the direct tax was going to fan class conflict in the North by favoring merchants, then it was going to fan class conflict in the South by favoring planters. By 1797, only one Federalist had glimpsed another solution. Oliver Wolcott, who had replaced Hamilton at the Treasury in 1795, had responded to an earlier request that he design a direct tax with his survey of the state tax systems (see chapter 3). Sensitive to New England tax issues (he was from Connecticut), Wolcott had proposed that the direct tax include a levy on luxury houses. Congress would not be able to tax commercial or financial assets. Efforts to locate and value this property "are either arbitrary, or they require an inquisition into the circumstances of individuals, to which free governments are incompetent." But Congress could reach the merchants by using their houses as "indices" of their standards of living ("expense"). Wolcott obscured this proposal in the same roundabout language that marred the rest of his report, but his point was significant. The Federalists could pursue tax equity in the North by exempting the houses of "farmers and laborers" and taxing the houses of elites.[63]

Congress rejected the direct tax in 1797, addressing its immediate needs with tariff hikes. A year later, however, the Federalists were ready to take the plunge. Tariff revenue had started to slide, from $7.5 million in 1797 to $7.1 million in 1798—and then down to $6.6 million in 1799. In response to French attacks on American merchant shipping, Congress was preparing for war: constructing frigates, enlarging the army, building fortifications. From 1798 to 1800, the United States deployed its expensive new navy in the Quasi-War against France (a series of naval engagements in the West Indies). Meanwhile, France's pressure on its puppet government in the Netherlands destroyed the Amsterdam credit market—which meant that the United States no longer could borrow abroad. Despite all the partisan reasons that the Republicans had called for direct taxes, the Federalists now conceded that the emergency situation had arrived.[64]

The Federalists also figured out how to protect their party's stake in the design of the tax. The Ways and Means Committee proposed a tax "laid by uniform assessment, on lands, houses, and slaves." This formula did not solve the northern tax equity problem, since it taxed all houses rather than only expensive houses. It also introduced a new southern problem: an assessment of the "value" of enslaved human beings. After a desultory discussion, Congress sent it back to the committee. Now, Wolcott intervened with a better idea. He proposed to tax slaves at a flat rate (38 cents per slave), noting that Congress probably would want to exempt "the aged and infirm." He proposed to tax houses worth more than $80 at a scale of flat rates: 50 cents on houses worth $80 to $200, $1.50 on houses worth $200 to $600, and so on to $60 on houses worth $10,000 to $25,000 and $120 on houses worth over $25,000.[65]

The kicker was Wolcott's plan for the land. After the slaves were counted and the houses assigned to brackets *in each state,* the Treasury would subtract the yields of these taxes from the state quotas and then levy the balances on land "at such a rate ad valorem in each State, as, with the sums assessed on houses and slaves, will produce the entire amount of the sums apportioned to the respective States." The tax rate on land in any state would depend on the yields from the taxes aimed at elites, and there might be no land tax where the slave and house taxes met a state's quota. This plan favored small farmers everywhere in the country. Wolcott estimated that land would bear less than one-fourth of the burden, which not only was less "than would be payable in most of the States, if the State systems should be adopted," but which "must also appear to be a tax really moderate, when the immense value of that species of property [land] in the United States is duly considered."[66] Wolcott had learned from Gallatin. He had figured out how to exploit the within-state effects of the apportionment rule to craft a Federalist direct tax.

With Federalist majorities in both houses of Congress, Wolcott's plan became the nucleus of the 1798 direct tax. The House of Representatives adopted his scheme to protect farmers from land taxes, though it modified his slave and house taxes. The result was complicated. The 1798 direct tax was a $2 million levy that was :

1. apportioned to the states by the three-fifths population rule;
2. levied on all slaves ("whether negroes, mulattoes or mestizoes") at the flat rate

of 50 cents, exempting children (12 and under), seniors (50 and over), and "such as from fixed infirmity, or bodily disability, may be incapable of labor;"

3. levied ad valorem on houses worth more than $100 at progressive rates (0.2 percent on houses worth $100 to $500, 0.3 percent on houses worth $500 to $1,000, and so on up to 0.9 percent on houses worth $20,000 to $30,000 and 1.0 percent on houses worth over $30,000); and

4. levied ad valorem on land at rates fixed to raise the balances of the state quotas after the slave and house tax yields had been determined in each state.[67]

Federalists were enthusiastic about the progressive house tax. Samuel Sewall (F-MA) praised it "as a remedy to the defect acknowledged to exist in a system of this kind, of not being able to reach personal property. This bill does not go to the property of persons in business, or to any kind of money-property, and laying a tax upon a man, in proportion to the size and goodness of his house, will, in some degree, remedy the omission." Nor did Sewall neglect its windfall for farmers. The tax "would principally fall on houses in the cities," which "would be taxed much higher than houses in the country." John Williams (F-NY), from a "frontier" district in upstate New York, liked it for the same reason. "The riches of the country lie in the cities, and the taxes ought, therefore, principally to fall there." This direct tax would "fall very lightly, indeed, upon the new settlers of the country, who, in general, are men unable to bear any considerable portion of taxes." Williams, who thought these settlers (his constituents) "should be exempt from public burdens," saw the progressive house tax as "not only calculated to do this, but also to relieve the poorer class of our citizens, who, he thought, were entitled to notice."[68]

The Federalists had beaten Gallatin at his own game. Through the progressive house tax, they had framed an apportioned direct tax to court rather than alienate northern farmers. Sewall gloated: "[F]armers would see the reasonableness of taxing people as nearly as possible according to their ability to pay, which is the object of this bill." Gallatin responded by attacking the house tax. He argued that rural houses could not be valued separately from land, predicted equalization problems ("what security would the people of Pittsburgh have that the assessors of Philadelphia would value the houses there . . . upon the same principle with their own assessors?"), and then dismissed the tax as a fraud ("a mere take-in, and nothing more than a Treasury plan, in order to raise more money"). Even if the house tax was not a hypocritical scheme to oppress the farmers, "those who live in a part of the country where they can get the least information" would believe that it was. "Such people, when they saw their houses and lands valued separately, contrary to the custom of the State [Pennsylvania], would apprehend a double tax was about to be laid upon them, and such an idea might excite great discontent"—which is exactly what happened in one Pennsylvania district, in an incident known as the Fries Rebellion (1799).[69]

Southerners said little during this debate, as Federalists and Republicans fought about the impact of the tax in the North. Finally, however, one Virginian realized what the Federalists had done in the South. If both the progressive house tax *and* the slave tax were levied before the land tax, wealthy planters might find themselves paying the entire quotas in southern states. Virginia Republicans had demanded the slave tax to show yeoman farmers that the slaveholding elite was paying its share. New England Federalists had added the house tax, using houses as proxies for commercial assets to show yeoman farmers that the merchant elite was paying its share. But, in the South, the slave tax already reached the "personal property" of elites. Abraham Venable (R-VA) got it. With the "houses being taxed as the representatives of other property," the slave tax became "a double tax" on "the large slaveholders, as they generally occupied the largest houses." In a tax "laid so heavily on houses and slaves, there would be nothing left for land to pay. And, if this should be the case, certain districts of the State of Virginia [tidewater] will pay almost the whole of the tax, and others [backcountry] scarcely any."[70]

The House of Representatives passed the tax bill by a lopsided vote of 62 to 18, with five of the Virginia Republicans abstaining and ten (including Venable) voting yes. The Federalists had outmaneuvered the Republicans. They had exploited the implications of the apportionment rule to design a tax that favored farmers over merchants in the North and that especially favored them over slaveholding planters in the South. As Robert Goodloe Harper (F-SC) told the voters of his southern backcountry district, "the burden is made to fall on those who are able to bear it, and on every one in proportion to his ability."[71] Where the "founding fathers" of the 1780s had barely understood the provision for "direct taxes" that they had inserted into the Constitution, the Republicans and Federalists of the 1790s had figured out how to exploit it for partisan advantage. Gouverneur Morris and Charles Pinckney, Rufus King and Samuel Nasson, James Madison and Patrick Henry—and perhaps even Alexander Hamilton—had only the vaguest ideas about what it might mean to levy an apportioned direct tax. Albert Gallatin, Oliver Wolcott, and their partisan allies in the 1790s finally defined "direct taxes," decided how Congress would levy them, and infused political meaning into the apportionment rule.

Legacies

Thomas Jefferson grasped a simpler truth. For the purpose of winning votes, promises of tax equity are less effective than promises of tax cuts. Today, it is obvious that many voters will sacrifice their interests to generalized antitax appeals—that people who pay large chunks of their incomes in payroll taxes (for Social Security) will support tax breaks for millionaires (estate tax abolition). Jefferson saw that the Federalists would gain nothing from the progressive house tax. The fact that they imposed a direct tax would be more obvious than the details of its design. In 1797, Uriah Tracy (F-CT) attributed the Republicans' demand for a direct tax to a "satanic hope, that they can enjoy the fulfillment of their prophecies concerning the administration." When Congress levied the tax in 1798, Jefferson declared victory. The "disease of the imagination" known as Federalism would now pass. "Indeed, the Doctor is now on his way to cure it, in the guise of a tax gatherer."[72]

After the Republicans took over the government in 1801, they abolished the internal taxes and the collection apparatus. They relied on the tariff, even as tariff receipts continued to depend on the vicissitudes of the war in Europe. Luckily for the Jeffersonians, receipts surged from $9.1 million in 1800 to $12.9 million in 1805. After peaking at $16.3 million in 1808, however, they sank to $7.2 million in 1809 and then fluctuated wildly (see fig. 1 above). As president, Jefferson undermined the only source of federal tax revenue through a foreign policy. Starting in 1807, the United States tried to compel Britain and France to stop attacking American shipping by shutting down American shipping—at a huge cost to the economy as well as the revenue. Jefferson's embargo might have echoed the "nonimportation" movements of the 1760s, which won the repeal of the Stamp Act and Townshend duties. It actually echoed the Coercive Acts of the 1770s. With the navy sealing the New England ports (searching and seizing without warrants or trials) and the army battling smugglers on the Canadian border in New York and Vermont, President Jefferson and Treasury Secretary Gallatin made Washington and Hamilton look like civil libertarians in the Whiskey Rebellion episode.[73]

Gallatin stayed at Treasury through Madison's first term. In 1812, just before the United States declared war on Britain, he tried to persuade Congress to create a tax program to meet the inevitable costs of the War of 1812. Predictably, a Republican lambasted him for "treading in the muddy footsteps of his official predecessors, in attempting to strap round the necks of the people this odious system of taxation, adopted by them, for which they have been condemned by the people and dismissed from power." Gallatin's plan did look familiar. It consisted of tariff hikes, a whiskey excise, a sales tax on auctions, an excise on sugar (but not snuff), licenses for retailers of imported liquor and other goods, a carriage tax, and a direct tax on land, houses, and slaves. Gallatin also proposed a stamp tax on legal documents, like one that the Federalists had imposed in 1797 (and the British had tried to impose in 1765).

Congress did nothing in 1812, but, in the summer of 1813, with the war in progress, it enacted Gallatin's plan wholesale—ten tax bills through the entire legislative process in six weeks.[74]

The most significant innovations involved the direct tax. The 1813 tax was apportioned to counties within the states, although it permitted state legislatures to amend the county quotas. It also offered 15 percent discounts to states that assumed their quotas and raised the money on their own. It dropped the crucial features of the 1798 tax, the progressive house tax and the prior taxation of houses and slaves, and added a new feature: assessments of the "value" of individual enslaved human beings. Except in states that assumed their quotas, the 1813 tax was levied on all tracts of land "with their improvements," all houses, and all slaves "at the rate each of them is worth in money." This was the Jeffersonian direct tax. It not only laid a larger proportion of the burden on farmers than its Federalist predecessor, but it left the issue of how much of the burden would fall on slaveholders to appointed local assessors, or, really, to the slaveholders themselves. Congress doubled this tax and imposed it as an annual levy in 1815 and then abolished it in 1817 with the rest of the internal revenue system.[75]

The Republicans also created new taxes in 1815. They levied excises on the manufacture of a range of goods—iron, nails, cigars, candles, saddles, boots, hats, umbrellas, and jewelry—and "an annual duty" on watches and household furniture. The watch tax imposed $2 on a gold watch and $1 on a silver watch. The furniture tax was more interesting. It was pegged at a scale of flat rates on "all household furniture kept for use . . . in any one family, with the exception of beds, bedding, kitchen furniture, family pictures, and articles made in the family from domestic materials." It exempted holdings of taxable furniture worth less than $200 and then levied $1 on $200 to $400 of furniture, $1.50 on $400 to $600, $3 on $600 to $1,000, and so on up to $75 on $6,000 to $9,000 and $100 on more than $9,000. This tax looked like the old Federalist house tax, but it was not intended as a tax break for farmers in the same way because it was not part of an apportioned direct tax. It was aimed at elites, but levied in addition to the direct taxes and other internal duties. Congress abolished all of these taxes in 1816.[76]

The 1815 furniture tax actually was a legacy of the *Hylton* decision. Alexander Hamilton had organized the *Hylton* case in 1795 to elicit a Supreme Court ruling that would authorize a tax of this kind. If the Court ruled that an unapportioned carriage tax was constitutional, Congress might be able to avoid apportioned direct taxes altogether by levying "internal duties" on various forms of property. Hamilton had crafted the fictitious "facts" of the *Hylton* case to ensure that the Supreme Court would have jurisdiction to rule on the constitutional issue (these "facts" were that Daniel Hylton of Virginia owned 125 chariots that he "kept exclusively for [his] own private use" and had failed to pay the tax on them). Hamilton then argued the case before the Supreme Court and won, which was a predictable outcome given that Washington had appointed all of the justices. Once the Court endorsed the carriage tax, Hamilton sent Wolcott a series of plans for progressive house taxes to be levied as internal duties. It was Wolcott's own innovation to levy the progressive house tax as part of the 1798 direct tax.[77]

The *Hylton* litigation had another legacy. Hamilton initiated the case in an attempt to narrow the scope of the apportionment rule so that Congress could tax without it. While the Virginians who took the other side agreed to participate in an attempt to broaden the scope of the rule, their agenda was not exactly the opposite of Hamilton's. They were thinking about a different issue from Hamilton's concern for a robust federal tax power. They were thinking about a prohibitive slave tax. They wanted a guarantee that Congress could not abolish slavery simply by calling a prohibitive slave tax an "internal duty." At the circuit court phase in Virginia, Hylton's lawyer was John Taylor of Caroline, who already had published two hyperbolic "country" attacks on Hamilton (one charging his "political papacy" with corrupting the people by "eternally selling its *paper indulgencies*"). Taylor later became a prominent proslavery constitutional theorist and champion of the doctrine of "strict construction"—the idea that the powers of Congress under the Constitution ought to be construed in the narrowest possible way.[78]

Where Patrick Henry and George Mason had worried about a prohibitive slave tax under the apportionment rule, Taylor now endorsed Madison's position that the rule protected slavery. The southern delegates at Philadelphia would not have signed the Constitution and the southern states would not have ratified it without this insurance against prohibitive slave taxes. The direct tax clauses were intended to protect slavery. "[I]f the southern states are allowed not to have been grossly duped," Taylor reasoned, "it is not improbable, that this species of property, had its influence . . . to produce the rule of numerical proportion." But the carriage tax opened a loophole and, as a tax on a form of property, created a dangerous precedent: "for if Congress can assess or rate one species of property . . . it follows that they may assess or rate every species of property." Nor did Taylor stop with this abstract language. He was talking about slavery, and he did not want to be misunderstood. "Unhappily for the southern states, they possess a species of property, which is peculiarly exposed, and upon which if this law stands, the whole burden of government may be exclusively laid." If an unapportioned carriage tax was constitutional, Congress could "effect a general emancipation, by imposing upon the property thus intended to be secured [the slaves intended to be freed], an excise or duty so exorbitant as to deprive it of its value."[79]

Taylor lost in 1796. The Supreme Court ruled that the carriage tax was not a "direct" tax, with all three justices who wrote opinions stressing the absurdity of apportioning it (rates based on the number of carriages in a state). One of these justices was William Paterson of New Jersey, who had opposed three-fifths representation at the Philadelphia convention. Able to cite the original intent of the framers with authority, Paterson recalled that "the principal, I will not say, the only, objects, that the framers . . . contemplated as falling within the rule of apportionment" were land taxes and poll taxes. He added a more interesting argument, combining "original intent" with "strict construction" to reject the creation of a new safeguard for slavery. The apportionment of direct taxes, Paterson explained, originated as a by-product of the representation debate. Three-fifths representation "was the work of compromise" at Philadelphia, but it "is radically wrong; it cannot be supported by any solid reasoning." Because the term "direct taxes" had entered the Constitution as part of this concession to slavery, it "ought not to be extended by construction." The slaveholders had won a constitutional protection against direct taxes at Philadelphia. They would have to take their chances with internal duties in Congress.[80]

The risk turned out to be minimal. Congress would not levy another "internal duty" on a specific form of property for twenty years. With Madison in the White House and Republicans holding commanding majorities in Congress (63 percent in the House, 78 percent in the Senate), there was no danger that the 1815 tax on watches and household furniture would be extended to threaten the South's "peculiarly exposed" form of property. The real security against prohibitive slave taxes lay in the political arena. It lay in three-fifths *representation* rather than in limitations on the federal tax power. It lay in the rules that created the majorities rather than in the ones that limited how the majorities could tax. The real security lay in the South's extra seats in the House of Representatives and extra votes in the electoral college. The slave states kept this advantage until mass immigration increased the northern free populations enough to swamp the three-fifths representation of slaves. Then, they clung to parity in the Senate through the balanced admission of new states.[81] When the North finally asserted its majority power in 1860—electing Abraham Lincoln to the presidency with no southern votes—the South responded by seceding from the Union and bombarding the U.S. army garrison at Fort Sumter.

The framers of the Constitution intended the apportionment of direct taxes as a limitation on the power of majorities to decide how to tax. They did not understand precisely what kind of a limitation it was, mainly because they were thinking more about the state quotas than about the actual taxes. The apportionment rule did preempt debates about the quotas.[82] It did not preempt debates about slavery. In the 1790s, when the two-party system of Federalists and Republicans emphasized the sectional interests of New Englanders and Virginians, Congress debated about the tax implications of slavery. In 1813, when the Republicans could ram a tax package through a Congress they dominated, the marginalized faction of New England Federalists (who opposed the war) sat silently and then voted against every Republican tax bill. The death of the Federalist party after 1815 inaugurated what historians used to call the Era of Good Feelings. With almost all politicians calling themselves Republicans and tariff receipts soaring (the defeat of Napoleon in 1815 having brought long-term peace to Europe), Congress no longer waged the debates about taxes that had politicized slavery in the past. Other issues created controversies about slavery, especially the application of Missouri for admission as a slave state in 1819, but congressional tax debates after 1817 consisted solely of debates about protective tariff schedules. They were debates about industrial policy rather than tax policy.

Southerners sometimes attacked the tariff as an assault on the institution of slavery, but it was nothing of the kind. It was about northern industry rather than southern slavery. Because the tariff forced southern planters and farmers across the country to subsidize the "infant industries" of the Northeast, moreover, it created an issue on which wealthy slaveholders—such as John Taylor—could pose plausibly as defenders of the "common man." The tariff burdened the South, but its productivity granted the South the political safeguard that the impost had always promised. Just as the framers had intended, the tariff confined the threat of a tax to "compel the Southern States to liberate their negroes" to the doomsday fantasies of slaveholders "who substitute unsupported suspicions to reasons." In their demands for "security," the slaveholding "founding fathers" had loaded the Constitution with restraints on majority rule because they feared that these majorities would be northerners. Madison may have said it best in his defense of the electoral college at Philadelphia. Three-fifths representation had to extend to presidential elections because slavery reduced the number of southern voters. "The right of suffrage was much more diffusive in the Northern than the Southern States," he explained, "and the latter could have no influence in the election [popular vote] on the score of the Negroes."[83] The slaveholders of the South had to be protected against the liberty and democracy of the North. As the most capable politician of his generation, James Madison ensured that they were.

PART III

The Synthesis in the States

As anyone who has perused a recent U.S. history textbook will have noticed, the "Age of Jackson" is not what it used to be. The traditional themes remain present—egalitarian rhetoric, mass political parties, ambitious reformers, the Bank War, Tocqueville's visit, rural expansion, urban class conflict—but many of them have come to look different. The abolition of property qualifications for the suffrage is inseparable from the spread of an explicit racial qualification (the word "white"). Westward settlement has more to do with the genocide of Indian Removal and the hideous interstate slave trade (coffles on the roads, pens in New Orleans) than with "free land" or the eventual Homestead Act. For radical thinking, we read David Walker's *Appeal to the Coloured Citizens of the World* (1829) rather than Thomas Skidmore's *The Rights of Man to Property* (1829) and, for radical action, we look to Nat Turner rather than to the Workingmen's Party of New York, much less the utopian socialists of Oneida. The major parties, the Whigs and Democrats, still fought about economic policies (banks, tariffs, internal improvements) and cultural regulation (immigrant rights, liquor laws, religion in the schools), but fewer historians are inclined to take sides on the contests that evaded the elephant in the room: the entanglement of a celebration of equality with a massive institution of slavery.[1]

Taxation has never been a major theme in this history. Nor should it be. Tax grievances did not inspire the movement for "white male democracy" or generate the national debates about slavery that pulled this polity toward its destruction. The single exception, the tariff struggle that climaxed in the Nullification Crisis of the early 1830s, ended in compromise because, outside of the peculiar hothouse of South Carolina, most southerners still thought they could win within the U.S. political system—and they actually won big tariff cuts in the 1830s and 1840s. From 1817 until the cataclysm of 1861, Congress levied no taxes except the tariff. As a result, the history of antebellum taxation is primarily the history of state and local taxation. State legislatures enacted the laws, local governments collected the money, and the conventions that wrote and revised the state constitutions delimited the power to decide how to tax.[2]

This history synthesized patterns we have already seen. In the antebellum era, northern taxes were still more sophisticated than southern taxes, espe-

cially in their more comprehensive use of ssments. Northern tax policies
still depended on local decision making le principle of local responsibility"), while southern policies still min ed both the administrative and the
political roles of local institutions. where, legislatures tried to exploit
nontax revenues to reduce or repl their regular levies. The most striking
antebellum development, howe was constitutional. By 1860, more than
half of the state constitutions (s the 33) contained clauses that prescribed
the design of state and local t Most of these clauses (15 of the 20), known
as "uniformity clauses," re ed that different forms of property be treated
"uniformly": that they be ssed in the same way and taxed at the same rate.[3]
Like the "direct tax" cla s of the U.S. Constitution—and like the clause that
Maryland adopted in 76, requiring that every person be taxed "according
to his actual worth real or personal property"—the antebellum clauses
were intended to eempt the decision-making power of legislatures. They
were intended t ock the design of tax structures against the potentially dangerous prefere es of majorities.

Few historians have looked closely at the adoption of the uniformity clauses. Although e legal historian Morton J. Horwitz has recognized that this "movement to onstitutionalize the taxing power" had antidemocratic implications—because it inspired judges to encroach on what otherwise was a legislative prerogative—most students of the uniformity movement have seen the clauses as expressions of majority sentiment rather than as restraints on majority rule. This view rests on the democratizing reforms that reshaped American politics in the early decades of the nineteenth century: the abolition of property qualifications for voting and officeholding and the extraordinary mobilization of the white male electorate that began in the 1830s (regular voter turnouts in the 80 percent range). The uniformity clauses, it is argued, "appealed to the spirit of equality" and reflected "the radical democratic spirit of the times."[4]

The antebellum constitutionalization of state and local taxation was indeed connected to the democratizing reforms of the "Age of Jackson," but it originated in efforts to limit the power of the newly democratized majorities rather than as a triumph of the majorities themselves. In this light, it is especially significant that the movement originated in the South. Map 1 identifies the states that adopted uniformity clauses before 1860, dividing the uniformity states into early adopters (1776–1845) and late adopters (1848–1860). While the map's most obvious feature is the "western" character of the uniformity movement, its southern origin is also clear. Except for Illinois, every early adopter was a southern state while every late adopter was a northern state.[5] Nor was the earlier southern action a mere artifact of the earlier achievement of statehood in the southern "west" than the northern "west"—since five uniformity

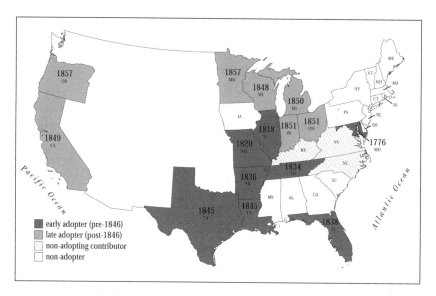

Map 1. Adoption of Uniformity Clauses, 1776–1860

states adopted these clauses in revised rather than original state constitutions: Ohio (statehood 1802, uniformity 1851), Indiana (1816, 1851), Michigan (1837, 1850), and, in the South, Tennessee (1796, 1834) and Louisiana (1812, 1845). As the map also notes, three southern nonadopters participated in the early phase of the movement: Virginia by elaborating its political logic (1829), North Carolina by devising a characteristically idiosyncratic variation (1835), and Kentucky by adopting the mandate through a judicial ruling rather than a constitutional clause (1839).[6]

There are other important features of the uniformity map, such as the absence of action in the Northeast and much of the Deep South. Yet to introduce the historical problem posed by the uniformity clauses, the crucial point is their transit from the South to the Northwest—the states now referred to as the Midwest plus California and Oregon. In southern states, uniformity emerged from bargains that resembled the ones that had placed the "direct tax" clauses into the U.S. Constitution. Nonslaveholding yeomen demanded democratizing reforms (broader suffrage, more equitable legislative apportionments) to win power commensurate with their numbers. Slaveholding planters responded by demanding "security" against the danger that nonslaveholding majorities would impose heavy or prohibitive slave taxes. Uniformity clauses compromised these demands by ensuring that democratized legislatures taxed slaves at the same rates as other forms of property—such as the land and livestock of the yeomen. "If you think your slaves will be unjustly taxed" by nonslave-holding majorities, as a Virginian put it in 1829, "prescribe in the Constitution a proper limit upon the legislative power: fix the ratio between the tax on slaves and real estate . . . declare that the tax shall be *ad valorem*, and equal on both, and that the one shall never be taxed without the other."[7]

The question is why this southern bargain to protect slavery would have been attractive in Ohio, Michigan, Wisconsin, and other western free states—a puzzle that only deepens when we notice that the westerners often were attempting to increase rather than cap the tax liabilities of elites. The answer is that while the southern political deal was irrelevant in the Northwest, the constitutional formula was highly attractive. The constitution writers of the Northwest looked at the southern language of "uniformity" and interpreted it as an American language of "equality." In Wisconsin, the point of a uniformity clause was "to have the legislature bound by some rules which would secure equal taxation." In Ohio, it was "equitably to fix in the fundamental law the great principles of taxation," and particularly the principle that "the property of the State ought to bear the burdens of the State" regardless of whether it belonged to individuals or corporations. A Michigan convention delegate identified uniformity with "equality" most directly: "[T]he question involved was one of mere justice—of equal rights—of uniform taxation."[8]

This effort to restrain majority rule by constitutional mandate in order to protect the "equal rights" of majorities turned out to be a grave mistake. The significance of the uniformity clauses would be worked out in the courts, where judges invoked them to shield elites from what state legislatures and local governments determined to be "equal taxation." The judges interfered aggressively in the local assessment process, quashing taxes at the behest of powerful taxpayers (such as railroad corporations) who claimed that assessors had overvalued their holdings and thereby violated the uniformity mandates. On the same justification, the judges also quashed tax legislation aimed at the wealth of elites: income taxes, inheritance taxes, various kinds of corporation taxes, and taxes levied at progressive rates.[9] This outcome made a mockery of the intentions of the men who had championed the uniformity clauses in the Northwest. They had meant to protect "the poor man's little supply of comforts, for his helpless, and, perhaps, suffering family" against tax exemptions for the "immense, and, in most instances, useless or injurious hoards [of the] millionaire."[10] They had *not* intended to grant the millionaire a constitutional shelter against the power of the majority to decide how to tax.

Their mistake was very significant. Misreading a defense of slavery as a defense of equality, the constitution writers of the antebellum Northwest did not even suspect that they were establishing privileges for their homegrown elites.

The northerners who accepted the direct tax clauses (and other proslavery provisions) of the U.S. Constitution as the price of its adoption did not confuse the outcome with "democracy." The southern yeomen who accepted uniformity clauses as the price of suffrage and apportionment reforms also knew that they were sacrificing majority rule to the demands of slaveholding elites for "security." But the men who framed state constitutions in the antebellum Northwest simply did not understand. Because they did not realize that these constitutional restraints on majority rule were elitist restraints on "the people," they turned concessions to slaveholders into shelters for other elites. Like many other Americans of their time, they could not tell the difference between a democratic strategy to promote equality and an antidemocratic strategy to protect slavery. This confusion is one of the critical legacies of the Age of Jackson.

From the perspective of the late nineteenth century, the wave of antebellum uniformity clauses seemed to have created a tax policy. This policy, known as "general property taxation," attempted to distribute tax burdens to individuals in proportion to their total wealth. It defined "wealth" as both real estate and personal property and measured it through local assessments of everything from land and buildings to livestock, machinery, commercial inventories, furniture, vehicles, jewelry, and the financial assets called "intangibles" (stocks, bonds, loan instruments). No assessors ever valued all of this property, few taxpayers reported even large fractions of it, and assessments rarely captured the true value of any of it. Many state officials found this situation intolerable. In dozens of angry reports, they exposed scandalous levels of everyday tax evasion across the country, most spectacularly in the case of the financial assets. The general property tax, a typical report proclaimed, was "debauching to the conscience and subversive of the public morals—a school for perjury, promoted by law." It "may be a burden on the conscience of the many," another lamented, "but it is a burden on the property of the few; not because there are few who ought to pay, but because there are few who can be made to pay."[1]

This was the voice of the Progressive Era, directing an outraged moralism at a practical problem of political economy. We hear echoes of this voice in exposés of the legion of special-interest provisions in our federal income tax code. The fine line between "tax avoidance" (legal) and "tax evasion" (illegal), whose navigation supports armies of accountants and lawyers, ought to tell us that taxation is a political process rather than a test of morality. Still, matters were out of hand in the late nineteenth century—creating a field day for the judges who cited assessment irregularities to quash the taxes of elites. Massive games of competitive underassessment pitted urban against rural districts to produce ridiculously low real estate valuations, enterprising towns advertised themselves as tax havens with illegally lenient assessors, and municipal bond markets rose and fell in tandem with state assessment deadlines as wealthy owners of taxable intangibles exchanged them for tax-exempt securities annually. "Before the enactment of Prohibition," the leading historian of these practices concludes, "probably nothing in American life entailed more calculated and premeditated lying than the general property tax."[2]

There was also another voice of the Progressive Era. In the cosmopolitan voice of social science expertise, the first generation of academic economists—led by Richard T. Ely of Johns Hopkins University and E. R. A. Seligman of Columbia University—urged Americans to replace "the happy-go-lucky system of property valuation" with taxes suited to the "complex industrial society of the present, with its delicate machinery and its subtle interrelations of all kinds." General property taxation may have been practical in the past (though the economists were skeptical), but in the "modern conditions" of the late nineteenth century, attempts to fix it by tinkering with its details "usually prove fruitless or render a bad matter worse." "The truth is, the existing system is so radically bad, that the more you improve it, the worse it becomes." After decades of energetic agitation, the economists finally won. Most states abolished general property taxation in the early decades of the twentieth century. They separated their state and local revenue bases, reserved real estate taxes for local use, and replaced the personal property taxes with state-level income taxes. This reform package established the outline of our present system of state and local taxation.[3]

Uniformity clauses posed obstacles to the reform agenda because they *required* state and local governments to tax the value of both real estate and personal property. To the economists, therefore, it seemed reasonable to treat the histories of the taxes and clauses as two sides of the same phenomenon. States had adopted both in the Jacksonian era in response to "the progress of democratic thought," and particularly to the idea "that all should contribute in proportion to their abilities."[4] Ely and Seligman recognized that general property taxation was much older than the uniformity clauses. They knew, for example, that the Massachusetts "country rates" had directed town assessors to make "a true estimation of all personall & real estates" in the 1640s. But they missed a large piece of the puzzle. Drawing pictures of American economic history that ignored slavery, they did not realize that the origin of the clauses had very little to do with the origin of the taxes.[5] They did not notice that the states that established pioneering general property taxes did not adopt uniformity clauses, while the states that adopted pioneering uniformity clauses did not levy general property taxes. They did not realize that the "personal property" at issue in the adoption of the first clauses—the property that had to be taxed in the same way as real estate—actually consisted of slaves in the South rather than financial assets in the North.[6]

The development of general property taxation and its constitutionalization were separate historical processes. They unfolded simultaneously, but they unfolded in different places and for different reasons. The pioneering general property tax legislation was enacted in the Northeast. Building on traditions dating from the colonial era, states such as Massachusetts, New York, and Pennsylvania revised their tax laws to drop flat-rate valuations and differential rate schedules, expand lists of taxable objects to include broad ranges of financial assets, and add procedures to handle the property owned by corporations. In theory, the resulting taxes were "uniform" and "universal," imposing the same ad valorem rates on all kinds of property and taxing all kinds of property except limited exemptions. In practice, they distributed burdens to individuals through the local assessment process—in the northern policy tradition that Oliver Wolcott had called "the principle of local responsibility." Legislatures created the ground rules, but the assessors and taxpayers who jockeyed over their local implementation made the real decisions.

The pioneering uniformity clauses, meanwhile, appeared in the South. Maryland was the true pioneer, acting during the Revolution, followed by states such as Missouri, Tennessee, and Louisiana in the antebellum era. These states, and also Virginia and North Carolina, faced the political dilemma of being slave states in which slaveholders were small minorities of the white population. When nonslaveholding small farmers in these states (and city people in Louisiana) called for legislative reapportionments to translate majority status into majority power, they had to persuade slaveholding minorities that they would not impose heavy or prohibitive slave taxes. Uniformity clauses offered these guarantees. "No one species of property from which a tax may be collected," as Tennessee phrased it, "shall be taxed higher than any other species of property of equal value."[7] These clauses had nothing to do with general property taxation. The southern uniformity states preserved cherry-picking lists of taxable property and "license" schedules that levied particularistic taxes on groups of taxpayers. Across the South, these practices meant that legislatures made the decisions that distributed tax burdens. Uniformity clauses limited the ways they could distribute the burdens to slaveholders.

The misleading development was the synthesis of these northern and southern practices in the Northwest, in states that adopted general property taxes *and* uniformity clauses. Although Illinois adopted the region's first clause in 1818, the synthesis did not happen until the 1840s and 1850s—Illinois levied flat per acre land taxes until 1839 even though its constitution stipulated that "the mode of taxation shall be by valuation." By the 1840s, however, the older northwestern states had switched to general property taxation by revising their tax laws, while the newer ones were copying their laws from eastern statute books to institute it immediately. In the Northwest, therefore, uniformity clauses actually did constitutionalize general property taxes. Ely criticized these decisions as hopelessly naive, made at a time when "people were more inclined to abolish or restrict power than to learn how to use it properly." Forty years later, when Ely was writing, this "fossilization of laws and institutions" had turned the living into "slaves of the dead" and condemned the "vast majority of the people" to "be ruled by a small but determined minority which finds profit in governmental imperfections."[8]

The minority that most troubled Ely consisted of the "vast corporations" of the late nineteenth century. "Unless the people are willing to trust themselves in financial matters, they must always expect to be worsted in contests" with these opponents.[9] But Ely missed the larger irony, that the elite of his own industrialized ("modern") society was exploiting a mechanism originally designed to protect another elite. The people who did not trust themselves in the Northwest had amplified the significance of a constitutional device framed for slaveholders who did not trust the people. The uniformity clauses of the state constitutions reflected the same political imperative as the direct tax clauses of the U.S. Constitution. Slaveholders simply would not allow nonslaveholding majorities to decide how to tax. Both of these fossilizations of their antidemocratic demands would outlive them. Both would shelter the wealth of industrial elites into the twentieth century. The direct tax clauses effectively required Congress to rely on the tariff by allowing the U.S. Supreme Court to block federal income taxation. The uniformity clauses frustrated similar attempts to secure "equal taxation" in the states.

General property taxation had never been intended to produce either moral perfection or scientific precision. It was intended to distribute burdens to individuals through the local politics of local assessments. Even the Puritans had not been shocked by large gaps between the results and "a true estimation of all personall & real estates." When glaring biases demanded attention, the Puritans had added incremental reforms such as rules for handling "marchants, shopkeepers and factors." Uniformity clauses, however, were reactions against politics. They were intended to take the politics out of an inherently political decision—who pays the taxes—by setting it in constitutional stone. The history of antebellum property taxation is the story of these different visions of politics, of institutional arrangements that were and were not based on majority rule, local self-government, and a basic acceptance of everyday politics on the ground.

The Antebellum Moment

The United States was a very different place in the antebellum era than it had been in the 1790s. With boundaries spanning the continent, population growth reflecting mass immigration (particularly from Ireland and the German states), a politics in which national parties (Whigs and Democrats) mobilized an almost universally enfranchised white male electorate, an economy in which large-scale manufacturing was beginning to displace artisan production, and a commercial popular culture that made celebrities of its actors and musicians, this society is more familiar to us than its predecessors. It was still a society that held millions of African Americans in chattel slavery (2 million in 1830, 4 million in 1860). It was still a society that excluded women from electoral politics and large sectors of the economy. It was still a society in which white demands for Indian land produced constant warfare, now capped by the formal ethnic cleansing campaigns known as Indian Removal. It was also a society careening toward its destruction. It was a kind of Weimar in blackface—with high levels of everyday violence punctuated by extraordinary outbreaks in the places where rebellious slaves, proslavery Border Ruffians, and divinely inspired abolitionists forced everyone else to recognize the central conflict of American life.[10]

The overwhelming fact about the antebellum United States was its growth. There were 13 states in 1790, 24 in 1830, and 33 in 1860. A population of 3.9 million in 1790 reached 12.9 million in 1830, and 31.4 million in 1860. Another crucial fact is that most of this growth was rural. In every part of the country, most people either lived and worked on farms or performed local services for neighbors who did.[11] Even in the Northeast, only 36 percent of the population lived in towns larger than 2,500 in 1860; the national figure was 20 percent. Americans were impressed by, and wary about, the explosive growth of the largest cities: New York to 814,000, Philadelphia to 565,000, Brooklyn to 267,000, and Baltimore to 212,000, with Boston and New Orleans not far behind and the western cities (Cincinnati, St. Louis, Chicago) seeming to shoot from the ground. They were also impressed and appalled by industrialization when they saw it, from the textile factories that employed large numbers of women and children in New England to the "bastardized crafts" that turned skilled artisans into semiskilled workers in the cities (in shoes, clothing, furniture, and so on). Yet these dramatic developments must not obscure the general picture. More than half the populations of Massachusetts (51 percent) and Rhode Island (56 percent) lived in towns larger than 2,500 in 1860, but this figure was still under one-third in *every* other state—and towns of 2,500 obviously were not all that "urban," even when residents worked in textile mills. The stereotype of an "industrial North" meeting an "agrarian South" on the battlefields of the Civil War is misleading. The growth of the antebellum United States was the expansion of an overwhelmingly rural society.[12]

It actually was the expansion of two rural societies, or many more if we consider regions smaller than the North and South.[13] The northern rural society was essentially the "Jeffersonian" society of small farmers, skilled artisans (millers, coopers, blacksmiths), and handfuls of doctors, lawyers, and shopkeepers. In the Northeast, farmers increasingly specialized in wool, dairying, meat, and market gardening for urban consumption. In the Northwest, they specialized in wheat and corn for the Northeast, parts of the South, and export to Europe. The southern rural society combined family farming (often with a limited use of slave labor) with a slave-based plantation agriculture, especially in the cotton belt that stretched from South Carolina and Georgia to Texas. This rural society had fewer shopkeepers, but plenty of doctors, lawyers, and especially skilled artisans—though many of the artisans labored as slaves, either directly for owners or in rental ("hiring out") arrangements. Family farmers ("yeomen") dominated areas with poor soils and poor transportation links; slaveholding planters ("planters" owned twenty or more slaves) dominated areas with richer soils and river connections to ports. Slavery had been showing signs of decline in the Upper South (Maryland, Virginia) since the mid-eighteenth century, as farmers who grew more wheat and less tobacco came to prefer hiring free people of color on a seasonal basis to owning slaves year around. Even so, Virginia still had more slaves (490,000) and slaveholders (52,000) in 1860 than any other state, despite the fact that it had fallen to fifth in total population.[14]

The Louisiana Purchase (1803) established U.S. control of the Mississippi River and the War of 1812 established U.S. control of the Great Lakes, though settlers had been trickling into Kentucky and Tennessee since the 1770s and Ohio since the 1780s. Once the claims of Britain, France, and Spain were extinguished—leaving the Indian nations of these areas on their own for military purposes—this movement accelerated dramatically. In the 1830s, the army supervised forced removals of Indians from lands white settlers wanted, on parallel "trails of tears" running from the North into Kansas and the South into Oklahoma. The United States acquired Florida by purchase in 1819, Texas by voluntary annexation in 1845 (after American settlers there staged a revolution against Mexico in 1836), Oregon by treaty in 1846, and California and New Mexico by conquest in 1848. The Gadsden Purchase of southern Arizona and New Mexico (1853) completed U.S. acquisition of what became the lower 48 states, though Indians still controlled much of the territory from the Mississippi to the Sierra Nevada.

The big story of American economic growth in this era was the rise of the Deep South "cotton kingdom." In 1790, Georgia was tiny (83,000, 35 percent slave), while Alabama and Mississippi were Creek and Choctaw country, partially under the jurisdiction of Spain. South Carolina had been expanding since the defeat of the Cherokees in the French and Indian War opened its backcountry to a population mainly of nonslaveholding farmers, but its population was still under 250,000 (43 percent slave) in 1790. By 1860, this region looked different. South Carolina had reached 700,000 (57 percent slave), with the spread of upcountry cotton plantations muting the earlier geographical split. Georgia stood at 1 million (44 percent slave), Alabama at 960,000 (45 percent slave), and Mississippi at 790,000 (55 percent slave). Louisiana, Arkansas, Florida, and Texas were smaller, but added another 1.9 million people (680,000 slaves) to the kingdom. The causes of this boom are well known. In the 1790s, the mechanical cotton gin made short-staple cotton economically viable just as the Industrial Revolution in Britain created vast new demand. While long-staple cotton (profitable even when ginned by hand) required rich coastal soils, the short-staple plant grew well across the region, its profitability limited only by the adequacy of transportation facilities.[15]

For the 38,000 Cherokees, Creeks, Choctaws, and Chickasaws "removed" to make way for it, the rise of the cotton kingdom was catastrophic. For the one million African Americans relocated by migrating masters or sold out of the Upper South, it was a disaster comparable to the Atlantic slave trade itself. It produced a relentless disruption of families and communities, and, for slaves "sold down the river" into the commercial trade (two-thirds of those who were moved), it produced searing experiences of what Walter Johnson has called the "chattel principle": the commodification of people that defined the institution of slavery.[16] For whites, meanwhile, the cotton kingdom produced booming prosperity. We often think of northern businessmen as the richest Americans of this era, but economic historians have shown that the title belonged to the cotton-belt planters—because the people they owned were expensive. "A man who owned two slaves and nothing else," Gavin Wright explains, "was as rich as the average man in the North." In the South as a whole in 1860, 25 percent of the white households owned slaves. In the cotton kingdom, *half* of them did. Holdings were concentrated: 60 percent of all slaveholders owned five or fewer, while the 8,000 owners of 50 or more owned 1 million of the 4 million slaves in the United States. James L. Huston illustrates the magnitude of these holdings by showing that more wealth was owned in the form of enslaved African Americans in 1860 ($3 billion) than in railroad and manufacturing assets combined ($2.2 billion). Even counting land, as well as livestock, railroads, factories, and bank capital, slaves comprised 20 percent of *all* American wealth.[17]

The other big story was the rise of New York, the state even more than the city. In 1787, when the large- and small-state delegates debated about representation at Philadelphia, New York was a small state. At 340,000 in 1790, it was only slightly larger than Maryland, and even this figure reflected very recent growth. In the colonial era, most of what is now New York was Iroquoia. Through a combination of military power and artful diplomacy, the Six Nations of the Iroquois Confederacy had defended their land more successfully than most other Indians. As a result, the colony barely extended beyond the Hudson River. It consisted of two commercial towns (New York and Albany), vast manors owned by aristocratic landlords and worked by tenant farmers along the Hudson, and town-based communities of landowning farmers (often slaveholding) on Long Island and in what are now the outer boroughs of New York City. The Iroquois weathered the French and Indian War, but they could not weather the Revolution. The Revolutionary War was a civil war in Iroquoia. It splintered the confederacy and its constituent nations, destroyed dozens of prosperous towns (one U.S. invasion in 1778 leveled forty of them), and culminated in huge land cessions and emigrations (to Canada and Wisconsin).[18]

The transformation of New York occurred in two phases. In the first, New Englanders streamed into New York in the 1780s and 1790s to seize the same opportunity their descendents would seize in Ohio, Michigan, and Oregon: to replicate the town-based family farming pattern on land newly wrested from Indians. Speculators tried to replicate the manorial relations of the Hudson Valley, in which tenants owed landlords deference and labor in addition to rent, but the settlers won full ownership rights in western New York and, after decades of struggle, finally in the Hudson Valley.[19] New York also abolished slavery slowly. There was more slavery in and around New York City in 1790 than anywhere else in the North. Merchants and artisans owned slaves in the city, while 40 percent of the white households owned them in rural Kings, Queens, and Richmond counties. New York enacted a "gradual abolition" law in 1799. Slaves born after its passage would be freed as adults (men at 28, women at 25)—as long as owners or kidnappers had not sold them illegally into the South before then. There were 10,000 slaves and 29,000 free people of color in 1820, but that was the end of the line. In 1830, there were 45,000 free people of color but only 75 slaves. Meanwhile, with a population of 1.3

million in 1820, New York had overtaken Virginia to become the largest state, a status it kept for the next 150 years.[20]

But it was the second phase that built the Empire State. By the 1850s, New York was the top producer of almost everything made in the United States except corn, tobacco, and cotton. It exported most of the nation's grain and much of its cotton; imported and manufactured the goods that went west and south in return; and led the nation in banking, insurance, and publishing. One source of this economic power was the cotton trade, in which New York City merchants handled much of the South's shipping and financing. Another was immigration. New York City was the leading entry point for European immigrants, many of whom settled there or in other parts of the state. New York's leadership in the Transportation Revolution added further advantages. The state's aggressive construction of roads, canals, and then railroads stimulated massive growth in New York, linking fertile lands to markets and turning towns such as Rochester into major cities. It also shaped the growth of the Northwest, directing its produce to New York via Cleveland, Detroit, and Chicago and changing the source of its settlers, so that large northern and immigrant migrations swamped earlier migrations from the Upper South. The decisive project was the Erie Canal. Completed in 1825, the Erie was a triumph of engineering, sheer labor, and public enterprise. State officials managed the project, creating a British market for American bonds, deploying the state's capital to cushion its economy against shocks, and earning enough income from canal tolls to finance further transportation arteries. Other states emulated this growth strategy, with mixed results in the initial "canal mania" and more consistent success in the ensuing railroad boom.[21]

The political story of the antebellum era was the rise of mass political parties.[22] The Whigs and Democrats were different from the Federalists and Republicans. Where the first parties had deployed careful uses of patronage, populist rhetoric, and some partisan pageantry, the Whigs and Democrats turned these practices into art forms, stimulated much higher levels of voter participation among a larger electorate (most states had abolished property qualifications for the suffrage), and added a new level of organizational mastery. They also produced a new kind of politician, who expected his constituents to value his party loyalty over his ability to think for himself. Both parties included serious people—Andrew Jackson, Martin Van Buren, Henry Clay, Daniel Webster—but both also included men like the six-term Indiana congressman Ratliff Boon. In 1836, this Democratic "party man" boasted that he was "one of the true collar dogs" with "the entire confidence of their masters." Boon was "proud to wear the collar of such a man as Andrew Jackson, whose collar is the collar of democracy." By the 1840s, this aggressively unreflective style had become typical, especially though not only in the Northwest.[23]

The crucial fact about the Whigs and the Democrats is that they were national rather than sectional parties. For the life of this party system (roughly 1834 to 1852), they were competitive in every state except South Carolina, where a different alignment prevailed. Formed around the struggle over Jackson's "war" against the Second Bank of the United States—his veto of the bill to recharter it in 1832 and removal of the Treasury deposits to "pet banks" in 1833—the parties coalesced around opposing views on economic policy and presidential power. In the 1840s, as the magnitude of a huge upsurge in immigration became clear, the parties also stressed cultural issues. North and South, Whigs favored a national bank to regulate the currency, expanded state bank facilities to provide credit, subsidies for transportation projects ("internal improvements") to link farmers to markets, and protective tariffs to stimulate industry. Democrats opposed the banks, tariffs, and most transportation subsidies, arguing that they handed "special privileges" to elites and, at the national level, threatened slavery by strengthening the federal government. On the cultural issues (liquor laws, religion in the schools, naturalization policies), Whigs favored natives over immigrants and Protestants over Catholics, with Democrats on the other side. Most generally, Whigs favored stronger governments and Democrats favored stronger presidents.[24]

The parties had complicated constituencies. In many southern states, Whigs ran better among planters and Democrats among yeoman farmers, though this relationship was reversed in Virginia and parts of North Carolina, Kentucky, and Tennessee—where the Whigs championed yeoman demands for schools, roads, and credit facilities, as well as democratized suffrage and apportionment rules (most states had abolished property qualifications by the early 1820s, but Virginia held out until 1851 and North Carolina until 1854).[25] In the Northeast, Whigs ran best in rural areas and Democrats in the cities, mainly because there were more immigrant voters in the cities (urban elites often were Whigs). In the Northwest, however, where there were many rural immigrant voters, Whigs ran best among "Yankees" from the Northeast while Democrats crafted coalitions between southern migrants (from Virginia and North Carolina, often by way of Kentucky and Tennessee) and European immigrants (particularly but not only Catholics). The glue in this coalition was resistance to Yankee "moral reform" projects, though racism also was critical. Throughout the North, the Democrats were more deeply committed to white supremacy. They promoted "black laws" that disfranchised African Americans, excluded them from juries and sometimes from testifying in court, barred them from public schools, and prohibited them even from settling in four states (Illinois, Indiana, Iowa, Oregon). In some parts of the North, Whigs had to adopt antiracist positions to prevent defections to the abolitionist Liberty Party.[26]

Because the Whig and Democratic parties were national, competing in both the North and the South, they took very similar positions on slavery—that silence was the best way to hold their parties together and that compromise was necessary when silence was impossible. Three issues made silence impossible. In the 1830s, abolitionists flooded the South with antislavery pamphlets and Congress with antislavery petitions. The Post Office stopped the pamphlets with outright censorship and Congress quashed the petitions with the notorious "gag rule." At the same time, South Carolinians attacked a very high tariff as an abolitionist plot to undermine the profitability of slave labor. Congress defused the ensuing Nullification Crisis with a compromise tariff. The decisive issue was the westward expansion of slavery. Dramatized in the Missouri Crisis (1819–21), when northern congressmen attempted to force Missouri to abolish slavery as a condition of statehood, and revived in 1836 over the admission of Texas (rebuffed by leaders of both parties), this problem intensified with the territorial conquests of the Mexican War (1846–48). Historians disagree about exactly what destroyed the Whigs, split the Democrats, and forged a Republican party that existed only in the North in the 1850s, but the difficult compromises over slavery in the territories (Compromise of 1850, Kansas-Nebraska Act of 1854) clearly played major roles. Until the 1850s, however, the Whigs and Democrats often managed to suppress national-level debate about slavery. In the South, both were strongly proslavery. In the North, both balanced general antislavery sentiments against a willingness to tolerate the institution in the South.[27]

Aside from the tariff, where the issue was protectionism rather than revenue, the Whigs and Democrats articulated no consistent positions on tax policy. Whigs were more enthusiastic about transportation and education spending, but both parties preferred to avoid general taxes at the state level by drawing revenue from banks and transportation projects until a major depression, the Panic of 1837, brought states to the verge of bankruptcy. In 1842, Democrats in New York developed a "Stop and Tax" policy to ban state borrowing for internal improvements. Making arguments just like the ones the Jeffersonians had made in the 1790s, they championed heavy taxation to compel people to "feel" the costs of transportation spending. Whigs answered predictably. Horace Greeley condemned Stop and Tax as a partisan scheme "to render Internal Improvements unpopular with the people" and "a wanton aggravation of the public burthens at a time of great and general depression." In 1846, the New York Democrats inserted Stop and Tax into their state constitution, as Louisiana Democrats had done in 1845. The result was a partisan agenda for the consti-

218 | Chapter 6

tutional reform of public finance, though not for the constitutional reform of taxation. The same New York Democrats who crusaded to limit the borrowing power dismissed an effort to limit the tax power (a uniformity clause) out of hand. Their allies in the Northwest would be less discriminating.[28]

In hindsight, no political story of the antebellum United States is nearly as significant as the one that has named it (in Latin) as the polity that would collapse in 1861. This is the story of antislavery violence, from the everyday arsons and poisonings on the plantations, along with the consistently ferocious white responses, to the Denmark Vesey conspiracy (1822), the Nat Turner rebellion (1831), the guerilla warfare of Bleeding Kansas (1855–56), and John Brown's raid on Harper's Ferry (1859). This is the story of the slaveholders' radicalization, as the Virginia rhetoric conceding the moral point to win the political point (which angered northerners) gave way to the cotton kingdom rhetoric of fire-eaters declaring that slavery was "a positive good" (which disgusted northerners). This is the story of the sectional conflict overwhelming class conflicts, of partisan alliances crumbling, and of the premise that the nation could endure half slave and half free dissolving in the *Dred Scott* case (1857), when the U.S. Supreme Court ruled that the sanctity of southern property rights was the law of the nation itself.[29]

The story of antebellum taxation has very little to do with this story. It does not lead to the battlefields where the Union defeated the Confederacy. Nor does it lead to the home front where African Americans brought slavery to an end whenever the regimes that enforced it showed signs of weakness.[30] The tax story is about the states rather than the nation. It is also about convergence rather than divergence, as northern states made minor reforms and southern states made major reforms, including the introduction of ad valorem taxes and local assessments. Most of all, it is a story about synthesis, as northern taxation met southern constitutionalism in the Northwest.

Taxes

By the antebellum era, the government systems of the North and South were more similar than they had ever been. Every state had a governor and bicameral legislature, and many created administrative boards for specific tasks. Voters elected governors and other top officials in most states, though legislatures chose the governors of Georgia until 1824, North Carolina until 1835, Maryland until 1837, New Jersey until 1844, Virginia until 1851, and South Carolina until 1865. Local governments exhibited more variation. The New England states continued to rely on town government, while the Pennsylvania county-and-township model and a similar New York system spread across the Northwest. In the South, new states adopted the Virginia county court model, though most democratized it immediately with elected rather than appointed (or co-opted) JPs and sheriffs. Among the laggards, Tennessee switched to elections in 1834 (for sheriffs but not JPs), Louisiana in 1845, North Carolina in 1848 (sheriffs but not JPs), Kentucky in 1850, and, finally, Virginia itself in 1851. South Carolina maintained its unique colonial-era regime of appointed local commissions, now for roads and bridges, poor relief, schools, and public buildings. Even there, however, voters elected their local sheriffs and tax collectors.[31]

Tax levels followed similar trends across the country, falling sharply in the early republic and then rising in the antebellum years. The least well-documented part of this story is the first one. State and local taxes must have plummeted everywhere after 1790, as the U.S. government assumed the outstanding costs of the Revolution and the states disestablished religion. While the assumption of the state debts is the famous piece of Alexander Hamilton's program to establish the "public credit" of the United States, the critical piece was the assumption of the *national* debt. That debt was the reason the states owed unpayable requisitions in the 1780s and its assumption established the "public credit." The disestablishment of religion, meanwhile, freed the states and especially local governments from the costs of church buildings and clerical salaries. Each state acted individually and some acted in stages, but when Massachusetts made its final concession in 1833, religious taxation was gone for good. Several states avoided property taxation for decades: Pennsylvania from 1788 to 1831, Maryland from 1790 to 1842 (except small levies in the 1830s to finance the deportation of "free negroes and mulattoes" to Liberia), and New York for most of the same period. Local taxation continued, but burdens clearly fell across the board.[32]

Many states found lucrative alternatives to taxation. Most of the western states received land grants for schools (one section in each township) and funds for roads (2 percent of land sale receipts), often supplemented with further land grants. In a variation on this theme, Connecticut built a rich school fund from land it owned in Ohio. Transportation projects also sometimes paid off. Like New York, Ohio built canals that generated tremendous economic growth, leveraging its ability to service its debt from canal tolls to sell new bonds to finance more canals. Georgia's investment in a railroad corporation enabled it to cut and then cancel its taxes. Other states were less successful—Virginia because it refused to hire professional engineers or invest real money, Pennsylvania because its program was too grandiose (a canal over the Appalachians), and Illinois because it launched its (also grandiose) program on the eve of the Panic of 1837. Eastern states often did better with banking. Some established state banks, some earned dividends from investments in banks, some taxed banks, and some required banks to pay bonuses for corporate charters. At one time or another between 1820 and 1860, bank income produced 35 percent of the state-level revenue in Connecticut, Pennsylvania, North Carolina, and South Carolina; 60 percent in Rhode Island and Delaware; and 80 percent in Massachusetts.[33]

But sectional differences persisted. First of all, especially after 1830, northern taxes were higher than southern taxes. Using state-level data compiled by the economic historians Richard Sylla and John Wallis, figure 2 compares state-level property tax burdens in the North and South from 1810 to 1850.[34] The high southern figures for the early part of the period, and particularly the peak in 1815, reflect state decisions to assume the quotas of the U.S. direct taxes for the War of 1812, which more southern states did because some northern legislatures, especially in New England, opposed the war. After 1830, however, when these data consist of state-level taxes for state-level purposes, the northern figures are higher. Northerners paid 9 cents per capita in 1830, 15 in 1840, and 36 in 1850. Southerners paid 5 cents per capita (free) in 1830, 11 in 1840, and 26 in 1850. The southern figures fall further when they are calculated on a true per capita basis (including slaves): to 3 cents in 1830, 7 in 1840, and 13 in 1850.

The post-1835 tax increases reflected decisions to expand public services, but they also reflected the economy's collapse in the Panic of 1837. A very deep depression from 1839 into the mid-1840s, the panic caught states that had inaugurated ambitious transportation programs with huge debts, unfinished

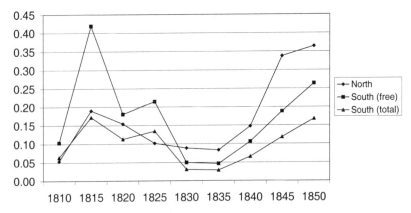

Figure 2. State Property Taxes per Capita, 1810–1850 (selected states). SOURCE: Calculated from Richard Sylla and John Joseph Wallis, "The Anatomy of Sovereign Debt Crises: Lessons from the American State Defaults of the 1840s," *Japan and the World Economy* 10 (1998): 281; Seventh Census, 1850, ix.

projects, and no near-term prospects of resuming construction. Nine defaulted at least temporarily (Pennsylvania, Maryland, Indiana, Illinois, Michigan, Mississippi, Louisiana, Florida, and Arkansas), while even those that remained solvent had to increase taxes or revive taxes they had not levied for decades. Following the New York "Stop and Tax" strategy, many states amended their constitutions to prevent legislatures from incurring onerous debts in the future. These provisions fixed debt ceilings, required debts to be secured by taxes dedicated to the debt service, and prohibited legislatures from lending the state credit to or otherwise investing in corporations. They also instituted general incorporation, allowing banks and other businesses to incorporate if they met general qualifications rather than requiring them to obtain special acts from legislatures. As John Wallis has pointed out, these reforms forced states to impose higher taxes by abolishing the lucrative alternatives of the past.[35]

State taxes are only part of the story. Local governments also levied higher taxes in the North. Unfortunately, we have nothing resembling comprehensive data on the taxes of counties, townships, cities, and other local government units in this period. What we have, from the 1850 census, is some suggestive data about local school taxes (see table 7). In 1850, these taxes were almost as high as state taxes in the North, but much lower than state taxes in the South. Northern local governments levied 31 cents per capita; southern local governments levied 5 cents.[36] The southern figure rises to 8 cents if we count only the free (or white) population, since the southern governments obviously did not tax for the education of slaves, but 8 cents is still only one-fourth of the northern figure. School taxes were higher in the East than the West and in more urbanized than less urbanized states. Indeed, the presence of big cities probably accounts for the relatively high figure in Maryland and the very high figure in Louisiana (California's zero is an artifact of recent statehood and a gold rush population with few children).[37] But the sectional pattern is clear. If other local taxes resembled the school taxes, local governments levied much higher taxes than states in the North, widening the already large gap between the North and the South.

The higher local taxes of the northern states reflected a more general structural difference between northern and southern tax institutions. In the North, the property tax was essentially a local tax, with assessment and collection machinery that functioned even when the states were relying on bank taxes, investment earnings, and other revenue sources. When northern states had to supplement these sources with property taxes, state officials simply directed local officials to add state rates to the local rates they were already levying. In the South, meanwhile, the property tax was essentially a state tax. With local governments relying on fees, fines, licenses, and poll taxes (on "tithables"),

Table 7: Local Government School Taxes, 1850

	Total (dollars)	Per Capita white	free	total
NORTHEAST	**3,506,005**	**0.41**	**0.41**	**0.41**
Connecticut	41,205	0.11	0.11	0.11
Maine	269,723	0.46	0.46	0.46
Massachusetts	935,241	0.95	0.94	0.94
New Hampshire	141,791	0.45	0.45	0.45
New Jersey	76,149	0.16	0.16	0.16
New York	761,505	0.25	0.25	0.25
Pennsylvania	1,120,246	0.50	0.48	0.48
Rhode Island	62,296	0.43	0.42	0.42
Vermont	97,849	0.31	0.31	0.31
NORTHWEST	**654,525**	**0.14**	**0.14**	**0.14**
California	0	0.00	0.00	0.00
Illinois	100,694	0.12	0.12	0.12
Indiana	76,746	0.08	0.08	0.08
Iowa	16,549	0.09	0.09	0.09
Michigan	88,879	0.22	0.22	0.22
Ohio	285,266	0.15	0.14	0.14
Wisconsin	86,391	0.28	0.28	0.28
UPPER SOUTH	**236,521**	**0.06**	**0.06**	**0.04**
Delaware	14,422	0.20	0.16	0.16
Kentucky	41,276	0.05	0.05	0.04
Maryland	86,663	0.21	0.18	0.15
Missouri	3,024	0.01	0.01	0.00
North Carolina	42,936	0.08	0.07	0.05
Tennessee	4,730	0.01	0.01	0.00
Virginia	43,470	0.05	0.05	0.03
LOWER SOUTH	**252,430**	**0.12**	**0.12**	**0.06**
Alabama	800	0.00	0.00	0.00
Arkansas	250	0.00	0.00	0.00
Florida	0	0.00	0.00	0.00
Georgia	21,520	0.04	0.04	0.02
Louisiana	194,984	0.76	0.71	0.38
Mississippi	33,676	0.11	0.11	0.06
South Carolina	1,200	0.00	0.00	0.00
Texas	0	0.00	0.00	0.00
NORTH	**4,160,530**	**0.31**	**0.31**	**0.31**
SOUTH	**488,951**	**0.08**	**0.08**	**0.05**
TOTAL	**4,649,481**	**0.24**	**0.23**	**0.20**

SOURCE: J. D. B. DeBow, *Statistical View of the United States* (1854), 142–43; Seventh Census, 1850, ix.

there were no regular assessment and collection procedures apart from the ones the states established for particular levies. Because the southern states increasingly allowed local governments to add their own local rates to the state rates, this distinction tended to blur in practice. By the 1840s and 1850s, when most states levied property taxes every year, it survived only as a feature of the tax legislation itself. Northern states supplemented detailed "permanent" laws outlining procedures with brief annual laws setting rates. Southern states established rates and procedures together in detailed annual laws. Still, this merely formal distinction expressed a more basic reality. States piggybacked on local property taxes in the North. Local governments piggybacked on state property taxes in the South.

The northern and southern tax systems also differed in more practical ways. By 1860, every state assessed the value of at least some forms of property. Every state assessed financial assets, every state but South Carolina assessed real estate (South Carolina still classified land by region and quality, ignoring buildings and improvements), and most states assessed livestock, commercial inventories, and luxury possessions (carriages, pianos, plate). Kentucky, Tennessee, Missouri, and Arkansas even assessed the "value" of enslaved human beings.[38] Still, there were important structural differences. Northern states taxed "all" property at uniform rates. Southern states taxed specified objects at specified rates. Aside from the earnings of certain corporations (principally banks and railroads), northern states now rarely taxed business profits, professional incomes, or salaries—having dropped the colonial-era "faculty" taxes that defined these items as taxable assets. Now, northern states taxed individuals and businesses, including corporations, by taxing their property. Southern states, in contrast, usually limited property taxation to individual assets. They taxed commerce and the professions with elaborate schedules of business "license" taxes, some intended to tap profits and some intended to be shifted to consumers.[39]

For a sense of what a northern tax structure looked like, consider New York's, which influenced a number of other states. "All lands and all personal estate within this state, whether owned by individuals or by corporations, shall be liable to taxation, subject to the exemptions hereinafter specified." Land consisted of all real estate: the land itself, buildings, other improvements, trees, mines, minerals, quarries, and fossils (presumably coal). Personal estate was "all household furniture; moneys, goods; chattels, debts due from solvent debtors, whether on account, contract, note, bond or mortgage; public stocks; and stocks of monied corporations." New York exempted the assets of governments, churches, schools, libraries, agricultural societies, $1,500 of the property of ministers and priests, property on reservations of the Seneca

Nation, and all property that the state also sheltered from liability for private debts. The last exemption protected a basic standard of living: food ("pork, beef, fish, flour and vegetables, actually provided for family use"), clothing, bedding, housewares (a table, six chairs and place settings, cooking and serving utensils), heating stoves with fuel for 60 days, minimal holdings of tools and livestock, family bibles and pictures, church pews, schoolbooks, and $50 of other books. Local assessors were directed to value all of the taxable property "at its full and true value, as they would appraise the same in payment of a just debt due from a solvent debtor," but taxpayers could reduce their assessments of personal property by swearing to lower figures (a loophole that millionaires abused notoriously into the twentieth century). County boards equalized the local assessments and then various government bodies— counties, towns, highway commissions, and the state—levied ad valorem rates on the result.[40]

For a southern example, consider Mississippi. The state levied ad valorem rates on each $100 of the value of particular items: 16 cents on land; 20 cents on money-at-interest, goods of out-of-state merchants, currency from out-of-state banks, and sales of "slaves, horses and mules" by professional traders; 25 cents on pianos and receipts of ferries, toll bridges, and turnpikes; 30 cents on bank stock; 50 cents on carriages, clocks, watches, and gold and silver plate (exempting the first $50); 75 cents on race, saddle, and carriage horses; $1 on liquor sales; and $3 on sales by auctioneers and transient peddlers. Mississippi also levied flat rates: 40 cents on slaves under age sixty, a 40 cent poll tax on white men (21 to 50), and a $1 poll tax on "free colored" men (21 to 50); one cent per head on cattle (exempting the first twenty); $1 on each bowie knife, dirk knife, and sword cane; and $25 on bowling alleys, theaters, race-tracks, and circuses. Taxpayers assessed their own holdings, with degrees of supervision linked to types of property. Assessors were not permitted to touch the land valuations. Owners estimated the "intrinsic value" of their own land, "taking into consideration the improvements, also the proximity to navigation, or to any town, city, village or road, and any other circumstance that may tend to enhance its value"—and that was it. For personal property, assessors who suspected undervaluations of 20 percent notified county boards, which could raise them "to such a standard as they may deem just and proper." For the money-at-interest and bank stock, finally, assessors could replace self-assessed figures with the sums they had "reason to believe correct according to the best information [they] can procure." Counties levied taxes as proportions of the state assessments.[41]

Each state had its own peculiarities (the swearing loophole for personal property in New York, the untouchable self-assessments of land in Mississippi, not to mention the Tennessee tax on exhibitions for profit of "persons of unusual size [and] persons or animals deformed").[42] Yet most northern taxes looked pretty much like New York's and most southern taxes looked pretty much like Mississippi's. The New York tax was a general property tax. It established one rule for the taxation of "all" property, leaving the details to be worked out in the assessment process. The Mississippi tax discriminated explicitly among the owners of specific kinds of property. It favored land-holders with the lowest ad valorem rate (16 cents per $100) and slaveholders with a flat rate that was even lower. If the average slave cost $774 in 1860 (as estimated by economic historians Roger Ransom and Richard Sutch), a 40 cent flat tax was an ad valorem tax of only 5 cents per $100. Mississippi almost doubled its slave tax in 1860, to 75 cents, but this was still an ad valorem tax of only 9.7 cents per $100.[43]

Southern states with uniformity clauses in their constitutions dropped the discriminatory rate schedules but achieved similar results through their li-cense taxes. Louisiana perfected this strategy. It levied a uniform property tax of one-sixth of one percent (16.7 cents per $100) on the "full cash value" of real estate (land, city lots, buildings, improvements, machinery), slaves (not assessed, but valued at realistic flat rates such as $850 for men aged 15 to 45), horses and other animals, carriages, ships (including shares in steamboats and other vessels), corporate stock, and the capital invested in "any kind of commerce."[44] A northern state would have stopped there, but Louisiana added $500 on insurance agents ($1,000 on agents of out-of-state companies); $300 on slave traders; $200 on theaters; $100 on money brokers, pawn brokers, liquor retailers, circuses, menageries, racetracks, and peddlers operating from boats; $50 on billiard tables; $30 on factors, commission merchants, whole-salers, cotton pressers (for shipment), restaurants, coffeehouses, and bars; $25 on brokers of real estate, slaves, freight, notes, produce, and merchandise, as well as bowling alleys and peddlers operating from stalls or traveling on horse-back; $20 on breweries and pubs; $15 on warehouses, livery stables, parking garages ("carriage warehouses"), furniture stores, retailers (not of liquor), and peddlers traveling on foot; $10 on lawyers, notaries, doctors, dentists, and druggists; and 50 cents per room on hotels and boardinghouses. Louisiana's heavy school taxes were state-mandated taxes: 10 cents per $100 on local property plus a $1 poll tax on white men over 21 (levied statewide but spent in the parish where it was paid).[45]

The point of a tax structure like this was to fix the relative burdens of coun-try versus city, agriculture versus commerce, favored versus stigmatized occu-pations, and slaveholders versus nonslaveholders. The Louisiana planter who owned twenty slaves in 1860 undoubtedly knew that he paid a higher tax than his counterpart in Mississippi: about $20 at one-sixth of one percent on the legislated valuations versus $8 at a flat 40 cents (or $15 at 75 cents).[46] Yet the Louisiana planter probably also knew, at least in general terms, that $20 plus the taxes on his land and other assets was moderate when a peddler on horseback paid $25 plus the taxes on his horse and inventory (capital invested in commerce) and a coffeehouse operator in New Orleans paid $30 plus the tax on choice urban real estate (perhaps as a landlord shifted it into his rent).[47] Northern states did not legislate the distribution of burdens in this obvious way. Their general property taxes were intended to be neutral among the taxpayers in various sectors of the economy. Although they may have favored commercial over agricultural holdings in practice (in New York through the swearing loophole), they aimed at the wealth of individuals rather than at the presumed incomes, cultural virtues, or political power associated with their occupations.

In the Northeast, tax reforms in this era modified older structures to add comprehensive descriptions of intangible wealth and abolish remnants of discriminatory rates. New York acted in 1823, adopting the language (quoted above) that it would maintain into the twentieth century. Massachusetts acted in 1829, dropping its 1781 tax break for unimproved land (assessment at 2 percent of value versus 6 percent for other property) and an 1817 tax break for its textile industry (exempting machinery in cotton and woolen factories). After 1829, Massachusetts assessed all real and personal property, including property owned by corporations, at "the just and true value thereof." Pennsylvania acted in 1844 by adopting a long description of intangible and corporate assets, though it retained flat taxes on carriages and gold or silver watches and a limited income tax. Connecticut acted in stages. In 1824, it replaced a series of valuation ratios (from 2 percent for houses and houselots up to 25 and 50 percent, respectively, for carriages and clocks) with only two ratios: 3 percent for real estate and 6 percent for personalty. Connecticut instituted a true general property tax in 1851 by applying the 3 percent ratio to everything. Northeastern states imposed additional taxes on banks and some other businesses, but, at least in theory, they now taxed "all" property beyond basic subsistence needs—unless it was owned by governments, churches, and so on—and taxed it all at the same rates ("uniformly").[48]

The key feature of tax reform in the Northeast was its incremental character. These states could build their general property taxes on long traditions of sophisticated property taxation that not only reached back into the colonial era, but that local governments employed throughout the post-revolutionary decades. Their tax reforms accommodated new economic institutions such as corporations and abolished old tax incentives such as for textile manufacturing, but they did not institute radically new practices or intergovernmental arrangements. New York actually moved further than its neighbors. Its 1823 general property tax capped decades of experimentation. In the colonial era, the New York assembly had acknowledged the patchwork character of colonial society (commercial towns, sprawling manors, town-based communities) by framing separate assessment rules for each county. Meanwhile, it acknowledged the demands of its quasi-feudal landlord class by relying heavily on imposts and excises instead of land taxes at the colony level. During the Revolutionary War, the legislature created an odd system that vested local assessors with extraordinary power over individual taxpayers. Instead of valuing any actual holdings of property, this system instructed assessors to determine "the estate and other circumstances, and ability to pay taxes, of each respective person collectively considered"—a formula that probably was intended to encourage them to slap disproportionately heavy taxes on Tories. In the early republic, New York tried a detailed schedule of flat-rate property taxes and piggybacked on the federal valuation for the 1798 direct tax before settling on its general property tax in 1823. Even in New York, however, the legislature could build on long traditions of local assessment.[49]

The New York experience is also interesting for another reason. When the state launched its Erie Canal project in 1817, legislators decided to buy off opposition by distributing the initial costs according to the "benefit" principle. On the assumption that the main beneficiaries, at least in the first instance, would be New York City merchants and western farmers along the canal line, the legislature funded its original debt issues with auction duties aimed at the merchants and salt taxes aimed at the western farmers (who were presumed to be large-scale consumers of salt). The legislature also decided to levy higher property taxes in "canal counties" than other counties, on the assumption that property values in these counties would climb disproportionately, but this expedient turned out to be unnecessary. New York was able to build the Erie Canal without any state-level property taxes. British investors snapped up the state's bonds and, as the completed sections of canal opened for navigation, toll revenues began rolling in. New York revived state-level property taxation only after a combination of overbuilding (new canal lines to please every possible constituency) and the Panic of 1837 brought the state to the verge of bankruptcy. Across the country, cities used another device based on the idea that beneficiaries should bear the costs of public works projects. Known as a "special assessment," this tax allowed cities to charge the costs of streets, sidewalks, and similar projects to the owners of "benefited" property.[50]

In the South, the antebellum reforms instituted more dramatic changes, mainly because the early southern tax systems were so primitive. Louisiana did not even assess land until 1846, Alabama until 1847, and Mississippi until 1850.[51] Virginia, as we have seen, emerged from the Revolution with an ad valorem tax on land and flat taxes on slaves, horses, carriages, and liquor licenses. When it assumed its quota of the first U.S. direct tax for the War of 1812, Virginia built onto this system without rethinking it. In 1814, it added flat licenses on merchants, peddlers, cigar factories, foundries, doctors, druggists, auctioneers, and exhibitors, plus an absurd furniture tax (repealed in 1816) with so many categories that assessment would have been simpler.[52] Nor had Virginia kept its land tax up to date. It used the 1782 equalization by "John Pendleton, junior, and Samuel Jones, gentlemen" until ordering its first reassessment in 1817—and then taking another three years to complete it. By the mid-1840s, Virginia had completed another assessment, scaled some of its license taxes to charge more for higher business volumes, and authorized counties to finance roads and bridges by adding taxes based on the state tax to their poll taxes on "tithables." By the 1850s, it was taxing financial assets ("all moneys and credits") and licenses on a schedule that made Louisiana's look straightforward. But Virginia continued to tax slaveholders "by the poll." In 1860, it charged $1.20 on every slave over age 12, with unique antievasion provisions. Slaves were taxable at the state level regardless of county exemptions for "bodily infirmity" or the otherwise tax-exempt status of the "company, institution, or person" owning or renting them.[53]

North Carolina moved further. It had emerged from the Revolution with a flat per acre land tax, poll and slave taxes equal to each other and to the tax on 300 acres, and a tax on urban real estate setting each £100 of value equal to 300 acres. Perhaps in deference to the memory of its performance during the Revolution, North Carolina did not assume its quotas for the War of 1812, but it adopted a major reform in 1814 anyway: an ad valorem tax on real estate and license taxes on merchants, peddlers, exhibitors, billiard tables, and toll roads. By the 1850s, it imposed ad valorem taxes on "all the real property, with the improvements thereon" (12 cents per $100), on the capital invested in slave trading (25 cents) and other commerce (10 cents), on interest and dividend income (30 cents), and on the inheritances of people other than lineal relatives (1 to 3 percent, depending on the relationship). Its flat taxes included levies on men's (but not women's) jewelry and on weapons (pistols, bowie knives, dirks, sword canes) "used, worn, or carried about the person," while its extensive license list made special mention of turpentine distillers (a major industry in North Carolina), "Ethiopian serenaders," and patent medicine peddlers. One feature of its revolutionary-era settlement endured. In North Carolina, the slave tax always equaled the poll tax on free male adults. The result was a slave tax even lower than Mississippi's: 40 cents per slave over 12 and under 50 (Mississippi levied its 40 cents on all slaves under 60).[54]

In the Northwest, finally, the antebellum reforms culminated in general property taxation, after statehood in the older regions (Ohio, Illinois, Indiana) and in the territorial era in the newer ones (Michigan, Wisconsin, Iowa, Minnesota, Oregon). Ohio, Illinois, and Indiana taxed land at flat rates in three "quality" categories until 1825, 1839, and 1842, respectively (a practice copied from neighboring Kentucky), and Michigan used licenses to tax some businesses throughout the period.[55] Nevertheless, by the 1850s, the tax systems of the Northwest not only resembled those of the Northeast but essentially had been copied from the northeastern statute books. Wisconsin (1849) was typical. "All property, real and personal, within this state, not expressly exempted therefrom, shall be subject to taxation," with the normal exemptions for governments, churches, and the rest, Indians who lived under tribal authority (unless they bought otherwise taxable land), and a $200 exemption for personal property. Wisconsin based its real estate list on New York's (dropping the trees, keeping the fossils) and, for personalty, combined phrases from New York and Massachusetts: "all goods and chattels, money and effects, all boats and vessels, whether at home or abroad, and all capital invested therein, all debts due, or to become due, from solvent debtors, whether on account, contract, note, mortgage, or otherwise, all public stocks, and stocks or shares in all incorporated companies." Township assessors valued real and personal property at its "full cash value," county boards equalized the local assessments, and each government unit (state, county, township, school district, road district) levied a rate on the result.[56]

In his classic study of Trempealeau County, Wisconsin, Merle Curti marveled at the idea of "simple frontiersmen" navigating "this fantastic labyrinth of intergovernmental finance" in the 1850s. "While subduing a wilderness, they managed somehow to apportion, collect, and forward these various taxes properly and according to plan." Curti attributed their success to the fact that as "loyal Americans" they "could express themselves politically" only in this "civic grammar" of American governance.[57] But this grammar actually was *northern* rather than "American." The Wisconsin settlers were acting in a northern political tradition in which robust local institutions did the heavy lifting of everyday governance, not only by managing the assessment process but also by imposing significant burdens for local purposes. Although southern local governments had become more democratic, they still did not exert anything like the power of their northern counterparts. Legislatures did much more of the governing in the South.

It would be nice to have aggregate data from the thousands of local government units that taxed in the United States before the Civil War, and particularly from the rural areas where most Americans lived.[58] The hints in the accessible record, however, all point to the conclusion that local governments taxed much more heavily in the North. The 1850 school tax data are only the beginning. New York and Massachusetts made their major reforms at moments when state-level property taxation was trivial (New York, 1823) or nonexistent (Massachusetts, 1829). Similarly, in the Northwest, territorial governments adopted their first general property taxes to raise local rather than territorial funds. The most striking evidence is from the Wisconsin "frontiersmen." In 1839, the legislature of the Wisconsin Territory created a "territorial revenue" by instructing county boards to forward 5 percent of their local tax receipts. If the idea of local taxes twenty times higher than state (or territorial) taxes seemed reasonable in Wisconsin, it would have seemed bizarre in the South. Several southern states capped local tax rates at or below the state tax rate, though no other state treated its local institutions with quite the contempt of Virginia—where a county tax could be rescinded on the petition of twenty-four "interested persons."[59]

The general property tax was a northern tax in the antebellum era, instituted through the reform of older taxes in the Northeast and the adaptation of northeastern taxes in the Northwest. Northern states relied on the local assessment of "all" property—which actually meant that local communities assessed what they decided to assess at the values they decided to assign, subject only to equalizations of the overall results across local jurisdictions. Many northern states drew further revenue from banking and transportation investments, more successfully in the East and more successfully before the Panic of 1837. By 1860, however, general property taxes financed the state and local governments of the North. Southern states also reformed their tax systems in the antebellum era, with a similar westward diffusion, a similar preference for nontax revenue, and a similar attention to financial and commercial wealth. But the southern states did not levy general property taxes. They used differential rates and elaborate license schedules to legislate the distribution of burdens. The results varied from state to state and within states over time. Most important, southern results varied for different reasons than northern results. In the North, the distribution of burdens depended on local politics. In the South, it depended much more on the centralized decision making of legislatures.

Clauses

The constitutionalization of taxation through the adoption of uniformity clauses followed a different trajectory. This innovation began in the South, moved to the Northwest, and bypassed the Northeast altogether (see map 1 above). Uniformity clauses required legislatures to tax "real estate" and "personal property" at the same ad valorem rates. They sometimes also required legislatures to tax all forms of property (a mandate called "universality"), but their main purpose was to ban particularistic schedules of property tax rates. They did not affect the southern license taxes on commerce, which often were authorized by the separate "power to tax merchants, pedlars, and privileges."[60] Nor did they affect the regressive poll taxes on free men. The uniformity clauses regulated property taxation, with special reference to the treatment of "personal property." As the history of taxation in the Northeast suggests, no legislature needed a constitutional mandate to tax property uniformly. General property taxes *were* uniform taxes. The point of adopting a constitutional mandate was to limit the power of a legislature to decide how to tax.

The meaning of a uniformity mandate depended on the nature of the "personal property" to be taxed at the same rates as real estate. When northerners used this term, they were talking mainly about financial and corporate assets, though also about livestock, mercantile inventories, machinery, and luxury possessions (jewelry, furniture, and so on). When southerners used the same term, however, they also were talking about enslaved human beings. This was the form of "personal property" at issue in the early (southern) uniformity clauses. Southerners linked slave taxes to taxes on real estate in order to bar their legislatures from levying higher taxes on slaves. The irony of this constitutional history is not just that a mandate framed to protect southern elites (owners of slaves) ended up protecting northern elites (owners of financial and corporate assets), but that the northern elites never asked for the protection. The later (northwestern) clauses—the ones that would protect northern elites—were adopted by men who thought they were banning elitist exemptions and tax breaks. The northwestern conventions adopted uniformity clauses, in short, because champions of the "common man" misunderstood them. They thought they were prohibiting *lower* taxes on financial and corporate assets. They actually were prohibiting *higher* taxes on these assets, exactly as the southern conventions had done with slaves.

Judges would explicate the real meaning of the northern clauses. In a series of cases in which wealthy individuals and corporations claimed that their tax bills violated the uniformity mandates, judges glossed the clauses as protections for elites. By the time Thomas M. Cooley, the influential Michigan jurist, issued his *Treatise on the Constitutional Limitations Which Rest Upon the Legislative Power of the States of the American Union* (1868), this reasoning was so firmly entrenched that Cooley could apply it even to states without clauses. "[I]n providing for uniformity and equality," he asserted, the clauses "have done little more than to state in concise language a principle of constitutional law which, whether declared or not, would inhere in the power to tax."[61] Cooley's precedent for this jump was an 1839 ruling by the Kentucky court of appeals that taxation "must be general and uniform . . . to secure every citizen against spoilation by a dominant faction, or by a rapacious public power." The Kentucky constitution included no uniformity clause, but it did include a clause barring the legislature from freeing slaves "without the consent of their owners . . . and a full equivalent in money for the slaves so emancipated." In the tax case, *Lexington v. McQuillan's Heirs* (1839), the court defined uniformity the same way: as a guarantee "that the public shall not take the property of any citizen . . . without his consent or an equivalent in money." While other antebellum southern courts were more direct, offering slippery slope arguments in which any nonuniform taxes opened the door to prohibitive slave taxes, Cooley chose the Kentucky case to formalize the expansion of this "principle of constitutional law." Now, Cooley explained, judges would protect all elites against "spoilation by a dominant faction, or by a rapacious public power."[62]

Slaveholders worried about dominant factions and rapacious majorities whenever they thought they would not dominate legislatures, just as they had worried about northern majorities at the federal level when they thought they would not dominate Congress. In the early republic, slaveholders dominated the southern legislatures. By refusing to reapportion them to reflect the growth of western (backcountry) yeoman populations, eastern (tidewater) planters maintained disproportionate power for decades. Slaveholders also would dominate their legislatures in the 1850s, this time as a result of the sectional crisis, in which the southern yeomen generally rallied behind the enemies they knew better.[63] But sporadically in the early republic, consistently in the 1820s and 1830s, and primarily in the Upper South states with large nonslaveholding majorities, yeomen mobilized to challenge planter rule. They demanded that legislatures be reapportioned, that suffrage restrictions (property qualifications) be abolished, and that their interests begin to be taken seriously. This was the essence of Jacksonian Democracy in the South, and planters responded by refusing to budge without new guarantees of "security."

Class struggles between southern yeomen and planters had a history stretching back to Bacon's Rebellion in seventeenth-century Virginia and the Regulator revolt in eighteenth-century North Carolina. In the early republic, Baptist and Methodist missionaries spread an antislavery gospel across the southern backcountry, endowing yeoman resistance with a religious authority. At the Virginia ratification convention in 1788, one yeoman delegate condemned slavery in a tone very different from the "lament" rhetoric of the gentry. Complaining that tidewater elites oppressed the backcountry with unfair taxes, Zachariah Johnston minced no words on the source of their power: "Slavery has been the foundation of that impiety and dissipation that have been so much disseminated among our countrymen. If it were totally abolished, it would do much good."[64] The line from Zachariah Johnston in the 1780s to Hinton Rowan Helper in the 1850s was direct. Although the North Carolina abolitionist cared more about economics than morality, he shared Johnston's concern about the impact of slavery on the white southern yeoman. In *The Impending Crisis of the South: How to Meet It* (1857), Helper proposed to rescue "the millions of down-trodden non-slaveholders" from "the diabolical excesses of the oligarchy" by taxing slavery out of existence. First, the southern legislatures would levy $60 per year "on every Slaveholder for each and every Negro in his Possession" to finance "the transportation of the Blacks to Liberia." Later and more radically, they would levy another $40 "to be paid into the hands of the Negroes so held in Slavery . . . to be used by them at their own option."[65]

This was the nightmare scenario that made everyday political negotiations so difficult in the slaveholding South. Planters saw threats to their "property" in any political action they did not control, even if yeomen actually were demanding roads, schools, and other mundane public services. For this reason, they continued to demand disproportionate power in their legislatures through slave representation.[66] In fact, the planters usually could count on the yeomen to protect the institution of slavery, just as they usually could count on northerners to leave it alone. Yeomen served in the "patrols" that terrorized African American communities and the militias that responded to revolts and alarms. Most recognized slaveholding as an integral part of their society and a reward in the American promise of upward mobility. These considerations were decisive in the cotton kingdom, with its very high rates of slaveholding. In the Upper South, however, they were not always sufficient to suppress serious grievances. Many yeomen resented the slaveholding elites who dominated their legislatures, dismissed their calls for services, and treated them with aristocratic disdain. These grievances occasionally provoked full-blown abolitionism. More often, they provoked demands to whiten the state populations through "gradual abolition" schemes—in which future deadlines would encourage slaveholders to move or sell slaves down the river.[67]

These conflicts climaxed at the conventions that wrote and revised state constitutions. In all, states adopted seventy new or radically revised constitutions between 1776 and 1860, as well as more limited amendments (see table 8). States held constitutional conventions for two main reasons: to democratize the governments of the existing states, especially by abolishing property

Table 8: State Constitutions, 1776–1860

	NORTH		SOUTH
New Hampshire	1776, 1784, 1792, 1852	Delaware	1776, 1792, 1831
Connecticut	1818	Maryland	**1776, 1851**
Massachusetts	1780, 1822	Virginia	1776, 1830, 1851
Rhode Island	1842	North Carolina	1776, 1835
New Jersey	1776, 1844	South Carolina	1776, 1778, 1790, 1808
New York	1777, 1801, 1821, 1846	Georgia	1777, 1789, 1798
Pennsylvania	1776, 1790, 1838		
Vermont	1777, 1786 [admitted 1791],	Kentucky	1792, 1799, 1850
	1793, 1828, 1836, 1850	Tennessee	1796, **1834**
Ohio	1802, **1851**	Louisiana	1812, **1845, 1852**
Indiana	1816, **1851**	Mississippi	1817, 1832
Illinois	**1818, 1848**	Alabama	1819
Maine	1820	Missouri	**1820**
Michigan	1835, **1850**	Arkansas	**1836**
Iowa	1846, 1857	Florida	**1838** [admitted 1845]
Wisconsin	**1848**	Texas	**1845**
California	**1850**		
Minnesota	**1857**		
Oregon	**1857** [admitted 1859]		

Bold constitution contained uniformity clause. NOTE: Table omits several constitutional amendments and several conventions whose products were not ratified.

qualifications for the suffrage, and because constitutions were prerequisites for the admission of new states. By the 1840s, conventions also met to deal with the fallout from the Panic of 1837, adopting the debt limits and corporation provisions intended to avert future defaults. While the early conventions kept only slim and uninformative journals of their proceedings, the later ones published transcripts of their debates. Maine, Massachusetts, and New York blazed this trail in 1819, 1820, and 1821, followed by Virginia in 1829–30. The Virginia convention was a national spectacle, featuring two elderly ex-presidents (Madison and Monroe), the sitting Chief Justice (John Marshall), and a galaxy of celebrated orators. By the 1840s, with publication the norm, partisan politicians were addressing ever longer speeches to their constituents and posterity.[68]

No convention met for the purpose of addressing tax policy issues. The early (southern) uniformity clauses emerged as by-products of other debates, usually about representation, while the later (northwestern) clauses often reflected the simple fact that these clauses had entered the repertoire of American constitutionalism. Most conventions supplied delegates with handbooks that collected the existing state constitutions. Eastern conventions that were amending previous documents rarely cited the handbooks, but western conventions that were starting from scratch relied on them heavily. They favored particular models on the grounds that states were similarly situated, that delegates hailed from them, that clauses had been framed by party allies, and that recent constitutions represented the latest in American constitutional thinking. This cutting-and-pasting produced constitutions with similar if not identical provisions about everything from the structure of legislative, executive, and judicial authority to more specific mandates about slavery (protecting it in the South, prohibiting it in the North), debts, duels, banks, schools, and property taxes.[69] Southern conventions adopted uniformity clauses to limit the power of nonslaveholding majorities. Northwestern conventions did it largely because other conventions already had. Yet with the possible exception of Maryland in 1776—which invented constitutional uniformity—none did it because tax reform was a pressing constitutional problem in its own right.

Indeed, the "founding fathers" of Maryland had had other very weighty concerns. The elites who dominated the Maryland patriot movement in 1776 were trying to establish the Revolution. As Ronald Hoffman has shown, they also were facing widespread slave revolts, the activities of Lord Dunmore (recruiting slaves into the British army), and open threats by poor whites to ally with slaves against the revolutionary regime, and all this in the long-term economic context of the shift from tobacco to wheat that was reducing the reliance even of prosperous white farmers on slavery.[70] The Maryland framers adopted the most elitist constitution of the Revolution: high property qualifications for voting and officeholding, a senate chosen by an electoral college, and appointed local officials. On taxation, however, the elites cut a deal with their (free) opponents by abolishing the colonial poll tax on "tithables." Proclaiming that "the levying of taxes by the poll is grievous and oppressive," Maryland abolished both sides of the old tax: the levy on free men and the levy on slaves of both sexes. Maryland abolished all poll taxes, shifted slaves into the property tax (as "personal property"), and, through the uniformity clause— every taxpayer to be charged "according to his actual worth, in real or personal property"—required that slaves be taxed at the same rates as other property. Later observers would miss the role of slavery in this bargain by construing the phrase "taxes by the poll" as a reference only to the regressive poll tax on free men. Maryland abolished that tax *and* protected slaveholders against the unpredictable legislatures of the future.[71]

Two early victories for the yeomen of the southern backcountry raised similar problems in the early republic. The stakes were lower when Kentucky split off from Virginia (1792) and Tennessee split off from North Carolina (1796) than they had been in Maryland, in part because smaller slave populations made the threat of rebellion less potent. Slaves were 30 percent of the Maryland population in 1776, but 16 percent in Kentucky and 13 in Tennessee in the 1790s. The danger lay in the other side of the picture: very small populations of slaveholders. The Kentucky constitution was the first in the nation to protect slavery explicitly: "The legislature shall have no power to pass laws for the emancipation of slaves without the consent of their owners, previous to such emancipation, and a full equivalent in money for the slaves so emancipated." One of the most influential delegates also called for a regulation of slave taxes, but the Kentucky convention demurred.[72] The Tennessee convention acted. It struck a primitive version of the Maryland deal, requiring all land to be taxed at one per acre rate (calling this "equal and uniform," since "no one hundred acres shall be taxed higher than another"), capping the slave tax at the tax on 200 acres, and capping the poll tax on free men at the tax on 100 acres. These ratios represented a win for the Tennessee yeomen (the poll and slave taxes were equal in North Carolina), but the critical decision was to adopt the Maryland strategy of constitutionalizing the bargain.[73]

The convention that staged the fullest debate about a uniformity clause ultimately decided not to adopt one. The 1829–30 Virginia convention was an apportionment struggle. Backcountry farmers had been calling for a reapportionment of the Virginia legislature since the 1780s. When Zachariah Johnston attacked slavery in 1788 ("foundation of that impiety and dissipation . . ."), he was talking about a representation system that consistently favored eastern planters over western yeomen. Because the malapportioned legislature determined the distribution of convention seats, the westerners lost again in 1829–30. Map 2 presents the data that structured the debate. The crucial political fact was that half the white population lived west of the Blue Ridge, in the Valley and Trans-Allegheny districts where there was relatively little slavery. Slaves were half the population in the Tidewater and Piedmont, 20 percent in the Valley, and only 9 percent in the Trans-Allegheny (which included most of what would become West Virginia). These figures meant that if the convention adopted an apportionment rule based on the distribution of the white population, as the westerners demanded, half the legislators could represent nonslaveholding constituencies. If it also abolished the property ("freehold") qualification for the suffrage, democratized urban electorates in Richmond and Norfolk might choose similarly untrustworthy representatives.[74]

The Virginia convention was renowned in its own time for its rhetorical

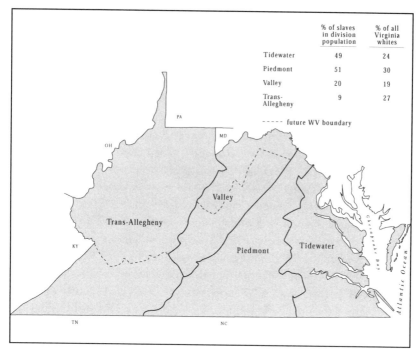

Map 2. The Four "Divisions" of Virginia, 1830

fireworks and celebrity delegates: Madison, Monroe, Marshall, and the extraordinary John Randolph, who had been bullying colleagues in Congress for decades by tossing off devastating insults while dressed in riding clothes, complete with dogs and whip. But historians usually remember it for another reason: the openly antidemocratic arguments of its eastern members. In 1788, nobody bothered to answer Zachariah Johnston. In 1829–30, the planters took turns lecturing the yeomen on the political prerogatives of the rich. "We are . . . your equals in intelligence and virtue, moral and political," a westerner proclaimed. No, an easterner scoffed, you would "select the first Mons'r Egalite who presents himself as the professed guardian of the rights of property." In response to the western demand for a "white basis" apportionment, the easterners proposed plans to count slaves: the "federal number" (three-fifths rule) to count them directly and a "combined ratio" of white population and taxation to count them indirectly (by counting slave taxes). The yeomen rejected both of these plans to reserve power for eastern elites: "If there is any rule in political sentiment common to [Americans], it is, that the majority ought to rule." But the elites refused to accept anything that would "put the power of controlling the wealth of the State, into hands different from those which hold the wealth."[75]

The yeoman agenda did not involve slavery. The westerners wanted roads and schools in their districts and an internal improvement program including more than an endlessly unfinished James River Canal (in the east). They knew they could never win major policy changes without a major democratization. Hence their calls for the white-basis apportionment and the abolition of the property qualification. They also wanted a new local government system: elected county boards to replace the county court oligarchies. The planters rejected it all. Madison urged the convention to count slaves in the apportionment ("incorporate that interest into the basis of our system") to protect slaveholders against "excessive taxation" and bolster the national proslavery victory he had won forty years earlier: "[I]f we reject a doctrine in our own State, whilst we claim the benefit of it in our relations to other States, other disagreeable consequences may be added to the charge of inconsistency, which will be brought against us." Monroe, who had been the U.S. ambassador in Paris during the French Revolution, regaled the convention with bloody stories, including one in which a mob killed a legislator "and cutting off his head, marched with it on a pike to the President's Chair"—the point being the importance of "some reasonable protection for property." Randolph fantasized about western legislators inviting the abolitionist "to put a torch to my property, that he may slake it in the blood of all that are dear to me."[76]

But the most striking aspect of this debate was that every defense of the eastern interest in slave representation cited the same threat: that a legislature under western control would overtax slaveholders. It would "burthen that species of property with excessive taxes, for the relief of other property from taxation," levy "unequal taxes on this species of property, to the exoneration of property of a different kind," lean heavily on "this oppressive mode of taxation—this *poll-tax* on slaves." As most easterners saw it, "*we* have a species of property which *they* have not; and on which they may lay what tax they please, without themselves paying under that law, a single dollar." One easterner rejected any slave tax: "No such tax is laid upon the white labourer of the West, and yet the product of his labour is of no more importance to the general welfare, than the same product from the labour of slaves." The others accepted slave taxes in principle, worrying only that a western majority would increase them. "The interest of the west is contrary to ours in regard to *slaves* considered as a subject of taxation, certainly and obviously," as the eastern floor leader (Benjamin Watkins Leigh) put it. While some of the easterners accused the westerners of being abolitionists, which the westerners denied, even the most extreme advocates of slaveholder power had to "admit that we have no danger to apprehend, except from oppressive and unequal taxation; no other injustice can reasonably be feared."[77]

From the opening days of the Virginia convention, the westerners proposed a uniformity clause to reconcile the easterners to majority rule. They followed the Maryland model:

> That the power of the Legislature to impose taxes, ought to be so limited, as to prohibit the imposition on property, either real or personal, of any other than an "*ad valorem*" tax; and that in apportioning this tax, either for State or county purposes, the whole visible property (household furniture and wearing apparel excepted) of each individual in the community, ought to be valued, and taxed only in proportion to its value.[78]

By prohibiting "the disproportionate taxation of slaves," they explained, this formula promised "security against the apprehension that the whole weight would be thrown on the slave property." "The effect of this must of course be, what all will acknowledge to be just, to reduce the tax on slaves to precisely the same level with all the other taxes of the State." Easterners dismissed it as a "paper guarantee." Leigh, the eastern leader, also punched a hole in its logic. Because eastern planters were richer than western yeomen (because their land was more valuable and they owned many more slaves) a western majority could, "by a uniform taxation, impose oppressive burdens on the east, which its own population will hardly feel the weight of." Westerners replied with the obvious. Because eastern planters were richer they *should* pay higher taxes: "[W]hen you look to *taxation,* you look to the ability to pay."[79] In the end, however, the easterners who controlled the convention won a favorable apportionment. Where there was no deal to be made, a uniformity clause was superfluous.

No other convention left a rhetorical legacy quite like Virginia's, though the same issues soon arose in Tennessee (1834) and North Carolina (1835). Ironically, the Virginia debate ended eighteen months before the Nat Turner rebellion (August 1831). Six months after that, many of the men who had debated about democracy debated about slavery itself. Westerners favored the adoption of gradual abolition plans, but they lost the slavery battle largely because they already had lost the apportionment battle. But in the other states, the planters and yeomen faced off after the Turner rebellion. In North Carolina, the outcome was straightforward and highly regressive: increased western representation in return for a uniform *poll tax* (constitutionalizing the old poll tax on "tithables"). The 1835 North Carolina constitution required the legislature to impose this tax on all free men (21 to 45) and slaves of both sexes

(12 to 55) at a rate "equal throughout the State, upon all individuals subject to the same." This deal was struck before the convention met. When a westerner who had not been privy to the negotiations criticized the uniform poll tax on symbolic (racist) grounds—"as slaves were property, and not persons, he was opposed to putting them on a footing with the whites in any shape"—an easterner pointed to "the compromise, by which it was hoped to settle the Convention question." "To soothe eastern fears that the growing power of the west would undermine the stability of the slave regime," as historian Marc Kruman summarizes it, "they limited the taxes placed upon slaves."[80]

The Tennessee convention met chiefly to reform the state courts, though delegates from yeoman areas also wanted to drop other parts of the 1796 constitution: its property qualification for officeholding, its apportionment by "taxable inhabitants" (including slaves), and its flat-rate land tax. But, once they arrived, the yeoman delegates spent three weeks reading out petitions (thirty in all) for a gradual abolition of slavery. Then, incredibly, they wrote a report attacking all laws that "assign to men their rights according to the different shades of color." Faced with this yeoman revolt, planters demanded security. They won a clause prohibiting the legislature from abolishing slavery, but only in a close vote (30–27) with most of the yeomen voting no. They also called for slave representation: a senate "on the compound bases of population and taxation combined . . . to prevent unreasonable taxation by the democratic branch of the Legislature."[81] The planters lost on representation (both houses were apportioned by eligible voters, the property qualification was dropped) but won a favorable tax deal. The 1834 constitution instituted an ad valorem land tax, shifted slaves into the property tax, required the exemption of all slaves under 12 and over 50, and added the uniformity clause: "All property shall be taxed according to its value . . . so that the same shall be equal and uniform throughout the state. No one species of property from which a tax may be collected shall be taxed higher than any other species of property of equal value." It also lifted the 1796 cap on the poll tax: "A tax on white polls shall be laid, in such manner and of such amount as may be prescribed by law."[82] The Tennessee yeomen paid for their antislavery petitions, for their manifesto about equal rights, and for their representation.

These Upper South deals had few parallels in the Deep South and none in the Northeast or Northwest. Conventions fought about apportionments everywhere, but nobody worried about a link between taxation and representation anywhere in the North. Apportionment battles in the North were about two issues: rural efforts to limit urban representation—by capping the big city delegations—and partisan efforts to gerrymander the legislatures.[83] Tax debates in the northern conventions, meanwhile, addressed every imaginable issue *ex-*

cept the idea of majorities trying to overburden elites. Northern delegates did not sound at all like the southern planters and yeomen. They zeroed in on the details of incidence and administration, usually trying to figure out how to increase the progressivity of their tax systems. They debated about whether to abolish road labor levies on all male adults (which especially favored men who could pay cash instead), how to tax people who did business in one county but lived in another (a struggle between New York City and Brooklyn), the fairness of charging resident owners the taxes on mortgaged real estate when lenders actually owned most of the equity (as American property taxes still do today), whether to levy school taxes at the state level in order to equalize the income of rich and poor districts, abuses of the tax-exempt status of wealthy churches and charities, exemptions for railroads and other corporations, and the thorny question of how to define the taxable assets of a bank.[84] These are the kinds of issues we normally think of as "tax issues." Northern tax debates were recognizably modern debates about policy details.

Northerners who could argue cogently about these issues found it harder to explain why they belonged in the state constitutions. Uniformity went nowhere in the Northeast. Delegates proposed clauses in New Jersey (1844) and New York (1846), but could defend them only by citing vague wishes, as one New Jersey delegate phrased it, "to establish a principle in matter[s] of taxation, based upon the principle of our government, which is *equality*." This was not good enough. Their constituents were sophisticated about taxes, a New Yorker declared. "Any thing that touched the pockets of the people they understood very well. These were matters they had looked into, and they wanted no proposition of this kind in the Constitution."[85] The New Jersey case involved a partisan maneuver. When Jonathan Pickel, a "true collar" Democrat from rural Mount Pleasant, proposed a clause drawn from Tennessee ("No one species of property . . . shall be taxed higher than any other species of property of the same value"), Richard Stockton Field, a Princeton Whig (and bank president), explained what it would do to the New Jersey tax system: "relieve the Banks very materially, for if any one species of tax was unequal, it was that on the Banks. . . . Adopt this rule, and instead of the Banks paying some twenty-five or thirty thousand dollars a year . . . they would pay only three or four." Pickel said he was "only tenacious as to the principle, and exceptions might easily be made if the Convention saw proper," but Francis Child, a moderate Morristown Democrat, accused him of proposing the clause "for the purpose of obtaining political capital"—so that "gentlemen would appear as voting against a principle which they approved." They voted against it anyway. In a convention with nearly equal Whig and Democratic delegations, uniformity lost by a two-to-one margin.[86]

But uniformity clauses prevailed across the Northwest. One after another, northwestern conventions adopted them in the 1840s and 1850s, sometimes without pausing to reflect on their practical implications. Unfortunately, the origin of the first northwestern clause is obscure. The "founding fathers" of Illinois (1818) may not have discussed it at all, though their journal is one of the sketchiest of the period.[87] Illinois in 1818 was more like Kentucky in 1792 than like New York or New Jersey in the 1840s—or even Illinois in the 1840s. Its controversial issue was slavery. Despite the Northwest Ordinance, governments in the Northwest Territory had allowed slavery by the subterfuge of calling the slaves "indentured servants." The servants were African Americans, bound for terms such as 50 or 90 years, barred from making contracts or testifying in court, and liable to be moved or sold to slave states at any time. Ohio (1802) and Indiana (1816) abolished this form of slavery at statehood, but Illinois guaranteed its survival: persons "bound to service" in the territory "shall be held to a specific performance of their contracts or indentures" along with their "children hereafter born," who would be freed as adults (men at 21, women at 18)—if they were still in Illinois. Slaves were only 3 percent of the Illinois population in 1818 (about 1,000 slaves). Even so, pressure to turn Illinois into a full-fledged slave state built until 1824, when a plan to call a new constitutional convention failed at the polls, with 43 percent of the electorate voting for slavery. This context does not prove that the Illinois uniformity clause was intended to protect slaveholders, though it certainly leaves that possibility open.[88]

By the 1840s and 1850s, however, uniformity clauses had nothing to do with slavery in the Northwest. They were intended to address the complaint that Jonathan Pickel articulated in New Jersey: "The poor man, as it is now, pays almost all the tax, while rich men, who are living on their thousands, pay almost no tax at all." Or, as William Sawyer (another "true collar" type) argued during the Ohio convention (1850–51), that favorable treatment of elites was "throwing the burden of taxation upon farmers, mechanics and laborers." While the point of uniformity in the South was to limit the taxes that majorities could impose on elites, the point in the North was to increase the taxes on elites, or, as another Ohioan put it, to tax "the millions in the hands of the wealthy . . . for the very purpose of relieving the poor." Since these were debates about property taxes, as opposed to regressive poll taxes or sales taxes, the "poor men" at issue actually were landowning farmers rather than propertyless "laborers." The problem was that these farmers were bearing heavy tax burdens, especially as a result of the fiscal crises unleashed by the Panic of 1837, while the elite owners of certain corporate assets enjoyed tax exemptions. In the words of yet another Ohioan, it was that legislators "have been bargaining with particular classes of men how their property should be taxed, whilst they have left other property belonging to the people of the State to be taxed under a general law."[89]

No other northern delegates took this problem nearly as seriously as the Ohioans. Next to their lengthy debate, the brief discussions of uniformity in Wisconsin (1848), California (1849), and the other "frontier" states were downright cavalier. Delegates in Michigan (1850) struggled about school finance, but hardly anyone in Michigan presented uniformity, which they adopted, as the solution to any particular tax problem.[90] In Ohio, however, delegates thought they could protect ordinary taxpayers from "unscrupulous and abandoned Shylocks" by constitutionalizing "the principle of taxing all property alike." They thought "everything should be taxed, without exception," that "all property in the state, whatever its description, [should] be taxed alike," and that the constitution had to limit a power that legislators had "grossly abused." They would not allow the legislature "to tax the property of corporations in one way, and the property belonging to the citizens of the State generally in another way"—because "honor, integrity, good faith to the people, and republican equality, *all* demand that we should tax the money of the capitalists, however or wherever invested, as we tax all other property."[91]

These concerns could not have been more different from those of Virginia, Tennessee, or North Carolina. A Virginia planter could insult his yeoman inferiors with sarcasm about "Mons'r Egalite," but one Ohio delegate actually quoted Robespierre and declared the Ohio convention "a revolutionary body, bound to inquire into the original elements of society, to rectify the errors of the past, and provide new safeguards for the people."[92] The Ohioans, of course, were Democrats rather than Jacobins. Their real agenda, a response to the fiscal crisis of the 1840s, drew on the New York "Stop and Tax" model. They banned state debts for internal improvements, mandated general incorporation, and required a referendum for the legislature to authorize the formation of banks. Backed by a strong Democratic majority, the "true collar" types ridiculed every argument they could identify with elites. Several delegates tried to explain that it made no sense to tax the assets of banks in the same way as the assets of farmers and country storekeepers, but practical considerations were beside the point where ignorance was a virtue: "Nobody, I believe, but his Satanic majesty himself, is capable of understanding the deep dark iniquity of those institutions [banks]." Others tried to explain that detailed restraints on the legislature would benefit elites in the end ("every word of detail is a word of weakness"), but, as Richard T. Ely would note in the 1880s, these Ohioans were the prototypical people who did not trust themselves.[93]

They constitutionalized a rigorous uniformity structure. Other northwestern states had kept their clauses fairly vague. Wisconsin (1848): "The rule of taxation shall be uniform, and taxes shall be levied upon such property as the legislature shall prescribe." California (1849): "Taxation shall be equal and uniform . . . All property in the State shall be taxed in proportion to its value, to be ascertained as directed by law." Michigan (1850): "The legislature shall provide for a uniform rule of taxation . . . on such property as shall be prescribed by law" with property assessed "at its cash value."[94] The Ohio convention went much further. "Laws shall be passed taxing by a uniform rule all moneys, credits, investments in bonds, stocks, joint-stock companies, or otherwise; and also all real and personal property according to its true value in money." The legislature could exempt only churches, schools, charities, cemeteries, and $200 of the personal property of individual taxpayers. Nor was this all. "The property of corporations, now existing or hereafter created, shall forever be subject to taxation, the same as the property of individuals," and the assets of banks—"notes and bills discounted or purchased, moneys loaned, and all other property, effects, or dues of every description (without deduction)"— had to be taxed "so that all property employed in banking shall always bear a burden of taxation equal to that imposed on the property of individuals."[95]

This was asking for trouble, which arrived immediately. Like Ohio's earlier tax laws, the first property tax under the 1851 constitution permitted individual taxpayers (but not banks) to subtract their debts from their holdings of financial assets. Now, a bank sued the state, arguing that the constitution banned such discrimination. The Ohio Supreme Court agreed. In *Exchange Bank v. Hines* (1853), it ruled that any law "throw[ing] a proportionably greater burden . . . on property employed in banking, than is imposed on individuals" was now unconstitutional. Even though the convention had intended to prohibit *lower* taxes on banks, it actually had prohibited *higher* taxes on banks. The Ohio court retreated from the disruptive implications of its ruling. It rejected the bank's demand that it annul the unconstitutional assessment (and all taxes based on it) with a tendentious claim that local assessors might not have permitted individuals to subtract debts—they "may have had a correct understanding of their official duties, and in obedience to their oaths to support the constitution, disregarded the void provision" of the tax law.[96] Looking back from the Cooley era, the Ohio court's interpretation of uniformity would be more important than its refusal to impose its consequences in 1853. Regardless of the intentions of their framers, uniformity clauses did in the Northwest precisely what they had been framed to do in the South: protect elites against the tax decisions of "dominant factions" and "rapacious" majorities.

Determined Minorities

Today, when Americans think of the role of the courts in defending "minority rights," we are thinking of groups defined by race, religion, gender, sexuality, disability, and other markers of social disadvantage, though never by the economic disadvantage of poverty. We are thinking of judges voiding discriminatory legislation (segregation, compulsory religious observance) and deciding what actions count as discrimination in employment, housing, college admissions, and so on. This understanding of "minority rights" emerged in the twentieth century. It is not what James Madison was describing in the *Federalist* (1788), when he predicted that the many cross-cutting political factions of a large republic would ensure "that the rights of individuals or of the minority, will be in little danger from interested combinations of the majority." Nor is it what Alexis de Tocqueville was describing in *Democracy in America* (1835), when he saw lawyers curbing the "tyranny of the majority" ("the vices inherent in popular government") by filtering "the nation's democratic instincts" through their own "aristocratic propensities."[97]

The modern understanding of "minority rights" is certainly not what Sidney Breese of the Illinois Supreme Court had in mind when he ruled, in *Bureau County v. the Chicago, Burlington, and Quincy Railroad Company* (1867), that the uniformity clause of the Illinois constitution (the "cardinal principle of uniformity of taxation") meant that corporations "stand upon the platform of equality before the law, and no greater burden for the support of government can be imposed upon them than can be placed upon the individual taxpayer." Nor is it what Thomas Cooley had in mind when he introduced his *Treatise on the Law of Taxation* (1876) with a tirade against the tendency of elected officials to turn taxation into "confiscation"—because they were dishonest ("fraud and corruption"), because they were inept ("the ignorant action of assessors"), and most of all because they would try to soak the rich ("imposing the whole burden of government on the few who exhibit the most energy, enterprise, and thrift"). Cooley's solution was an aggressive judicial supervision. "[W]hen one considers how vast is this [tax] power, how readily it yields to passion, excitement, prejudice or private schemes, and into what incompetent hands its execution is usually committed, it seems unreasonable [for the courts] to treat as unimportant, any stretch of power—even the slightest—whether it be on the part of the legislature which orders the tax, or of any of the officers who [administer it]." Breese and Cooley were activist judges dedicated to the protection of minority rights. Like Madison and Tocqueville before them, however, they also were heirs to a long tradition in political thought, going back to Aristotle, that defined the "minority" as the elite and "minority rights" as property rights.[98]

Progressives understood "minorities" the same way. Hence Richard T. Ely's attack on a system in which the "vast majority of the people" were "ruled by a small but determined minority which finds profit in governmental imperfections." Since the activist judges were the ones who defined the imperfections (at the behest of litigious elites), they could undermine the decisions of legislative majorities dramatically—as the U.S. Supreme Court did in the *Pollock* case by ruling that the 1894 federal income tax violated the direct tax clauses (governmental imperfections by any standard). Although the Ohio court had refused to nullify the unconstitutional assessment in *Exchange Bank*, late-nineteenth-century judges did not flinch from the results of punishing "any stretch of power—even the slightest." In *Bureau County v. the C.B.Q.*, the Illinois court voided the tax because local officials *may have* assessed the railroad's property at a higher fraction of its actual value than the property of other taxpayers.[99] The Illinois court was among the pioneers of the strict scrutiny that Cooley promoted in his treatises. In *Lawrence v. Fast* (1858), it annulled an assessment roll solely because there were no dollar signs in front of its columns of numbers! Breese dissented in *Lawrence* ("[C]an any reasonable man doubt that dollars and cents, or cents only, were intended?"), but was less forgiving in *Bureau County* when the issue was the distribution of burdens: corporations, and particularly banks and railroads, standing "on the platform of equality before the law." The Ohio delegate who argued that "every word of detail [in a constitution] is a word of weakness" clearly had this emerging legal order in mind.[100]

Before the 1850s, the courts had treated taxation permissively. In the widely cited case of *Portland Bank v. Apthorp* (1815), the Massachusetts Supreme Court did exactly what the U.S. Supreme Court had done in *Hylton v. U.S.* (1796). The bank claimed that a tax levied on bank capital but not other property violated the rule in the Massachusetts constitution requiring taxes to be "proportional and reasonable." As the U.S. Supreme Court had defined the carriage tax as an "internal duty" rather than a "direct tax," the Massachusetts court defined the bank tax as an excise rather than a property tax (which did have to be "proportional").[101] Nor were the courts more exacting in states with full-blown uniformity clauses. In Maryland, which avoided state-level property taxes for decades, the uniformity clause reached the court only in the bizarre case of *Waters v. Maryland* (1843), in which a county collector who had stolen the proceeds of the colonization tax (to deport free people of color to Liberia) said he should be allowed to keep the money because the tax had been levied in an unconstitutional manner! The court dismissed this claim out of hand, but used the case to emphasize its deference to the legislature. The collector argued that the tax violated the uniformity clause because the legislature had set county quotas arbitrarily. In language that would be inconceivable in the Cooley era, this court ruled that "in the absence of evidence" about how the legislature had set the quotas, "we must suppose" it had used a valuation of real and personal property.[102] Even the Illinois court was permissive at first. Faced with a blatant contradiction—a flat per acre land tax in three "quality" categories when the constitution said that "the mode of levying a tax shall be by valuation"—it held in *Rhinehart v. Schuyler* (1845) that in the frontier conditions in which the tax had been levied (in 1830) the flat rates were more equitable than valuations would have been.[103]

Yet there were dissenters. The Kentucky case that Cooley would emphasize, *Lexington v. McQuillan's Heirs* (1839), struck down a local street-paving assessment that seemed to raise the threat of "spoilation by a dominant faction, or by a rapacious public power." The Arkansas Supreme Court nullified a tax on billiard tables in *Stevens and Woods v. State* (1840), since if it accepted that tax it would be authorizing the legislature "to inhibit the culture and acquisition of cotton or corn, or the acquisition of horses or negroes, or any other article, species, or description of property."[104] A Missouri judge made this point with hysterical excess in *Crow v. State* (1851). In a long opinion citing everything from Magna Carta to the Spanish Inquisition to Tocqueville on the tyranny of the majority, he struck down a merchant license to prevent any future tax from "practically emancipating" slaves. Only the courts could bar "the predominating interest, or the coalesced and combined interests and prejudices of an accidental and unchecked majority of the Legislature" from "enacting that no citizen should purchase, or sell, or hire, or even own a slave" without a license priced at "such sum as the legislative wisdom or virtue may enact."[105] Virginia was more restrained—but only because its judges reasoned forward from slave taxes rather than backward from other taxes. In *Slaughter v. Commonwealth* (1856), involving a tax on insurance agents, the Virginia court held that because a qualified uniformity clause adopted in 1851 (when the west finally won its reapportionment) was framed "with the intention of preventing onerous taxes upon slaves," it applied only in the context of the east-west struggle over slave taxes.[106]

We rarely think of Kentucky, Arkansas, and Missouri as the pioneering centers of public policy development in American history. By the late nineteenth century, however, the stringent approach of their courts to uniform taxation—and the property rights of an elite minority—had displaced the permissive approach in most of the state courts. As Morton Horwitz has noted, the uniformity clauses accelerated this transition. They gave activist judges constitutional warrants to prevent rapacious majorities from turning taxation into "confiscation" (Cooley), or, to subject the decisions of majorities to the vetoes of "a small but determined minority which finds profit in governmental imperfections" (Ely). By the 1880s, judges were citing the uniformity clauses not only to discipline local assessors and ban minor taxes that could set unwelcome precedents but also to strike down major reforms: income taxes, inheritance taxes, corporation taxes, and taxes at progressive rates. In states without clauses, judges disciplined legislatures and local officials by invoking "implied" uniformity mandates.[107] In the name of "equal taxation," the courts held the legislatures in a vise. They rejected alternatives to general property taxation, which southern states had adopted during Reconstruction, meanwhile exacerbating the already massive evasion problem by endorsing the claims of elites to have been targeted in a discriminatory way—when assessors managed to reach their wealth in the first place. As the Sixteenth Amendment (1913) voided the *Pollock* decision by authorizing the federal income tax (to supplement and ultimately replace the tariff), another wave of state constitutional revision in the 1910s and 1920s freed the legislatures from the stranglehold of the state supreme courts. Major aspects of our current tax regime date from this era: income and corporation taxes for the states, real estate taxes for local governments, and no taxes on "personal property."

The economists were right about general property taxation. Because most of the wealth in a modern economy is mobile and fungible, "ability to pay" is more closely related to streams of income than stocks of wealth—making income taxes more equitable even before considering their administrative advantages. Today, the states also enjoy the administrative benefit of being able to piggyback on the federal system that verifies individual tax returns against independent income reports (the W2s and 1099s). Our income taxes have serious problems, many of which involve the power of elites to profit from "governmental imperfections." At this writing (2005), Congress is considering a radical scheme to replace the federal income tax with a national sales tax, which might produce a level of regressivity that Americans have not seen since the days of the late-nineteenth-century tariff. Yet no matter what kinds of tax reforms Congress decides to adopt, it has the power to adopt major reforms and, if its composition changes in the future, to exchange these reforms for different ones. The direct tax clauses still lurk in the background, though presumably without the power they once posed as impediments to majority rule.[108]

The same cannot be said for our local real estate taxes. In the 1970s, a new generation of people who did not trust themselves slapped new constitutional restraints on the power of local majorities to decide how to tax. Exemplified by California's Proposition 13 (1978), these "tax-expenditure limitations" not only repeated the mistakes of the 1840s and 1850s but repudiated "the principle of local responsibility" altogether. Proposition 13 caps the increase of real estate assessments at 2 percent per year, except that when real estate changes hands it is reassessed at its full market value (there are also caps on the tax rates). Californians understand some of the resulting inequities. Because real estate values have skyrocketed since the late 1970s, owners who bought identical neighboring houses at different times pay wildly different property taxes. Other inequities are less well known, such as that the reassessment cap also covers commercial holdings (for example, corporate office towers), which change hands less often than residential real estate. A delegate in frontier Wisconsin (1848) captured the mood of the California voters who would endorse Proposition 13 more than a century later. The Wisconsin convention should adopt a uniformity clause, he argued, because it had to take *some* action to protect the ordinary taxpayer. "If gentlemen expected to get a good constitution without having anything in it, they would find themselves mistaken in the end."[109]

But the northwesterners *were* mistaken in the end. "Uniformity" had nothing to do with the "equality" they envisioned. It had been devised in a completely different political context to accomplish a completely different goal. Wanting to do *something* to protect "the people" did not justify doing absolutely anything. Constitutional limitations are suited to protect minority rights, whether the "minorities" are the socially disadvantaged groups of today or the elites of classical political thought. The rights and interests of majorities, however, are best secured by democratic institutions with the power to act. This is why defenders of minority rights have mistrusted these institutions, as James Madison explained in his most famous *Federalist* essays (numbers 10 and 51) and John C. Calhoun explained in *A Disquisition on Government* (1851). While Madison's discussion has been open to interpretation, in part because he was writing for a northern audience (to persuade New York to ratify the Constitution), nobody has been confused about the identity of the "minority" that Calhoun wanted to protect.[110] When Calhoun declared that constitutional restraints were insufficient, that minorities also needed "the power of preventing or arresting the action of government," he was talking about southern slaveholders and the northern majority. Constitutional restraints were not intended to protect majorities: "The ballot box, of itself, would be ample protection to them."[111] This was the point the northwestern champions of the "common man" misunderstood. Unwilling to trust themselves, they donned a constitutional shackle forged to protect slaveholders—and did it in the name of "equality."

Slavery had profoundly antidemocratic effects on American politics, not just for the most obvious reason—it was *slavery*—but because, in the post-

Enlightenment world of the eighteenth and nineteenth centuries, it was inherently vulnerable. Slaveholders would not permit majorities, even of southern white men, to make decisions affecting their "property." Most of the southern state constitutions prohibited legislatures from emancipating slaves. Some provided for slave representation in schemes resembling the national three-fifths rule, while some limited the tax power with uniformity clauses resembling the national direct-tax rule. Slaveholders were not always unwilling to pay taxes. Sometimes, they supported lavish spending for which they paid large parts of the tab.[112] But slaveholders would not allow nonslaveholders to decide how to tax. Majority rule as a general principle has its own limitations. Even so, it was and is preferable to the rule of determined elites—either the ones who create the governmental imperfections or the ones who merely exploit them.

James Madison on Slave Taxes

In the midst of the 1829–30 Virginia constitutional convention, James Madison made an astonishing claim: that slaveholder power benefited enslaved African Americans. At the age of seventy-eight, Madison had come out of retirement to attend this convention as a delegate from his home county of Orange (in the eastern Piedmont), whose population consisted of 6,456 whites, 7,983 slaves, and 198 free people of color. Madison was supporting a legislative apportionment that would grant the white men of counties like Orange more power than the white men of counties like Brooke (in the Trans-Allegheny, later West Virginia), whose population consisted of 6,774 whites, 228 slaves, and 39 free people of color. Orange was obviously larger than Brooke and, from a white perspective, obviously richer. While Madison and his eastern colleagues wanted to favor Orange over Brooke through slave representation, Brooke county leader Philip Doddridge insisted that the 6,744 whites of Brooke deserved at least as much power as the 6,456 whites of Orange. The representation of wealth was fundamentally undemocratic, Doddridge argued, no matter what form the wealth took. Were the eastern planters also prepared to grant "the largest capitalists, the largest suffrage in the State?"[1]

Because they were not prepared to extend wealth representation to capitalists, the planters could answer Doddridge only by explaining why slaves entitled owners to political power while commercial, financial, and manufacturing assets did not. They had to explain why slaveholding was different from the ownership of other wealth. Most of the planters agreed with Madison that the problem was the peculiar vulnerability of the slaveholders to taxation. "It is apprehended, if the power of the Commonwealth shall be in the hands of a majority, who have no interest in this species of property, that, from the facility with which it may be oppressed by excessive taxation, injustice may be done to its owners." Robert Stanard, representing a county similar to Madison's (6,384 whites, 8,053 slaves, 697 free people of color) cited another problem. Slaveholders could not permit "the transit of power to hands not acquainted with our situation and dangers . . . and who know not how to adapt laws to the wants, the condition, the feelings, and the passions of the slaves in regard to those who retain them in bondage." The security of the master class, Stanard argued, involved "interests, not of property merely, but of life itself." In retrospect, however, it was Littleton Tazewell of Norfolk (5,130 whites, 3,756 slaves, 928 free people of color) who answered Doddridge and the other westerners most effectively—not by complaining about the vulnerability of the slaveholders but by exposing the racism in the western case for democracy. "Gentlemen assert, that according to an eternal rule of right, the majority must govern, and then instantly exclude from the enumeration, all except free *white* persons."[2]

Tazewell was talking about free people of color. It made no sense to define the majority in a way based "not upon the condition of the population as bond or free, but upon the accidental circumstance of the colour of their skins." The crucial point was the institution of slavery itself. To be logical, the apportionment could exclude "slaves of every sort, whether black or white," but only "under the idea that they ought not to be considered as persons, but as property merely."[3] For Madison, this was a very old game by 1829. He had mastered the manipulation of the terms "persons" and "property"—to defend whatever concessions slaveholders were demanding at any particular moment—in his struggles with northerners in the 1780s. Tazewell may have hoped to embarrass the westerners into submission by calling them on their racism, but Madison knew he could call them on their toleration of slavery. The "last of the founders," who had outlived the allies and opponents of his glory days, told the young Virginians what he had not told the New Englanders, Pennsylvanians, and New Yorkers: that nonslaveholding whites who actually were defending their own political interests had no right to pretend that they cared about the plight of the enslaved.[4]

Since slaves were "persons," Madison now argued, they had interests in policy decisions that should be taken into account, including interests in the distribution of tax burdens. Virginia should apportion its lower house (house of delegates) by white population and its senate by the three-fifths rule because "such an arrangement might prove favourable to the slaves themselves." Madison could mix the "persons" and "property" views in the same sentence:

It may be, and I think it has been suggested, that those who have themselves no interest in this species of property, are apt to sympathise with the slaves, more than may be the case with their masters; and would, therefore, be disposed, when they had the ascendancy [in the house of delegates], to protect them from laws of an oppressive character, whilst the masters, who have a common interest with the slaves, against undue taxation, which must be paid out of their labour, will be their protectors when they have the ascendancy [in the senate].[5]

This was "trickle-down" economics with a vengeance. It is one thing for a modern trickle-down theorist to argue that workers are the real victims of taxes on employers because employers will "create jobs" only when they have funds to invest. In a slaveholding context, however, Madison could only have been saying that slaves and masters shared an interest in low slave taxes because slaveholders would respond to tax increases by shifting them to the slaves: forcing them to work harder, reducing their living standards (spending less on food, clothing, and shelter), and selling them or their children down the river. This analysis had nothing to do with a "common interest." It was about the conflict of interest at the heart of the institution of slavery. In reality, if masters tried to shift their tax increases to slaves, they could expect the slaves to respond—in a struggle that would involve "interests not of property merely, but of life itself."

Madison was also saying something else. When the interests of slaves were considered, the most progressive tax structure would be one that taxed the yeomen (who could not shift their burdens to slaves) and exempted the slaveholders (who could). Madison was not urging Virginia to adopt a progressive tax structure. He was pointing out that the yeomen were not "the poor" in a slave state. Western empowerment would not produce egalitarian economic policies any more than a "white basis" apportionment would produce majority rule. Equality was not on the table at this convention. Neither was democracy. The entire table was occupied by the institution of slavery. Madison may have intended his trickle-down argument to sound whimsical. He cared about the power to decide how to tax much more than he cared about the practical distribution of tax burdens. He wanted Virginia to adopt slave representation ("incorporate that interest into the basis of our system") in order to guarantee the power of the slaveholders—over their slaves but also over everyone else.[6] Egalitarian demands could not possibly make sense in a slave society. The institution rendered them fatuous from the beginning.

Yet the really odd thing about Madison's argument is that the westerners at the 1829–30 Virginia convention never claimed to be "apt to sympathise with the slaves." They did not try to justify their demands by pointing to the immorality of slavery, as northerners had in the early republic. They did not try to play on the slaveholders' fears, as Benjamin Franklin did in 1776 ("Sheep will never make any insurrections"). Nor did they try to play on the slave-holders' guilt, as George Thatcher did in 1789 ("If the pernicious effects of New England rum have been justly lamented, what can be urged for negro slavery?"). What they did say was that they resented the slaveholders' insistence that "we must obey you." "Do I misrepresent or exaggerate when I say your doctrine makes me a slave? I may still live in the west; may pursue my own business and obey my own inclinations, but so long as you hold political dominion over me, I am a slave," as Doddridge put it.[7] In a sense, Madison may not have been talking to the Virginians in the room. He may have been addressing long-dead political opponents from the North. Nobody had ever guilt-tripped Madison successfully. In 1829–30, however, he was ready to say so. He not only refused to accept the power of a nonslaveholding majority to decide how to tax his "species of property," but he also revealed his resentment of the idea that he *should* pay higher taxes because some northerner (or westerner) claimed to have cleaner hands.

Nat Turner would revive an antislavery politics among the yeomen of Virginia and other Upper South states, the same politics that had led Zachariah Johnston to endorse abolition at the ratification convention in 1788. In 1829–30, however, the yeomen insisted only that *they* not be treated like slaves. By the 1840s, increasing numbers of northerners were saying the same thing. Some of these northerners actually were Upper South yeomen—who had moved to the Northwest to escape a slave regime that imposed "great trials and vexations to the poor, who are perpetually harassed and fatigued with the servile drudgery of patroling through the neighborhood of a night, in order to keep rich people's slaves at home." Others were easterners, including David Wilmot of Pennsylvania, who defended his 1846 Proviso (banning slavery in territory the United States acquired from Mexico) by "plead[ing] the cause of the rights of white freemen" for access to land "where the sons of toil, of my own race and own color, can live without the disgrace which association with negro slavery brings upon free labor." By 1860, Republican politicians could campaign in the North by ridiculing the long series of ultimatums in which southerners warned about what could happen if northerners refused to subordinate their own interests to the defense of southern slavery—believing, as Henry Wilson of Massachusetts did, that the South actually "could not be kicked out of the Union."[8]

In the end, Philip Doddridge was right about the demands of the slave-holders. A regime based on preferential treatment for a vulnerable elite ultimately favored "the largest capitalists," who inherited many of the slaveholders' political prerogatives after the Civil War. For decades, Americans have thought that we dismantled that elitist regime in the twentieth century. In the early twenty-first, however, Madison and the other slaveholding founders are back. It is not just that powerful judges think we have only the rights that the slaveholders intended to grant us. It is that our invocations of "democracy" are coming to sound fatuous once again. There can be no solutions to these problems as long as we are Doddridges attempting to argue with Madisons—who portray their own power as victimization and then call us on our toleration of the injustice that sustains it. We must purge the legacies of the slaveholders and their demands for "security" from our public life. We must reclaim the other part of our political tradition, the one in which people who were willing to trust themselves regulated their society through everyday political jockeying. That is the tradition of democratic self-government in the United States.

How to Talk about Taxes

You know a tax politics is impoverished when politicians assume that the citizens lack the mental capacity to consider anything more complicated than the words "high" and "low"—when they talk about "tax relief" without specifying which taxes they are discussing and reduce complex policy choices to what advertisers call branding (Republicans renaming the estate tax the "death tax," linguist George Lakoff urging Democrats to call the national debt a "baby tax"). The size of the overall tax burden is certainly important, though it is a product of choices about spending rather than choices about taxation itself. The choices we make about taxes actually are about *how* to raise the public money we have decided to spend. They are about how heavily we rely on each of the taxes in our tax system. To make these choices in an informed way, we need access to the language that describes tax equity and tax incidence.[1]

For centuries, there have been two basic approaches to tax equity, known as "benefit" and "ability to pay." In the "benefit" approach, individuals should pay in proportion to the benefits they receive from government, with the "benefits" generally defined to emphasize protection. In the "ability to pay" approach, the distribution of benefits is irrelevant and individuals should pay in proportion to their income or wealth, which measure their "ability." Although these two ways of defining equity may sound different, they have similar implications—because, except in very extreme formulations, the "protection" at issue in the benefit approach involves property as well as personal security.[2] Since, in most "benefit" analyses, richer people (who have more property to protect) derive greater benefits from government than poorer people (who have less property to protect), measures of benefit usually end up being very similar to measures of ability. Benefit taxes remain important for some public services (entrance fees at national parks, gasoline excises spent on road maintenance and construction). Nevertheless, for most public spending—from national defense, local police protection, and jails to education, poor relief, and the basic costs of having any government at all (salaries and buildings from the county courthouse to the White House)—"ability" has been the dominant way of thinking about tax equity in the modern era.[3]

The controversial issue is not the choice between "benefit" and "ability," except in certain cases (how much of the cost of the national parks should come from entrance fees? how much of the cost of airport security should come from taxes on plane tickets?).[4] Rather, the controversial phrase is "in proportion to"—regardless of whether it is followed by "benefit" or "ability." In a "benefit" context, the controversial question is *how much* more the government spends to protect richer people than poorer people. In an "ability" context, it is *how much* more the richer people are able to pay. Some would answer both questions by saying "a whole lot more." Others would say "very little more." In a benefit context, extreme commentators have even said "possibly less" (a result that depends on emphasizing things like schools and welfare while ignoring the protection of property). There is no need to review the conclusions of particular theorists here. Anyone can work out these arguments by thinking about the things government does for richer and poorer people (benefit) and about how people tend to spend higher and lower incomes (ability).[5] Here, the point is merely that even if everyone agreed that taxes should be levied "in proportion to" benefit or ability, we would be no closer to an agreement about what would constitute an equitable tax structure.

So far, we have been talking about the normative question of how tax burdens *should* be distributed. Yet the answers to this question become meaningful only once we have recovered the conceptual vocabulary that addresses two empirical issues: (1) how tax burdens are actually distributed, and (2) how each of the taxes that comprise the tax system (income taxes, property taxes, sales taxes, payroll taxes, and so on) affect this distribution. These empirical questions are addressed by the language of *tax incidence*. The politics of taxation cannot be democratic unless the citizens have a basic familiarity with this language.

The *incidence* of a tax is the distribution of its burden across a society. It can refer to the distribution among any kinds of groups (men and women, old and young, by race or ethnicity), but it usually refers to the distribution of burdens among groups defined by levels of personal or household income. These income groups are most commonly defined by breaking the range of the income distribution into deciles (richest tenth, second-richest tenth, and so on to the poorest tenth of the population). Significantly, the burdens on the people in each decile are expressed as tax rates, or, as the *percentages of their income* that they pay in taxes. Thus, a description of the incidence of taxation in the United States might sound something like this: "The richest tenth pays an average of 22 percent of their income in taxes, while the poorest tenth pays an average of 28 percent." The expression in percentages is very important. In a sales tax, for example, the rich will pay larger numbers of dollars than the poor because they buy more of the taxed stuff, while they will pay much lower percentages of their income because they spend less *of that income* on the taxed stuff (applying more to services, investments, and other uses). An excise—a tax on the production or sale of a particular commodity—works in the same way. The rich may pay more dollars in gasoline excise if they buy more gasoline (say, for large SUVs), but the poor will pay this tax at higher rates because it will take larger shares of their smaller incomes. When we talk about tax incidence, it is the percentages of income that count.

The incidence of a tax or a tax system can be described as proportional, progressive, or regressive. Taxes are *proportional* if richer and poorer people pay the same percentages of their income in taxes. Taxes are *progressive* if richer people pay higher percentages and *regressive* if poorer people pay higher percentages (see fig. 3). In the real world, tax incidence rarely will resemble any of these descriptions completely. While most taxes and tax systems in history have been sharply regressive, the incidence of a tax system usually cannot be graphed as a line that is upward-sloping (progressive), downward-sloping (regressive), or flat (proportional) for its entire length. Instead, tax incidence usually takes the form of a shallowly U-shaped or a shallowly upside-down U-shaped distribution (fig. 4), in which the very rich and very poor pay more (or less) than the people in the middle of the income distribution. Note that we are talking about the averages for the deciles instead of the actual burdens on any particular individuals. People who buy more liquor, tobacco, and gasoline than average will pay higher than average taxes (for their deciles) because of the excise taxes on these commodities. By the same token, people who can claim certain tax breaks (say, because their dividend income comes from tax-exempt securities) will pay lower than average taxes (for their deciles).

These technical terms (incidence, progressivity, regressivity) plainly have huge political implications. When politicians argue that the "middle class" is especially oppressed by taxation, they are arguing that the incidence curve has the upside-down U shape (fig. 4-B) in which the middle deciles pay heavily while the rich and poor get off more cheaply. When they say that the poor are overtaxed, they are saying either that the curve is downward-sloping (fig. 3-C) or that the U shape (fig. 4-A) is too sharp in the low-income deciles.

One political implication is frequently misunderstood. The distribution of tax burdens must not be confused with the distribution of income or wealth in

A. Proportional

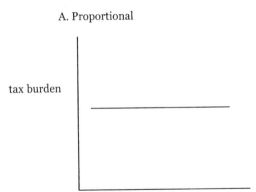

B. Progressive

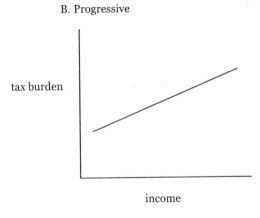

C. Regressive

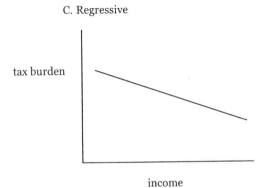

Figure 3. Theoretical Incidence of Taxes

A. U shape (higher for poor and rich)

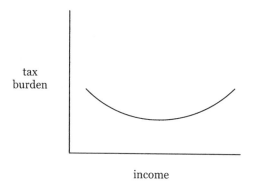

income

B. Upside-down U shape (higher for middle class)

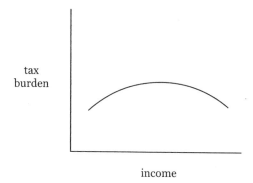

income

Figure 4. More Likely Incidence of Taxes

society. The distribution of tax burdens will usually *affect* the distribution of income or wealth—progressive taxes will reduce inequality while regressive taxes will increase it. Still, arguments that conflate the distribution of tax burdens with the general distribution of income or wealth are misleading. The most popular arguments about progressive taxation illustrate this point. The case for a progressive tax is often portrayed as resting on the idea that there is an intolerable level of inequality in the society, that the progressive tax is intended to "soak the rich" in order to redistribute income or wealth. The real issue, however, is usually whether to include a progressive tax in a larger system in which the other taxes are regressive. Here, the case for adopting the progressive tax actually rests on a desire to redistribute *tax burdens,* such as by using a progressive income tax to offset the impact of regressive sales taxes and excises. Despite rhetoric to the contrary, this was the point of the 1894 income tax and 1913 income tax amendment: to use income taxes to offset the regressive impact of very high tariffs. Similarly, the case against progressive taxation is often portrayed as resting on the injustice of "confiscation"—on the idea that it is inherently unfair to tax the rich at higher rates than the poor. Again, however, the real issue is usually adding a progressive tax to a larger tax system. Even if it makes sense to argue that high-income people have a right to keep what they earn in the economy (assuming that their high incomes do not depend on government spending), nobody "earns" the right to profit from regressive taxation—since it can be no more fair to tax the poor at higher rates than to tax the rich at higher rates. There is nothing remotely confiscatory about a tax that redistributes the overall burden to stop *subsidizing* the rich.[6]

All of these arguments depend on basic empirical data about how tax burdens are actually distributed: about whether the poor are subsidizing the rich, the rich are subsidizing the poor, or the middle is subsidizing both extremes. Before turning to measures of the actual distribution of tax burdens, however, we must notice a complicating factor. Tax incidence covers more than the taxes for which we write checks, endure withholding from paychecks, or pay an additional eight percent or so at the cash register. It covers taxes that we pay indirectly as well as taxes that we pay directly—or, taxes that are *shifted* to us by the people who pay them initially so that we pay them ultimately. We can pay these shifted taxes in various ways, but we pay them most often in the "invisible" form of higher prices for goods or services.

The nineteenth-century tariff is an obvious example. Importers paid the tariffs on goods they imported and then shifted these taxes to consumers by raising prices. Thus, the importers paid the tariff initially, but the consumers paid it ultimately. (When the tariff was protective—that is, set at very high rates to subsidize domestic manufacturing—manufacturers could raise prices without delivering any tax revenue to the government.) Today, the primary examples of this kind are the excises on liquor, tobacco, and gasoline in the United States and, in Europe, the value-added taxes (VATs) that are levied on producers and shifted to consumers. The retail sales taxes of the American state and local governments work somewhat differently. They are levied on consumers at the cash register and then paid over by the retailers who collect them. Yet aside from critical policy details such as which goods are exempted from taxation (most often food), the incidence of American sales taxes is similar to the incidence of European VATs.[7] The difference is the "visibility" of these taxes from the perspectives of the consumers who pay them in both cases. While the European VATs shift silently into consumer prices, the American sales taxes are listed separately on receipts and levied only after a consumer has agreed to pay a particular price—a procedure that is intended to ensure that we feel the burden.

Many other taxes are also shifted. One example would be the real estate tax on a building that a landlord rents out as apartments. The landlord will pay the tax initially and then try to shift it to tenants in the form of higher rents. Taxes on businesses can often be shifted. We might call a business tax a "corporation income tax," for example, but the corporation will treat it as one of the many "costs" that get factored into decisions about how to price the corporation's goods and services and about how to bargain with workers over wages. In a sense, *all* taxes can be shifted under certain economic conditions. If the higher after-tax prices produced by a sales tax curtail consumer spending, we can say that consumers are shifting the burdens to retailers or further to manufacturers. One of the most clever arguments about the logic of shifting was Adam Smith's claim in *The Wealth of Nations* (1776) that even a poll tax could be shifted. Levied at a flat sum regardless of wealth or income, a poll tax is often considered the paradigmatically regressive tax. Smith argued, however, that because poor laborers might not have enough money to spend on food and other necessities after paying a poll tax, their employers would be compelled to raise wages. The people who ultimately paid a poll tax, therefore, were the employers—who should oppose the use of poll taxes because they were not all that regressive after all![8]

Whether a tax can be shifted depends on economic conditions. The importer will not be able to shift his tariff payments into prices when there is a glut of the goods he is selling on the market. The landlord will not be able to shift his real estate tax into rents when a high vacancy rate creates competition for tenants or rent control laws prevent him from doing so. The corporation will not be able to shift its income taxes when recessions reduce prices in general or strong unions defend the wage rates of workers. Consumers will not be able to shift sales taxes or excises when they want the taxed goods more than they resent their increased prices. Finally, Adam Smith's eighteenth-century laborer could not have shifted his poll tax into higher wages when he was competing with others for work or when his wages were already above the subsistence level that Smith was envisioning. And even if the laborer could shift his poll tax, the employer might be able to shift it again to consumers.

Because all this shifting is going on, the measurement of tax incidence requires a series of assumptions about who is able to shift which taxes to whom in practice. Everyone will try to shift tax burdens, just as everyone will try to shift other costs (as in the case of a manufacturing company that tries to force its neighbors or the taxpayers to assume the costs of its dumping and other pollution). There is also a distinction to be made between short-term and long-term effects. Landlords might be able to shift local property tax increases to tenants, but, as rents increase over time in the town with the higher taxes, tenants may start moving to other towns where taxes (and therefore rents) are lower. Then, the landlords who are losing money may decide to invest less in maintenance and the construction of new units, so that the less-mobile tenants who stay in town pay higher rents for lower-quality apartments. This is not the only possible scenario. The higher taxes may finance high-quality local services (such as excellent public schools) that attract tenants and spur new construction. For economists who care primarily about long-term economic outcomes, thought experiments of this kind are what make tax incidence interesting. Yet to recover a tax equity language that is essentially *political*, models of the long run (in which we are all dead) are not helpful.[9] What we need are serviceable assumptions that make sense of the shorter terms in which tax policies and tax politics (really all politics) actually operate in the real world.

The most important work in this area was done by Joseph A. Pechman and his colleagues at the Brookings Institution from the 1960s through the 1980s, published initially as *Who Bears the Tax Burden?* (1974) and then updated to describe the effects of policy changes in *Who Paid the Taxes, 1966-1985?* (1985).[10] Pechman and the Brookings economists solved the problem of disagreements about the proper shifting assumptions by calculating multiple estimates based on different sets of assumptions. They surmounted facile discussions of equity based on only one tax (usually the federal income tax) by estimating the incidence of the entire structure including the panoply of federal, state, and local taxes. Finally, they compiled data about income sources, asset ownership, and consumption patterns in order to trace the impact of each tax across the income distribution. Who (which deciles) tended to pay income taxes only on wage and salary ("earned") income versus the interest, dividend, and capital gains ("unearned") income that was favored in various ways (to promote investment)—and that meanwhile also was exempted from payroll taxes? Who tended to own commercial real estate and who owned or rented their homes? Which groups spent what fractions of their incomes on goods covered by retail sales taxes? Who tended to buy what amounts of liquor, tobacco, and gasoline? How was each group was affected by the estate and gift taxes (the gift tax, imposed on large transfers of wealth by the living, is intended to block the obvious form of estate tax evasion)?

Figure 5 and table 9 present some of Pechman's results for 1985. Starting with the total tax burden, these results show a sharp regressivity at the very bottom of the income distribution, a gently progressive curve through most of the rest, and a regressive drop at the very top (for the richest tenth of the population). The more interesting result, however, comes from breaking the total into its components. Income taxes on individuals were quite progressive in 1985 (except in the bottom decile). They took 4.0 percent of the incomes of the poorest tenth of the population and 14.5 percent of the incomes of the richest tenth.[11] The other taxes were more regressive—most dramatically (but predictably) in the case of the sales taxes and excises. Sales taxes and excises took 7.2 percent of the incomes of the poorest tenth but only 1.9 percent of the incomes of the richest tenth. Thus, to the extent that the American tax system was progressive in 1985, it was progressive because progressive income taxes accounted for a large fraction of the total tax burden (43.1 percent). Tax changes since 1985 have reduced the progressivity of the federal income tax. Tax changes since 2000 have been intended both to reduce the progressivity of the federal income tax and to reduce the role of this tax in the larger tax system.

There is another implication of these data. Proposals to weaken the federal government by decentralizing its functions will tend to make the tax system more regressive because the federal taxes are (or were in 1985) more progressive than the state and local taxes. Federal taxation in table 9 includes most of the income taxes, all of the payroll taxes, and some of the excise taxes. State

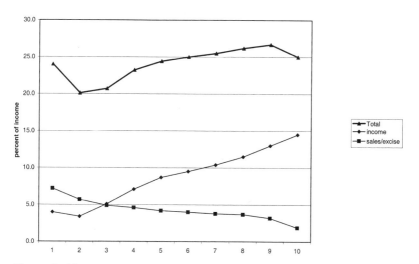

Figure 5. Incidence of U.S. Tax Burdens, 1985 (for deciles of income distribution). SOURCE: Joseph A. Pechman, *Who Paid the Taxes, 1966–85?* (Washington, 1985, 2nd printing), 92.

Table 9: Incidence of U.S. Tax Burdens, 1985

	Total Taxes	Individual Income	Corporation Income	Payroll	Property	Sales and Excise
Income deciles						
First (poorest)	24.0	4.0	3.6	5.1	3.9	7.2
Second	20.1	3.4	2.8	5.1	3.0	5.7
Third	20.7	5.1	2.4	5.9	2.4	4.9
Fourth	23.2	7.1	2.2	6.9	2.3	4.6
Fifth	24.4	8.7	1.9	7.3	2.1	4.2
Sixth	25.0	9.5	1.9	7.2	2.1	4.0
Seventh	25.5	10.4	1.8	7.1	2.1	3.8
Eighth	26.2	11.5	1.8	6.9	2.1	3.7
Ninth	26.7	13.0	1.7	6.6	2.1	3.2
Tenth (richest)	25.0	14.5	2.2	4.0	2.2	1.9
Overall	25.3	10.9	2.1	6.5	2.3	3.4
Percentage of overall burden	43.1	8.3	25.7	9.1	13.4

SOURCE: Joseph A. Pechman, *Who Paid the Taxes, 1966–1985?* (Washington, 1985, 2nd printing), 92. Data as reported for assumptions 3b. The last row is calculated from the overall burden row. Note that it is the percentage of the *burden*, as reported in the table, rather than the percentage of the total revenue raised from each tax.

and local taxation in table 9, meanwhile, includes some of the income taxes, some of the excises, all of the property taxes, and all of the sales taxes. Weakening the federal government by decentralizing its functions, therefore, means reducing the impact of the more progressive federal taxes and increasing the impact of the more regressive state and local taxes. It means reducing the tax burdens of the rich and increasing the tax burdens of the poor.

Unfortunately (one might even say criminally), no similar data are available for the period since the mid-1980s. Data from the Organization for Economic Co-operation and Development (OECD), however, can fill in some details (see table 10). The OECD reports that income taxes on individuals raised 37.7 percent of American tax revenue in 2002. This figure was high in a comparative perspective, although it is undoubtedly lower now (in 2005). Only four OECD countries (Denmark, New Zealand, Iceland, and Australia) raised larger fractions of their total tax revenue from individual income taxes in 2002. The American income taxes were less progressive than some of the others, but the United States relied on them heavily—mainly because it levied no VAT. As a result, the American tax system was relatively progressive in 2002.[12]

The OECD data also permit us to return to the question of the size of the tax burden. The table ranks countries according to the per capita tax burden (the average burden per individual). It places the United States about one-third of the way down, with eleven countries imposing higher tax burdens and eighteen countries imposing lower ones. Yet most social scientists would consider it more appropriate to rank the OECD countries by tax burden as a percentage of GDP (essentially the size of the economy) than by the nominal burdens on individuals. This ranking places the United States near the bottom. While the United States raised 26.4 percent of its GDP in taxes in 2002, Germany raised 36.0 percent, France raised 44.0 percent, and Sweden raised a huge 50.2 percent. In fact, the United States raised less of its GDP in taxes in 2002 than any other OECD countries except Japan, Korea, and Mexico. What this means is that even though the taxpayers in relatively poor countries (such as Poland and Turkey) paid fewer dollars than Americans did in 2002, they paid larger fractions of their (smaller) incomes. Given the size of the American economy, in short, American taxes were extraordinarily low.

The OECD data shed light on significant empirical questions by illustrating the relative incidence of American taxes and the relative size of American taxes. Like the Pechman data, however, they provide only a framework for addressing the crucial normative issues: how high or low and how progressive or regressive our taxes *should* be. The answers to these questions are inherently political. There are no "right answers" that are not connected to other inherently political issues: who should benefit from government spending and who should pay for it. On the spending side, they are questions about how much we prefer to spend on what kinds of public services and other costs (such as wars). On the tax side, they are questions about tax equity and tax incidence: how we want to modify particular taxes and how heavily we want to rely on the different taxes in our larger tax system. Polling data seem to show that Americans think our tax structure should be more progressive than it is.[13] Election returns, however, seem to show that we are fairly comfortable with tax "reforms" that increase burdens on the poor and middle class in order to reduce burdens on the rich. If there is indeed a disconnect between the policies we want and the policies we are getting, it is the responsibility of the voters to say so.

Table 10: Tax Revenue in OECD Countries, 2002

| | Per Capita Burden (dollars) | Tax Burden as Percent of GDP | Percentage of Total Tax Burden | | | | |
			Individual Income	Corporation Income	Social Security	Property	Sales and Excise
Luxembourg	19,842	41.8	16.2	20.5	26.9	8.0	27.9
Norway	18,275	43.5	24.8	18.9	22.7	2.3	31.2
Denmark	15,675	48.9	53.2	5.8	3.4	3.5	33.1
Sweden	13,570	50.2	30.4	4.8	30.1	3.2	26.4
Finland	11,615	45.9	31.2	9.3	26.6	2.4	30.2
Switzerland	11,315	30.3	34.4	8.8	25.6	8.6	22.6
Iceland	11,255	38.1	38.6	3.0	8.1	7.4	40.3
Austria	11,237	44.0	22.8	5.1	33.4	1.3	28.2
Belgium	10,980	46.4	31.7	7.6	31.6	3.1	24.6
France	10,331	44.0	17.3	6.6	37.0	7.5	25.4
Netherlands	10,167	39.2	18.3	8.8	35.5	5.3	30.8
United States	**9,569**	**26.4**	**37.7**	**6.7**	**26.1**	**11.9**	**17.6**
United Kingdom	9,444	35.8	29.8	8.1	17.0	12.0	32.7
Ireland	8,837	28.4	26.2	13.1	15.0	5.3	39.5
Italy	8,699	42.6	25.5	7.6	29.4	5.1	26.9

Country						
Germany	8,668	36.0	25.1	2.9	40.3	2.3	29.2
Canada	8,125	33.9	35.0	10.1	15.2	9.8	26.3
Japan	8,035	25.8	18.4	12.2	38.3	10.8	20.1
Australia	6,532	31.5	38.5	16.8	0.0	9.0	30.3
Spain	5,752	35.6	19.4	9.1	35.3	6.6	28.6
New Zealand	5,300	34.9	42.3	12.1	0.0	5.0	35.2
Greece	4,363	35.9	14.0	10.4	32.8	4.7	37.3
Portugal	3,987	33.9	27.6	0.0	27.1	3.4	37.3
Korea	2,801	24.4	12.8	12.8	18.8	12.7	38.8
Czech Republic	2,680	39.3	12.8	11.8	44.1	1.5	29.7
Hungary	2,446	38.3	20.3	6.2	30.3	1.9	37.4
Poland	1,631	32.6	22.9	6.3	29.0	4.3	36.9
Slovak Republic	1,488	33.1	10.2	8.2	43.3	1.6	34.1
Mexico	1,155	18.1	28.9	0.0	17.9	1.7	49.0
Turkey	822	31.1	17.6	7.1	19.8	2.9	46.8
Unweight Average	8,153	36.3	26.0	9.3	25.4	5.5	31.9

NOTE: For Portugal and Mexico, corporation income tax is included with individual income tax.

SOURCE: Organization for Economic Co-operation and Development, *Revenue Statistics, 1965–2003* (Paris, 2004), 68, 70, 72–74, 78–79, 84.

Introduction

1. On the masters' control of national politics, see Leonard L. Richards, *The Slave Power: The Free North and Southern Domination, 1780–1860* (Amherst, 2000). On the senses in which they were and were not overthrown during and after the Civil War, see Eric Foner, *Reconstruction: America's Unfinished Revolution, 1865–1877* (New York, 1988). See also David Brion Davis, "Free at Last: The Enduring Legacy of the South's Civil War Victory," *New York Times,* Aug. 26, 2002, sec. 4, p. 1.

2. For a different take on this theme, Eric Foner, *The Story of American Freedom* (New York, 1998).

3. J. R. R. Tolkien, *The Lord of the Rings. Part One, The Fellowship of the Ring* (1955; New York, 1973), 27.

4. My approach to political history is an "institutionalist" or "policy history" approach, known in political science as "American political development." This mode of analysis directs attention to the structures of political institutions. For the period I am examining, it is a useful corrective to biographical, ideological, and behavioral approaches that often allow the subjects of historical research to frame the questions and thereby to dictate the conclusions. See especially Richard R. John, "Governmental Institutions as Agents of Change: Rethinking American Political Development in the Early Republic," *Studies in American Political Development* 11 (1997): 347–80; Theda Skocpol, "Bringing the State Back In: Strategies of Analysis in Current Research," in *Bringing the State Back In,* ed. Peter B. Evans et al. (New York, 1985), 3–43; and, more generally, the research published in *Studies in American Political Development* and the *Journal of Policy History.*

5. Historians have made withering criticisms of every aspect of this "liberal" story, but especially of its portrait of the early twentieth century. That era is now usually described as a time of incredible racial violence, rampant nativism, the rise of a corporate culture that subordinated most people to large-scale organizations, and elitist political reforms that undermined democracy. See especially Alan Dawley, *Struggles for Justice: Social Responsibility and the Liberal State* (Cambridge, MA, 1991); and Nell Irvin Painter, *Standing at*

Armageddon: The United States, 1877–1919 (New York, 1987). For the political side of this interpretation, Robert H. Wiebe, *The Search for Order, 1877–1920* (New York, 1967), was foundational. Still, the idea that there was a "progressive era" seems to be making a comeback: Daniel T. Rodgers, *Atlantic Crossings: Social Politics in a Progressive Age* (Cambridge, MA, 1998); Elizabeth Sanders, *Roots of Reform: Farmers, Workers, and the American State, 1877–1917* (Chicago, 1999); and, for taxation, W. Elliot Brownlee, *Federal Taxation in America: A Short History* (Cambridge, 1996).

6. For recent critiques of such taxes, see William F. Shughart II, ed., *The Predatory Politics of Fiscal Discrimination* (New Brunswick, NJ, 1997).

7. For an excellent synthesis of research on slavery itself, see Ira Berlin, *Many Thousands Gone: The First Two Centuries of Slavery in North America* (Cambridge, MA, 1998). From a growing literature on slavery in political history, one might start with Don E. Fehrenbacher, *The Slaveholding Republic: An Account of the United States Government's Relations with Slavery* (New York, 2001); and Richards, *Slave Power.*

8. Joseph A. Schumpeter, "The Crisis of the Tax State," trans. W. F. Stolper and R. A. Musgrave, *International Economic Papers* 4 (1954): 5–38; Rudolf Goldscheid, "A Sociological Approach to Problems of Public Finance," in *Classics in the Theory of Public Finance,* ed. Richard A. Musgrave and Alan T. Peacock (London, 1964).

9. This point is made for the period from the Revolution to the Civil War in classic studies: Oscar Handlin and Mary Flug Handlin, *Commonwealth: A Study of the Role of Government in the American Economy, 1774–1861,* rev. ed. (1947; Cambridge, MA, 1969); Louis Hartz, *Economic Policy and Democratic Thought: Pennsylvania, 1776–1860* (Cambridge, MA, 1948); Harry N. Scheiber, *Ohio Canal Era: A Case Study of Government and the Economy* (Athens, OH, 1968).

10. For similar findings in larger comparative studies of the Americas, see Kenneth L. Sokoloff and Eric M. Zolt, "Inequality and Taxation: Evidence from the Americas on How Inequality May Influence Tax Institutions," *Tax Law Review* 58 (forthcoming 2005); Stanley L. Engerman and Kenneth L. Sokoloff, "Factor Endowments Inequality, and Paths of Development among New World Economies," *Economia* 3 (2002): 41–109; idem, "The Evolution of Suffrage Institutions in the New World," *Journal of Economic History* 65 (2005): 891–921.

11. Two historians have written crucial correctives; neither has been taken seriously enough: Staughton Lynd, *Class Conflict, Slavery, & the United States Constitution: Ten Essays* (Indianapolis, 1967), chaps. 6–10; Paul Finkelman, *Slavery and the Founders: Race and Liberty in the Age of Jefferson,* 2nd ed. (Armonk, NY, 2001). See also William W. Freehling, *The Road to Disunion: Secessionists at Bay, 1776–1854* (New York, 1990); Duncan J. Macleod, *Slavery, Race, and the American Revolution* (London, 1974); and Donald L. Robinson, *Slavery in the Structure of American Politics, 1765–1820* (New York, 1971).

12. Note to social historians. This study does not analyze tax lists. It analyzes the political history that shaped them. On their weaknesses as social history sources, see James T. Lemon and Gary B. Nash, "The Distribution of Wealth in Eighteenth-Century America: A Century of Change in Chester County, Pennsylvania, 1693–1802," *Journal of Social History* 2 (1968): 1–24; G. B. Warden, "Inequality and Instability in Eighteenth-Century Boston: A Reappraisal," *Journal of Interdisciplinary History* 4 (1976): 585–620; Edward

Pessen, *Riches, Class, and Power before the Civil War* (Lexington, MA, 1973), chap. 2. Gaps between the assessed valuation and actual value of property result from legislation and local assessment decisions—that is, from the political history of taxation.

Prologue

1. This and the next two paragraphs rely on George T. Matthews, *The Royal General Farms in Eighteenth-Century France* (New York, 1958), supplemented by Jean-Pierre Poirier, *Lavoisier: Chemist, Biologist, Economist,* trans. Rebecca Balinski (Philadelphia, 1996). The Farmers General was also one of the monarchy's chief lenders. This contributed immeasurably to its power, as an unpayable royal debt ensured that the tax farming contracts, allegedly awarded through competitive bidding, always were awarded to the Farmers General.

2. In U.S. history, the terms "direct" and "indirect" have a complex legal history because of the use of the term "direct taxes" in the Constitution (see chap. 5). Although there are also complex European definitions (especially the French physiocratic idea that because all taxes fall ultimately on land, only land taxes are "direct"), the normal usage in European history applies the term "direct" to income and property taxes and "indirect" to consumption taxes that are paid in the first instance by businesses and then shifted to consumers in higher prices of the taxed goods. See the appendix for more discussion of the shifting and incidence of taxation.

3. This paragraph and the next rely on Michael Kwass, *Privilege and the Politics of Taxation in Eighteenth-Century France: Liberté, Egalité, Fiscalité* (Cambridge, 2000), supplemented by James C. Riley, *The Seven Years War and the Old Regime in France: The Economic and Fiscal Toll* (Princeton, 1986).

4. Kwass, *Privilege,* 201.

5. Except as noted, my entire discussion of Britain relies on John Brewer, *The Sinews of Power: War, Money, and the English State, 1688–1783* (Cambridge, MA, 1988).

6. Thomas Paine, "Case of the Officers of Excise," in Philip S. Foner, ed., *The Complete Writings of Thomas Paine,* 2 vols. (New York, 1945), 1: 3–15.

7. Adam Smith, *An Inquiry into the Nature and Causes of the Wealth of Nations,* ed. Edwin Canaan (1776; New York, 1937), 833.

8. On the Customs Service in the colonies, see Thomas C. Barrow, *Trade and Empire: The British Customs Service in Colonial America, 1660–1775* (Cambridge, MA, 1967).

9. I will refer to the imperial wars by their American names in this book. In Europe, Queen Anne's War was called the War of the Spanish Succession.

10. On this comparative point, see Peter Mathias and Patrick O'Brien, "Taxation in Britain and France, 1715–1810: A Comparison of the Social and Economic Incidence of Taxes Collected for the Central Governments," *Journal of European Economic History* 5 (1976): 601–50, esp. the discussion of sources at the end of the article.

11. For these quotations (and many others), see Raymond Turner, "The Excise Scheme of 1733," *English Historical Review* 42 (1927): 46, 51; and Paul S. Boyer, "Borrowed Rhetoric: The Massachusetts Excise Controversy of 1754," *William and Mary Quarterly,* 3rd. ser., 21 (1964): 341.

12. On the politics of the excise, in addition to Brewer, *Sinews,* see Paul Langford, *The Excise Crisis: Society and Politics in the Age of Walpole* (Oxford, 1975). There is a vast literature on the "court" versus "country" dispute and especially its impact in the colonies. Most of this work sympathizes with the "country." For the stakes, see P. G. M. Dickson, *The Financial Revolution in England: A Study in the Development of Public Credit, 1688–1756* (London, 1967); Isaac Kramnick, *Bolingbroke and His Circle: The Politics of Nostalgia in the Age of Walpole* (Cambridge, MA, 1968); and Raymond Williams, *The Country and the City* (New York, 1973). On the American side, Bernard Bailyn, *The Ideological Origins of the American Revolution* (Cambridge, MA, 1967), is foundational.

13. John Lynch, *Bourbon Spain, 1700–1808* (Oxford, 1989), quotation on 344; see also Jan de Vries and Ad van der Woude, *The First Modern Economy: Success, Failure, and Perseverance of the Dutch Economy, 1500–1815* (Cambridge, 1997), chap. 4; David Brading, *Miners and Merchants in Bourbon Mexico, 1763–1810* (Cambridge, 1971); Barbara A. Tenenbaum, *The Politics of Penury: Debts and Taxes in Mexico* (Albuquerque, 1986); Philip Lawson, *The East India Company: A History* (London, 1993); H. V. Bowen, *Revenue and Reform: The Indian Problem in British Politics, 1757–1773* (Cambridge, 1991). For an overview of early modern Europe, see Carolyn Webber and Aaron Wildavsky, *A History of Taxation and Expenditure in the Western World* (New York, 1986), chap. 5. For long-term outcomes in the Americas, see Kenneth L. Sokoloff and Eric M. Zolt, "Inequality and Taxation: Evidence from the Americas on How Inequality May Influence Tax Institutions," *Tax Law Review* 58 (forthcoming 2005).

14. Smith, *Wealth of Nations,* 899–900.

15. Economic historians agree with Smith. See John J. McCusker and Russell R. Menard, *The Economy of British America, 1607–1789* (Chapel Hill, 1991), 354; and Edwin J. Perkins, *The Economy of Colonial America* (New York, 1980), 128–29, 139. On American contributions to the French and Indian War, see Fred Anderson, *Crucible of War: The Seven Years' War and the Fate of Empire in British North America, 1754–1766* (New York, 2000).

16. This story is told in many places. See, for example, Robert Middlekauff, *The Glorious Cause: The American Revolution, 1763–1789* (New York, 1982), 1–273.

17. Edmund S. Morgan and Helen M. Morgan, *The Stamp Crisis: Prologue to Revolution,* rev. ed. (1953; Chapel Hill, 1995), 35, 39, 111, 146.

18. There were a handful of resident aristocrats in the colonies, such as Sir William Johnson of New York. See Richard R. Beeman, *The Varieties of Political Experience in Eighteenth-Century America* (Philadelphia, 2004), esp. chap. 4.

19. Even where the colonial suffrage rule was the same as Britain's, a 40 shilling freehold, many more Americans were able to qualify because of a broader distribution of land ownership. See Alexander Keyssar, *The Right to Vote: The Contested History of Democracy in the United States* (New York, 2000), 5–7.

20. The most famous version of this argument is Louis Hartz, *The Liberal Tradition in America: An Interpretation of American Political Thought since the Revolution* (New York, 1955).

Introduction to Part 1

1. Contrast Richard Buel, Jr., *Dear Liberty: Connecticut's Mobilization for the Revolutionary War* (Middletown, CT, 1980), against Woody Holton, *Forced Founders: Indians,*

Debtors, Slaves, and the Making of the American Revolution in Virginia (Chapel Hill, 1999); Ronald Hoffman, *A Spirit of Dissension: Economics, Politics, and the Revolution in Maryland* (Baltimore, 1973); Sylvia R. Frey, *Water from the Rock: Black Resistance in a Revolutionary Age* (Princeton, 1991).

2. Roger H. Brown, *Redeeming the Republic: Federalists, Taxation, and the Origins of the Constitution* (Baltimore, 1993); E. James Ferguson, *The Power of the Purse: A History of American Public Finance, 1776–1790* (Chapel Hill, 1961).

3. Brown, *Redeeming*, 14.

4. Ibid., 155. Brown also makes a third argument: that the Federalists who supported the adoption of the Constitution wanted to use a powerful national government to discipline an unruly populace by forcing them to pay heavy taxes. For the failure of requisitions causing the adoption of the Constitution, see also Max Edling, *A Revolution in Favor of Government: Origins of the U.S. Constitution and the Making of the American State* (New York, 2003); and Calvin H. Johnson, *Righteous Anger at the Wicked States: The Meaning of the Founders' Constitution* (New York, 2005).

5. Brown, *Redeeming*, 154, 166, 167.

6. The major study of this difference, Robert A. Becker, *Revolution, Reform, and the Politics of American Taxation, 1763–1783* (Baton Rouge, 1980), takes a more charitable view of the southern tax reforms, in part because it stops in 1783 rather than continuing through the next several years, when many of these reforms were rolled back. Along with several journal articles, which will be cited below, Brown, *Redeeming*, and Becker, *Revolution*, comprise the existing literature on colonial taxation and state taxation during the Revolution. Brown emphasizes administrative capacity (ability to collect the taxes). Becker emphasizes tax equity (economic incidence of the burden). My main disagreements with these rich histories—both steeped in the details of local political conflicts—stem from the longer time period considered here.

7. See especially Edmund S. Morgan, "Slavery and Freedom: The American Paradox," *Journal of American History* 59 (1972): 5–29; and Edmund S. Morgan, *American Slavery, American Freedom: The Ordeal of Colonial Virginia* (New York, 1975). Recent synthetic works tend to downplay differences between North and South. See Richard R. Beeman, *The Varieties of Political Experience in Eighteenth-Century America* (Philadelphia, 2004); Jack P. Greene, *Pursuits of Happiness: The Social Development of Early Modern British Colonies and the Formation of American Culture* (Chapel Hill, 1988).

Chapter 1

1. On sovereign mastership, see Ira Berlin, *Many Thousands Gone: The First Two Centuries of Slavery in North America* (Cambridge, MA, 1998), 117–18. The classic work on gentry politics is Charles S. Sydnor, *Gentlemen Freeholders: Political Practices in Washington's Virginia* (Chapel Hill, 1952), which is updated in Rhys Isaac, *The Transformation of Virginia* (Chapel Hill, 1982); and Woody Holton, *Forced Founders: Indians, Slaves, and the Making of the Revolution in Virginia* (Chapel Hill, 1999).

2. The best discussion of tobacco inspection is Allan Kullikoff, *Tobacco and Slaves: The Development of Southern Cultures in the Chesapeake, 1680–1800* (Chapel Hill, 1986), 104–16. On flour inspection in Pennsylvania, see Mary M. Schweitzer, *Custom and Contract: Household Government and the Economy in Colonial Pennsylvania* (New York, 1987), 175–90.

3. Unless otherwise noted, the following sketch relies on Edmund S. Morgan, *American Slavery, American Freedom: The Ordeal of Colonial Virginia* (New York, 1975), supplemented by Gary B. Nash, *Red, White, and Black: The Peoples of Early America*, 3rd ed. (Englewood Cliffs, 1992); and Wesley Frank Craven, *The Southern Colonies in the Seventeenth Century, 1607–1689* (Baton Rouge, 1949).

4. See especially John J. McCusker and Russell R. Menard, *The Economy of British America, 1607–1789* (Chapel Hill, 1991), chap. 6.

5. In addition to the sources already cited, see David W. Galenson, *White Servitude in Colonial America: An Economic Analysis* (New York, 1981).

6. Stephen Saunders Webb, *1676: The End of American Independence* (New York, 1984), provides information that supplements the account in Morgan, *American Slavery, American Freedom*.

7. See especially Berlin, *Many Thousands Gone*, chap. 5.

8. If "hopelessly corrupt" sounds extreme, it is the consensual view of historians of seventeenth-century Virginia politics, not only the highly critical Morgan, *American Slavery*, and Webb, *1676*, but also the gentler (and older) Craven, *Southern Colonies*, and Philip Alexander Bruce, *Institutional History of Virginia in the Seventeenth Century*, 2 vols. (1910; Gloucester, MA, 1964)—but "primitive" in the eighteenth century is my own conclusion. The following sketch of government structure relies on these works and the laws collected in Virginia, *The Statutes at Large*, ed. William Waller Hening, 13 vols. and supplement (1819–23; Charlottesville, 1969, 1971), which will be cited hereafter as Hening, *Statutes*.

9. Virginia Constitution (1851), art. 6, sec. 26. Historians of colonial Virginia all notice the self-perpetuating county courts, but nobody seems impressed by the fact that this was a radically undemocratic system of local government. For a typical gloss, see Robert Wheeler, "The County Court in Colonial Virginia," in *Town and County: Essays on the Structure of Local Government in the American Colonies*, ed. Bruce C. Daniels (Middletown, CT, 1978), 111–33.

10. On the vestries, see William H. Seiler, "The Anglican Church: A Basic Institution of Local Government in Colonial Virginia," in *Town and County: Essays on the Structure of Local Government in the American Colonies*, ed. Bruce C. Daniels (Middletown, CT, 1978), 134–59. The rotation also reflected an effort to discipline the sheriffs by holding the justices responsible for their defaults (when they failed to pay the taxes they collected). Hening, *Statutes*, 2: 78.

11. Thomas C. Barrow, *Trade and Empire: The British Customs Service in Colonial America 1660–1775* (Cambridge, 1967); Beverley W. Bond, Jr., *The Quit-Rent System in the American Colonies* (New Haven, 1919), chap. 8, and, for the 1762 incident, 242.

12. Hening, *Statutes*, 1: 295, 297, 2: 19, 280, 412, 3: 47–50, 7: 140, 539, 8: 178, 381.

13. The quotation is from a classic on machine politics, William L. Riordon, *Plunkitt of Tammany Hall: A Series of Very Plain Talks on Very Practical Politics*, ed. Terrence J. McDonald (1905; Boston, 1994), 49.

14. Morgan, *American Slavery*, 367; A. Roger Ekirch, *"Poor Carolina": Politics and Society in Colonial North Carolina, 1729–1776* (Chapel Hill, 1981), 82–83, 111. The quota-

tions are from arguments attributing North Carolina's corruption to the fact that it lacked these attributes of Virginia.

15. The Robinson affair is complicated not only because it coincided with the Stamp Act crisis, but because it was the culmination of a struggle in which the crown had been demanding a separation of the offices of colony treasurer and speaker of the House of Burgesses. Robinson had held both, using the combination to exert great political power. See Joseph Albert Ernst, *Money and Politics in America, 1755–1775: A Study in the Currency Act of 1764 and the Political Economy of Revolution* (Chapel Hill, 1973), chap. 6; and Richard R. Beeman, *The Varieties of Political Experience in Eighteenth-Century America* (Philadelphia, 2004).

16. Hening, *Statutes,* 1: 491, 498, 2: 131–32, 280, 468, 3: 23–24, 88, 229, supp.: 47, 67, 130, 4: 143, supp., 237, 291, 4: 394, 5: 26, 28, 6: 251, 7: 265, 8: 343.

17. For details on the handling of race and gender, see Kathleen M. Brown, *Good Wives, Nasty Wenches, and Anxious Patriarchs: Gender, Race, and Power in Colonial Virginia* (Chapel Hill, 1996), 116–28.

18. Hening, *Statutes,* 1: 124, 159, 281, 284, 286–88, 292. The quoted language on tithables is from 1645, but see also a 1643 version: "[T]hat is to say, as well for all youths of sixteen years of age as vpwards, as also for all negro women at the age of sixteen years." Ibid., 1: 243.

19. Brown, *Good Wives,* 116–28.

20. Hening, *Statutes,* 1: 242.

21. The most controversial of these exempted members of the colony's council "and 10 servants each," an elitist rule that was abolished during Bacon's Rebellion. Ibid., 1: 228, 279, 307, 445, 2: 32, 84–85, 360, 391–92. In 1633, in an effort to encourage artisans to migrate, new migrants who were not planters or agricultural workers were exempted. Ibid., 1: 222, 2: 85, 179, 392.

22. Ibid., 1: 284, 295, 297, 329–30, 2: 19, 170, 296, 3: 47. Unfree white women were exempted again in 1663: "[T]hat women servants be excepted out of this act [about concealed tithables], which whether they are tythable or not is referred to the county courts to judge and determine." Ibid., 187. The racial basis became more explicit in 1668 ("[T]hat negro women, though permitted to enjoy their ffredome yet ought not in all respects to be admitted to a full fruition of the exemptions and impunities of the English, and are still lyble to payment of taxes") and in 1680 in a law declaring Indian women servants to be tithable. Ibid., 2: 267, 492.

23. The taxes rose to pay for the French and Indian War. See below for details, but note the 1757 complaint that since the tax laws were revised, "the more ignorant are liable to be imposed upon by the sheriffs who collect the said taxes and levies." Ibid., 7: 140. There was an especially creative tax scam in 1738: taxpayers failing to turn in their lists of tithables, then "covinously" suing each other to claim informants' rewards. There was also a more prosaic evasion: moving tithables across county lines temporarily to avoid taxes in a county financing a new building. Ibid., 5: 35.

24. Morgan, *American Slavery,* 346.

25. Hening, *Statutes,* 1: 305–6.

26. Ibid., 1: 305–6, 329–30, 337, 342–43, 356.

27. Ibid., 1: 491, 469, 498, 513–14, 523, 535–37.

28. Ibid., 2: 131–36, 176–77. Initially, the governor appointed council members to collect the tax. Because they also enforced the Navigation Acts, they had to be confirmed in England. In 1671, the crown took over the appointment of customs officers; now these new officers collected the tax. Morgan, *American Slavery,* 201; Barrow, *Trade and Empire,* 11–13; Bruce, *Institutional History,* 2: 592–95; and J. M. Sosin, *English America and the Restoration Monarchy of Charles II: Transatlantic Politics, Commerce, and Kingship* (Lincoln, 1980), 163. The two-shilling tobacco tax usually is discussed in another context, the struggle between the crown and assembly over the establishment of a "permanent revenue." The assembly lost in 1679, which meant it lost the right to renew this tax on a regular basis, a major source of assembly power against governors. Benjamin Woods Labaree, *Royal Government in America: A Study of the British Colonial System before 1783* (New York, 1930), 275.

29. Hening, *Statutes,* 2: 178, 204. The land tax might have been a strategy to improve quitrent collection by making the colony depend on a tax that piggybacked on the quitrents. There is no evidence for this interpretation, though it would solve the puzzle of why the governor and council suggested the land tax.

30. Quoted in Bruce, *Institutional History,* 2: 542–43.

31. Or, at least, it started over this issue. See Morgan, *American Slavery;* Webb, *1676.*

32. Hening, *Statutes,* 2: 468, 3: 23–24, 88, 212–13, 225, 229, and for the quotations: supp.: 47, 237–38, 4: 393–94, 6: 251, 8: 343. Starting in 1691, the assembly also taxed exported hides, wool, and iron, which quickly became a tax on hides and furs, since Virginia exported no wool or iron. Ibid., 3: 62–63, 123, 129, 189.

33. Virginia, *Executive Journals of the Council,* ed. H. R. McIlwaine et al., 6 vols. (Richmond, 1925–66), 4: 40; Hening, *Statutes,* supp.: 237–38.

34. Virginia, *Executive Journals,* 4: 75, 116, 149, 257, 5: 346, 6: 149–50, 396; Hening, *Statutes,* 4: 143, supp.: 285, 291, 4: 278, 310–17, 317–22, 393–94, 470–73. For the slave duties as efforts to restrict importations, see Holton, *Forced Founders,* 66–73. The slave trade also inspired other regulations, such as this one from 1748: "whereas the masters of ships or vessels importing negroes, frequently cause such as die on board, to be cast into the water, to the great annoyance of adjacent inhabitants," bodies were to be brought ashore for burial. Hening, *Statutes,* 6: 100–1.

35. Francis Jennings, *Empire of Fortune: Crowns, Colonies, and Tribes in the Seven Years' War in America* (New York, 1988); Philip Lawson: *The East India Company: A History* (London, 1993), chaps. 4–6; John Brewer, *The Sinews of Power: War, Money, and the English State, 1688–1783* (Cambridge, 1990); and James C. Riley, *The Seven Years War and the Old Regime in France: The Economic and Financial Toll* (Princeton, 1986). On the reimbursements, see Lawrence Henry Gipson, *The British Empire before the American Revolution,* 15 vols. (New York, 1936–70), vol. 10, chap. 2.

36. See E. James Ferguson, *The Power of the Purse: A History of American Public Finance, 1776–1790* (Chapel Hill, 1961), chap. 1.

37. Hening, *Statutes,* 6: 552, for the quotation and, more generally, 6: 435–38, 461–66,

471–72, 522–30, 7: 9–11, 77–78, 81–86, 174–78, 258–63, 274, 281, 333–37, 349–53, 359–63, 497–501. Most of the tax hikes were framed to kick in over a series of years and, in one case (7: 497–501), to stop immediately when the British reimbursement arrived. For Virginia's tax system after the Revolution, see chap. 6 below.

38. Richard Buel, Jr., *In Irons: Britain's Naval Supremacy and the American Revolutionary Economy* (New Haven, 1998), 30–37.

39. Hening, *Statutes,* 9: 67–70, 143–45, 220–25. On the black troops, Berlin, *Many Thousands Gone,* 256–58; Holton, *Forced Founders,* 156–61.

40. Hening, *Statutes,* 9: 349–51, 361–62, 365–66, 369.

41. Ibid., 9: 351–55.

42. Ibid., 9: 547–49.

43. Ibid., 10: 10–12, emphasis added.

44. Ibid., 10: 242–44, 285. The Williamsburg and Jamestown plan came in a law that introduced a window tax and others (279–86).

45. Thomas Jefferson, "Bill to Amend an Act for Raising a Supply of Money," Oct. 14, 1778, in Julian P. Boyd, ed., *The Papers of Thomas Jefferson,* 29 vols. (Princeton, 1950–2000), 2: 223–24, a footnote to the bill itself, including the quoted language and identifying the opinion poll as Jefferson's "innovation." The legislature rejected this proposal when Jefferson proposed it initially but adopted it the next year. On Jefferson and arithmetic, see Daniel Scott Smith, "Population and Political Ethics: Thomas Jefferson's Demography of Generations," *William and Mary Quarterly,* 3rd ser., 56 (1999): 591–612. See also Herbert E. Sloan, *Principle and Interest: Thomas Jefferson and the Problem of Debt* (New York, 1995).

46. Hening, *Statutes,* 10: 9–10.

47. Ibid., 10: 79, 404, 490.

48. Ibid., 10: 501–5; 11: 112–13.

49. Ibid., 11: 140–42.

50. Ibid., 12: 431. See chap. 6 below.

51. For the trade tax program, see ibid., 12: 413–15. For an introduction to the 1790 financial deal, see Ferguson, *Power of the Purse,* chap. 14.

52. Hening, *Statutes,* 11: 114.

53. John Adams, "A Defence of the Constitutions of Government of the United States of America," in Charles Francis Adams, ed., *The Works of John Adams,* 10 vols. (Boston, 1852–65), 4: 393; and Thomas Jefferson to Samuel Kercheval, July 12, 1816, quoted in A. G. Roeber, *Faithful Magistrates and Republican Lawyers: Creators of Virginia Legal Culture, 1680–1810* (Chapel Hill, 1981), 163. George Mason reported that tax commissioners were being appointed even while the law still mandated elections, Roeber, *Faithful Magistrates,* 178.

54. For overseers of poor, Hening, *Statutes,* 12: 27–30. Roeber, *Faithful Magistrates,* is a study of the court reform. For the fiscal significance of the disestablishment of religion, see H. James Henderson, "Taxation and Political Culture: Massachusetts and Virginia, 1760–1800," *William and Mary Quarterly,* 3rd ser., 47 (1990): 90–114.

Chapter 2

1. Thomas Jefferson to William Smith, Nov. 13, 1787, in Julian P. Boyd, ed., *The Papers of Thomas Jefferson*, 29 vols. (Princeton, 1950–2000), 12: 356; Leonard L. Richards, *Shays's Rebellion: The American Revolution's Final Battle* (Philadelphia, 2002); Van Beck Hall, *Politics without Parties: Massachusetts, 1780–1791* (Pittsburgh, 1972); Roger H. Brown, *Redeeming the Republic: Federalists, Taxation, and the Origins of the Constitution* (Baltimore, 1993), chap. 8; and David P. Szatmary, *Shays' Rebellion: The Making of an Agrarian Insurrection* (Amherst, 1980). There were also some additional casualties. Richards, *Shays'*, 74–83, emphasizes that the decision to pay the state debt at par actually was an outrageous decision to "transfer wealth from ordinary citizens to wealthy speculators living in Boston, Salem, and other port cities" (81).

2. Quoted in Hall, *Politics*, 282.

3. Massachusetts Constitution (1780), chap. 1, sec. 1, art. 4, in Oscar and Mary Handlin, eds., *The Popular Sources of Political Authority: Documents on the Massachusetts Constitution of 1780* (Cambridge, MA, 1966), 450. Massachusetts actually had made valuations more often throughout the eighteenth century.

4. For these laws in 1769, see Massachusetts, *Acts and Resolves, Public and Private, of the Province of Massachusetts Bay*, 21 vols. (Boston, 1869–1922), 5: 18, 21. This source will be cited hereafter as Massachusetts, *Acts, Province*. I will remove editorial interpolations when quoting from it. For the persistence of this tax system, see Charles J. Bullock, *Historical Sketch of the Finances and Financial Policy of Massachusetts, 1780–1905* (New York, 1907).

5. The four were Quakers; Massachusetts already had banished them twice. Richard S. Dunn, *Puritans and Yankees: The Winthrop Dynasty of New England, 1630–1717* (Princeton, 1962), 106–7. For this sketch of seventeenth-century society, I am relying especially on Virginia DeJohn Anderson, *New England's Generation: The Great Migration and the Formation of Society and Culture in the Seventeenth Century* (New York, 1991); James D. Drake, *King Philip's War: Civil War in New England, 1675–1676* (Amherst, 1999); and John Murrin, "Review Essay," *History and Theory* 11 (1972): 226–75.

6. Alfred A. Cave, *The Pequot War* (Amherst, 1996), 43–48.

7. Drake, *King Philip's War*. Both Indians and English lived in settled agricultural villages, but the Indians hunted where the English raised livestock, a difference that created conflicts over land use and especially fences. Virginia DeJohn Anderson, "King Philip's Herds: Indians, Colonists, and the Problem of Livestock in Early New England," *William and Mary Quarterly*, 3rd ser., 51 (1994): 601–24. See also Richard R. Johnson, "The Search for a Usable Indian: An Aspect of the Defense of Colonial New England," *Journal of American History* 64 (1977): 623–51.

8. Drake, *King Philip's War*, 119–20; Cave, *Pequot War*, 147–51.

9. See especially Perry Miller, *Errand into the Wilderness* (Cambridge, MA, 1956), 1–15.

10. John Frederick Martin, *Profits in the Wilderness: Entrepreneurship and the Founding of New England Towns in the Seventeenth Century* (Chapel Hill, 1991); Bernard Bailyn, *The New England Merchants in the Seventeenth Century* (Cambridge, MA, 1955); and Stephen Innes, *Labor in a New Land: Economy and Society in Seventeenth-Century Springfield* (Princeton, 1983).

11. For the servants, Anderson, *New England's Generation*, 24–25, 108–12. Anderson (p. 173) describes "a broadly shared, comfortable style of life," but see also William D. Piersen, *Black Yankees: The Development of an Afro-American Subculture in Eighteenth-Century New England* (Amherst, 1988).

12. Bailyn, *New England Merchants*, 174–89; Richard R. Johnson, *Adjustment to Empire: the New England Colonies, 1675–1715* (New Brunswick, 1981); Gary B. Nash, *The Urban Crucible: Social Change, Political Consciousness, and the Origins of the American Revolution* (Cambridge, MA, 1979); T. H. Breen, *Puritans and Adventurers: Change and Persistence in Early America* (New York, 1980), chap. 5; Paul S. Boyer and Stephen Nissenbaum, *Salem Possessed: The Social Origins of Witchcraft* (Cambridge, MA, 1974); Richard L. Bushman, *King and People in Provincial Massachusetts* (1985; Chapel Hill, 1992); and William Pencak, *War, Politics, and Revolution in Provincial Massachusetts* (Boston, 1981).

13. Nash, *Urban Crucible*, 107, 171–76, 180–97, 245–46, 402.

14. The following sketch relies on Murrin, "Review Essay," whose modest title is misleading. Also, Robert Zemsky, *Merchants, Farmers, and River Gods: An Essay on Eighteenth-Century American Politics* (Boston, 1971). There has been much debate about "communalism" in early New England, but the fact that a rhetoric disapproving of divisive politics remains appealing today should caution us against trusting it as a description of how politics actually worked. See Nash, *Urban Crucible*, on the vibrancy of Boston politics.

15. Even by the 1760s, when top royal appointees distributed valuable patronage, cronies on the payroll still did their jobs. On patronage, see Bernard Bailyn, *The Origins of American Politics* (New York, 1967).

16. Murrin, "Review Essay," 253–57, 260–61, 267–70; and David Thomas Konig, *Law and Society in Puritan Massachusetts: Essex County, 1629–1692* (Chapel Hill, 1979).

17. Kenneth A. Lockridge and Alan Kreider, "The Evolution of Massachusetts Town Government, 1640 to 1740," *William and Mary Quarterly*, 3rd ser., 33 (1966): 549–74. For a summary of the issues involved in evaluating the suffrage, see Alexander Keyssar, *The Right to Vote: The Contested History of Democracy in the United States* (New York, 2000), 5–7.

18. Murrin, "Review Essay," quotation on 234, 248–50. The best account of a minister and congregation fighting over money is in Boyer and Nissenbaum, *Salem Possessed*. The classic study emphasizing residential dispersion is Richard L. Bushman, *From Puritan to Yankee: Character and the Social Order in Connecticut, 1690–1765* (Cambridge, MA, 1967).

19. This paragraph is based on Martin, *Profits,* quotation on 193. The comparison to condo associations is my own.

20. Ibid., 281. On Andros and the dominion, see Bailyn, *New England Merchants*, 174–89; Johnson, *Adjustment,* chap. 12; and Dunn, *Puritans and Yankees,* chaps. 10–11.

21. Edward M. Cook, Jr., *The Fathers of the Towns: Leadership and Community Structure in Eighteenth-Century New England* (Baltimore, 1976), 33–34.

22. See especially Bailyn, *New England Merchants,* 154–67.

23. Breen, *Puritans,* especially 84–91. On schools and literacy, see Kenneth A. Lockridge, *Literacy in Colonial New England: An Enquiry into the Social Context of Literacy in the Early Modern West* (New York, 1974); Robert Middlekauff, *Ancients and Axioms: Secondary Education in Eighteenth-Century New England* (1963; Salem, NH, 1988), chaps.

1–4; and David D. Hall, *Worlds of Wonder, Days of Judgment: Popular Religious Beliefs in Early New England* (Cambridge, MA, 1990), chap. 1.

24. Breen, *Puritans*, 88; Nash, *Urban Crucible*, 60–63, 173–75, 241–43; and Robert A. Becker, *Revolution, Reform, and the Politics of American Taxation, 1763–1783* (Baton Rouge, 1980), 12.

25. Herbert L. Osgood, *The American Colonies in the Seventeenth Century*, 3 vols. (New York, 1904), 1: 398–406, 414–15. The alliance apportioned costs to each colony by its male population from the ages of sixteen to sixty; accordingly, Massachusetts ordered a census of these "polls" in 1643. The fact that they counted the polls for this reason does not seem sufficient to explain the poll tax, although it may have influenced the decision. For the census, see Nathaniel B. Shurtleff, ed., *Records of the Governor and Company of the Massachusetts Bay in New England*, 5 vols. (Boston, 1853–54), 2: 37, 151. This source will be cited hereafter as *Mass. Recs.;* I will be modernizing its most distracting spelling and abbreviation conventions when quoting from it.

26. *Mass. Recs.*, 1: 77, 82, 89, 93, 103, 110.

27. Ibid., 1: 120, 166, 168, 262, 330. A study of the town tax lists finds evidence of an earlier poll tax in a fragment from the Cambridge town records, which apparently assessed 138 men 20 pence per head in 1635. H. H. Burbank, "The Taxation of Polls and Property in Massachusetts, I," New England Tax Materials, 1658–1850 Collection, vol. 1, Baker Library, Harvard Business School, 16.

28. *Mass. Recs.*, 2: 173–74.

29. Massachusetts, *Laws and Liberties* (1648), ed. Max Farrand (Cambridge, MA, 1929), 9–10.

30. Ibid., 10; Burbank, "Taxation," 14. In the debate about the constitutionality of the 1894 federal income tax, which ended with the 1913 adoption of the Sixteenth Amendment, this "faculty tax" was treated as a precedent for modern income taxation. This claim was demolished in Edwin R.A. Seligman, *The Income Tax: A Study of the History, Theory, and Practice of Income Taxation at Home and Abroad* (New York, 1914), 367–87.

31. Adam Smith, *The Wealth of Nations*, ed. Edwin Cannan (1776; New York, 1937), 777. For the intellectual history of "ability to pay," see Walter J. Blum and Harry Kalven, Jr., *The Uneasy Case for Progressive Taxation* (Chicago, 1953).

32. Massachusetts, *Laws and Liberties* (1648), 10.

33. *Mass. Recs.*, 3: 221, but quoted from version in *Laws and Liberties* (1660), 14, *Records of the States of the United States of America: A Microfilm Compilation*, ed. William Sumner Jenkins (Washington, 1949–51), Mass. B.1, reel 1, unit 8. Also, *Mass. Recs.*, 3: 320, 426. The livestock cut actually raised the horse valuations (poorer farmers would have used oxen rather than horses), but see also *Mass. Recs.*, 3: 298–99.

34. Martin, *Profits*, 161–68, quotation on 168.

35. Burbank, "Taxation," 16–19b.

36. Breen, *Puritans*, 88–89, 103.

37. Ibid. Note that the revival of apportionment did not impose an English practice. In England, joint-stock companies assessed their members for capital in proportion to investments, while local governments levied "rates" on property. The joint-stock model probably

influenced the pre-1646 apportionments; before 1691, the Massachusetts General Court technically was a stockholders meeting of the Massachusetts Bay Company. But the synthesis of apportionment with the rating was a colonial innovation. No English practice resembled the apportionments the Massachusetts General Court crafted, particularly after 1694: long lists of towns with assigned tax liabilities. I thank Thomas Barnes for help with this point.

38. Massachusetts, *Acts, Province,* 1: 30, 91–92.

39. Ibid., 167, 199, 213–14, 240.

40. Ibid., 413; Burbank, "Taxation," 21a–b, 23a–25a; Edwin Canaan, *The History of the Local Rates in England in Relation to the Proper Distribution of the Burden of Taxation,* 2nd ed. (1896; London, 1912).

41. Massachusetts, *Acts, Province,* 1: 92, 167, 2: 572; Burbank, "Taxation," 24–25.

42. For the number of towns, *Mass. Recs.,* 1: 129, 3: 28; Massachusetts, *Acts, Province,* 1: 177–79, 5: 210–11. For the quotations, *Mass. Recs.,* 1: 294; *Journals of the House of Representatives of Massachusetts, 1715–1771,* 47 vols. (Boston, 1919–78), 2: 239, 13: 68. For the high winds, *Acts, Province,* 4: 631. For a complicated apportionment fight, ibid., 5: 209. For examples of town petitions, ibid., 4: 336, 544–45, 783.

43. Burbank, "Taxation," 32–35. Nash, *Urban Crucible,* 117–18, notes that Boston's assessors were exempting up to one-fourth of that town's polls in the early 1740s.

44. Burbank, "Taxation," 36–54a. For the 1772 valuation, see Massachusetts, *Acts, Province,* 5: 210–11.

45. By 1835, towns were to levy one-sixth of their quotas on polls, but the tax was capped at $1.50 per poll, including all town, county, and state taxes, with the rest levied on property. Massachusetts had tried a version of this strategy during the Revolution. A 1779 law directed the officials of towns where the legislated poll tax exceeded one-third of the quota to reduce the poll tax rate so that it yielded one-third, turning to property for the rest. Massachusetts, *Revised Statutes* (Metcalf, Mann 1836), 79; Massachusetts, *Acts, Province,* 5: 955–56. For the abolition of the poll tax, Massachusetts, *Acts and Resolves* (1963), 90–92.

46. Massachusetts, *Acts, Province,* 5: 581, 799; Massachusetts, *Acts and Resolves* (1792–1793), 372; Massachusetts, *Acts and Resolves* (1804–1805), 268–69.

47. Massachusetts, *Acts, Province,* 5: 756, 1110, 1163; Massachusetts, *Acts and Resolves* (1780–1781), 519–20. Bostonians tried to impose price controls and criminal penalties for "forestalling" (holding supplies off the market in anticipation of higher prices, which was a good bet amid rampant currency inflation). Richard Buel, Jr., *In Irons: Britain's Naval Supremacy and the American Revolutionary Economy* (New Haven, 1998), 127–30. The 1781 tax law also initiated what would remain a poll tax exemption for Indians.

48. Massachusetts, *Acts, Province,* 5: 828–37 (quotation on 831). For the valuations, ibid., 5: 799–801, 865, 1184–88; Massachusetts, *Acts and Resolves* (1780–1781), 153–54, 289–90, 359, 435, 903–6; *Acts and Resolves* (1784–1785), 57–60; *Acts and Resolves* (1786–1787), 323–30. See also Hall, *Politics,* 113–14.

49. Massachusetts, *Acts and Resolves* (1780–1781), 525–33; Paul S. Boyer, "Borrowed Rhetoric: The Massachusetts Excise Controversy of 1754," *William and Mary Quarterly,* 3rd ser., 21 (1964): 328–51.

50. Brown, *Redeeming the Republic,* chap. 8; Hall, *Politics Without Parties,* chaps. 6–10.

51. Ira Berlin, *Many Thousands Gone: The First Two Centuries of Slavery in North America* (Cambridge, MA, 1998), 229.

52. Massachusetts Constitution (1780), chap. 1, sec. 2, art. 1, and chap. 1, sec. 3, art. 2, in Handlin and Handlin, *Popular Sources,* 450, 454.

Chapter 3

1. Oliver Wolcott, Jr., "Direct Taxes," Dec. 14, 1796, in Walter Lowrie and Matthew St. Clair Clark, comps., *American State Papers: Documents, Legislative and Executive, of the Congress of the United States,* 10 vols. (Washington, 1832–61), 3rd ser., *Finance,* 1: 414–65, quotation on 437.

2. For the New London incident, see Charles J. Hoadley, comp., *The Public Records of the Colony of Connecticut,* 15 vols. (Hartford, 1850–90), 1: 392, 405, 411; and Frances Manwaring Caulkins, *History of New London, Connecticut* (New London, 1895), 135. Bruce C. Daniels, *The Connecticut Town: Growth and Development, 1635–1790* (Middletown, CT, 1979), 75, notices the accusation. For the elaborate valuation schedule, see Hoadley, *Public Records,* 4: 334–35, 8: 131–33. No historian has analyzed this peculiar tax structure directly. For context, see Daniels, *Connecticut Town;* Lawrence Henry Gipson, *Connecticut Taxation, 1750–1775* (New Haven, 1933); Harold E. Selesky, *War and Society in Colonial Connecticut* (New Haven, 1990); and Charles S. Grant, *Democracy in the Connecticut Frontier Town of Kent,* 2nd ed. (1961; New York, 1972).

On North Carolina's tax problems, see Marvin L. Michael Kay, "Provincial Taxes in North Carolina during the Administration of Dobbs and Tryon," *North Carolina Historical Review* 42 (1965): 440–53; idem, "The Payment of Provincial and Local Taxes in North Carolina, 1748–1771," *William and Mary Quarterly,* 3rd. ser., 26 (1969): 218–40; A. Roger Ekirch, *"Poor Carolina": Politics and Society in Colonial North Carolina* (Chapel Hill, 1981), esp. 157–61; Marjoleine Kars, *Breaking Loose Together: The Regulator Rebellion in Pre-Revolutionary North Carolina* (Chapel Hill, 2002), "Fee-Bill" quotation on 169. See also ibid., 144–45, quoting a Regulator leader saying a local official forced him to promise "never to give your Opinions of the Laws . . . nor shew any Jealousies of the Officers taking extortionary Fees;—and if you hear any others speaking disrespectfully, or hinting at any Jealousies of that Nature, of Officers, that you will reprove and caution them; and that you will tell the People that you are satisfied all the Taxes are agreeable to Law,—and do everything in your Powers to moderate and pacify them."

3. Hoadley, *Public Records,* 13: 513–14; Charles J. Hoadley and Leonard Woods Labaree, comps., *The Public Records of the State of Connecticut,* 11 vols. (Hartford, 1894–1967), 1: 365–66 (quotations), 471, 2: 172–73, 3: 11, 5: 340–41; Connecticut, *Acts and Laws* (1796), 277–78. Also, Richard Buel, Jr., *Dear Liberty: Connecticut's Mobilization for the Revolutionary War* (Middletown, CT, 1980).

4. Walter Clark, ed., *The State Records of North Carolina,* 26 vols. (Raleigh, 1886–1907), 24: 6–9, 109–10, 200–2, 317, 429, 543–44, 556. The poll tax applied to free men over 21, enslaved men and women from 12 to 50, and also to "male servants" over 21.

5. Wolcott, "Direct Taxes," 438. Perhaps doubting that this was polite enough, Wolcott also criticized the northern states: their more sophisticated tax instruments were "frequently dilatory" and sometimes "impracticable."

6. In 1800 there were still 12,000 enslaved African Americans in New Jersey (6 percent of the population) and 20,000 in New York (3 percent), but only 1,700 in Pennsylvania (0.3 percent). There were still 951 slaves in Connecticut, 381 in Rhode Island, 8 in New Hampshire, and zero in Massachusetts. The slow death of northern slavery must not obscure the difference between North and South. In Virginia, 346,000 slaves were 39 percent of the population; in South Carolina, 146,000 were 42 percent; in North Carolina, 133,000 were 28 percent; in Maryland, 106,000 were 31 percent. U.S. Census Bureau, *Seventh Census of the United States: 1850* (Washington, 1853), ix.

7. Data on the size of the colonial tax burdens are impressionistic at best. David Hackett Fischer, *Albion's Seed: Four British Folkways in America* (New York, 1989), 815, estimates that the average tax burden per capita in 1765 was 12 pennies in Massachusetts and Virginia and 5 pennies in the "Delaware Valley," defined as New Jersey, Pennsylvania, Delaware, and northern Maryland. Fischer offers no sources. The figure that applies to Pennsylvania would have been even lower before the French and Indian War. R. R. Palmer, *The Age of Democratic Revolution: A Political History of Europe and America, 1760–1800,* 2 vols. (Princeton, 1959–64), 1: 155, assigns the 12 pennies to Massachusetts and Pennsylvania and the 5 pennies to Virginia.

8. Penn quoted in Gary B. Nash, *Red, White, and Black: The Peoples of Early America,* 2nd ed. (1974; Englewood-Cliffs, NJ, 1982), 97. For the Long Peace, see James H. Merrell, *Into the American Woods: Negotiators on the Pennsylvania Frontier* (New York, 1999); and Francis Jennings, "The Indian Trade of the Susquehanna Valley," *Proceedings of the American Philosophical Society* 110 (1966): 406–24. For the politics of pacifism, see Gary B. Nash, *Quakers and Politics: Pennsylvania, 1681–1726* (Princeton, 1968), 127–43, 202–5, 252–54; Alan Tully, *William Penn's Legacy: Politics and Social Structure in Provincial Pennsylvania, 1726–1755* (Baltimore, 1977), 153–60; James H. Hutson, *Pennsylvania Politics, 1746–1770: The Movement for Royal Government and Its Consequences* (Princeton, 1972); and Jack D. Marietta, *The Reformation of American Quakerism, 1748–1783* (Philadelphia, 1984), chaps. 6–8.

9. Marietta, *Reformation;* Barry Levy, *Quakers and the American Family: British Settlement in the Delaware Valley* (New York, 1988); and Sally Schwartz, *"A Mixed Multitude": The Struggle for Toleration in Colonial Pennsylvania* (New York, 1987). Nor did Pennsylvania create public schools; Fischer, *Albion's Seed,* 533–38. For the costs of established religion, see H. James Henderson, "Taxation and Political Culture: Massachusetts and Virginia, 1760–1800," *William and Mary Quarterly,* 3rd ser., 47 (1990): 90–114.

10. Mary M. Schweitzer, *Custom and Contract: Household, Government, and the Economy in Colonial Pennsylvania* (New York, 1987), chaps. 4–5; E. James Ferguson, *The Power of the Purse: A History of American Public Finance, 1776–1790* (Chapel Hill, 1961), chap. 1; Theodore Thayer, "The Land-Bank System in the American Colonies," *Journal of Economic History* 13 (1953): 145–59; and Edwin J. Perkins, *American Public Finance and Financial Services, 1700–1815* (Columbus, 1994), chap. 2.

11. Fischer, *Albion's Seed,* 421–24; U.S. Department of Commerce, Bureau of the Census, *Historical Statistics of the United States: Colonial Times to 1970,* 2 vols. (Washington, 1976), 2: 1168.

12. Levy, *Quakers;* James T. Lemon, *The Best Poor Man's Country: A Geographical*

Study of Early Southeastern Pennsylvania (New York, 1972); Stephanie Grauman Wolf, *Urban Village: Population, Community, and Family Structure in Germantown, Pennsylvania, 1683–1800* (Princeton, 1976); Farley Ward Grubb, "Immigration and Servitude in the Colony and Commonwealth of Pennsylvania: A Quantititative and Economic Analysis" (Ph.D. diss., University of Chicago, 1984); Sharon V. Salinger, *"To Serve Well and Faithfully": Labor and Indentured Servants in Pennsylvania, 1682–1800* (Cambridge, 1987); Gary B. Nash and Jean R. Soderlund, *Freedom by Degrees: Emancipation in Pennsylvania and Its Aftermath* (New York, 1991), chap. 1; Alan Tully, "Patterns of Slaveholding in Colonial Pennsylvania: Chester and Lancaster Counties, 1729–1758," *Journal of Social History* 6 (1973): 284–305; and Lucy Simler, "Tenancy in Colonial Pennsylvania: The Case of Chester County," *William and Mary Quarterly*, 3rd. ser., 43 (1968): 542–69. For Philadelphia, see Gary B. Nash, *The Urban Crucible: Social Change, Political Consciousness, and the Origins of the American Revolution* (Cambridge, 1979).

13. Nash, *Quakers and Politics;* Tully, *Penn's Legacy;* Hutson, *Pennsylvania Politics;* Marietta, *Reformation.* See also Richard Beeman, *The Varieties of Political Experience in Eighteenth-Century America* (Philadelphia, 2004), chap. 8.

14. Nash, *Quakers and Politics* (Penn quoted on 49); Tully, *Penn's Legacy;* Alan Tully, *Forming American Politics: Ideas, Interests, and Institutions in Colonial New York and Pennsylvania* (Baltimore, 1994), 69–85, 89–90; Beeman, *Varieties,* chap. 8; and Richard Alan Ryerson, *The Revolution Is Now Begun: The Radical Committees of Philadelphia, 1765–1776* (Philadelphia, 1978), chap. 1.

15. Three boroughs (Chester, Lancaster, and Bristol) also elected clerks and councils. See Lucy Simler, "The Township: The Community of Rural Pennsylvania," *Pennsylvania Magazine of History and Biography* 106 (1982): 41–68; Wayne L. Bockelman, "Local Government in Colonial Pennsylvania," in *Town and County: Essays on the Structure of Local Government in the American Colonies,* ed. Bruce C. Daniels (Middletown, CT, 1978), 216–37; Judith M. Diamondstone, "The Government of Eighteenth-Century Philadelphia," in *Town and County,* 238–63; and Wolf, *Urban Village,* chap. 5. On urban "closed corporations," also Jon C. Teaford, *The Municipal Revolution in America: Origins of Modern Urban Government, 1650–1825* (Chicago, 1975).

Outright theft seems to have been minimal. There were two embezzlements from the GLO, in 1730 and 1766. The 1766 case has been compared to Virginia's Robinson affair, but it involved only £3,000 and one person. The Robinson affair involved £100,000 and a large chunk of the Virginia elite. Schweitzer, *Custom,* 213–15; and Edwin B. Bronner, "The Disgrace of John Kinsey, Quaker Politician, 1739–1750," *Pennsylvania Magazine of History and Biography* 75 (1951): 400–15. Lancaster County had a longer-term problem; twenty-eight officials overbilled the county for a total of more than £1,700 in the 1760s. Charles F. Hoban, ed., *Pennsylvania Archives,* 8th ser., 7: 6513–14 (Feb. 17, 1770), 6533–34 (Sept. 17, 1770). The activities of James Logan are of another order. As the Penns' agent for over forty years, Logan ran the proprietary land office and dominated the Indian trade. Jennings, "Indian Trade," shows that he defrauded both the Delawares and the Penns. His most famous coup was the Walking Purchase (1737). The Delawares agreed to grant a tract of land that a man could walk in a day and a half. Logan, with Thomas and John Penn, had a path cleared through the woods and sent athletes to run it, despite

Delaware objections. The Delawares never forgot this insulting rip-off. Merrell, *Into the American Woods*, 36, 176, 292.

16. Hence Wolcott's survey of the states. For Pennsylvania tax legislation, see James T. Mitchell and Henry Flanders, comps., *The Statutes at Large of Pennsylvania from 1682–1801*, 18 vols. (Harrisburg, 1896–1915); and Gail McKnight Beckman, *The Statutes at Large of Pennsylvania in the Time of William Penn* (New York, 1976). For specific citations, see below. The liquor excise was levied on retailers by volume sold, but without English-style "gaugers." Pennsylvania required licensed retailers to give bonds for the tax, reserving search and seizure for cases of suspected evasion. In light of the fact that Pennsylvania would be the site of the Whiskey Rebellion (1794), note that this tax exempted the distillers who later found the U.S. whiskey excise so outrageous. Mitchell and Flanders, *Statutes*, 2: 106–9 (1700), 3: 26–30 (1713), 229–37 (1719), 280–88 (1722), 362–63 (1723), 408–17 (1723), 4: 68–73 (1727), 157–63 (1730), 238–48 (1734), 308–19 (1738), 395–407 (1744), 5: 249–61 (1756), 8: 210–20 (1772).

17. On the so-called "marriage penalty," see Edward J. McCaffery, *Taxing Women* (Chicago, 1997). It is not a penalty on marriage per se, but on married couples in which wives earn significant incomes. As a result, it penalizes only women in relatively high-income families. Part of its effect stems from the fact that the personal exemption for a married couple is lower than the exemptions for two single people. The significant part, however, stems from the fact that summing the incomes of a husband and wife can boost them into a higher tax bracket, producing a higher marginal rate on the joint income than would be levied on either income if they were single. Since one of the two incomes is usually substantially larger than the other, the result is a disproportionately heavy tax on the "second" (smaller) income—and since this smaller income is usually the wife's, the effect is to encourage married women in higher tax brackets to exit the paid labor force by slapping disproportionately heavy taxes on their earnings. The "penalty" does not apply to married women in low-income households. Its incentive to reproduce a "traditional" family (working dad, stay-at-home mom) is not extended to the poor, for whom the single-income household was never "traditional" in the first place.

18. Levy, *Quakers*, "garden" quotation on 116. See also Fischer, *Albion's Seed*, 485–517.

19. Beckman, *Statutes*, 203–4 (1693) 216 (1696), 219 (1696), 235 (1699); Mitchell and Flanders, *Statutes*, 2: 35 (1700, quotation), 114–15 (1700), 280 (1706), 374 (1711, which dropped the exemption of household goods and tools), 389–90 (1711), 3: 83 (1715, which restored the exemption), 128 (1717).

20. Beckman, *Statutes*, 204 (1700), 219 (1696); Mitchell and Flanders, *Statutes*, 4: 14 (1725). According to James T. Lemon and Gary B. Nash, "The Distribution of Wealth in Eighteenth-Century America: A Century of Change in Chester County, Pennsylvania, 1693–1802," *Journal of Social History* 2 (1968): 11, the poorest tenth of taxpayers owned an average of £36 of taxable property in 1730 and £24 in 1748. This does not tell us the minimum taxed in Chester County, though it is likely to have been the minimum in 1748. In 1730, the average holding in the second decile was more than double the holding in the bottom decile, the result we would expect if each decile included a range of values. In 1748, the bottom and second decile averages were equal (at £24), meaning that many people must have been taxed for exactly £24.

21. Mitchell and Flanders, *Statutes,* 4: 14 (1725). As the laws were elaborated, great attention was lavished on the problem of finding the single men and collecting their taxes. Generally, employers were made responsible.

22. Beckman, *Statutes,* 204 (1693); Mitchell and Flanders, *Statutes,* 3: 129 (1717), 4: 14 (1725); 5: 205 (1755).

23. Hutson, *Pennsylvania Politics,* 17–40, 59–85; Mitchell and Flanders, *Statutes,* 4: 14 (1725), 5: 340, 342 (1758). For enforcement of the tax on trades, see R. Eugene Harper, *The Transformation of Western Pennsylvania, 1770–1800* (Pittsburgh, 1991), 212–13n.

24. Mitchell and Flanders, *Statutes,* 6: 345–58 (1764), 7: 55–56 (1766), 8: 378 (1774), 9: 230–32 (1778), 360–61 (1779), 10: 210 (1780), 326–27 (1781); and Robert A. Becker, *Revolution, Reform, and the Politics of American Taxation, 1763–1783* (Baton Rouge, 1980), 56–59.

25. Ibid., 9: 23 (1776), 101–2 (1777), 362 (1779, quotation), 10: 330 (1781, quotation), 389 (1782).

26. Local democracy also could frustrate collection, as it did in the 1780s. See Terry Bouton, "A Road Closed: Rural Insurgency in Post-Independence Pennsylvania," *Journal of American History* 87 (2000): 867–76.

27. Roger H. Brown, *Redeeming the Republic: Federalists, Taxation, and the Origins of the Constitution* (Baltimore, 1993), 14. The national average was 37 percent.

28. Thomas Cooper and David J. McCord, *The Statutes at Large of South Carolina,* 14 vols. (Columbia, 1836–73), includes some Tax-Acts but omits others, which are available in the microfilmed *Records of the States of the United States* and will be cited below as *Tax-Act* (year). For the quitrent collectors using the colony's tax lists, see Robert M. Weir, *Colonial South Carolina: A History* (Millwood, NY, 1983), 139.

29. Peter H. Wood, *Black Majority: Negroes in Colonial South Carolina from 1670 through the Stono Rebellion* (New York, 1974), 132; Philip D. Morgan, *Slave Counterpoint: Black Culture in the Eighteenth-Century Chesapeake and Lowcountry* (Chapel Hill, 1998), 97; Peter A. Coclanis, *The Shadow of a Dream: Economic Life and Death in the South Carolina Lowcountry, 1670–1920* (New York, 1989), 122; Ira Berlin, *Many Thousands Gone: The First Two Centuries of Slavery in North America* (Cambridge, MA, 1998), 154–61; and Jack P. Greene, *Pursuits of Happiness: The Social Development of Early Modern British Colonies and the Formation of American Culture* (Chapel Hill, 1988), 178–79.

30. Joyce E. Chaplin, *An Anxious Pursuit: Agricultural Innovation and Modernity in the Lower South, 1730–1815* (Chapel Hill, 1993); Weir, *Colonial South Carolina,* 123 ("garrison"); Rachel N. Klein, *Unification of a Slave State: The Rise of the Planter Class in the South Carolina Backcountry, 1760–1808* (Chapel Hill, 1990), 20; Jerome J. Nadelhaft, *The Disorders of War: The Revolution in South Carolina* (Orono, 1981), 3; Alice Hanson Jones, *The Wealth of a Nation to Be: The American Colonies on the Eve of the Revolution* (New York, 1980), 58; Coclanis, *Shadow,* 125. The South Carolinians remain richer if we count only nonhuman wealth: three times the southern average, four times the middle colonies average, and five times the New England average. For mortality, Coclanis, *Shadow,* 38–47; Greene, *Pursuits,* 142. For coping, Chaplin, *Anxious Pursuit,* chap. 3; Sally E. Hadden, *Slave Patrols: Law and Violence in Virginia and the Carolinas* (Cambridge, MA, 2001);

Robert M. Weir, "The Harmony We Were Famous for': An Interpretation of Prerevolutionary South Carolina Politics," in Weir, *"The Last of American Freemen": Studies in the Political Culture of the Colonial and Revolutionary South* (Macon, GA, 1986), 131; Weir, *Colonial South Carolina*, 123 ("Domestic Enemy").

31. M. Eugene Sirmans, *Colonial South Carolina: A Political History, 1663–1763* (Chapel Hill, 1966), 9–16; Coclanis, *Shadow*, 23–26; Cooper and McCord, *Statutes*, 2: 153–54 (1698).

32. Nash, *Red, White, and Black*, 128–40; James H. Merrell, *The Indians' New World: Catawbas and Their Neighbors from European Contact through the Era of Removal* (Chapel Hill, 1989); Alan Gallay, *The Indian Slave Trade: The Rise of the English Empire in the American South, 1670–1717* (New Haven, 2002).

33. Wood, *Black Majority*, chap. 4.

34. Morgan, *Slave Counterpoint*, chaps. 1–4; Berlin, *Many Thousands Gone*, chap. 6, quotation on 146.

35. Wood, *Black Majority*, chap. 12; Berlin, *Many Thousands Gone*, 73–74, 147; Morgan, *Slave Counterpoint*, 59; Sirmans, *Colonial South Carolina*, 167–68; Weir, *Colonial South Carolina*, 207–11; Klein, *Unification*, 10–36; and Robert L. Meriwether, *The Expansion of South Carolina, 1729–1765* (Kingsport, TN, 1940). Revenue from the tax on imported slaves was dedicated to the township subsidies.

36. Sirmans, *Colonial South Carolina;* Weir, "Harmony." See also Rebecca Starr, *A School for Politics: Commercial Lobbying and Political Culture in Early South Carolina* (Baltimore, 1998).

37. Richard Waterhouse, "The Responsible Gentry of Colonial South Carolina: A Study in Local Government, 1670–1770," in Daniels, ed., *Town and County*, 160–85; Nadelhaft, *Disorders*, 13; Richard Maxwell Brown, *The South Carolina Regulators* (Cambridge, MA, 1963); Rachel N. Klein, "Ordering the Backcountry: The South Carolina Regulation," *William and Mary Quarterly*, 3rd ser., 38 (1981): 661–80; Klein, *Unification*, chaps. 2–3. Note that the South Carolina Regulators were totally different from their North Carolina namesakes: elitist vigilantes versus poor farmers in revolt against corrupt elites.

38. Cooper and McCord, *Statutes*, 3: 384 (1734), 438–39 (1736), 473 (1737), 502 (1738, which dropped the poll tax); *Tax-Act* (1758), 4; Morgan, *Slave Counterpoint*, 490–91; Berlin, *Many Thousands Gone*, 154, 319–20. The Tax-Acts provided for the seizure of assets for nonpayment generally but said nothing specific about free blacks.

39. Cooper and McCord, *Statutes*, 2: 16 (1686), 207–8 (1703). See also ibid., 2: 24 (1687), 64 (1691), 86 (1695), 96 (1695), 110 (1696), 162 (1700), 177–78 (1701), 182–83 (1701), 229–31 (1703).

40. Ibid., 2: 257–59 (1704), 324–27 (1708, instructing soldiers to sell Indian slaves), 341 (1710), 352–54 (1711), 618 (1713, title but not text), 627–29 (1715, quotation on 628), 663 (1716).

41. Ibid., 2: 666–671 (1716), 3: 71–77 (1719). It would be nice to have the record of a discussion of exactly why South Carolina could not value the plantations. The existing record is more elliptical. South Carolina, Commons House of Assembly, *Journal* (1716), *Records of the States of the United States*, unpaginated MS. The assembly began with a bill

to use the "old and usual method of raising Tax in this Province with some Regulations & Amendm[ent]s." When the governor and council rejected that, the Commons House framed the new tax in a series of votes. They first adopted the flat-rate land tax, with an affirmative answer to the question, "if a Tax be laid on Land, whether the same shall be Taxed equally?" Next, they defined the tax base, deciding that "the tax to be Levied, shall be levied upon Lands & Negroes." After fixing the size of the tax at £35,000 (later changed to £95,000 over three years), they turned to the land tax rate, rejecting "one penny per Acre" and adopting 5 shillings per hundred acres (0.6 pennies per acre). Finally, they established the separate Charleston tax by resolving to levy £6,000 (one-sixth of the total) on "those Persons who inhabit within the Bounds of Charles Town Platts." When the governor and council saw the bill, they insisted that land south of the Edisto River be taxed at half the normal rate. The Commons held firm. All rural land would be taxed "equally."

42. Cooper and McCord, *Statutes,* 2: 667 (1716); 3: 92 (1719).

43. Ibid., 3: 73 (1719), 207–10 (1723), 308–9 (1731), 319–22 (1732), 320–22 (1733, quotation on 320), 439 (1736); *Tax-Act* (1747), 4–5, 8–11; *Tax-Act* (1752), 10–11 (quotations). The assembly went back and forth on a slightly more complex slave tax rule, exempting owners for children and the elderly, but usually taxed all slaves.

44. *Tax-Act* (1755), 3–4; *Tax-Act* (1756), 4; *Tax-Act* (1758), 4–5; *Tax-Act* (1759), 4–5.

45. Becker, *Revolution,* 99–104; Brown, *South Carolina Regulators,* 139–40, quotation on 139; Nadelhaft, *Disorders,* 13. The direct cause of the tax holiday was the assembly's £1,500 donation to the legal defense fund of the London radical John Wilkes. Angry crown officials instructed governors to block Tax-Acts with unauthorized spending; the assembly insisted on its power of the purse; the colony's government essentially shut down. Weir, *Colonial South Carolina,* 305–12; Jack P. Greene, *The Quest for Power: The Lower Houses of Assembly in the Southern Royal Colonies, 1689–1776* (New York, 1963), 403–16.

46. Cooper and McCord, *Statutes,* 4: 365–66 (1777), 413–14 (1778), 487–88 (1779), 529 (1783); Nadelhaft, *Disorders,* chap. 3; Becker, *Revolution,* 206–10.

47. Cooper and McCord, *Statutes,* 4: 627–28 (1784); Nadelhaft, *Disorders,* 126–27, 135–38, quotation on 127. Two categories were left to the discretion of assessors: certain pine barren, valued "according to its relative value in the judgment of the assessors," and agricultural land in the Charleston parishes, "assessed in the same manner and upon the same principles as houses and lots in Charleston, and in a relative proportion to the lands in the country." I am following Becker, *Revolution,* 210, in using the currency equivalents in the 1783 Tax-Act to convert to dollars.

48. U.S. Department of Commerce, Bureau of the Census, *Statistical Abstract of the United States: 2004–2005* (Washington, 2004), 61, available at http://www.census.gov/prod/2004pubs/04statab/stlocgov.pdf.

49. Cooper and McCord, *Statutes,* 3: 160 (1721), 556–57, 560–61 (1740). The use of height survived the major rate reduction (to £10, £5, £2), and, in a modified form, also survived the Revolution. Ibid., 3: 739 (1751), 4: 577 (1783). For the complexities of the questions and answers in slave sales, see Walter Johnson, *Soul by Soul: Life Inside the Antebellum Slave Market* (Cambridge, MA, 1999), 172–87.

50. Massachusetts Constitution (1780), chap. 1, sec. 1, art. 4; Pennsylvania Constitution (1776), sec. 41; Maryland Declaration of Rights (1776), sec. 13. The constitutions are col-

lected in several places, e.g., Ben. Perley Poore, ed., *The Federal and State Constitutions,* 2nd ed., 2 vols. (Washington, 1878). My count of the states with limits on the tax power does not include Massachusetts or other states that copied its language, though courts eventually interpreted this language in restrictive ways. See Wade J. Newhouse, *Constitutional Uniformity and Equality in State Taxation,* 2nd ed., 2 vols. (Buffalo, 1984).

51. Maryland, *Laws* (1781), chap. 4, in Jenkins, ed., *Records of the States.* For real estate, this law followed Virginia in directing assessors to estimate what it "would have sold for" in 1774.

52. The key works are classics: Greene, *Quest for Power;* Bernard Bailyn, *The Origins of American Politics* (New York, 1967); Leonard Woods Labaree, *Royal Government in America: A Study of the British Colonial System before 1783* (New Haven, 1930); Edmund S. Morgan and Helen M. Morgan, *The Stamp Act Crisis: Prologue to Revolution,* rev. ed. (1953; Chapel Hill, 1995). This dynamic was basically the same in proprietary colonies (especially Pennsylvania and Maryland), where governors were the proprietors' instead of the crown's men.

53. There have been many studies of local government in single colonies, but the introduction to Daniels, *Town and County,* parts of Fischer, *Albion's Seed,* and Beeman, *Varieties,* stand alone as comparative approaches.

Introduction to Part 2

1. On the bank taxes, see especially Richard Sylla, John B. Legler, and John J. Wallis, "Banks and State Public Finance in the New Republic: The United States, 1790–1860," *Journal of Economic History* 47 (1987): 391–403.

2. For overviews, see John Joseph Wallis, "A History of the Property Tax in America," in *Property Taxation and Local Government Finance: Essays in Honor of C. Lowell Harris,* ed. Wallace E. Oates (Cambridge, MA, 2001), 123–47; and Richard T. Ely, *Taxation in American States and Cities* (New York, 1888).

3. On "gradual emancipation," see especially Joanne Pope Melish, *Disowning Slavery: Gradual Emancipation and "Race" in New England, 1780–1860* (Ithaca, 1998); Gary B. Nash and Jean R. Soderlund, *Freedom by Degrees: Emancipation in Pennsylvania and Its Aftermath* (New York, 1991); and Shane White, *Somewhat More Independent: The End of Slavery in New York City, 1770–1810* (Athens, GA, 1991).

4. This paragraph and the next rely mainly on Bernard Bailyn, *The Ideological Origins of the American Revolution* (Cambridge, MA, 1967); Isaac Kramnick, *Bolingbroke and His Circle: The Politics of Nostalgia in the Age of Walpole* (Cambridge, MA, 1968); P. G. M. Dickson, *The Financial Revolution in England: A Study in the Development of Public Credit, 1688–1756* (London, 1967); and Raymond Williams, *The Country and the City* (New York, 1973). See also Daniel T. Rodgers, "Republicanism: The Career of a Concept," *Journal of American History* 79 (1992): 11–38.

5. "Corruption" was a technical term in republican ideology. It referred to the bribery of legislators with salaries and contracts to ensure that they voted for bills that the crown wanted Parliament (or the colonial assemblies) to pass. In this book, I have been using the term in the more familiar sense of theft and extortion by public officials.

6. David Brion Davis, *The Problem of Slavery in Western Culture* (Ithaca, 1966), 3.

7. Thomas Jefferson, *Notes on the State of Virginia* (New York, 1999), 170–71. Jefferson may have noticed that slavery was relevant to this romance of agricultural labor. The book contains a long and notorious rumination about slavery, whose point was that while slavery was morally wrong and a curse for the slaveholders, it could be abolished only if African Americans were deported and replaced with an equal number of white Europeans. This massive population transfer was necessary to prevent interracial sex from compromising the "dignity and beauty" of whites. Jefferson seems to have meant this literally, bolstering it with such salutary details as the "very strong and disagreeable odour" of black people and their animalistic sexuality: "Their love is ardent, but it kindles the senses only, not the imagination"—and a good deal more just like this (146, 147, 151). From a large literature on the issues raised by this material, see especially Clarence Walker, *Mongrel Nation: Thomas Jefferson and Sally Hemings and the Racial Origins of the American Republic* (Charlottesville, forthcoming), chap. 1.

8. See especially Lance Banning, *The Jeffersonian Persuasion: Evolution of a Party Ideology* (Ithaca, 1978). For the harpies, see *Annals of Congress*, 1st Cong., 3rd sess., 1891–92 (Josiah Parker of Virginia). For identical language from Antifederalist opponents of the Constitution in 1788, see Frederick Arthur Baldwin Dalzell, "Taxation without Representation: Federal Revenue in the Early Republic" (Ph.D. diss., Harvard University, 1993), 36–42.

9. I am arguing here primarily with Edmund S. Morgan, "Slavery and Freedom: The American Paradox," *Journal of American History* 59 (1972): 4–29; Michael Merrill and Sean Wilentz, "William Manning and the Invention of American Politics," in *The Key of Liberty: The Life and Democratic Writings of William Manning, "A Laborer," 1747–1814*, ed. Michael Merrill and Sean Wilentz (Cambridge, MA, 1993); Alfred F. Young, *The Democratic Republicans of New York: The Origins, 1763–1797* (Chapel Hill, 1967); and Paul Goodman, *The Democratic-Republicans of Massachusetts: Politics in a Young Republic* (Cambridge, MA, 1964). See also Gordon S. Wood, *The Radicalism of the American Revolution* (New York, 1993). For an important corrective (though for a later period), see James L. Huston, *Calculating the Value of the Union: Slavery, Property Rights, and the Economic Origins of the Civil War* (Chapel Hill, 2003), chaps. 2–3.

Chapter 4

1. For the tax data, see U.S. Department of Commerce, Bureau of the Census, *Historical Statistics of the United States: Colonial Times to 1970* (Washington, 1975), 2: 1106. For the Nullification Crisis, see William W. Freehling, *Prelude to Civil War: The Nullification Controversy in South Carolina, 1816–1836* (New York, 1966). For details on the antebellum tariffs, see F. W. Taussig, *The Tariff History of the United States*, 2nd ed. (New York, 1892), 1–153; and Edward Stanwood, *American Tariff Controversies in the Nineteenth Century*, 2 vols. (Boston, 1903), 1: 1–410, 2: 1–108.

2. The classic discussions of elite attitudes toward slavery in this era are Winthrop D. Jordan, *White over Black: American Attitudes toward the Negro, 1550–1812* (1968; New York, 1977); David Brion Davis, *The Problem of Slavery in Western Culture* (Ithaca, 1966); and idem, *The Problem of Slavery in the Age of Revolution 1770–1823* (1975; New York, 1999). The classics on the politics of slavery are Donald L. Robinson, *Slavery in the Struc-*

ture of American Politics, 1765–1820 (New York, 1971); Duncan J. MacLeod, *Slavery, Race and the American Revolution* (London, 1974); and Staughton Lynd, *Class Conflict, Slavery, and the United States Constitution: Ten Essays* (Indianapolis, 1967), chaps. 6–10. See also Paul Finkelman, *Slavery and the Founders: Race and Liberty in the Age of Jefferson,* 2nd ed. (Armonk, NY, 2001); and Joseph J. Ellis, *Founding Brothers: The Revolutionary Generation* (New York, 2000), chap. 3.

3. For the quotations, Articles of Confederation, art. 5; U.S. Constitution, art. 2, sec. 1. For representation under the Constitution, see especially Leonard L. Richards, *The Slave Power: The Free North and Southern Domination 1780–1860* (Baton Rouge, 2000). Jack N. Rakove, *The Beginnings of National Politics: An Interpretive History of the Continental Congress* (Baltimore, 1979), 140–41, calls representation by states the only practical option for the First Continental Congress (1774). As Patrick Henry noted, official population data could only mean "attestations of officers of the Crown," whom Congress could hardly ask to help organize the colonial resistance movement. John Adams' Notes of Debates, Sept. 6, 1774, in Paul H. Smith et al., eds., *Letters of Delegates to Congress, 1774–1789,* 25 vols. (Washington, 1976–98), 1: 29 (hereafter cited as *LDC*).

4. See Max Edling, *A Revolution in Favor of Government: Origins of the U.S. Constitution and the Making of the American State* (New York, 2003); Calvin H. Johnson, *Righteous Anger at the Wicked States: The Meaning of the Founders' Constitution* (New York, 2005); E. James Ferguson, *The Power of the Purse: A History of American Public Finance, 1776–1790* (Chapel Hill, 1961), 239–50; Rakove, *Beginnings,* 337–42. Historically, the difference between the impost and tariff was the protectionism of the latter. Linguistically, an impost was any trade tax and a tariff any list of enumerated rates (as in the word's archaic usage to describe any price list, such as a restaurant menu). Thus, a tariff was an impost whose rates were enumerated. See James Madison's description of a proposal not designed to protect manufacturing: "to turn the 5 perCt. ad valorem into a Tariff founded on an enumeration of the several classes of imports." James Madison's Notes of Debates, March 11, 1783, *LDC,* 19: 782. The proposal is printed in Robert Morris to Congress, March 8, 1783, in E. James Ferguson et al., eds., *The Papers of Robert Morris,* 9 vols. (Pittsburgh, 1973–99), 7: 529–30.

5. David Howell to Nicholas Brown, July 20, 1783, *LDC,* 20: 483; Jonathan Arnold to William Greene, Jan. 8, 1783, ibid., 19: 560; Jonathan Arnold to Welcome Arnold, Feb. 11, 1783, ibid., 19: 669; Jonathan Arnold to David Howell, March 8, 1783, ibid., 19: 777. For Rhode Island's interests, see Forrest McDonald, *We the People: The Economic Origins of the Constitution* (Chicago, 1958), 324–28.

6. For Lynch, see John Adams' Notes of Debate, July 30, 1776, *LDC,* 4: 568. For the draft clause, Rakove, *Beginnings,* 157. The phrase "Indians not paying Taxes," which would appear in the three-fifths clause of the Constitution as "Indians not taxed," referred to two groups: Indians living under sovereign tribal governments (i.e., those not conquered by English settlers) and Indians living under English jurisdiction in colonies (such as Massachusetts) whose tax laws exempted Indians. The rest of the quotations in this section are from Adams's Notes, July 30, Aug. 1, 1776, *LDC,* 4: 568–69, 592; and Thomas Jefferson's Notes of Proceedings in Congress, July 12–Aug. 1, 1776, ibid., 4: 438–41.

7. For the vote, see Jefferson's Notes, ibid., 4: 441. For the slave populations in 1770, Ira

Berlin, *Many Thousands Gone: The First Two Centuries of Slavery in North America* (Cambridge, MA, 1998), 369.

8. Note that this was not an abolitionist argument. It was about how slavery would shape the relative tax burdens on northern and southern *whites*. Wilson also complained that under Chase's amendment "the Southern colonies would have all the benefit of slaves, whilst the Northern ones would bear the burthen. That slaves increase the profits of a state, which the Southern states mean to take to themselves; that they also increase the burthen of defence, which would of course fall so much the heavier on the Northern." Jefferson's Notes, *LDC*, 4: 440. Wilson's analysis of underconsumption by slaves was not novel. See, for example, T. H. Breen, *The Marketplace of Revolution: How Consumer Politics Shaped American Independence* (New York, 2004), 94.

9. Ellis, *Founding Brothers*, 14–15: "[H]istorians have essentially been fighting the same battles, over and over again, that the members of the revolutionary generation fought originally among themselves." The foundational text for the "ideological" view is Bernard Bailyn, *The Ideological Origins of the American Revolution* (Cambridge, MA, 1967). Rakove, *Beginnings*, 185, offers another view: what the revolutionaries could not imagine were logistical solutions. For Valley Forge, see Robert Middlekauff, *The Glorious Cause: The American Revolution, 1763–1789* (New York, 1982), 411–17. See also E. Wayne Carp, *To Starve the Army at Pleasure: Continental Army Administration and American Political Culture, 1775–1783* (Chapel Hill, 1984). For the ways in which the organizational rules of Congress itself contributed to the problems, see Calvin Jillson and Rick K. Wilson, *Congressional Dynamics: Structure, Coordination, and Choice in the First American Congress, 1774–1789* (Stanford, 1994).

10. Among the amendment suggestions from the states in 1778 was a proposal by South Carolina to insert the word "white" between "free" and "inhabitants." Congress rejected this and every other proposed amendment (see below). Worthington Chauncey Ford et al., eds., *Journals of the Continental Congress 1774–1789*, 37 vols. (Washington, 1904–37), June 25, 1778, 11: 652. Cited hereafter as *JCC*, this source is also available in a searchable World Wide Web format at the Library of Congress page "A Century of Lawmaking for a New Nation: U.S. Congressional Documents and Debates, 1774–1873," available at http://memory.loc.gov/ammem/amlaw/lwjclink.html. A version of Madison's notes on the debates is included with the journals.

11. Roger H. Brown, *Redeeming the Republic: Federalists, Taxation, and the Origins of the Constitution* (Baltimore, 1993). The major difference between the financing of the Revolution and that of modern wars is that the revolutionary generation absorbed far more of the cost of its war, as the currency depreciation acted on the currency holders as a massive debt repudiation. This is the conclusion of Ralph Volney Harlow, "Aspects of Revolutionary Finance, 1775–1783," *American Historical Review* 35 (1929): 46–68.

12. For the British blockade, see Richard Buel, Jr., *In Irons: Britain's Naval Supremacy and the American Revolutionary Economy* (New Haven, 1998).

13. *JCC*, July 29, 1775, 2: 21–22; Dec. 26, 1775, 3: 458; Nov. 22, 1777, 9: 955. See also Ferguson, *Power of the Purse*, chap. 1.

14. Ferguson, *Power of the Purse*, chaps. 2–4 (quotation on 49); Rakove, *Beginnings*, especially 277. For the commodity requisitions, *JCC*, Feb. 9, 1780, 16: 143–46; Feb. 25,

1780, 16: 198–99; Nov. 4, 1780, 18: 1011–18. For the devaluation, ibid., March 18, 1780, 16: 262–67.

15. For the colonial and revolutionary state tax systems, see chaps. 1–3 above.

16. Rakove, *Beginnings*, 161, calls these the three "insurmountable" issues. While the tax conflict hinged on slavery, the representation conflict would have addressed slavery if delegates from large states had persuaded delegates from small states to consider representation by population rather than one-state-one-vote. The representation debate never reached the problem of counting slaves, although Patrick Henry gave a hint in 1774 of how it might have gone when he defended Virginia's large-state interest by proposing to exclude slaves from the count: "Slaves are to be thrown out of the Question, and if the freemen can be represented according to their Numbers I am satisfyed." Adams' Notes of Debates, Sept. 6, 1774, *LDC*, 1: 28. On the western land issue, see especially Peter S. Onuf, *Statehood and Union: A History of the Northwest Ordinance* (Bloomington, 1987).

17. *JCC*, Oct. 9, 1777, 9: 788–89; Oct. 13, 1777, 9: 800 (quotation); Cornelius Harnett to Richard Caswell, Oct. 10, 1777, *LDC*, 8: 98; William Williams to Jonathan Trumbull, Sr., Oct. 11, 1777, ibid., 8: 108; Henry Laurens to John Laurens, Oct. 10, 1777, ibid., 8: 100. See also Nathaniel Folsom to Meshech Weare, Oct. 27, 1777, ibid., 8: 198. On the reasons Congress revived the Articles at this time, see Rakove, *Beginnings*, 177–79.

18. *JCC*, Oct. 14, 1777, 9: 801; Cornelius Harnett to William Wilkinson, Nov. 30, 1777, *LDC*, 8: 349; Nathaniel Folsom to Meshech Weare, Nov. 21, 1777, ibid., 8: 299. Folsom also was angry about article 9, which favored the South by requiring Congress to set state troop quotas "in proportion to the number of white inhabitants."

19. *JCC*, June 22, 1778, 11: 631–32; June 23, 1778, 11: 636–40 (Massachusetts quotation on 638); June 25, 1778, 11: 647–56 (South Carolina quotation on 654); for Congress's dispatch, Rakove, *Beginnings*, 186–89.

20. James Madison's Notes of Debates, March 27, 1783, *LDC*, 20: 117.

21. Rakove, *Beginnings*, 177–78; Richard Henry Lee to Roger Sherman, Nov. 24, 1777, *LDC*, 8: 319–20.

22. Roger Sherman to Richard Henry Lee, Nov. 3, 1777, quoted in ibid., 8: 320–21n.

23. *JCC*, Feb. 3, 1781, 19: 112–13; for the draft language, ibid., Aug. 22, 1780, 17: 758; on the weakening blockade, Buel, *In Irons*, chaps. 6–9.

24. *JCC*, Sept. 19, 1778, 12: 929 (Morris); March 18, 1780, 16: 261 (Burke); Aug. 22, 1780, 17: 758 (tax exports); Dec. 18, 1780, 18: 1162–63 (enumerated rate schedule); Dec. 22, 1780, Jan. 19–Jan. 31, 1781, 11: 1183, 19: 72, 73, 74, 77, 85, 87, 91–92, 97–98, 102–3 (committee of the whole deliberates); Feb. 1–3, 1781, 19: 105–6, 109, 110–13 (debate and passage). At the end, there was a dispute about whether Congress should ask the states to "pass laws granting" Congress the right to collect the impost or, as the final language said, ask the states to "vest a power in Congress, to levy [the impost] for the use of the United States." Ferguson, *Power of the Purse*, 116–17; and H. James Henderson, *Party Politics in the Continental Congress* (New York, 1974), 273–75, treat this as a weighty conflict about centralizing power in the national government. Yet the main issue in the committee of the whole deliberations probably was whether to use the impost to regulate trade. The version with enumerated rates was part of a bullionist scheme to discourage luxury imports (hence the enumeration) in order to stem specie flows from the United States. This scheme also

included encouragement for exports, the power to lay trade embargos, a bank, and the collection of gold and silver plate from individuals to coin into money. See John Sullivan's Committee Notes, Nov. 7–23, 1780, *LDC*, 16: 305–13; Jesse Root to Jonathan Trumbull, Sr., Jan. 29, 1781, ibid., 16: 639–40; James M. Varnum to John Innes Clark, Feb. 3, 1781, ibid., 16: 671–72. Perhaps in reference to the "pass laws granting" versus "vest a power" dispute, Varnum (who had just arrived in Congress) complained about the more experienced delegates: "And if a Word in a Report should not exactly suit their mechanical genius's a long Debate ensues." Ibid., 16: 672.

25. This turned out to be true in the 1790s. See Frederick Arthur Baldwin Dalzell, "Taxation without Representation: Federal Revenue in the Early Republic" (Ph.D. diss., Harvard University, 1993).

26. *JCC*, April 19, 1781, 19: 425–25. For the retail arrangements, see Breen, *Marketplace*, 115–47.

27. James Madison to Edmund Randolph, Nov. 19, 1782, *LDC*, 19: 399; Rakove, *Beginnings*, 313–14, 316. For the chronology, *Morris Papers*, 1: 396, 401. For South Carolina and Georgia, *JCC*, Feb. 7, 1781, 19: 124–25; Samuel Huntington to the States, Feb. 8, 1781, *LDC*, 16: 687. By October 1782, South Carolina had ratified, leaving only Rhode Island and Georgia, though it was Rhode Island that mattered. *JCC*, Oct. 10, 1782, 23: 643.

28. Ibid., April 19, 1781, 19: 422–23; April 1, 1782, 22: 159.

29. William Ellery to Nicholas Cooke, Nov. 30, 1777, *LDC*, 8: 326; *JCC*, Nov. 2, 1781, 21: 1089–90, April 1, 1782, 22: 159, Sept. 10, 1782, 23: 565–71.

30. Morris was widely known as the "Financier." Most historians now accept the generally favorable appraisal of his efforts in Clarence L. Ver Steeg, *Robert Morris: Revolutionary Financier* (Philadelphia, 1954). On the 1779 dispute among the envoys, known as the "Lee-Deane Affair," see Rakove, *Beginnings*, 249–74. For Morris's tax proposals, Robert Morris to Congress, Feb. 27, 1782, July 29, 1782, March 8, 1783, in *Morris Papers*, 4: 317–18, 6: 65–69, 7: 527–28.

31. Rakove, *Beginnings*, 310–11, 317–19; Ferguson, *Power of the Purse*, 149–64. For the evidence about Newburgh, see the debate in the *William and Mary Quarterly:* Richard H. Kohn, "The Newburgh Conspiracy: America and the Coup D'Etat," 3rd ser., 27 (1970): 187–270; Paul David Nelson, "Horatio Gates at Newburgh: A Misunderstood Role," 3rd. ser., 29 (1972): 143–51, with "Richard H. Kohn's Reply," 151–58; C. Edward Skeen, "The Newburgh Conspiracy Reconsidered," 3rd. ser., 31 (1974): 273–90, with "Richard H. Kohn's Rebuttal," 290–98.

32. David Howell to Theodore Foster, Oct. 9, 1782, *LDC*, 19: 245; David Howell to Theodore Foster, Oct. 12, 1782, ibid., 19: 253; Rhode Island Delegates to William Greene, Oct. 15, 1782, ibid., 19: 264 (written by Arnold, signed by him and Howell). See also David Howell to Welcome Arnold, Aug. 3, 1782, ibid., 19: 6; David Howell to Welcome Arnold, Aug. 23, 1782, ibid., 19: 91; David Howell to Nicholas Brown, Sept. 19, 1782, ibid., 19: 175; David Howell to Welcome Arnold, Oct. 9, 1782, ibid., 19: 243; David Howell to Nicholas Brown, Oct. 12, 1782, ibid., 19: 251–52; David Howell to Nicholas Brown, Oct. 30, 1782, ibid., 19: 329–30. On Howell, Rakove, *Beginnings*, 314–17.

33. Robert Morris to Congress, Nov. 5, 1781, *Morris Papers*, 3: 142–47; *JCC*, Feb. 20,

1782, 22: 83–84; Ferguson, *Power of the Purse,* 210. For the states failing to act on this resolution, *JCC,* Feb. 26, 1783, 24: 152.

34. Ibid., April 18, 1783, 24: 256–60; April 26, 1783, 24: 277, 279–80. Congress framed a complex package. It sent the population amendment and western land resolution to the states independently, but linked the impost and long-term requisition so that neither would go into effect until both "shall be acceded to by every State." Ibid., April 18, 1783, 24: 259. The linkage was a mistake. When the impost came far closer to ratification than the long-term requisition, Congress asked the states to decouple them. Ibid., Feb. 15, 1786, 30: 71, 75–76.

35. For the impost, ibid., April 18, 1783, 24: 257–58. For Rhode Island's complaint, ibid., Dec. 12, 1782, 23: 788.

36. Ibid., April 18, 1783, 24: 258–59; April 26, 1783, 24: 278. For an explicit acknowledgment that Congress was using the 1775 population guess, Madison's Notes, April 7, 1783, *LDC,* 20: 144.

37. North Carolina Delegates to Alexander Martin, Oct. 22, 1782, ibid., 19: 291; Samuel Osgood to John Lowell, Nov. 23, 1783, ibid., 19: 415. Osgood, however, wished that article 8 had used population, "including Whites & Blacks; there is no good Reason why Blacks should not be included." Ibid., 19: 414. Also Hugh Williamson to Alexander Martin, Sept. 2, 1782, ibid., 19: 120–21. On the end of the 1781 impost, see Rakove, *Beginnings,* 316; and Ferguson, *Power of the Purse,* 152–53.

38. *JCC,* Feb. 6, 1783, 24: 113.

39. Madison's Notes of Debate, Jan. 9 and 10, Jan. 31, 1783, *LDC,* 19: 569, 649. Madison first arrived in Congress in March 1780. Hamilton arrived in November 1782. Neither had participated in drafting the Articles. Their teamwork is clear in Madison's notes, as are their vigorous efforts to defend the interests of their own states in the settlement of accounts. Hamilton demanded "abatements" to compensate New York for the period when the British occupied New York City. Madison insisted on including state war spending Congress had not authorized, of which Virginia claimed a large amount. Congress rejected both. Madison also remained alert to southern interests more generally. For example, when Hamilton suggested that, instead of the states doing full valuations, Congress class land into categories (arable, pasture, wood, etc.), ask the states to report numbers of acres in each category, and apply uniform rates to estimate "their comparative values," Madison balked. "This mode," he commented, "would have been acceptable to the more compact & populous States, but was totally inadmissible to the Southern States," which opposed anything that involved counting acres. Madison's Notes, Jan. 14, 1783, ibid., 19: 582.

40. Madison's Notes, Jan. 31, 1783 (Hamilton and Dyer), Feb. 7, 1783 (Madison), ibid., 19: 650, 663. When they had to explain why they abandoned the real estate plan, the North Carolina delegates repeated Madison's comparison of the Virginia and Pennsylvania data. North Carolina Delegates to Alexander Martin, March 24, 1783, ibid., 20: 90.

41. *JCC,* Feb. 17, 1783, 24: 136–37; Madison's Notes, Feb. 17, 1783, *LDC,* 19: 698; Alexander Hamilton to George Clinton, Feb. 24, 1783, ibid., 19: 727; James Madison to Edmund Randolph, Feb. 18, 1783, ibid., 19: 706; Hugh Williamson to James Iredell, Feb. 17, 1783, ibid., 19: 699. For the states, *JCC,* March 8, 1786, 30: 102: "[N]ot a single State

in the Union has, in any degree, complied therewith," except for "an unauthenticated account" from New Hampshire, "a part whereof was imperfectly formed from conjecture."

42. Madison's Notes, Jan. 14, 1783, Feb. 26, 1783 (Madison's preference for a two-to-one ratio), *LDC,* 19: 581, 583n., 742; North Carolina Delegates to Alexander Martin, March 24, 1783, ibid., 20: 90–91.

43. Madison's Notes, March 28, 1783, ibid., 20: 120–21. Hamilton urged Congress to permit public access to the debate. Madison thought his "true reason" for this was to enable the Philadelphia community of public creditors to pressure Congress. *JCC,* Feb. 18, 1783, 24: 140; Madison's Notes, Feb. 18, 1783, *LDC,* 19: 704; Jonathan Arnold to David Howell, March 8, 1783, ibid., 19: 777: the finance debate "by direction is now a secrecy."

44. Madison's Notes, March 28, 1783, ibid., 20: 121.

45. *JCC,* March 28, 1783, 24: 215–16, April 1, 1783, 24: 224; Madison's Notes, April 1, 1783, *LDC,* 20: 128. On April 1, Rhode Island voted no, the Massachusetts delegation divided (two yes, two no), and votes by single delegates from New Hampshire and Delaware (in favor) did not count. No Georgia delegates were present for any part of the 1783 debate. The other eight state delegations (Connecticut and the middle and southern states) endorsed the amendment. For the states, *JCC,* March 8, 1786, 30: 103, 107; for the further requisitions, ibid., Sept. 27, 1785, 29: 767, Aug. 2, 1786, 31: 462. The New England opponents later attacked the three-fifths bargain. Stephen Higginson to Samuel Adams, June 10, 1783, *LDC,* 20: 318: "[T]he allowance made for the Blacks is much too great;" southern slave labor produced more profit than northern free labor, "& in proportion to that excess is their Ability to pay Taxes." Rhode Island Delegates to William Greene, Sept. 8, 1783, ibid., 20: 642: "The nett produce of the labour of a black in those [southern] States is, at least, double to that of a common white labourer in the eastern States."

46. For the population figures, see Berlin, *Many Thousands Gone,* 264, 304.

47. Eliphalet Dyer to William Williams, Jan. 10, 1783, *LDC,* 19: 573; James Madison to Edmund Randolph, Feb. 25, 1783, ibid., 19: 733. Brown, *Redeeming the Republic,* does not look at the distribution of the requisition quotas but shows that the states could not pay them even when they tried.

48. Madison's Notes, Jan. 27–29, March 11, 1783, *LDC,* 19: 618–19, 624–25, 629–30, 641–45, 782 (quotation). The part of Morris's plan that drew the most censure was a proposal that Congress offer the states the alternatives of agreeing to a tax plan that included the impost plus other taxes or paying their quotas of the entire national debt immediately. See Morris to Congress, March 8, 1783, *Morris Papers,* 7: 526–27. There was also desultory talk of a house tax.

49. Morris to Congress, July 29, 1782, ibid., 6: 66–68. The idea of using flat-rate land taxes to penalize speculative holdings of unimproved land was not new. "The taxing Land by the Acre," a New York leader had argued in 1752, "is so apparently unjust, that no body denies the Inequality of this Method: But at the same Time they affirm, that it would be useful in obliging the Proprietors of large Tracks to procure their Settlement. If this is the Design in View, it should no longer be called a Tax but a *Penalty* laid on the Proprietors of large Tracts of Land, for their Negligince in Improving them." Beverly McAnear, "Mr. Robert R. Livingston's Reasons Against a Land Tax," *Journal of Political Economy* 48 (1940): 84.

50. Morris to Congress, July 29, 1782, *Morris Papers*, 6: 65, 67, 68. The suspicion that this report had a satiric dimension is bolstered by another circumstance. The editors of the *Morris Papers*, 6: 43, report that Robert Morris "delegated the task of deriving theoretical formulations and defenses of his policies" to Gouverneur Morris, who is widely described as too clever by half.

51. Madison's Notes, *LDC*, Jan. 28, 1783, 19: 630, 631n.

52. Joseph Jones to George Washington, Feb. 27, 1783, ibid., 19: 745; John Taylor Gilman to Josiah Bartlett, Jan. 9, 1783, ibid., 19: 567; John Francis Mercer to Henry Tazewell, March 18, 1783, ibid., 20: 53; Eliphalet Dyer to Jonathan Trumbull, Sr., March 18, 1783, ibid., 20: 45.

53. Dyer to Trumbull, March 18, 1783, ibid., 20: 45.

54. James Madison's Notes, Feb. 26, 1783, ibid., 19: 740–42, much of it repeated in James Madison's Memorandum on a Continental Revenue Plan, March 6, 1783, ibid., 19: 771–72; Stephen Higginson to Theophilus Parsons, April 7–10, 1783, ibid., 20: 141–43. The New York case involved a qualified ratification. Congress could have the impost, but only if merchants could pay in New York paper currency. This strategy would help New York retire its money but defeat the purpose of dedicating impost revenue to the national debt—since no foreign and few domestic creditors would accept payment in New York money. In August 1786, when the governor refused to call the legislature into session to repeal the currency qualification, the 1783 impost died. See John P. Kaminski, *George Clinton: Yeoman Politician of the New Republic* (Madison, WI, 1993), 89–96; and Linda Grant DePauw, *The Eleventh Pillar: New York State and the Federal Constitution* (Ithaca, 1966), 35–43.

55. The assumption of state debts was notoriously controversial in part because, by 1790, some states had little outstanding debt for the federal government to assume. Rhode Island, for example, had paid off its debt at heavily discounted rates, essentially repudiating much of it. Ferguson, *Power of the Purse*, 243–44. Virginia concentrated on—and succeeded in—inflating its claims against the nation in the settlement of accounts. Ibid., 206–8, 211–18, 322–25.

56. Alexander Hamilton, "Report on Manufactures," in Harold C. Syrett, ed., *The Papers of Alexander Hamilton*, 27 vols. (New York, 1961–87), 10: 296.

57. For Howell, see note 32 above. Madison does not notice this change in his *Federalist* essays. For more on his role in the framing and adoption of the Constitution, see chapter 5.

58. *Annals of Congress*, 1st Cong., 1st sess., 107, 111, 115, 119. Madison actually announced from the start that he intended to exploit the new legislative conditions, tacking "a clause or two on the subject of tonnage" onto the 1783 impost (107). The "tonnage" clauses were designed to favor French over British shipping and caused a long debate. See Stanley Elkins and Eric McKitrick, *The Age of Federalism: The Early American Republic, 1788–1800* (New York, 1993), 67–74. As a member of the Philadelphia convention that drafted the Constitution, Fitzsimons had predicted that Congress might want to tax exports "when America should become a manufacturing country," but even he did not anticipate a protective tariff on imports. Max Farrand, ed., *The Records of the Federal Convention of 1787*, 3 vols. (New Haven, 1911), 2: 386. Both Farrand and the *Annals* are available and searchable at the Library of Congress, "Century of Lawmaking" Web site.

59. For the political science highlights, see E. E. Schattschneider, *Politics, Pressures, and the Tariff* (New York, 1935); Raymond A. Bauer, Ithiel De Sola Pool, and Lewis Anthony Dexter, *American Business and Public Policy: The Politics of Foreign Trade,* 2nd ed. (1963; Chicago, 1972); Theodore Lowi, "American Business, Public Policy, Case-Studies, and Political Theory," *World Politics* 16 (1964): 677–715; John Mark Hansen, "Taxation and the Political Economy of the Tariff," *International Organization* 44 (1990): 527–51; and Richard Franklin Bensel, *The Political Economy of American Industrialization, 1877–1900* (Cambridge, 2000).

60. *Annals,* 1st Cong., 1st sess., 155 (Fitzsimons), 340 (Ames).

61. Ibid., 165–66 (Tucker), 168 (Laurence), 170 (Madison), 224 (Thatcher), 227 (Madison), 240 (Jackson).

62. Ibid., 224, 349 (Parker), 350 (Jackson, Sherman), 351 (Ames: "subject of some delicacy").

63. Ibid., 351 (Ames), 352 (Jackson).

64. Ibid., 352–56 (Madison quotation on 355, Sherman quotation on 356). In support of the Parker motion, Madison claimed that Congress could tax the slave trade out of existence with the 5 percent duty: "Our object in enumerating persons on paper with merchandise, is to prevent the practice of actually treating them as such." Ibid., 353. This was a strange claim in light of the fact that nobody thought 5 percent was high enough to discourage other imports. Generally, Madison's management of this debate looks suspiciously like an effort to collect discursive ammunition to guarantee that no federal collector tried to tax imported slaves in the residual 5 percent category. In other words, he said he was trying to ensure that the 5 percent applied to slaves, but he actually was doing the opposite. At the Philadelphia convention, Sherman had argued that the tax provision of the slave trade clause only "made the matter worse, because it implied they were *property.*" Farrand, *Records,* 2: 374.

65. Ellis, *Founding Brothers,* 96. For the second session debate, see also Howard A. Ohline, "Slavery, Economics, and Congressional Politics, 1790," *Journal of Southern History* 46 (1980): 351–52.

66. *U.S. Statutes at Large,* ch. 2, July 4, 1789, 1: 25–27.

Chapter 5

1. The standard reference is Davis Rich Dewey, *Financial History of the United States* (New York, 1939).

2. These clauses are art. 1, sec. 2, cl. 3 (three-fifths) and art. 1, sec. 9, cl. 4 (direct tax).

3. For the taxes, *U.S. Statutes at Large,* ch. 70, July 9, 1798, 1: 580–91; ch. 75, July 14, 1798, 1: 597–604; ch. 16, July 22, 1813, 3: 22–34; ch. 37, Aug. 2, 1813, 3: 53–72; ch. 21, Jan. 9, 1815, 3: 164–80; ch. 60, Feb. 27, 1815, 3: 216; ch. 24, March 5, 1816, 3: 255–56; ch. 45, Aug. 5, 1861, 12: 294–309. For states assuming them, A. J. Dallas, "Valuations of Real Estate and Slaves," Jan. 25, 1816, in Walter Lowrie and Matthew St. Clair Clark, comps., *American State Papers: Documents, Legislative and Executive of the Congress of the United States,* 10 vols. (Washington, 1832–61), 3rd ser., *Finance,* 3: 65 [hereafter cited as *ASP-F*]; William H. Crawford, "Direct Tax and Internal Duties," Feb. 11, 1817, *ASP-F,* 3: 190; and Frederic C. Howe, *Taxation and Taxes in the United States under the Internal*

Revenue System, 1791–1895 (New York, 1896), 85. The Nebraska and New Mexico territories assumed the 1861 tax by deduction from their U.S. appropriations, *Statutes at Large*, ch. 119, July 1, 1861, 12: 446, 488–89. Both the *Statutes* and *State Papers* are available in a searchable format at the Library of Congress Web site "A Century of Lawmaking for a New Nation," available at http://memory.loc.gov/ammem/amlaw/lawhome.html.

4. Dividing Internal Revenue Service collections (2002) by estimates of total income (per capita income in 2001 multiplied by resident population in 2000) shows that Connecticut actually paid more than Mississippi: 24.4 percent versus 14.4 percent. These tax rate estimates are higher than those in table 1 because total collections include payroll taxes (Social Security). Internal Revenue Service, "Table 6: Internal Revenue Gross Collections by State, Fiscal Year 2002" revised May 2003, http://www.irs.gov/pub/irs-soi/02db06co.xls, accessible through the Internal Revenue Web site "Tax Stats" page, available at http://www.irs.gov/taxstats/.

5. Calvin H. Johnson, "Apportionment of Direct Taxes: The Foul-Up in the Core of the Constitution," *William and Mary Bill of Rights Journal* 7 (1998): 1–103; Bruce Ackerman, "Taxation and the Constitution," *Columbia Law Review* 99 (1999): 1–58; Erik M. Jensen, "The Apportionment of 'Direct Taxes': Are Consumption Taxes Constitutional?" *Columbia Law Review* 97 (1997): 2334–419; Charlotte Crane, "Reclaiming the Meaning of 'Direct Tax,'" paper presented at Tax History Conference, UCLA School of Law, July 17, 2005. See also E. R. A. Seligman, *The Income Tax*, 2nd ed. (New York, 1914), 531–89; Charles J. Bullock, "The Origin, Purpose, and Effects of the Direct-Tax Clause of the Federal Constitution," *Political Science Quarterly* 15 (1900): 217–39, 452–81.

6. *Hylton v. U.S.*, 3 U.S. (3 Dall.) 171 (1796), quotation on 181. See below for further discussion of this case.

7. *Pollock v. Farmers' Loan and Trust Company*, 157 U.S. 429 (1895), 158 U.S. 601 (1895); *Springer v. U.S.*, 102 U.S. 586 (1880).

8. John Buenker, *The Income Tax and the Progressive Era* (New York, 1985); and Richard Franklin Bensel, *The Political Economy of American Industrialization, 1877–1900* (Cambridge, 2000). The Sixteenth Amendment is brief: "'The Congress shall have power to lay and collect taxes on incomes, from whatever source derived, without apportionment among the several States, and without regard to any census or enumeration.'"

9. The best analysis of the Philadelphia convention (by far) is Jack N. Rakove, *Original Meanings: Politics and Ideas in the Making of the Constitution* (New York, 1996), on which I have relied throughout this section.

10. Max Farrand, ed., *The Records of the Federal Convention of 1787*, 3 vols. (New Haven, 1911), 1: 486, searchable at the "Century of Lawmaking" page on the Library of Congress Web site.

11. Ibid., 1: 20. In the Virginia Plan, "the people" would elect the first branch and the first branch would elect the second after candidates had been nominated by the state legislatures.

12. Ibid., 1: 35–36.

13. Ibid., 1: 196, 533, 605. Besides, Wilson argued in an echo from 1776, population already reflected the wealth of the states: "the number of people was the best measure of their comparative wealth." Ibid., 1: 179–80.

14. Three of the most famous delegates, Franklin, Washington, and Hamilton, played minor roles. Franklin acted as elder statesman, but was so old and frail that Wilson had to read his speeches for him. Washington, whom everyone expected to be the first president, considered it unseemly to play a role in creating the job. Hamilton was there only for the beginning and end, just long enough to make a famously elitist speech. The Constitution, he argued, should reserve power for "the rich and well born" to check "the imprudence of democracy." "The people are turbulent and changing; they seldom judge or determine right." Ibid., 1: 299. For the list of delegates, ibid., 3: 557–59.

15. Ibid., 1: 594 (Pinckney, Randolph), 587 (Wilson).

16. Ibid., 1: 585 (Madison), 592 (Morris, Mason), 595 (Wilson). Three-fifths representation is often portrayed as an insult to enslaved African Americans ("three-fifths of a man"), but this view makes it sound far less pernicious than it actually was. Three-fifths representation did *not* grant African Americans three-fifths of a vote. It granted them zero, or, really, negative votes. Counting slaves to grant extra votes to their owners, it was intended to injure rather than merely to insult African Americans.

17. Ibid., 1: 596 (Pinckney), 605 (Butler), 602 (Madison), 2: 14 (adoption).

18. Ibid., 2: 106. See also 2: 350 (Daniel Carroll, Maryland), 358 (Oliver Ellsworth, Connecticut).

19. Ibid., 1: 243 (New Jersey Plan), 2: 26 (Morris, Sherman).

20. Rakove, *Original Meanings*, 84.

21. Farrand, *Records*, 2: 181–83, Rakove, *Original Meanings*, 86.

22. Ibid., 2: 220 (King), 222 (Morris).

23. Ibid., 2: 222–23.

24. Ibid., 2: 223 (Morris), 359 (Martin), 350 (King).

25. Ibid., 2: 307.

26. Ibid., 2: 607.

27. Ibid., 2: 618. For the details of the settlement, see Ferguson, *Power of the Purse*, chaps. 9–10, 14–15. In the end, after serious wheeling and dealing, a board appointed by the last Congress under the Articles weighed state claims of war spending, determined the total cost of the war, subtracted requisition payments, announced the balances due to and from each state, and then destroyed their records—so that nobody else ever knew how the "charges of war" finally were apportioned to the states!

28. The clauses are: art. 1, sec. 2, cl. 3 (three-fifths); art. 1, sec. 9, cl. 4 (direct tax); art. 5 (amendment); art. 1, sec. 8, cl. 1 (tax power); art. 1, sec. 9, cl. 5 (export tax); art. 1, sec. 10, cl. 2 (state imposts); art. 1, sec. 9, cl. 1 (slave trade).

29. Farrand, *Records*, 2: 306 (Madison). The "navigation act" problem was about shipping rather than industry, with southerners afraid of rules that would favor U.S. over foreign shippers, enabling the U.S. shippers (northerners) to gouge the staple-crop exporters on freight rates. On the incidence of consumption taxes, Madison ignored slavery to present the opposite argument from Morris's to a Virginia audience at his state's ratification convention. "The Southern States, from having fewer manufacturers, will import and consume more. They will therefore pay more of the imposts." Direct taxes were desirable to "lessen that inequality." Merrill Jensen, John P. Kaminski, and Gaspare J. Saladino, eds., *The Docu-*

mentary History of the Ratification of the Constitution, 19 vols. (Madison, 1976–), 9: 1146 (hereafter cited as *DHRC*). Quotations from *DHRC* can also be found in any of the many reprints of Jonathan Elliot, *The Debates in the Several State Conventions on the Adoption of the Federal Constitution,* 5 vols. (Philadelphia, 1836), including the searchable one at the "Century of Lawmaking" page on the Library of Congress Web site.

30. Farrand, *Records,* 2: 95.

31. Ibid., 2: 221 (Morris), 2: 370–71 (Mason, Ellsworth). Cf. Thomas Jefferson, *Notes on the State of Virginia* (New York, 1999), 168.

32. "The morality or wisdom of slavery," Ellsworth had said the previous day, "are considerations belonging to the States themselves—What enriches a part enriches the whole, and the States are the best judges of their particular interest." Farrand, *Records,* 2: 364.

33. Ibid., 2: 371 (Pinckneys), 370 (Mason).

34. Ibid., 1: 561 (Paterson), 1: 201 (Gerry).

35. On the politics of ratification, see Rakove, *Original Meanings,* chaps. 5–6; Robert Allen Rutland, *The Ordeal of the Constitution: The Antifederalists and the Ratification Struggle of 1787–1788* (Norman, 1966); Steven R. Boyd, *The Politics of Opposition: Antifederalists and the Acceptance of the Constitution* (Millwood, NY, 1979); and Saul Cornell, *The Other Founders: Anti-Federalism and the Dissenting Tradition in America, 1788–1828* (Chapel Hill, 1999), chaps. 1–3.

36. Art. 7, cl. 1.

37. Thus, when state conventions proposed amendments, they included one to revive requisitions, allowing states to opt out of "direct taxes" by assuming their quotas. A Virginia proposal included excises: "When the Congress shall lay direct taxes or excises, they shall immediately inform the Executive power of each State, of the quota of such State . . . which is proposed to be thereby raised; and if the Legislature of any State shall pass a law which shall be effectual for raising such quota at the time required by Congress, the taxes and excises laid by Congress, shall not be collected in such State." *DHRC,* 10: 1553–54.

38. Alexander Hamilton, "The Federalist No. 31," Jacob E. Cooke, ed., *The Federalist* (Middletown, CT, 1961), 198; *DHRC,* 9: 1045–46 (Henry).

39. Herbert J. Storing, ed., *The Complete Anti-Federalist,* 7 vols. (Chicago, 1981), 2: 122.

40. *DHRC,* 6: 1237 (King), 1239 (Nasson); Elliot, *Debates,* 4: 277 (Rutledge), 4: 30 (Goudy). Centinel (Samuel Bryan of Pennsylvania) combined Nasson's point with the underconsumption analysis of slavery: "When it is recollected that no poll tax can be imposed on five negroes above what three whites can be charged; when it is considered, that the impost on the consumption of the Carolina field negroes, must be trifling, and the excise nothing, it is plain that the proportion of contributions, which can be expected from the southern states under the new constitution, will be very unequal." Storing, *Complete Anti-Federalist,* 2: 160.

41. *DHRC,* 10: 1341, 1222; Hugh Blair Grigsby, *The History of the Virginia Federal Convention of 1788* (1890–91; New York, 1969), 157n. Grigsby, who wrote his account in the 1850s, cites his source as "a person on the floor of the Convention at that time," adding that after Henry had frightened his fellow delegates with the threat of emancipation, this "homely exclamation" led them "instantly from fear to wayward laughter."

42. *DHRC,* 9: 1161 (Mason), 10: 1503 (Madison). For another view of the difference

between Virginia and the Deep South, Jack P. Greene, "The Constitution of 1787 and the Question of Southern Distinctiveness," in *The South's Role in the Creation of the Bill of Rights*, ed. Robert H. Haws (Jackson, 1991), 21–31.

43. *DHRC*, 10: 1477.

44. Ibid., 10: 1476–77.

45. Ibid., 10: 1341. For the elastic clause, art. 1, sec. 8, cl. 18.

46. *DHRC*, 10: 1342 (Nicholas), 1339 (Madison).

47. Ibid., 9: 937 (Mason), 1022 (Randolph), 10: 1215, 1342 (Henry), 10: 1343 (Mason), 10: 1222 (Henry).

48. Ibid., 9: 1122, 1127 (Marshall), 1148 (Madison).

49. The best account of national politics in the 1790s, Stanley Elkins and Eric McKitrick, *The Age of Federalism: The Early Republic, 1788–1800* (New York, 1993), emphasizes this European context. For the impact on finance, see Herbert E. Sloan, "Hamilton's Second Thoughts: Federalist Finance Revisited," in *Federalists Reconsidered*, ed. Doron Ben-Atar and Barbara B. Oberg (Charlottesville, 1998), 61–76. Jacob E. Cooke, *Tench Coxe and the Early Republic* (Chapel Hill, 1978), is also very useful on the financial issues.

50. These controversial arrangements, usually summarized as Hamilton's program to establish the "public credit" of the United States, increased the total size of the domestic debt in three ways. First, the federal government assumed the outstanding war debts of the states, rescuing several states (especially Massachusetts and South Carolina) from crushing burdens. Second, the federal government funded all outstanding debt instruments at par (face value), handing windfall profits to speculators who had bought them from original holders (soldiers, army suppliers) at pennies on the dollar. Third, the settlement of the state accounts for the war proceeded with a permissive treatment of undocumented claims for state spending, favoring states that had kept poor records or no records during the war (especially Virginia and North Carolina). The first two decisions can be (and were) called "Hamiltonian." The third can only be called "Madisonian" in light of Madison's relentless efforts to win it. See especially Ferguson, *Power of the Purse*, chaps. 10–15.

51. *Annals of Congress*, 4th Cong., 2nd sess., 1939 (searchable at "Century of Lawmaking" page on the Library of Congress Web site). For party affiliations, I am following Kenneth C. Martis, *The Historical Atlas of Political Parties in the United States Congress, 1789–1989* (New York, 1989).

52. The quotation continues: "If I could not go to heaven but with a party, I would not go there at all." Joseph J. Ellis, *Founding Brothers: The Revolutionary Generation* (New York, 2002), 66. The classic work on anti-party attitudes in the early republic is Richard Hofstadter, *The Idea of a Party System: The Rise of Legitimate Opposition in the United States, 1780–1840* (Berkeley, 1969).

53. In addition to Elkins and McKitrick, *Age of Federalism*, and Ellis, *Founding Brothers*, see Lance Banning, *The Jeffersonian Persuasion: Evolution of a Party Ideology* (Ithaca, 1978); and on the press, Jeffrey L. Pasley, *"The Tyranny of Printers": Newspaper Politics in the Early Republic* (Charlottesville, 2001). Although it focuses on the next decade, Linda K. Kerber, *Federalists in Dissent: Imagery and Ideology in Jeffersonian America* (Ithaca, 1970), chap. 2, is indispensable.

54. Herbert E. Sloan, *Principle and Interest: Thomas Jefferson and the Problem of Debt* (New York, 1995), 178, 193 (Jefferson, Madison); *Annals of Congress,* 3rd Cong., 1st sess., 625 (Smilie).

55. *Annals of Congress,* 3rd Cong., 1st sess., 623 (Tracy); Jefferson to Madison, March 6, 1796, in James Morton Smith, ed., *The Republic of Letters: The Correspondence between Thomas Jefferson and James Madison, 1776–1826,* 3 vols. (New York, 1995), 2: 922.

56. *Statutes at Large,* ch. 45, June 5, 1794, 1: 373–75 (carriages); ch. 48, June 5, 1794, 1: 376–78 (retail licenses); ch. 51, June 5, 1794, 1: 384–90 (snuff and sugar); ch. 65, June 9, 1794, 1: 397–400 (auctions). For Alexander Hamilton recommending these and similar taxes, see his "State Debts," March 4, 1790, *ASP-F,* 1: 43–44; "Public Credit," Dec. 13, 1790, ibid., 1: 64–67; "Public Debt," Dec. 3, 1792, ibid., 1: 178, all also in Harold C. Syrett, ed., *The Papers of Alexander Hamilton,* 27 vols. (New York, 1961–87).

57. *Annals of Congress,* 4th Cong., 1st sess., 312, quoted in Frederick Arthur Dalzell, "Taxation with Representation: Federal Revenue in the Early Republic" (Ph.D. diss., Harvard University, 1993), 172. The "harpies" reference is from the 1791 whiskey excise debate (1st Cong., 3rd sess., 1891–92), but this rhetoric endured. In 1794, John Nicholas (R-VA) had to apologize for insulting internal revenue officers, "whom he represented as the dregs of society." "With some gentlemen, in the line referred to," it seems, "he had as strict a friendship as with any persons on earth." *Annals,* 3rd Cong., 1st sess., 700, 705. The auction, snuff, and sugar revenue was collected almost solely in Boston, New York, Philadelphia, and Baltimore. Tench Coxe, "Internal Revenues," Feb. 21, 1798, *ASP-F,* 1: 567.

58. There is a very large literature on the Whiskey Rebellion. See especially Elkins and McKitrick, *Age of Federalism,* 461–85; and Thomas P. Slaughter, *The Whiskey Rebellion: Frontier Epilogue to the American Revolution* (New York, 1986). On customs enforcement, Dalzell, "Taxation with Representation."

59. Raymond Walters, Jr., *Albert Gallatin: Jeffersonian Financier and Diplomat* (New York, 1957). After Gallatin served three years in the state legislature, his colleagues elected him to the U.S. Senate, but a Federalist Senate expelled him for not yet having lived in the United States long enough.

60. Albert Gallatin, *A Sketch of the Finances of the United States,* in Henry Adams, ed., *The Writings of Albert Gallatin,* 3 vols. (Philadelphia, 1879), 3: 160.

61. *Annals of Congress,* 4th Cong., 2nd sess., 1935 (Smith), 1936 (Potter).

62. Ibid., 1933 (Gallatin), 1937 (Claiborne), 1938–39 (Page), 1940–41 (Brent). Brent also described sectional divisions within southern states. "Almost the whole of the lower part of the country possessed property of this kind [slaves], whilst the upper parts had scarcely any. If a tax was, therefore, imposed upon land only, the upper part of the country would be extremely aggravated, and would murmur, and they would murmur with justice." Ibid., 1940. New Englanders could have said the same thing, since most commercial property was held in the seaboard cities.

63. Oliver Wolcott, Jr., "Direct Taxes," Dec. 4, 1796, *ASP-F,* 1: 439–40.

64. Dewey, *Financial History,* 112; Elkins and McKitrick, *Age of Federalism,* 643–60; Sloan, "Hamilton's Second Thoughts," 74. This Congress also enacted the Alien and Sedition Acts.

65. *Annals of Congress,* 5th Cong., 2nd sess., 1595–1630 (quotation on 1595); Oliver Wolcott, Jr., "Apportionment of Direct Taxes," May 25, 1798, *ASP-F,* 1: 589.

66. Ibid., 589–90.

67. *Statutes at Large,* ch. 70, July 9, 1798, 1: 580–91 (quotations on 585); ch. 75, July 14, 1798, 1: 597–604.

68. *Annals of Congress,* 5th Cong., 2nd sess., 1853 (Sewall), 1840–42 (Williams). See also Nathaniel Smith (F-CT): "Land carries with it evidence of no other property besides itself; but an elegant house carries an idea of something farther, and the possessor of it certainly ought to pay a heavier tax than the solitary possessor of land." Smith added an administrative argument: he wanted "to throw the tax principally upon the cities, where it would be most easily collected." Ibid., 1845.

69. Ibid., 1853 (Sewall), 1837–38, 1848–52, 1893–94 (Gallatin, quotations on 1838, 1850, 1894). On the rebellion, see Elkins and McKitrick, *Age of Federalism,* 696–700; and Paul Douglas Newman, *Fries's Rebellion: The Enduring Struggle for the American Revolution* (Philadelphia, 2004). Newman emphasizes ethnoreligious conflicts but also shows that Republican politicians spread the fear of double taxation. Note also that the tax law contained an equalization provision, *Statutes,* ch. 70, secs. 22–23, 1: 589. Gallatin's best argument against the direct tax actually was that Wolcott's estimate of the share that would fall on land rested only on a guess at the number of houses that would fall into each valuation category.

70. *Annals of Congress,* 5th Cong., 2nd sess., 2058.

71. Ibid., 2066–67; Robert Goodloe Harper, "Circular Letter," July 23, 1798, in Noble E. Cunningham, ed., *Circular Letters of Congressmen to their Constituents, 1789–1829,* 3 vols. (Chapel Hill, 1978), 1: 137. The actual incidence of the tax depended on the wealth of particular states (the number of expensive houses and slaves), and also on the assessments that treasury officials conducted. Thus, the land tax unsurprisingly raised the overwhelming bulk of the revenue in Vermont (92 percent), since it was a "frontier" state with no slaves and very few expensive houses. Land made the smallest contribution in New York (43 percent), since it not only had a major commercial city but also had assessors who seem to have valued houses at relatively high figures. The Virginia assessors, in contrast, seem to have treated plantation houses gently. No data are available from South Carolina, North Carolina, Georgia, or Rhode Island, but, among the other states, only New York raised less than half of its quota from land. The land tax raised 58 percent in Pennsylvania and Maryland, 68 in Massachusetts and Virginia, 70 in Kentucky, 72 in New Jersey, 74 in Delaware, 82 in Tennessee, 83 in Connecticut, and 85 in New Hampshire. Calculated from data in letters from Oliver Wolcott to the state revenue supervisors, vols. 36–38, Oliver Wolcott, Jr., collection, Connecticut Historical Society: John Overton (TN), June 13, 1799; John Chester (CT), Sept. 12, 1799; George Truitt (DE), Sept. 13, Dec. 9, 1799; Nathaniel Rogers (NH), Sept. 30, 1799; Aaron Dunham (NJ), Oct. 1, 1799; James Morrison (KY), Nov. 2, 1799; Nathaniel Brush (VT), Nov. 22, 1799; Jonathan Jackson (MA), Dec. 30, 1799; Henry Miller (PA), Feb. 17, Apr. 12, 1800; Edward Carrington (VA), Apr. 2, 1800; John Kilty (MD), May 2, 1800; and Nicholas Fish (NY), Sept. 1, 1800.

72. Tracy to Oliver Wolcott, Sr., Jan. 24, 1797, in George Gibbs, ed., *Memoirs of the Administrations of Washington and John Adams: Edited from the Papers of Oliver Wolcott,* 2 vols. (New York, 1846), 1: 439; Elkins and McKitrick, *Age of Federalism,* 724–25 (Jefferson).

73. Dewey, *Financial History,* 112, 126, 142; Leonard W. Levy, *Jefferson and Civil Liberties: The Darker Side* (1963; New York, 1973), chaps. 5–6. See also Henry Adams, *The History of the United States of America during the Administrations of Thomas Jefferson and James Madison,* 2 vols. (1890; New York, 1986), 1: 1031–238. For abolition of the Federalist tax system, *Statutes at Large,* ch. 19, Apr. 6, 1802, 2: 148–50.

74. *Annals of Congress,* 12th Cong., 1st sess., 1123 (quotation), 851–56 (Gallatin's plan). For the tax laws, *Statutes at Large,* ch. 16, July 22, 1813, 3: 22–34 (direct tax and collection); ch. 21, July 24, 1813, 3: 35–38 (sugar); ch. 22, July 14, 1813, 3: 39 (collection); ch. 24, July 24, 1813, 3: 40–41 (carriage); ch. 25, July 24, 1813, 3: 42–44 (whiskey); ch. 26, July 24, 1813, 3: 44–47 (auction); ch. 37, Aug. 2, 1813, 3: 53–72 (direct tax); ch. 39, Aug. 2, 1813, 3: 72–73 (retail license); ch. 53, Aug. 2, 1813, 3: 77–81 (stamp); ch. 56, Aug. 2, 1813, 3: 82–84 (collection). Congress narrowed the stamp tax to apply only to bank notes and other negotiable paper. Gallatin had recommended a tax that applied to a range of legal and commercial documents, as the 1797 tax had. Ibid., ch. 11, July 6, 1797, 1: 527–32.

75. Ibid., ch. 16, July 22, 1813, 3: 26 (quotation); ch. 21, Jan. 9, 1815, 3: 164–80; ch. 1, Dec. 23, 1817, 3: 401–3. For a glimpse at how the valuation of slaves proceeded, see John B. Clopton to A. J. Dallas, May 5, 1816, RG 58, entry 24, National Archives. Clopton was a principal assessor in tidewater Virginia (and son of a Republican congressman). At the state equalization meeting he was told to raise his slave valuations by 15 percent, but he was stymied by the arithmetic. "[M]y equalization then seemed to form a mystical point about, and in sight of which I was compelled to move, being unable either to approach it or to abandon it entirely . . . I was driven to the necessity of finding such unknown rates per centum, as would, by their addition to or deduction from, the original valuations in the several assessment districts," raise the slave figures but preserve the equalization. This required the "vast labour" of "five distinct calculations" per taxpayer. "I was thus laboriously proceeding in the work, when my progress was arrested by a violent and obstinate inflamation in the right eye," which partially blinded him and "compelled me to resort to a long course of medical prescription, and continual applications of blistering plaster about the head." He then hired a clerk, "whose labours I considered myself bound to revise, in order to assure accuracy in the calculations," although his vision "is yet obscured." Then, "my mother was suddenly seized with a violent indisposition so that her life was despaired of, and filial duty required it of me not to leave her until a favorable change had taken place." Hence his failure to send his returns to the Treasury or his tax lists to the collector. The flat slave tax the Federalists levied in 1798 had avoided administrative incompetence of this kind.

76. *Statutes,* ch. 22, Jan. 18, 1815, 3: 180–86 (excise); ch. 61, Feb. 27, 1815, 3: 217 (excise); ch. 23, Jan. 18, 1815, 3: 186–92 (watch and furniture, quotation on 186); ch. 18, Feb. 22, 1816, 3: 254 (repeal excises); ch. 41, Apr. 9, 1816, 3: 264 (repeal watch and furniture).

77. *Hylton v. U.S.,* 3 U.S. (3 Dall.) 171 (1796). The point of the 125 chariots was to bring Hylton's liability up to $2,000 in taxes and penalties. See legal literature in note 5, especially Crane, "Reclaiming." See also Syrett, *Hamilton Papers,* 17: 2, 18: 40–42, 201–2, 396–97; Julius Goebel, Jr. and Joseph H. Smith, eds., *The Law Practice of Alexander Hamilton: Documents and Commentary,* 5 vols. (New York, 1964–81), 4: 297–355. For Hamilton's house taxes, see Hamilton to Wolcott, June 6, 1797, *Hamilton Papers,* 21: 99–100, with "Enclosure," 20: 502–4 (flat tax rates by architectural features, levied prior to land in a di-

rect tax); Hamilton to Wolcott, June 8, 1797, ibid., 18: 103: "I regret that you appear remote from the idea of a house tax simply without combining the land." Also Hamilton to Wolcott, June 5, 1798, ibid., 21: 487 (proposing national duty on male household servants "by whatever name").

78. Robert E. Shalhope, *John Taylor of Caroline: Pastoral Republican* (Columbia, 1980), 78. There has been a modern Taylor revival, with reissues of his works. John Taylor, *Arator: Being a Series of Agricultural Essays, Practical and Political,* ed. M. E. Bradford (Indianapolis, 1977); John Taylor, *Tyranny Unmasked,* ed. F. Thornton Miller (Indianapolis, 1992). See also John Ashworth, *Slavery, Capitalism, and Politics in the Antebellum Republic* (Cambridge, 1995).

79. John Taylor, *An Argument Respecting the Constitutionality of the Carriage Tax* (Richmond, 1795), 15, 20, on a microcard format in *Early American Imprints* (Worcester, 1962), 1st ser., no. 29606. The Virginia lawyer on the other side at the circuit court level dismissed Taylor's anxiety: because slave taxes were "capitations," the fate of the carriage tax would not affect them. John Wickham, *The Substance of an Argument in the Case of the Carriage Duties* (Richmond, 1795), 15, *Early American Imprints,* 1st ser., no. 29889.

80. *Hylton v. U.S.,* 177–78. Paterson also repeated his 1787 question: "Why should slaves, who are a species of property, be represented more than any other property?" Ibid., 178. Ackerman, "Taxation and the Constitution," argues that this "taint" of slavery justifies adherence to the *Hylton* precedent of strict construction of the direct tax provision today.

81. See especially Leonard L. Richards, *The Slave Power: The Free North and Southern Domination, 1780–1860* (Baton Rouge, 2000).

82. In 1797 and 1798, debates about the quotas revolved entirely around the use of an old census (from 1790). The issue did not come up during the War of 1812, when the census was more recent. *Annals of Congress,* 4th Cong., 2nd sess., 1915–27; 5th Cong., 2nd sess., 1596–1601.

83. Farrand, *Records,* 2: 57.

Introduction to Part 3

1. The traditional view, Arthur M. Schlesinger, Jr., *The Age of Jackson* (Boston, 1945), is influentially updated in Charles Sellers, *The Market Revolution: Jacksonian America, 1815–1846* (New York, 1991); and Harry L. Watson, *Liberty and Power: The Politics of Jacksonian America* (New York, 1990). But see also Daniel Walker Howe, *The Political Culture of the American Whigs* (Chicago, 1979); and Daniel Feller, *The Jacksonian Promise: America, 1815–1840* (Baltimore, 1995). One very significant change has been a new appreciation of the depth of northern racism. See especially David Roediger, *The Wages of Whiteness: Race and the Making of the American Working Class* (London, 1991); Alexander Saxton, *The Rise and Fall of the White Republic* (London, 1990); and the truly pioneering Leon F. Litwack, *North of Slavery: The Negro in the Free States, 1790–1860* (Chicago, 1961). Another major revision has foregrounded women's participation. For an introduction, Paula M. Baker, "The Domestication of Politics: Women and American Political Society, 1780–1920," *American Historical Review* 89 (1984): 620–47.

2. It is likely that state and local governments also levied higher taxes than the federal government in this era, but the quantitative evidence is complicated by two facts: (1) we

have no comprehensive data on the local taxes, and (2) the total burden of the tariff included subsidies to domestic producers (who charged higher prices to consumers) as well as the customs receipts. For an important effort to weigh the intergovernmental shares, see Richard Sylla, "Long-Term Trends in State and Local Finance: Sources and Uses of Funds in North Carolina, 1800–1977," in *Long-Term Factors in American Economic Growth*, ed. Stanley L. Engerman and Robert E. Gallman (Chicago, 1986), 819–68.

3. The nonuniformity clauses were in the constitutions of Alabama (1819), Maine (1820), North Carolina (1835), Virginia (1851), and Iowa (1857). Alabama and Maine required land to be assessed ad valorem but did not mention other forms of property. Iowa came closer, requiring the property of corporations to be taxed "the same as that of individuals," but also did not mention the treatment of particular forms of property (real and personal). North Carolina adopted a uniform *poll tax* rather than property tax, while Virginia maintained "by the poll" taxation for slaves. Kansas adopted a uniformity clause in 1859, but was not granted statehood until 1861.

4. For the quotations, Morton J. Horwitz, *The Transformation of American Law, 1870–1960: The Crisis of Legal Orthodoxy* (New York, 1992), 22; Glenn W. Fisher, *The Worst Tax? A History of the Property Tax in America* (Lawrence, 1996), 62; Sumner Benson, "A History of the General Property Tax," George C.S. Benson et al., *The American Property Tax: Its History, Administration, and Economic Impact* (Claremont, CA, 1965), 34. For the suffrage, see Alexander Keyssar, *The Right to Vote: The Contested History of Democracy in the United States* (New York, 2000), chaps. 1–6. There is a huge literature on the electoral mobilization, but Joel H. Silbey, *The American Political Nation, 1838–1893* (Stanford, 1985), is a good place to start, along with the less sanguine Glenn C. Atschuler and Stuart M. Blumin, *Rude Republic: Americans and Their Politics in the Nineteenth Century* (Princeton, 2000); and Richard Franklin Bensel, *The American Ballot Box in the Mid-Nineteenth Century* (Cambridge, 2004).

5. This map is based on Robin L. Einhorn, "Species of Property: The American Property-Tax Uniformity Clauses Reconsidered," *Journal of Economic History* 61 (2001): 979–82. Previous studies of the sequence of adoptions had erroneously concluded that the northwestern states acted first. The Illinois case is complex; until 1824, the future of slavery in Illinois was far from clear. See especially Paul Finkelman, *Slavery and the Founders: Race and Liberty in the Age of Jefferson,* 2nd ed. (Armonk, NY, 2001), chap. 3.

6. For more detail on the early adopters, late adopters, and nonadopting contributors, see chap. 6

7. Virginia, *Proceedings and Debates of the Virginia State Convention of 1829–30* (Richmond, 1830), 290.

8. Wisconsin, *Journal of the Convention to Form a Constitution for the State of Wisconsin* (Madison, 1848), 196; Ohio, *Report of the Debates and Proceedings of the Convention for the Revision of the Constitution of the State of Ohio, 1850–51,* 2 vols. (Columbus, 1851), 2: 49–50; Michigan, *Report of the Proceedings and Debates of the Convention to Revise the Constitution of the State of Michigan* (Lansing, 1850), 765.

9. For the case law, see Wade J. Newhouse, *Constitutional Uniformity and Equality in State Taxation,* 2nd ed., 2 vols. (Buffalo, 1984).

10. Ohio, *Report,* 2: 60.

Chapter 6

1. C. K. Yearley, *The Money Machines: The Breakdown and Reform of Governmental and Party Finance in the North, 1860–1920* (Albany, 1970), 59, 86.

2. Ibid., 41. For other ways to game this system, see Robert P. Sweirenga, *Acres for Cents: Delinquent Tax Auctions in Frontier Iowa* (Westport, CT, 1976).

3. Edwin R. A. Seligman, *Essays in Taxation,* 10th ed. (New York, 1925), 391, 397; Richard T. Ely, *Taxation in American States and Cities* (New York, 1888), 142. On the reforms, see especially W. Elliot Brownlee, *Progressivism and Economic Growth: The Wisconsin Income Tax, 1911–1929* (Port Washington, NY, 1974); Glenn W. Fisher, *The Worst Tax? A History of the Property Tax in America* (Lawrence, 1996), chaps. 4–9; and Ajay K. Mehrotra, "Creating the Modern American Fiscal State: The Political Economy of U.S. Tax Policy, 1880–1930" (Ph.D. diss., University of Chicago, 2003).

4. Ely, *Taxation,* 139.

5. But see Seligman, *Essays,* 16. The *Pollock* case, which ruled a federal income tax unconstitutional in 1895, led Seligman to stress the significance of slavery in the context of federal taxation because of its role in causing the insertion of the direct tax clauses into the U.S. Constitution. See also E. R. A. Seligman, *The Income Tax,* 2nd ed. (New York, 1914), 531–89; and chap. 5 above.

6. The economists were not alone. The same conflation of "personal property" with financial assets lay at the heart of the influential work of the historian Charles A. Beard: *An Economic Interpretation of the Constitution of the United States* (New York, 1913); and *Economic Origins of Jeffersonian Democracy* (New York, 1915).

7. Tennessee Constitution (1834), art. 2, sec. 28. The state constitutions are available in Ben. Perley Poore, ed., *The Federal and State Constitutions,* 2nd ed., 2 vols. (Washington, 1878); Francis Newton Thorpe, ed., *The Federal and State Constitutions,* 7 vols. (Washington, 1909); and John Wallis, ed., *The NBER / Maryland State Constitutions Project,* available at http://129.2.168.174/constitution/.

8. Illinois Constitution (1818), art. 8, sec. 20; Robert Murray Haig, *A History of the General Property Tax in Illinois* (Champaign, 1914), 43, 79–80; Ely, *Taxation,* 146, 376, 378.

9. Ely, *Taxation,* 147.

10. For the everyday violence, see David Grimsted, "Rioting in Its Jacksonian Setting," *American Historical Review* 77 (1972): 361–97; idem, *American Mobbing, 1828–1861: Toward Civil War* (New York, 1998); William A. Link, *Roots of Secession: Slavery and Politics in Antebellum Virginia* (Chapel Hill, 2003); and John Hope Franklin and Loren Schweninger, *Runaway Slaves: Rebels on the Plantation* (New York, 1999).

11. This crucial point—that the North was rural—is a cornerstone in the first major reinterpretation of the causes of the Civil War since the 1970s: James L. Huston, *Calculating the Value of the Union: Slavery, Property Rights, and the Economic Origins of the Civil War* (Chapel Hill, 2003).

12. U.S. Department of Commerce, Bureau of the Census, *Historical Statistics of the United States: Colonial Times to 1970,* 2 vols. (Washington, 1975), 1: 24–38; Howard P. Chudacoff and Judith E. Smith, *The Evolution of American Urban Society,* 4th ed. (Engle-

wood Cliffs, NJ, 1994), 70. For small towns as sites of the early factories, see Jonathan Prude, *The Coming of Industrial Order: Town and Factory Life in Rural Massachusetts, 1810–1860* (Cambridge, 1983); and Anthony F. C. Wallace, *Rockdale: The Growth of an American Village in the Early Industrial Revolution* (New York, 1978). For an overview of antebellum industrialization, see Walter Licht, *Industrializing America: The Nineteenth Century* (Baltimore, 1995), chaps. 1–3.

13. "The terms 'North' and 'South' are, of course, figures of speech that distort and oversimplify a complex reality, implying homogeneity in geographical sections that, in fact, were highly variegated." Edward Pessen, "How Different from Each Other Were the Antebellum North and South?" *American Historical Review* 85 (1980): 1119.

14. Huston, *Calculating*, chaps. 2–3; Gavin Wright, *The Political Economy of the Cotton South: Households, Markets, and Wealth in the Nineteenth Century* (New York, 1978); Robert William Fogel, *Without Consent or Contract: The Rise and Fall of American Slavery* (New York, 1989); Barbara Jeanne Fields, *Slavery and Freedom on the Middle Ground: Maryland in the Nineteenth Century* (New Haven, 1985). Southern historians define "yeomen" in several ways: as nonslaveholding farmers, farmers with small farms and no slaves or few slaves, and small farmers pursuing a diversified agriculture that limited exposure to market risks. They define "planters" as owners of land and at least twenty slaves (3 percent of southern white household heads in 1860). I will use these terms as political labels rather than strict economic categories, following William W. Freehling, *The Road to Disunion: Secessionists at Bay, 1776–1854* (New York, 1990). For Virginia in 1860, see Link, *Roots of Secession*. In total population, Virginia had fallen behind Ohio and Illinois as well as New York and Pennsylvania.

15. In addition to the works cited in note 14, see especially Lacy K. Ford, Jr., *Origins of Southern Radicalism: The South Carolina Upcountry, 1800–1860* (New York, 1988); and J. Mills Thornton III, *Politics and Power in a Slave Society: Alabama, 1800–1860* (Baton Rouge, 1978).

16. Walter Johnson, *Soul by Soul: Life inside the Antebellum Slave Market* (Cambridge, MA, 1999). For an introduction to the Indian Removal, see Anthony F. C. Wallace, *The Long, Bitter Trail: Andrew Jackson and the Indians* (New York, 1993). For a foundational statement on cotton as a driver of economic growth in this era, see Douglass C. North, *The Economic Growth of the United States, 1790–1860* (Englewood Cliffs, NJ, 1961). Economic historians disagree about the relative significance of industrialization in this period. See, e.g., Licht, *Industrializing America*.

17. Wright, *Political Economy*, 35; Huston, *Calculating the Value*, 28–29. Also Fogel, *Without Consent or Contract*, 85: "Nearly two out of every three males with estates of $100,000 or more lived in the South in 1860." The cotton kingdom slaveholding figure is for the belt of *counties* instead of entire states, many of which included upcountry areas with few slaves. Harry L. Watson, "Slavery and Development in a Dual Economy: The South and the Market Revolution," in *The Market Revolution in America: Social, Political, and Religious Expressions*, ed. Melvyn Stokes and Stephen Conway (Charlottesville, 1996), 43–73.

18. Colin G. Calloway, *The American Revolution in Indian Country: Crisis and Diversity in Native American Communities* (Cambridge, 1995), chaps. 4–5; Barbara Graymont, *The Iroquois in the American Revolution* (Syracuse, 1972).

19. Edward Countryman, *A People in Revolution: The American Revolution and Political Society in New York, 1760–1790* (Baltimore, 1981); Reeve Huston, *Land and Freedom: Rural Society, Popular Protest, and Party Politics in Antebellum New York* (New York, 2000); Alan Taylor, *William Cooper's Town: Power and Persuasion on the Frontier of the Early American Republic* (New York, 1995). For continuities in the West, see especially Susan E. Gray, *The Yankee West: Community Life on the Michigan Frontier* (Chapel Hill, 1996).

20. See especially Shane White, *Somewhat More Independent: The End of Slavery in New York City, 1770–1810* (Athens, GA, 1991), chaps. 1–2.

21. Robert Greenhalgh Albion, *The Rise of New York Port, 1815–1860* (New York, 1939); Mary P. Ryan, *Cradle of the Middle Class: The Family in Oneida County, New York, 1790–1865* (Cambridge, 1981); Paul E. Johnson, *A Shopkeeper's Millennium: Society and Revivals in Rochester, New York, 1815–1837* (New York, 1978); Sean Wilentz, *Chants Democratic: New York City and the Rise of the American Working Class, 1788–1850* (New York, 1984); Peter Way, *Common Labor: Workers and the Digging of North American Canals, 1780–1860* (Cambridge, 1993); Nathan Miller, *The Enterprise of a Free People: Aspects of Economic Development in New York State during the Canal Period* (Ithaca, 1962); L. Ray Gunn, *The Decline of Authority: Public Economic Policy and Political Development in New York, 1800–1860* (Ithaca, 1988). For the West, see especially Harry N. Scheiber, *Ohio Canal Era: A Case Study of Government and the Economy, 1820–1861* (Athens, OH, 1968); and William Cronon, *Nature's Metropolis: Chicago and the Great West* (New York, 1991). See also George Rogers Taylor, *The Transportation Revolution, 1815–1860* (New York, 1951).

22. Key works include Joel H. Silbey, *The American Political Nation, 1838–1893* (Stanford, 1991); Ronald P. Formisano, *The Transformation of Political Culture: Massachusetts Parties, 1790s–1840s* (New York, 1983); Richard R. John, "Affairs of Office: The Executive Departments, the Election of 1828, and the Making of the Democratic Party," in *The Democratic Experiment: New Directions in American Political History*, ed. Meg Jacobs, William J. Novak, and Julian E. Zelizer (Princeton, 2003), 50–84; and Harry L. Watson, *Liberty and Power: The Politics of Jacksonian America* (New York, 1990). See also the essays in "Round Table: Alternatives to the Party System in the 'Party Period,'" *Journal of American History* 86 (1999): 93–166.

23. U.S. Congress, *Register of Debates*, 24th Cong., 1st sess., 3552. Cf. Glenn Atschuler and Stuart M. Blumin, *Rude Republic: Americans and Their Politics in the Nineteenth Century* (Princeton, 2000).

24. Watson, *Liberty and Power;* Michael F. Holt, *The Rise and Fall of the American Whig Party: Jacksonian Politics and the Onset of the Civil War* (New York, 1999). On banking, see also Robert V. Remini, *Andrew Jackson and the Bank War: A Study in the Growth of Presidential Power* (New York, 1967); Bray Hammond, *Banks and Politics in America, from the Revolution to the Civil War* (Princeton, 1957); James Roger Sharp, *The Jacksonians Versus the Banks: Politics in the States after the Panic of 1837* (New York, 1967); Naomi R. Lamoreaux, *Insider Lending: Banks, Personal Connections, and Economic Development in Industrial New England* (Cambridge, 1994).

25. Holt, *Rise and Fall;* Thornton, *Politics and Power;* William G. Shade, *Democratizing the Old Dominion: Virginia and the Second Party System, 1824–1861* (Charlottesville,

1996); Jonathan M. Atkins, *Parties, Politics, and the Sectional Conflict in Tennessee, 1832–1861* (Knoxville, 1997).

26. Holt, *Rise and Fall;* Kathleen Neils Conzen, "Pi-ing the Type: Jane Grey Swisshelm and the Contest of Midwestern Regionality," in *The American Midwest: Essays on Regional History,* ed. Andrew R. L. Cayton and Susan E. Gray (Bloomington, 2001), 91–110; Robert R. Dykstra, *Bright Radical Star: Black Freedom and White Supremacy on the Hawkeye Frontier* (Cambridge, MA, 1993); Nicole Etcheson, "Private Interest and Public Good: Upland Southerners and Antebellum Midwestern Political Culture," in *The Pursuit of Public Power: Political Culture in Ohio, 1787–1861,* ed. Jeffrey P. Brown and Andrew R. L. Cayton (Kent, 1994), 83–98; Eugene H. Berwanger, *The Frontier against Slavery: Western Anti-Negro Prejudice and the Slavery Extension Controversy* (Urbana, 1967); Jean H. Baker, *Affairs of Party: The Political Culture of the Northern Democrats in the Mid-Nineteenth Century* (Ithaca, 1983); Richard H. Sewall, *Ballots for Freedom: Antislavery Politics in the United States, 1837–1860* (New York, 1976).

27. Richard R. John, *Spreading the News: The American Postal System from Franklin to Morse* (Cambridge, MA, 1995), chap. 7; William Lee Miller, *Arguing about Slavery: The Great Battle in the United States Congress* (New York, 1986); Leonard L. Richards, *The Slave Power: The Free North and Southern Domination, 1780–1860* (Baton Rouge, 2000); David M. Potter, *The Impending Crisis, 1848–1861* (New York, 1976); Michael F. Holt, *The Political Crisis of the 1850s* (New York, 1978); Eric Foner, *Free Soil, Free Labor, Free Men: The Ideology of the Republican Party before the Civil War* (New York, 1970); William E. Gienapp, *The Origins of the Republican Party, 1852–1856* (New York, 1987); William J. Cooper, *The South and the Politics of Slavery, 1828–1856* (Baton Rouge, 1978).

28. Gunn, *Decline of Authority,* chaps. 5–6 (quotation on 165); Judith K. Schafer, "Reform or Experiment? The Constitution of 1845," in *In Search of Fundamental Law: Louisiana's Constitutions, 1812–1974,* ed. Warren M. Billings and Edward F. Haas (Lafayette, 1993), 21–36; New York, *Report of the Debates and Proceedings of the Convention for the Revision of the Constitution of the State of New York* (Albany, 1846; Bishop and Atree edition), 118–23, 128–29, 138–40, 175–76, 288–89, 1022, 1068–69. The critique of people who were not "willing to trust themselves" in Ely, *Taxation,* aimed at this entire movement to constitutionalize public finance—the stop and tax clauses as well as the uniformity clauses.

29. Potter, *Impending Crisis;* Holt, *Political Crisis;* Freehling, *Road to Disunion;* Link, *Roots of Secession;* Don E. Fehrenbacher, *Slavery, Law, and Politics: The Dred Scott Case in Historical Perspective* (New York, 1981).

30. Ira Berlin et al., *Slaves No More: Three Essays on Emancipation and the Civil War* (New York, 1992).

31. Ralph A. Wooster, *The People in Power: Courthouse and Statehouse in the Lower South, 1850–1860* (Knoxville, 1969); idem, *Politicians, Planters, and Plain Folk: Courthouse and Statehouse in the Upper South, 1850–1860* (Knoxville, 1975); Ford, *Origins,* 304–5.

32. Max M. Edling and Mark D. Kaplanoff, "Alexander Hamilton's Fiscal Reform: Transforming the Structure of Taxation in the Early Republic," *William and Mary Quar-*

terly, 3rd ser., 61 (2004): 713–44; T. K. Worthington, *Historical Sketch of the Finances of Pennsylvania* (Baltimore, 1887), 60–62; Robin L. Einhorn, "Species of Property: The American Property-Tax Uniformity Clauses Reconsidered," *Journal of Economic History* 61 (2001): 992–93; Gunn, *Decline of Authority*, 138–41. For disestablishment, see H. James Henderson, "Taxation and Political Culture: Massachusetts and Virginia, 1760–1800," *William and Mary Quarterly*, 3rd ser., 47 (1990): 90–114; Pauline Maier, "The Revolutionary Origins of the American Corporation," *William and Mary Quarterly*, 3rd ser., 50 (1993): 51–84; and Thomas E. Buckley, "Evangelicals Triumphant: The Baptists' Assault on the Virginia Glebes, 1786–1801," *William and Mary Quarterly*, 3rd ser., 45 (1988): 33–69.

33. Daniel Feller, *The Public Lands in Jacksonian Politics* (Madison, 1984); Scheiber, *Ohio Canal Era*; Peter Wallenstein, *From Slave South to New South: Public Policy in Nineteenth-Century Georgia* (Chapel Hill, 1987); John Lauritz Larson, *Internal Improvement: National Public Works and the Promise of Popular Government in the Early United States* (Chapel Hill, 2001); John Majewski, *A House Dividing: Economic Development in Pennsylvania and Virginia before the Civil War* (Cambridge, 2000); Richard Sylla, John B. Legler, John J. Wallis, "Banks and State Public Finance in the New Republic: the United States, 1790–1860," *Journal of Economic History* 47 (1987): 391–403 (figures on 401).

34. Richard Sylla and John Joseph Wallis, "The Anatomy of Sovereign Debt Crises: Lessons from the American State Defaults of the 1840s," *Japan and the World Economy* 10 (1998): 281. This data set covers 17 states and probably includes poll and other taxes levied along with the property taxes.

35. John J. Wallis, "State Constitutional Reform and the Structure of Government Finance in the Nineteenth Century," in *Public Choice Interpretations of American Economic History*, ed. Jac C. Heckelman et al. (Boston, 2000), 33–52. See also John Joseph Wallis, "A History of the Property Tax in America," in *Property Taxation and Local Government Finance: Essays in Honor of C. Lowell Harriss*, ed. Wallace E. Oates (Cambridge, MA, 2001), 131–39.

36. The census commissioner dismissed the data on total local taxes as unreliable: "[T]he returns are very incomplete." The school tax data were better despite categorization problems: "[T]he statistics upon the whole are imperfect, though the best that can be obtained." J. D. B. DeBow, *Statistical View of the United States* (Washington, 1854), 141, 190.

37. Other data in the same census tables flesh out the school finance picture. Local taxes raised 49 percent of the cost of public schools nationally, but 61 percent in the North and only 18 percent in the South. In both sections, "public funds" (income from state investments) supplied 27 percent and endowments 2 percent. The difference was "other sources"—presumably tuition: 54 percent South, 10 percent North, 22 percent nationally. Historians of education agree that schools were better and more plentiful in the cities. Ira Katznelson and Margaret Weir, *Schooling for All: Class, Race, and the Decline of the Democratic Ideal* (New York, 1985), chaps. 1–2, attribute this to working-class demand. For a more general argument, see John B. Legler, Richard Sylla, and John J. Wallis, "U.S. City Finance and the Growth of Government, 1850–1902," *Journal of Economic History* 48 (1988): 347–56.

38. Only archival research can reveal how these assessments went. Kentucky started as-

sessing slaves early, in 1814, requiring that each taxpayer list "the value of his or her slaves" with the value of livestock and carriages. Kentucky, *Statute Law,* 5 vols. (Littell 1809–19), 5: 110. Arkansas and Missouri also listed slaves among the forms of taxable property, assessing all property at "the true value thereof in ready money" (Arkansas) and "its full and true value in cash at the time of the assessment" (Missouri). Arkansas, *Revised Statutes* (Ball, Roane 1838), 673, 675; Missouri, *Revised Statutes,* 2 vols. (Hardin 1856), 2: 1322, 1334. Tennessee offered a guideline for slaves who were hired out: "assessed to the hirer for the amount of the hire." Tennessee, *Code* (Meigs, Cooper 1858), 179. In Louisiana, which taxed slaves ad valorem from 1846 to 1856, owners swore to "a description of them by age and sex," a hint that they were categorizing rather than valuing. Louisiana, *Revised Statutes* (Phillips 1856), 464. The law with the flat rates on age-and-sex categories was called an act "to equalize the rate of taxation on slaves." Louisiana, *Acts, 1856,* 180.

39. Most states also used more regressive tax instruments. They required male adults (including slaves in the South) to perform road labor for two or three days a year, burdens that often could be commuted to cash payments. In New England and the South, many states also imposed poll taxes on free male adults.

40. New York, *Revised Statutes,* 3 vols. (Parker, Wolford, Wade 1859), 1: 905–15, 2: 646 (quotations on 1: 905, 906, 911, 2: 646); New York, *Laws, 1823,* 390–97. For the swearing loophole, see Edward Pessen, *Riches, Class, and Power: America before the Civil War* (1973; New Brunswick, NJ, 1990), chaps. 2–3; Don C. Sowers, "The Financial History of New York State: From 1789 to 1912" (Ph.D. diss., Columbia University, 1914), 117–18. Michigan copied the loophole in 1827 and kept it until the mid-1850s. Michigan Territory, *Laws,* 4 vols. (1871–84), 2: 610, 3: 1151; Michigan, *Revised Statutes* (Green 1846), 104; Michigan, *Compiled Laws,* 2 vols. (Cooley 1857), 1: 294.

41. Mississippi, *Revised Code* (Sharkey et al. 1857), 71–78 (quotations on 73, 75, 76, 77). There was also a $200 tax on dealers in coin or paper money and licenses for peddlers and other traders. Ibid., 87–89.

42. Tennessee, *Code* (Meigs, Cooper 1858), 174. Georgia also forbade its local assessors to touch self-assessments. Thornton, "Fiscal Policy," 358.

43. Roger Ransom and Richard Sutch, "Capitalists without Capital: The Burden of Slavery and the Impact of Emancipation," in *Quantitative Studies in Agrarian History,* ed. Morton Rothstein and Daniel Field (Ames, 1993), 148; and J. Mills Thornton III, "Fiscal Policy and the Failure of Radical Reconstruction in the Lower South," in *Region, Race and Reconstruction: Essays in Honor of C. Vann Woodward,* ed. J. Morgan Kousser and James M. McPherson (New York, 1982), 357.

44. Louisiana, *Revised Statutes* (Phillips 1856), 459. The other flat slave valuations were $200 for children aged 1–5, $300 for children 5–10, $450 for children 10–15, $650 for women 15–45, and $300 for all adults over 45. Louisiana, *Acts, 1856,* 180.

45. Louisiana, *Revised Statutes* (Phillips 1856), 460–61.

46. I estimated the Louisiana planter's slave tax by assuming that the twenty slaves included seven men aged 15–45 (taxed at $1.42 each), five women aged 15–45 (at $1.08), three children aged 10–15 (at 75 cents), two children aged 5–10 (at 50 cents), one child aged 1–5 (at 33 cents), and two adults over the age of 45 (at 50 cents), for a total of $19.92. At the average price of $774 in 1860, a tax of one-sixth of one percent on the "cash value"

of twenty slaves would have been about $25.80. The Mississippi planter actually would have paid slightly less than $8 (or $15), since Mississippi exempted slaves over age 60.

47. The peddler and coffeehouse operator probably shifted their taxes into consumer prices. Planters would have tried to shift their taxes into the price of cotton and, more successfully, the price of sugar—a crop with little out-of-state competition and significant tariff protection. But, in anything except depression conditions, commercial landlords would have been able to shift their taxes into rents. Note that slave traders probably were expected to shift parts of their very high license taxes ($300) to out-of-state customers. See the appendix for further discussion of shifting.

48. New York, *Laws, 1823,* 390–97; Massachusetts, *Laws, 1829,* 289 (quotation); Massachusetts, *General Laws,* 2 vols. (Stearns, Shaw, Metcalf 1823), 2: 578, 581; Pennsylvania, *Purdon's Digest* (1853), 787–88; Worthington, *Historical Sketch,* 58; Connecticut, *Public Statute Laws* (Swift, Whitman, Day 1821), 446–48; Connecticut, *Public Statute Laws, 1824,* 44; Connecticut, *Statutes* (Dutton et al. 1854), 836–41. Pennsylvania turned its "faculty tax" into a full-fledged income tax by pulling incomes out of the property lists and taxing them separately. Pennsylvania, *Purdon's Digest* (1853): 788. Northern local governments licensed (taxed) taverns, ferries, and so on.

49. New York, *Laws of the State of New York Passed at the Sessions of the Legislature Held in the Years [from 1777 through 1801],* 5 vols. (Albany, 1886–87), 1: 223 (quotation), 227–28; 4: 402–3, 5: 493; idem, *Laws, 1815, 32;* idem, *Laws, 1817,* 347; Countryman, *People in Revolution,* 186–87, 211–16, 255–59; Robert A. Becker, *Revolution, Reform, and the Politics of American Taxation, 1763–1783* (Baton Rouge, 1980), chap. 2; Alexander Hamilton to Robert Morris, Aug. 13, 1782, in Harold C. Syrett, ed., *The Papers of Alexander Hamilton,* 27 vols. (New York, 1961–87), 3: 135–37.

50. For New York, Gunn, *Decline of Authority,* chap. 4; Miller, *Enterprise of a Free People,* 66–93. For special assessment, Robin L. Einhorn, *Property Rules: Political Economy in Chicago, 1833–1872* (Chicago, 1991).

51. Thornton, "Fiscal Policy," 356–57. See also Peter Wallenstein, "'More Unequally Taxed than any People in the Civilized World': The Origins of Georgia's Ad Valorem Tax System," *Georgia Historical Quarterly* 64 (1984): 459–87. Thornton argues that the shift to ad valorem in the Lower South benefited slaveholding planters; Wallenstein argues that it benefited urban interests.

52. Virginia, *Acts, 1814,* 5–7. The furniture tax imposed a long series of flat rates: clocks in five categories; bureaus, sideboards, wardrobes, chests, bookcases, beds, tables, chairs, and sofas depending on material (mahogany, bamboo, gold or silver leaf); pictures and portraits by size, framing, and medium (oil, crayon, or both); and so on for pianos, watches, mirrors, lamps, urns, pitchers, goblets, carpets, and curtains not "manufactured in the family" (10 cents per window if calico, marseilles, or dimity; 75 cents if worsted, silk, or satin; 25 cents per venetian blind). Virginia assumed only the first U.S. direct tax.

53. Frederick Tilden Neeley, "The Development of Virginia Taxation: 1775–1860" (Ph.D. diss., University of Virginia, 1956), 133–35, 137–41, 235–37; Virginia, *Code* (Patton, Robinson 1849), 213–14, 219–20, 277–78; Virginia, *Code* (Munford 1860), 194–96, 242–50 (quotation on 242).

54. North Carolina, *Laws,* 2 vols. (Potter, Taylor, Yancey 1821), 2: 1305–10; North Car-

olina, *Revised Code* (Moore, Biggs 1855), 503–20 (quotations on 503, 510, 514). North Carolina abolished its tax on weapons in May 1861, nine days before seceding from the Union. North Carolina, *Public Laws, 1861, first extra session,* 107.

55. Ohio, *Statutes,* 3 vols. (Chase 1833–35), 2: 1476–87; Illinois, *Laws* (1838), 1–23; Indiana, *Revised Statutes* (1843), 208–15; Michigan Territory, *Laws,* 4 vols. (1871–84), 2: 609–17, 3: 1150–52; Wisconsin Territory, *Statutes* (Whiton 1839), 384–88; Wisconsin Territory, *Laws, 1841,* 20–22; Iowa Territory, *Revised Statutes* (Stull 1843), 546–65; Minnesota Territory, *Revised Statutes* (Wilkinson 1851), 94–101; Oregon Territory, *Statutes* (1855), 431–38; Michigan, *Compiled Laws,* 2 vols. (Cooley 1857), 1: 329–37.

56. Wisconsin, *Revised Statutes* (1849), 138–48, 171–72, 199–200 (quotations on 138, 141).

57. Merle Curti, *The Making of an American Community: A Case Study of Democracy in a Frontier County* (Stanford, 1959), 270–71.

58. See Richard E. Sylla, John B. Legler, and John Wallis, "State and Local Government: Source and Uses of Funds, City and County Data, Nineteenth Century," data set 6305 (1985–), Inter-University Consortium for Political and Social Research, University of Michigan, available at http://www.icpsr.umich.edu/access/index.html.

59. Wisconsin Territory, *Statutes* (Whiton 1839), 43; Missouri, *Laws,* 2 vols. (1825), 2: 671; idem, *Revised Statutes,* 2 vols. (Hardin 1856), 2: 1349 (local taxes now up to double state taxes); Arkansas, *Digest of the Statutes* (English 1848), 857, 870; idem, *Digest of the Statutes* (Gould 1858), 916, 930; Florida Territory, *Compilation of the Public Acts* (Duval 1839), 317; Florida, *Acts and Resolutions* (1845), 65, 66 (exempting certain towns from caps); Texas, *Digest of the General Statute Laws* (Oldham, White 1859), 421; Virginia, *Code* (Patton, Robinson 1849), 278.

60. Tennessee Constitution (1834), art. 2, sec. 28. See also Arkansas Constitution (1836), art. 10, sec. 2; Louisiana Constitution (1845), art. 6, sec. 127; Texas Constitution (1845), art. 7, sec. 27.

61. Thomas M. Cooley, *A Treatise on the Constitutional Limitations Which Rest Upon the Legislative Power of the States of the American Union* (Boston, 1868), 613.

62. *Lexington v. McQuillan's Heirs,* 39 Ky. 513 (1839); Morton J. Horwitz, *The Transformation of American Law, 1870–1960: The Crisis of Legal Orthodoxy* (New York, 1992), 22; Thomas M. Cooley, *A Treatise on the Law of Taxation* (Chicago, 1876), 178–79.

63. Robert McColley, *Slavery and Jeffersonian Virginia,* 2nd ed. (1964; Urbana, 1973); Rachel N. Klein, *Unification of a Slave State: The Rise of the Planter Class in the South Carolina Backcountry, 1760–1808* (Chapel Hill, 1990), chap. 8; Wooster, *People in Power,* 125–53; idem, *Politicians, Planters, and Plain Folk,* 163–69.

64. Merrill Jensen, John P. Kaminski, and Gaspare J. Saladino, eds., *The Documentary History of the Ratification of the Constitution,* 19 vols. (Madison, 1976–), 10: 1533. For the antislavery gospel, see especially Christine Leigh Heyrman, *Southern Cross: The Beginnings of the Bible Belt* (New York, 1997).

65. Hinton Rowan Helper, *The Impending Crisis of the South: How to Meet It,* ed. George M. Fredrickson (Cambridge, 1968), 156–57.

66. As of 1860, five states bolstered slaveholder power with slave representation. South

Carolina used a "combined ratio" of white population and taxes (including slave taxes) in one house and a parish-and-district rule (favoring the lowcountry) in the other. South Carolina Constitution (1790), art. 1, secs. 3, 7 (as amended 1808). North Carolina used the three-fifths rule in one house and taxes in the other. North Carolina Constitution (1835), art. 1, sec. 1. Florida used the three-fifths rule in both houses, and Georgia used it for the lower house to distinguish large from small counties, granting the small counties one seat and the large counties two. Florida Constitution (1838), art. 9, secs. 1–2; Georgia Constitution (1798), art. 1, sec. 7 (as amended 1843). Louisiana was extreme: both houses by the *total* population (47 percent slave overall) plus draconian caps on the representation of New Orleans. Louisiana Constitution (1852), art. 2, secs. 8, 15.

67. Freehling, *Road to Disunion*, is the best work on these issues.

68. There was also another influential publishing event: the 1836 release of Madison's record of the 1787 Philadelphia convention, which he had held for posthumous publication.

69. See especially Christian G. Fritz, "The American Constitutional Tradition Revisited: Preliminary Observations on State Constitution-Making in the Nineteenth-Century West," *Rutgers Law Journal* 25 (1994): 945–98.

70. Ronald Hoffman, *A Spirit of Dissension: Economics, Politics, and the Revolution in Maryland* (Baltimore, 1973); David Curtis Skaggs, *Roots of Maryland Democracy, 1753–1776* (Westport, 1973); Paul G. E. Clemens, *The Atlantic Economy and Colonial Maryland's Eastern Shore: From Tobacco to Grain* (Ithaca, 1980).

71. Maryland Declaration of Rights (1776), sec. 13. Ohio Constitution (1802), art. 8, sec. 23, copied the Maryland poll tax language ("That the levying of taxes by the poll is grievous and oppressive . . .") in a free-state context. See also Jean H. Vivian, "The Poll Tax Controversy in Maryland, 1770–76: A Case of Taxation *with* Representation," *Maryland Historical Magazine* 71 (1976): 151–76; Einhorn, "Species of Property," 985–86, 991–93.

72. Joan Wells Coward, *Kentucky in the New Republic: The Process of Constitution-Making* (Lexington, 1979), 16–25, 35–45; Kentucky Constitution (1792), art. 9, which would be copied widely.

73. Tennessee Constitution (1796), sec. 26. Although the record is scanty, the Missouri Constitution (1820), art. 13, sec. 19 ("That all property, subject to taxation in this State, shall be taxed in proportion to its value"), probably reflected similar issues. Glover Moore, *The Missouri Controversy, 1819–1821* ([Lexington], 1953), 258–73; Floyd Calvin Shoemaker, *Missouri's Struggle for Statehood, 1804–1821* (Jefferson City, 1916), chaps. 2–4.

74. The best analysis is Alison Goodyear Freehling, *Drift toward Dissolution: The Virginia Slavery Debate of 1831–1832* (Baton Rouge, 1982), chaps. 1–3.

75. Virginia, *Proceedings and Debates of the Virginia State Convention of 1829–30* (Richmond, 1830), 53, 88, 129, 332. On this convention, in addition to Freehling, *Drift*, see Shade, *Democratizing*, chap. 2; Dickson D. Bruce, Jr., *The Rhetoric of Conservatism: The Virginia Convention of 1829–30 and the Conservative Tradition in the South* (San Marino, 1982); and Robert P. Sutton, *Revolution to Secession: Constitution-Making in the Old Dominion* (Charlottesville, 1989), chap. 4.

76. Virginia, *Proceedings*, 150–51, 538, 858.

77. Ibid., 75, 116, 158, 207, 306, 657.

78. Ibid., 41. This "plan had been tried in Maryland, and succeeded to entire satisfaction." Ibid., 626.

79. Ibid., 51, 75, 158, 170, 221, 626. See also the "benefit" argument: wealthy easterners "deriving three times as much benefit from the Government, ought to pay three times as much of the expense." Ibid., 233. From 1829 to 1831 the east-dominated legislature actually slashed slave taxes by 46 percent, or, from 28 percent of state tax revenue in 1828 to only 17 percent in 1831. Einhorn, "Species of Property," 995–96.

80. North Carolina Constitution (1835), art. 4, sec. 3; North Carolina, *Proceedings and Debates of the Convention of North-Carolina* (Raleigh, 1835), 81–83; Marc W. Kruman, *Parties and Politics in North Carolina, 1836–1868* (Baton Rouge, 1983), 12–13. This deal still rankled twenty-five years later. "In no [other] State in this Union," a politician declared in 1860, "is the poor white man's head put up as a shield to prevent the slaves from bearing their equal burden of taxation." Donald C. Butts, "The 'Irrepressible Conflict': Slave Taxation and North Carolina," *North Carolina Historical Review* 58 (1981): 64.

81. Tennessee, *Journal of the Convention of the State of Tennessee* (Nashville, 1834), 55 (quotation), 103 (quotation), 201 (vote). At the vote on final passage of the ban on emancipation, one delegate proposed a sarcastic proviso: "that horses, cows, and all other personal property, shall be secured to their respective owners in a similar manner." Ibid., 273. Chase C. Mooney, "The Question of Slavery and the Free Negro in the Tennessee Constitutional Convention of 1834," *Journal of Southern History* 12 (1946): 487–509, is essential on this convention.

82. Tennessee Constitution (1834), art. 2, sec. 28. The constitution also exempted "free men of color" from poll tax as a compensation for disfranchising them. Ibid., art. 4, sec. 1.

83. New York, Pennsylvania, and Rhode Island (with Maryland and Louisiana) capped big-city representation, while Connecticut and Delaware used arbitrary territorial apportionments (by town in Connecticut, by county in Delaware). By 1860, only one northern state apportioned by wealth at all; New Hampshire counted local tax payments for its senate (Massachusetts had dropped this rule in 1840). Cf. note 66 above on the South. For a suggestive discussion of apportionments, see Rosemarie Zagarri, *The Politics of Size: Representation in the United States, 1776–1850* (Ithaca, 1987), chap. 2.

84. Delegates debated about one or more of these issues in New Jersey (1844), New York (1846), Wisconsin (1848), Michigan (1850), Ohio (1850–51), Indiana (1850–51), and Iowa (1857).

85. New Jersey, *Proceedings of the New Jersey State Constitutional Convention of 1844*, comp. New Jersey Writers' Project, WPA ([Trenton?], 1942), 399; New York, *Report of the Debates, 1846*, 121. See also the earlier comment in New York, *Reports of the Proceedings and Debates of the New York Constitutional Convention, 1821* (reprint, New York, 1970), 358: "To pretend to shackle the legislature by constitutional embarrassments was nugatory and unavailing."

86. New Jersey, *Proceedings, 1844*, 343, 571–72. In the Northeast, only the Maine Constitution (1820), art. 9, sec. 8, included anything more specific than the Massachusetts "proportional and reasonable" and decennial reassessment rules from 1780. But Maine did not link taxes on different forms of property. It required taxes on "real estate" to be "apportioned and assessed equally, according to the just value thereof." This provision addressed a

local grievance. The Massachusetts tax break for land speculators (assess unimproved land at 2 percent of value versus 6 percent for other property) had applied chiefly to the absentee owners of land in Maine, removing two-thirds of the nonresident property from local tax rolls. Even so, the clause was an afterthought, suggested only in the convention's final days, after the ritual thanking of the president. The response was enthusiastic. "[N]o member . . . could possibly oppose it, who had witnessed the unequal system of taxation in . . . Massachusetts," and very few did. It passed "nearly unanimously." Maine, *The Debates, Resolutions, and Other Proceedings of the Convention of Delegates . . . for the Purpose of Forming a Constitution for the State of Maine* (Portland, 1820), 263–66. Alabama Constitution (1819), art. 6, sec. 8, was similar: "All lands liable to taxation in this State, shall be taxed in proportion to their value."

87. Illinois, "Journal of the Convention," *Journal of the Illinois State Historical Society* 6 (1913): 355–424. One Illinois resident praised general property taxation and the Maryland uniformity clause in a newspaper essay—"And this equitable system of taxation [is] engrafted into but one state constitution, and that contains very little else which is free and liberal"—but then ducked the issue of why Illinois needed the clause to levy the tax: "altho' some other states pursue a correct course in the practical operation of their taxation." *Illinois Intelligencer,* May 27, 1818.

88. Solon Buck, *Illinois in 1818* (Chicago, 1918); Paul Finkelman, *Slavery and the Founders: Race and Liberty in the Age of Jefferson,* 2nd ed. (Armonk, NY, 2001), chaps. 2–3; James Simeone, *Democracy and Slavery in Frontier Illinois: The Bottomland Republic* (DeKalb, 2000). Illinois listed slaves as taxable property even after it finally abolished slavery in 1848. Einhorn, "Species of Property," 980.

89. New Jersey, *Proceedings, 1844,* 397; Ohio, *Report of the Debates and Proceedings of the Convention for the Revision of the Constitution of the State of Ohio, 1850–51,* 2 vols. (Columbus, 1851), 2: 51, 60, 77.

90. For Wisconsin and California, Einhorn, "Species of Property," 1000–2. The exception in Michigan was a Detroit delegate who wanted railroads to pay real estate taxes in the city. Michigan, *Report of the Proceedings and Debates of the Convention to Revise the Constitution of the State of Michigan* (Lansing, 1850), 765.

91. Ohio, *Report, 1850–51,* 2: 51, 52, 81, 113, 754.

92. Ibid., 2: 87. The Robespierre quotation: "I have no confidence in the men that have such good memories of the catalogue of crimes charged upon the people."

93. Ibid., 2: 791, 828; Ohio Constitution (1851), art. 7, secs. 4–6, art. 8, secs. 1–7; Ely, *Taxation,* 139.

94. Wisconsin Constitution (1848), art. 8, sec. 1; California Constitution (1849), art. 11, sec. 13; Michigan Constitution (1850), art. 14, secs. 11–12. The Michigan clause included an exception for "specific taxes" on certain corporations. The California clause included a guarantee of local control over assessments, a demand of *Californio* (Mexican) delegates who worried about losing their lands to Anglo gold rush migrants, as many of them eventually did. See also Indiana Constitution (1851), art. 10, sec. 1, which was somewhat more detailed.

95. Ohio Constitution (1851), art. 7, secs. 2–3, art. 8, sec. 4. Minnesota Constitution (1857), art. 9, secs. 1, 3–4, copied this language.

96. *Exchange Bank v. Hines*, 3 Oh. St. 1 (1853).

97. James Madison, "The Federalist Number 51," in Jacob E. Cooke, ed., *The Federalist* (Middletown, CT, 1961), 351; Alexis de Tocqueville, *Democracy in America*, 2 vols. (New York, 1945), 1: 278. Tocqueville anticipated the modern conception of "minority rights" in a footnote citing the intimidation of African American voters in Pennsylvania as an example of majority tyranny. Ibid., 1: 261.

98. *Bureau County v. the C.B.Q.*, 44 Ill. 229 (1867); Cooley, *Taxation*, iv.

99. "For instance, while the valuation of the property of individuals ranged from one-fifth to one-third of its cash value, that of the [railroad] ranged from one-third to one-half of its value." *Bureau County v. the C.B.Q.*, 238. But see also *Kneeland v. Milwaukee*, 15 Wis. 454 (1862); 18 Wis. 411 (1864). In the first round, the court rejected a separate (lower) railroad tax, offering a ringing statement of the actual goal of the framers: "The small property owners who constitute the great mass of the people, usually pay their taxes without question, and seldom combine for the purpose of procuring any special privileges or exemptions. But capital, always keen-eyed and vigilant, always equally ready to grasp at the profit and shrink from the burden,—often able to bring to bear powerful and dangerous combinations of influence upon legislative bodies—will be sure to take advantage of [legislative discretion], and to shift upon others the burdens which itself ought to bear." In the second round, however, the Wisconsin court accepted the separate (lower) railroad tax, and *this* precedent informed its unusual approval of separate (higher) railroad taxes later. See Wade J. Newhouse, *Constitutional Uniformity and Equality in State Taxation*, 2nd ed., 2 vols. (Buffalo, 1984), 2: 1628–72.

100. *Lawrence v. Fast*, 20 Ill. 338 (1858). More generally, see Lawrence M. Friedman, *A History of American Law*, 2nd ed. (New York, 1985), 355–63; and Clyde E. Jacobs, *Law Writers and the Courts: The Influence of Thomas M. Cooley, Christopher G. Tiedeman, and John F. Dillon upon American Constitutional Law* (Berkeley, 1954).

101. *Portland Bank v. Apthorp*, 12 Mass. 252 (1815); *Hylton v. U.S.*, 3 U.S. (3 Dall.) 171 (1796). *Portland Bank* would be cited not for its outcome, but for a definition of the "proportional" rule that was not applied in this case.

102. *Waters v. Maryland*, 1 Gill 302 (1843). In the end, the collector won on a technicality involving his official bond. See also *Egan v. Charles County*, 3 H. & McH. 169 (1793), refusing to broaden the term "poll tax."

103. *Rhinehart v. Schuyler*, 7 Ill. 473 (1845). See also *Le Breton v. Morgan*, 4 Mart. (n.s.) 128 (1826), a Louisiana case that defended a permissive ruling on the grounds that the state constitution included no uniformity clause (Louisiana adopted its clause in the context of an apportionment fight in 1845).

104. *Lexington v. McQuillan's Heirs*, 39 Ky. 513 (1839); *Stevens and Woods v. State*, 2 Ark. 291 (1840).

105. *Crow v. State*, 14 Mo. 237 (1851).

106. *Slaughter v. Commonwealth*, 54 Va. 767 (1856). See also *Gilkeson v. Frederick Justices*, 54 Va. 577 (1856). Virginia Constitution (1851), art. 4, sec. 22: "Taxation shall be equal and uniform throughout the commonwealth, and all property other than slaves shall be taxed in proportion to its value, which shall be ascertained in such manner as may be prescribed by law." Historians often count this as a uniformity clause, even though its ex-

ception ("other than slaves") excluded a huge amount of property. The next three clauses (art. 4, secs. 23–25) set the slave tax equal to the tax on $300 of land, exempted slaves under age 12, allowed the legislature to exempt other property, required the legislature to levy a poll tax on free men over 21 equal to the tax on $200 of land (and to spend half its proceeds on schools), and authorized income and license taxes as long as the assets from which the taxed incomes and profits were derived had been exempted from property tax.

107. Horwitz, *Transformation,* 22. Newhouse, *Constitutional Uniformity,* reviews this case law. For a major implied mandate, *Washington Avenue,* 69 Pa. 352 (1871). See also *Oliver v. Washington Mills,* 93 Mass. 268 (1865).

108. But see the legal analyses of Johnson, Ackerman, Jensen, and Crane, cited in chapter 5, note 5 above.

109. Milo M. Quaife, ed., *The Attainment of Statehood* (Evansville, 1928), 402. Although the activists who framed Proposition 13 had different motives, many voters endorsed it to solve a specific problem. The inflation of the 1970s led to spiraling real estate assessments, which squeezed homeowners because officials failed to reduce the tax rates levied against the dramatically higher valuations. David O. Sears and Jack Citrin, *Tax Revolt: Something for Nothing in California* (Cambridge, MA, 1982); Robert Kuttner, *The Revolt of the Haves: Tax Rebellions and Hard Times* (New York, 1980). The constitutionalization of Proposition 13 is only one source of its political power. No politician can criticize it safely because every current homeowner already has stepped onto its underassessment escalator. Its disincentive to sell underassessed property also contributes to high real estate values generally. Combined with low voter turnout among the young—who are its real victims—these characteristics appear to render Proposition 13 invulnerable.

110. See Lacy K. Ford, Jr., "Inventing the Concurrent Majority: Madison, Calhoun, and the Problem of Majoritarianism in American Political Thought," *Journal of Southern History* 60 (1994): 19–58; Lacy K. Ford, "Republican Ideology in a Slave Society: The Political Economy of John C. Calhoun," *Journal of Southern History* 54 (1988): 405–24; and Robin L. Einhorn, "Patrick Henry's Case against the Constitution: The Structural Problem with Slavery," *Journal of the Early Republic,* 22 (2002): 567–69.

111. John C. Calhoun, *A Disquisition on Government,* ed. C. Gordon Post (Indianapolis, 1953), 26.

112. Thornton, *Politics and Power,* chap. 5; Thornton, "Fiscal Policy."

Epilogue

1. Virginia, *Proceedings and Debates of the Virginia State Convention of 1829–30* (Richmond, 1830), 84. All county population figures are from the 1830 census as reported in Alison Goodyear Freehling, *Drift Toward Dissolution: The Virginia Slavery Debate of 1831–1832* (Baton Rouge, 1982), 265–69.

2. Virginia, *Proceedings,* 538 (Madison), 307 (Stanard), 331 (Tazewell). Stanard was from Spotsylvania County. Tazewell was the elitist who ridiculed the yeomen as dupes of "the first Mons'r Egalite who presents himself as the professed guardian of the rights of property." Ibid., 332.

3. Ibid., 331. We can only wonder at the bizarre "whether black or white."

4. Drew R. McCoy, *The Last of the Founders: James Madison and the Republican Legacy* (Cambridge, 1989).

5. Virginia, *Proceedings,* 539.

6. Ibid., 538.

7. Ibid., 88.

8. Eugene H. Berwanger, *The Frontier against Slavery: Western Anti-Negro Prejudice and the Slavery Extension Controversy* (Urbana, 1967), 26; Leonard L. Richards, *The Slave Power: The Free North and Southern Domination, 1780–1860* (Baton Rouge, 2000), 152; David M. Potter, *Lincoln and His Party in the Secession Crisis* (1942; New Haven, 1962), 9, quoting Potter's paraphrase of "Sir, you cannot kick out of the Union the men who utter these impotent threats" (ibid., 9n).

Appendix

1. The loss of this language from our public debate is often blamed on economists, who dismissed tax equity as a merely "aesthetic" concern after World War II. See especially Dennis J. Ventry, Jr., "Equity versus Efficiency and the U.S. Tax System in Historical Perspective," in *Tax Justice: The Ongoing Debate,* ed. Joseph J. Thorndike and Dennis J. Ventry, Jr. (Washington, 2002), 25–70. For a major contemporary critique, Louis Eisenstein, *The Ideologies of Taxation* (New York, 1961). For the rise of our "low tax" discourses, Julian E. Zelizer, "The Uneasy Relationship: Democracy, Taxation, and State Building since the New Deal," in *The Democratic Experiment: New Directions in American Political History.* ed. Meg Jacobs et al. (Princeton, 2003), 276–300. For earlier versions, see Robin L. Einhorn, *Property Rules: Political Economy in Chicago, 1833–1872* (Chicago, 1991); and Terrence J. McDonald, *The Parameters of Urban Fiscal Policy: Socioeconomic Change and Political Culture in San Francisco, 1860–1906* (Berkeley, 1986).

2. The dissenters are on the extreme right of the political spectrum. Adam Smith, *The Wealth of Nations* (1776; New York, 1937), 670, asserted that governments exist for the very purpose of protecting the property of the rich: "The affluence of the rich excites the indignation of the poor, who are often both driven by want, and prompted by envy, to invade his possessions. It is only under the shelter of the civil magistrate that the owner of that valuable property . . . can sleep a single night in security. . . . The acquisition of valuable and extensive property, therefore, necessarily requires the establishment of civil government. Where there is no property, or at least none that exceeds the value of two or three days labour, civil government is not so necessary." I thank Brad DeLong for this reference.

3. For these and many of the issues that follow, see Richard A. Musgrave and Peggy B. Musgrave, *Public Finance in Theory and Practice,* 5th ed. (New York, 1989). See also Edwin R. A. Seligman, *The Shifting and Incidence of Taxation,* 2nd ed. (New York, 1902); idem, *Progressive Taxation in Theory and Practice,* 2nd ed. (Princeton, 1908).

4. We might ask these questions about other government spending—how much of the cost of conquering an oil-rich nation should be charged to oil companies, gasoline consumers, or corporate stockholders?—but the fact is that we do not. We usually identify such spending with the promotion of "democracy," expansion of "freedom," or defense of "our way of life," any of which would imply that everyone benefits more or less equally.

5. See especially Walter J. Blum and Harry Kalven, Jr., *The Uneasy Case for Progressive Taxation* (Chicago, 1953).

6. The most influential statement of the redistributive case for progressivity, to reduce a "distinctly evil or unlovely" inequality, was Henry C. Simons, *Personal Income Taxation* (Chicago, 1938), quoted in C. Eugene Steuerle, "And Equal (Tax) Justice for All?" in *Tax Justice: The Ongoing Debate*, ed. Joseph J. Thorndike and Dennis J. Ventry, Jr. (Washington, 2002), 265. Musgrave made the real case to Congress in 1963: for progressive income tax rates "since the rest of our tax structure is regressive." Ventry, "Equity versus Efficiency," 43. For the early mix of tax justice and social justice arguments for the income tax, see W. Elliot Brownlee, "Tax Regimes, National Crisis, and State-Building," in *Funding the Modern American State, 1941–1995: The Rise and Fall of the Era of Easy Finance*, ed. Brownlee (Cambridge, 1996), 51–60. See also Robert Stanley, *Dimensions of Law in the Service of Order: Origins of the Federal Income Tax, 1861–1913* (New York, 1993); and Mark H. Leff, *The Limits of Symbolic Reform: The New Deal and Taxation* (Cambridge, 1984). Regressive taxes traditionally have been defended for disciplining the poor (forcing them to work harder and spend less on luxuries inappropriate to their subordinate status) and to promote capital formation. Explanations of economic growth that emphasize consumer spending tend to support progressive taxation because the poor are more numerous than the rich and spend larger fractions of their incomes. Conversely, explanations of economic growth that emphasize saving tend to support regressive taxation because the rich can afford to save larger fractions of their incomes.

7. The details matter a lot. Retail sales taxes are less regressive, for example, when they exempt clothing as well as food. For the origin of the American sales taxes (early 1930s), see Robert Murray Haig and Carl S. Shoup, *The Sales Tax in the American States* (New York, 1934). For VAT provisions, Organization for Economic Co-Operation and Development, *Consumption Tax Trends: VAT / GST and Excise Rates, Trends, and Administrative Issues*, 2004 edition (Paris, 2005).

8. Smith, *Wealth of Nations*, 821. Smith certainly thought poll taxes were regressive, which is the reason they were common "in countries where the ease, comfort, and security of the inferior ranks of the people are little attended to." But, "so far as they are levied upon the lower ranks of the people, [they] are direct taxes upon the wages of labour, and are attended with all the inconveniencies of such taxes," meaning shifting to employers and also to consumers (ibid., 815–17). Smith also distinguished between poll taxes and slave taxes that were called poll taxes. Ibid., 808. Note that the notorious American poll taxes of the twentieth century were not really taxes; they were designed to prevent African Americans from voting rather than to raise money. Hence the Twenty-Fourth Amendment to the Constitution (1964): "The right of citizens of the United States to vote . . . shall not be denied or abridged . . . by reason of failure to pay any poll tax or other tax."

9. For classic analyses of the responses to local taxing and spending, Charles M. Tiebout, "A Pure Theory of Local Expenditures," *Journal of Political Economy* 64 (1956): 416–24; Paul E. Peterson, *City Limits* (Chicago, 1981). See also Laurence J. Kotlikoff and Lawrence H. Summers, "Tax Incidence," in *Handbook of Public Economics*, ed. Alan J. Auerbach and Martin Feldstein, 4 vols. (Amsterdam, 1987), 2: 1088, which explains that long-run considerations are what make tax incidence "fun" and includes a table projecting

outcomes 150 years into the future (ibid., 2:1081). It was John Maynard Keynes, of course, who said that in the long run we are all dead.

10. Joseph A. Pechman and Benjamin A. Okner, *Who Bears the Tax Burden?* (Washington, 1974); Joseph A. Pechman, *Who Paid the Taxes, 1966–85?* rev. ed. (Washington, 1985). For other work in this vein, see Edgar K. Browning and William R. Johnson, *The Distribution of the Tax Burden* (Washington, 1979); and Donald Phares, *Who Pays State and Local Taxes?* (Cambridge, 1980). For an illustration of why economists no longer do this work, see Donald Fullerton and Gilbert E. Metcalf, eds., *The Distribution of Tax Burdens* (Cheltenham, UK, 2003). The pivotal moment may well have been Henry J. Aaron, *Who Pays the Property Tax?: A New View* (Washington, 1975).

11. For more recent estimates of the incidence of federal taxes (especially the individual income tax), see the Web sites of the Congressional Budget Office (http://www.cbo.gov) and the Tax Policy Center of the Urban Institute and Brookings Institution (http://www.taxpolicycenter.org).

12. Organization for Economic Co-Operation and Development, *Revenue Statistics, 1965–2003* (Paris, 2004), 72. See also Sven Steinmo, *Taxation and Democracy: Swedish, British, and American Approaches to Financing the Modern State* (New Haven, 1993), chaps. 1–2.

13. Ventry, "Equity versus Efficiency," 56–58. Polling data show support for the idea that the rich should pay higher taxes than they currently do *and* support for a "flat tax"—an income tax with only one marginal rate (tax bracket) and without deductions, credits, or exemptions. As Ventry points out, this combination of responses reflects a widely held perception (most likely incorrect) that a "flat" federal income tax would be more progressive than the current income tax, in which a formal structure of mildly progressive rates is compromised by loopholes that favor the rich.